James Edward

Japan: its history, traditions and religions (1879)

with the narrative of a visit (Vol. II)

James Edward

Japan: its history, traditions and religions (1879)
with the narrative of a visit (Vol. II)

ISBN/EAN: 9783742840530

Manufactured in Europe, USA, Canada, Australia, Japa

Cover: Foto ©Lupo / pixelio.de

Manufactured and distributed by brebook publishing software
(www.brebook.com)

James Edward

Japan: its history, traditions and religions (1879)

MOUNT FUJI.

JAPAN:

ITS HISTORY, TRADITIONS, AND RELIGIONS.

WITH THE

NARRATIVE OF A VISIT IN 1879.

By Sir Edward J. REED, K.C.B., F.R.S., M.P.,

VICE-PRESIDENT OF THE INSTITUTION OF NAVAL ARCHITECTS;
MEMBER OF THE INSTITUTIONS OF CIVIL ENGINEERS AND MECHANICAL ENGINEERS;
KNIGHT OF THE IMPERIAL RUSSIAN ORDER OF ST. STANISLAUS, OF THE
AUSTRIAN ORDER OF FRANCIS JOSEPH, AND OF THE
TURKISH ORDER OF THE MEDJIDIÉ, ETC.

IN TWO VOLUMES.—Vol. II.

WITH ILLUSTRATIONS.

LONDON:

JOHN MURRAY, ALBEMARLE STREET.

1880.

LONDON :
PRINTED BY WILLIAM CLOWES AND SONS, LIMITED,
STAMFORD STREET AND CHARING CROSS.

CONTENTS.

(*VOL. II.*)

———◆———

CHAPTER I.

OUR ARRIVAL IN JAPAN—FIRST IMPRESSIONS.

CHAPTER II.

A MONTH IN THE EASTERN CAPITAL.

CHAPTER III.

LANGUAGE AND LITERATURE.

CHAPTER IV.

DRAWING AND PAINTING.

CHAPTER V.

PROVERBS AND PHRASES OF THE PEOPLE.

CHAPTER VI.

THE INLAND SEA AND NAGASAKI.

CHAPTER VII.

THE CITY OF OSAKA.

CHAPTER VIII.

THE SACRED CITY OF NARA.

CHAPTER IX.

KIOTO, OR SAIKIO, THE WESTERN CAPITAL.

CHAPTER X.

THE SACRED SHRINES OF ISÉ.

CHAPTER XI.

NAGOYA AND THE SHRINE OF THE SACRED SWORD.

CHAPTER XII.

TO SHIDZUOKA : THE HOME OF THE TOKUGAWAS.

CHAPTER XIII.

FUJI-YAMA AND THE HAKONÉ MOUNTAINS.

LIST OF ILLUSTRATIONS.

(*VOL. II.*)

Full-Page Engravings.

Minor Engravings.

JAPAN:

ITS HISTORY, TRADITIONS, AND RELIGIONS.

—◆◆◆—

CHAPTER I.

OUR ARRIVAL IN JAPAN—FIRST IMPRESSIONS.

Our first view of Japan—The sacred mountain Fuji-yama—Coast scenery
—Yokohama Bay—Our landing—Reception on shore—A small
summer palace of the emperor—Railways of Japan—Arrival in Tokio
—The residence of Admiral Kawamura—Memoranda by E. Tenn.
Reed—*Jinriki-shas*—Costumes of the people—Japanese shops—*Torii*—
A Shinto temple—Mode of worship—Shinto priests—A movable shop
—The police—The children—Shampooers—Outside the town—Country
scenery—Rice-fields—An inland town—Tea-drinking—The national
beverage, *saké*—A Buddhist temple—Buddhistic worship—The lotus
emblem—Japanese animals—Excursion vans.

IT was on a fine breezy morning early in the year (January
10) that we first saw the land of Japan proper. Approaching it from Hong Kong, and by the southern route, which
passes among the solitary Loo-choo Islands, the lordly and
beautiful Fuji-yama rose up before us long before any other
land was visible. Like a vast and splendid temple, it stood
high above the ocean-plain, white with snow, and glittering
in the sun. I shall have many occasions hereafter for
speaking in admiration of this wondrous object, and will
therefore only remark here that if one's memories of Japan
were destined to fade one by one, I believe the very last to
disappear would be that of Fuji-san,* as first seen from
the sea, at a distance of nearly one hundred miles.

---

* Fuji-san is more correct than   us) of Fuji-yama, but usage has
the more popular designation (among   justified the employment of either

With interest ever deepening, through the day we saw the picturesque shores of Japan gradually displayed as we approached, broken as they are, and as artists must exult to see them, into hills and headlands, valleys and sand-beaches, rocks and caves, in indescribable variety. On many an island and promontory stand lighthouses—those beacons of civilisation of which any nation may well be proud.* The days being short at this season of the year, night came on, and the lighthouses blazed forth long before we reached the roadstead of Yokohama, where steam-launches

---

term indifferently in this case. Yama, Taka, and San or Zan are all applied to mountains according to their position or importance.

* "The first view of the coast of Japan which one obtains after five or six days' voyage from Hong Kong is a very fair specimen of the coast scenery in general. Hills of peculiarly sharp outline, and which bear unmistakable signs of volcanic formation, send their rounded spurs out seaward in such a way as to form along the entire coast a series of small bays, in some of the more protected of which may be seen little nests of grey huts, with their inevitable accompaniment of single-masted junks lying at anchor close in to the shore. Every now and then a little white sail will be seen skimming along past the shore, the hull of the vessel often being out of sight to passengers on the mail steamers, which naturally give the coast a wide berth. At times the hills will fall away enough to give you a glimpse into the interior of the country, when you see others, range beyond range, of the same varied and picturesque forms, increasing apparently in height in proportion to their distance inland. With the exception of those nearest to the coast, these hills appear pretty thickly wooded, and even the barer

parts are overgrown with grass which in the winter is of a deep straw colour, the result of the scorching sun of the preceding summer. This scenery, varying slightly at times of course, repeats itself continually as you pass along towards the Gulf of Yedo. Now and then the shore becomes more rocky, and the surf forms a broken line of white as far as the eye can reach.

"Islands occasionally loom up on the seaward side, the last and finest being that of 'Vries,' or 'Ooshima,' an active volcano which continually pours forth smoke and occasionally flame. Soon after passing these islands the Gulf of Yedo is reached and the shores close in, the eastern one keeping very low right up the bay, the western one also being a little less hilly and more thickly wooded than before.

"The Gulf of Yedo is extremely well supplied with lighthouses of various kinds, by aid of which mail steamers are able to proceed straight to their moorings in Yokohama Bay, at whatever time they arrive.

"E. TENN REED."

This note, and some other notes which follow bearing corresponding initials, are from the pen of my son, who accompanied me on my visit to Japan.

were waiting to take us to the shore if we had chosen to land. But the hour was late, and we had previously determined to remain on board for the night, and therefore sent our compliments and apologies to the friends awaiting us, not doubting that their convenience, like our own, would thus be best secured.

Early on the morning of the 11th we went upon deck and saw the pleasant town of Yokohama, with its long line of European-looking buildings extending along the sea-front, and its charming residences high up on "The Bluff," on our left. In the roadstead or harbour were ships of all nations, including British, American, and German men-of-war, with the flag of Japan floating proudly from many a war-vessel, one of which, the ironclad frigate *Foo-so*, I had myself had the privilege to design and have built for his majesty the emperor. After breakfast the steam-launches were again alongside, and several young officers whom we had known in England had come out in them to escort us to the port-admiral's landing-place, where we were most cordially received by their excellencies Admiral Kawamura and Mr. Enouyé Kawori, the ministers of marine and of public works respectively, both of whom we had had the pleasure of knowing in England. With them were Admiral Ito and several naval and civil officers, some of whom we already knew, and others whose acquaintance we then made for the first time, as we did also that of Captain Hawes, an English officer who had established and brought to a condition of great excellence a corps of Japanese marines whose disbandment subsequent events had brought about.*

Our first entertainment in Japan was at a small but elegant little summer residence situated upon a hill overlooking the bay, which formerly belonged to Mr. Enouyé,

---

* To Capt. Hawes we were indebted for many kindnesses during our stay. I understand that, in conjunction with Mr. Ernest Satow, this accomplished officer is engaged in the preparation of a guidebook to Japan, which will be of the utmost service to visitors, and doubtless help to attract strangers to the Flowery Land.

but has of late years been employed as a temporary residence for the Mikado on the occasions of his visiting the fleet, or making a sea passage to or from his capital. Although built and provided in European style, the little palace bore throughout its fittings, furniture, and decorations the unmistakable impress of the Japanese artist and handicraftsman. The walls were hung with Japanese pictures, both ancient and modern; the curtains were of rich Japanese silk; the carpets and rugs of native manufacture; the furniture of woods and designs special to the country, while beautiful specimens of inlaid lacquer-work, Satsuma and Kiyomidzu *faïence*, and screens of Kioto embroidered silk adorned the several apartments. A luncheon of European type emphasised the welcome which had been given us, and assured us of the cordial hospitality with which we were to be treated. A brief visit to the club, the privileges of which were secured for us by the kindness of Captain Hawes, occupied the only time available before the departure of our train to the eastern capital.*

---

* "An Englishman arriving in Yokohama, looking at the town from a ship in the bay, will have some difficulty at first in discovering any very novel feature in its appearance. To the left on a hill he sees European houses in abundance; all along the shore are large stone buildings, hotels, store-houses, and clubs such as may be seen in any seaport town at home; and with a score or two of steamers of every kind in the foreground, it is indeed hard to realise that he is face to face with the land of the Mikados. But this disappointment does not last long. He has but to lift his eyes and look beyond, and there, towering above all the nearer hills, he sees Fuji-yama, the monster snow-capped mountain which forms a background for all the loveliest scenes in Japan. Steamers, hotels, and store-houses are forgotten in a moment, and he becomes for the time a Japanese, or at any rate a worshipper of Fuji.

"But now the boats which are to take him ashore crowd round, and he has to postpone further contemplation to a more suitable opportunity. The boatmen and boats are Japanese at any rate. The men are dressed in a loose sort of robe with hanging sleeves. They row with long sweeps tied to the side of the boat, and worked in a kind of sculling fashion with the blades nearly under the stern of the boat. On reaching the shore and having passed through the ordeal of the customs, a stranger finds himself in the midst of a curiously mixed population. Here he sees in the same minute Englishmen, Americans, Germans, Frenchmen, Chinamen, all of them feeling apparently at home, and seeming as if it was the most natural thing in the world for each of them to be there: the Japanese

Before proceeding with the narrative of our visit to Tokio it may be well to pause sufficiently long to mention the existing railway accommodation of Japan. There are but three lines of railway yet constructed, viz. that upon which we were about to travel from Yokohama to Tokio, a distance of 18 miles; a second, from the open port of Kobé to the great commercial city of Osaka, which is 22 miles long;

RAILWAYS OF JAPAN.

and a third, from Osaka to the western capital of Kioto, which is 26½ miles in length. These last-named being continuous, may be considered as one line of 48½ miles, from

---

going their own way quite unconcerned. As he moves farther into the town, however, the purely Japanese population appears in all its novelty and picturesquences;

and from this point all we shall see in Yokohama may be seen in any town throughout the country.
"E. T. R."

Kobé to Kioto. Several other lines have been laid out, as shown in the plan on the previous page, of which the parts drawn in a continuous black line have been completely planned and estimated for, the short piece from Kioto to Otsu being already in hand and well advanced; while the dotted lines indicate a much more extensive system, which can scarcely be said to have advanced much beyond the region of imagination, although the general routes indicated have been more or less examined and determined upon. While speaking of increased communication with the plan before us, it may be well to mention that it has been for centuries past the hope of thoughtful Japanese that a canal would be cut from Tsuruga to the northern extremity of Lake Biwa, for the purpose of admitting shipping from the ocean into the lake, and thus carrying sea-borne produce inland to Otsu, which is within nine or ten miles of the western capital. The whole length of projected railways above indicated is about 600 miles, of which 143 have been completely planned and in part commenced, the remaining 457 miles being at present but little more than talked of. The line from Yokohama to Tokio was commenced in 1867, and opened for traffic in October 1872. There are large stations at the termini, and smaller stations at several intermediate places. Extensive workshops exist at Tokio. It is said that the receipts for passenger traffic alone on this line reach nearly £100 per mile per week, and will therefore compare well with those of first-class English railways. English and Scotch enginemen and drivers are still employed upon the railway, but the management of the traffic and the working of the stations are conducted entirely by Japanese.

About five in the afternoon of the 11th we reached Tokio, where a crowd awaited our arrival, attracted doubtless by the circumstance that one of the carriages in waiting belonged to the government, and bore among its decorations the imperial crest. A few minutes' drive, during which we could not but be struck by the characteristic features alike of the city and of the people, brought us to the residence of Admiral Kawamura, where we found ourselves delightfully

located in the midst of a purely Japanese household, but
with an adjoining building of European style, newly erected
for the use of foreign visitors, and furnished with the
choicest art-furnishings of Japan, as in the case of the little
Yokohama palace already adverted to.

In place of giving my own general impressions resulting
from our first views of this extraordinary country and people,
I will take the following from the memoranda jotted down by
my son—in whose youth (his age being but nineteen) the
friendly reader will find sufficient excuse for any literary
crudeness that he may detect :—

"Among the first things we see on entering a Japanese
town is a line of *jinriki-sha* men, with their hand-carriages,
waiting for a job. The shafts of the two-wheeled carriages
are resting on the ground, and their proprietors are standing
by, or sitting on the now sloping seat. Their dress consists
in most cases (in this winter time) of a pale-blue shirt with
hanging sleeves tucked in at the waist, and tight-fitting
breeches of the same colour, reaching just below the knee.
Legs and feet are bare, with the exception of straw sandals
fastened on by means of straw cords, one passing round the
ankle and another between the toes. They are most of
them holding their rough scarlet rugs round their necks and
shoulders, but as soon as they get a job the rug will be
transferred to the knees of the fare.

"But let us look for a moment at the dresses of the
passers-by. Here comes a young man, probably an assistant
in a shop. His dress consists of a thick-striped silk robe
reaching down to the ankles, or nearly so. The colour of this
is a quiet grey, with narrow mauve or black stripes in it. It
crosses on his breast, and inside it shows an under-garment
crossing in the same way, made of a different shade of grey
from the other. The outer dress is fastened at the crossing
with a thick cord of cream-coloured silk. He wears white
socks, which only reach to the ankle, and which separate
between the big toe and the rest of the foot, so as to allow
the strap of his clogs to pass between. These clogs consist
of a flat sole of wood about half an inch thick, which rests on

two broad wooden uprights at toe and heel. A straw cord comes up between the big toe and the next one, and separates into two parts, which join the clog halfway along. As there is no fastening at the back, a continual drag has to be kept on the clog or it would fall off, the result of which is that very shambling gait which is one of the peculiarities noticed in walking through a Japanese town. This young man, like most others now, has allowed his hair to grow all over his head in European fashion.

" But before going further we must notice the arrangement of the hair which is peculiar to the Japanese men. The head

HAIR OF LABOURER.

is shaved, from the forehead to a little behind the crown. The hair is grown at the sides and back, then a kind of short pigtail is made of the upper part of the back-hair, which is stuck together with cosmetic, doubled, and the point brought partly over the shaved part of the head, as in the engraving above. This practice is fast dying out, though, and even now is almost confined to the working classes.

" Let us now take a glance at a shop or two, and see in what they differ from those we are accustomed to. Here on our right we see a low-built wooden house. We go inside the door; the proprietor is sitting on his heels on the floor, which

is raised about a foot and a half above the ground, and is
smoothly covered with clean matting. He has his bronze
hibashi, or brazier, before him. One arm is resting on it,
while one hand is spread over the fire of red-hot ashes. In
his other hand is his small silver pipe, with its diminutive bowl.
The moment we enter he taps the ashes out of this pipe into
the *hibashi*, and makes his reverence with his forehead on the
ground. If we wish to purchase anything, a certain amount of
preliminary incredulity and subsequent beating down is often
necessary here as in most other places in the East. He asks
us to be seated, and pushes some flat cushions to the edge of
the floor so as to enable us to keep our feet on the ground,
and thus avoid taking off our boots, which would be necessary
if we were to mount on to his floor. He calls to some one
in the back room of the house, which is shut off by a paper
partition with wooden framework, and in a few minutes a boy
appears with tea, which we are invited to take while we look
over some of his stock. After making a few purchases and
drinking the tea, with which the cups are continually re-
plenished, we wish him good-day, and leave him repeating
his obeisance, and producing that remarkable sound which is
so common in Japan, of sucking in the breath between the
teeth and lips, and terminating in a noise made with the
throat, which is rather suggestive of asthma. These sounds
almost always accompany a bow either on meeting or leaving
a person. Passing on, every shop is a picture, even though
it be for the sale of casks or wine-bottles. The clean white
ribs of the cask held together by rings of green willow; the
masses of common blue and white china *saké* bottles, shelf
above shelf, and layer above layer, are pleasing to the eye,
and so help in their way to increase that fascination with
the country which every foreigner feels after a short stay
in Japan, and which is of course contributed to by every
evidence of taste and artistic sense in the Japanese in things
however trifling and unimportant.

"But what is that curious structure at the end of the
street? Well, it does look curious at first, but before many
days have passed it will seem as familiar as a church-spire at

home. It is the sign that you are approaching a Shinto temple, and if you look beyond you will see nestled among the trees the steep thatched roof of the temple itself, which is entered by a flight of steps, at the foot of which may be seen a little group of devotees making their obeisances before the shrine. Even at this distance, if we look carefully into the shadow cast by the overhanging roof, we can see the glimmer of the round mirror which appears to be one of the symbols of the Shinto faith.*

"As we draw nearer we find that the archway we have noticed consists of two large upright posts some two and a half feet in diameter, across the tops of which is laid a beam, projecting over them and curving slightly upward. A few inches below this is a second and smaller beam, parallel to it, and which bears a framed board on which is inscribed in Japanese characters the name of the temple. The whole structure is painted a bright red,† and is altogether about fifteen or eighteen feet high. We can now distinctly see the mirror in the centre of the temple, surrounded by those wands with curiously cut tassels of white paper which are called *gohei*, and which are seen in every Shinto temple. The original idea of them might have been that of a duster, as it is the custom of the priests to make two or three passes with them in the air before praying, apparently for the purpose of clearing the atmosphere from any impurities before invoking the god. Here, too, are the worshippers, some kneeling, some standing at the foot of the steps. Let us watch this new-comer for a moment. He walks to the foot of the steps, throws a coin on to them, and stands for some seconds gazing into the temple, then raises his hands and claps them sharply three times. He then places them together and bends his head, muttering a short prayer. After another prolonged gaze at the sacred mirror and its surroundings,

---

* "The mirror, we afterwards found, although a sacred Shinto emblem, was not displayed in early Shinto temples. Its public use came in with Buddhism, according to Mr. Ernest Satow. "E. T. R."

† "This painting of the *torii* appears also to be traceable to Buddhism, but it is not at all unfrequent now. "E. T. R."

he moves off to make room for other equally devout worshippers, who present their offerings, go through the same
ceremony, and in their turn make way for others, and so on.
The clapping of the hands is only saved from appearing
ridiculous to foreigners by the thoroughly reverent and
earnest looks of the worshippers.   The object of this, we are
told, is to attract the attention of the *kami*, or god, to the
prayers which are to follow.   As we turn to leave we take a
final glance at the temple, and notice for the first time
that the richly coloured chickens amongst the carving under
the roof are moving their heads and wings in a decidedly
natural manner.   We are told to our astonishment that these
birds are sacred, and so are allowed to take their roost on
the very temple itself; but we have no doubt that were
we to scatter a little food on the ground, their strictly religious proclivities would be, at any rate for the time,
overcome, and that they would show themselves worldly
enough to give way to temptation, and leave their exalted
perch.

   " Near the *torii*, or archway, we meet two men in curious-
looking dresses, whom we discover to be priests of the temple.
One is dressed in flowing white robes, with baggy sleeves,
the ordinary socks and clogs, and wears a stiff headdress of
linen or silk, somewhat resembling a peaked nightcap doubled
backwards with the peak hanging down.   The other wears
richer-looking robes, made apparently of brocaded silk, but
of the same shape as the first; his headdress is quite different, however, consisting of a lacquered black hat, the
shape of which is roughly rectangular, but has a deep dent
in the front, and is crinkled all over.   It is about four inches
high, and projects beyond the head at the back with a slight
curve upwards.   They make a polite bow as we pass, and
wish us good-day.   We are told that the first is an ordinary
Shinto priest, while the second is the chief priest of the
temple.

   " Just after leaving the temple we meet an object which
looks like a very large cabinet of some sort with legs and
feet taking a quiet stroll through the town.   On nearer

approach this resolves itself into two tall narrow boxes, through which, about three fourths of the way up, passes a stout bar of wood, which rests on the shoulder of the man to whom the legs belong. At first this appears an enormous load for one man to carry, but on closer examination we find that it is merely a framework of light wood barely strong enough to support its contents. If we watch this man for a few moments he will probably very soon find a suitable place for depositing his shop, for such it is; when we shall see the two boxes quickly opened and converted into stands on which to place his wares.

" But we must continue our walk, for there is much to see and wonder at. Every few hundred yards we pass one of the best results of the introduction of European customs in the form of a neatly dressed and business-like policeman. His uniform consists of a dark-blue coat reaching below the knees, with collar and cuffs of bright yellow cloth. He wears a white belt, and a peaked cap with a yellow band and a silver badge in front. Under his arm he carries an ominously thick stick some four feet long, which gives to the mildest and most harmless-looking policeman that appearance of latent power which is so necessary to their profession.

" Most of the people we pass now are of the lower classes, as we are approaching the poorer quarter of the town. The men are mostly dressed in a short sort of cloak of dark blue material with hanging sleeves, which is open down the front. The lower part of this is ornamented with a white pattern, often resembling the Greek key. On the back is a large Japanese character surrounded by a white ring. This is generally the emblem or sign adopted by their employer. Under this cloak an inner garment of darker material is worn, the thickness of this varying according to the time of year. They wear tight-fitting trousers of dark blue. They go generally with the head bare, but sometimes wear a light-blue figured handkerchief tied under the chin. While walking along between the low wooden houses with their heavily tiled roofs, we have abundant opportunities of seeing every phase of domestic life. Here we see a party of little children with their bright dresses of imitation crape (*chirimen*), and their little heads clean shaved with the exception of four little tufts, one in front, one behind, and one at each side. Some are flying kites made in the shape of diminutive men with outspread arms, while the smaller ones are confining their attention to the perilous occupation of climbing down from the raised floor of the houses to the road, and there making their first attempts at walking in clogs; and as they always secure the biggest ones at hand, their endeavours are often extremely amusing. The moment a *jinriki-sha* is seen approaching, the children immediately show a strong desire to be on the opposite side of the road, the result of this generally being a series of narrow escapes, which would in many cases be bad accidents were it not that the *jinrika-sha* is so quickly swerved aside or stopped.

"In passing a side street we are struck by the doleful notes of some instrument, which is evidently approaching us by the increasing clearness of the sound. We will stay a moment and find out whence it comes. In a few moments a figure appears, which halts every now and then, and each time the sound we first heard is repeated, and is followed by a low droning cry. As it gets nearer we find it is a blind man, who feels his way with a stick and carries a reed-pipe. On inquiry we learn that this man's profession is that of a shampooer. The system of shampooing has become quite an institution in Japan. Any one suffering from rheumatism or any pain which rubbing would relieve calls in one of these men, who are continually passing, and undergoes a course of kneading and hammering and pinching in the part affected, or all over the body if he wishes it. The few notes on the pipe and the low cry of "amma" (great stress being laid on the m's, which causes the peculiar droning sound) combine to form one of the most plaintive street cries imaginable. Our curiosity being satisfied we pass on, and in a few minutes find ourselves approaching the open country. Here on the roadside is a square stone column about six feet high, on which is carved in Japanese characters the name of the town we are leaving, and probably also that of the Ken, or prefecture.

"We will now take a glance at scenery of a type which is common to most parts of Japan. The road runs on an embankment, some five or six feet high, between rice- (or paddy-) fields, which are almost invariably under two or three inches of water, and which cover all the level ground. Beyond these rise hills of marked outline, but of no great height, up which the rice-fields climb terrace above terrace until there is not a square foot of available ground unoccupied. At intervals we pass clusters of wooden huts, apparently deserted; but if we look carefully over the surrounding fields, we shall probably see the owners with their wives and children, with wicker baskets in their arms, up to their knees in mud and water. They are evidently working hard, but what the exact nature of their work is it is difficult to see. *Jinriki-shas* occasionally pass us on the road, their occupants being often asleep, and remaining so with a determination which is truly remarkable, considering the faulty nature of the road. Occasionally the monotony of the fields is broken by a bamboo-forest, over which the faintest breath of wind sends a wavy sheen as it reveals the silvery under-side of the leaves. Now and then the road is bordered on either side by those lofty pines of distorted shape which are so often represented in Japanese art. They twist and turn and stretch out their crooked arms in every direction, at times joining hands with their comrades on the opposite side of the road, as if taking part in some weird, fantastic dance, which is only interrupted for the moment to allow us to pass.

"Gradually the wooden huts become more frequent, and at last become almost continuous, developing finally into a long straggling town of one street. As we get farther into it, the huts improve gradually in size and style, until the middle portion of the town consists of a series of well-to-do-looking shops. Here we see the one European house, which we now recognise immediately as the police-station. Opposite this is the principal *chaya*, or tea-house, which

corresponds to an inn in Europe. The raised lower floor
seems one vast expanse of matting, stretching far back from
the street. We stop here for some tea, while our *jinriki-shas*
are changed and a relay of men is obtained. We are
welcomed by the girl-attendants of the place, who bow low
and conduct us to a back room, where we ensconce ourselves
on the floor round the *hibashis*, or ash fires. The girls
then bring us tea, in the diminutive cups peculiar to the
country, and sit down to watch for an opportunity to
replenish them, endeavouring meanwhile to tempt us to
taste some of the curious, and at first uninviting, cakes
which usually accompany the Japanese tea, and the most
common form of which resembles square blocks of 'Turkish
delight.' Meanwhile the *jinriki-sha* men are making the
most of their time outside. Each man has his bowl of rice
in hand, and is transferring its contents as fast as possible
to his mouth by means of chopsticks. The bowl is held
close up to the mouth, so that the process is simple and the
transfer rapid. This rice, with the addition of a cup or two
of *saké* (the spirituous drink of the country), will fit him
for several hours of steady running over any country you
please. We are soon in our *jinriki-sha* and off again. The
inhabitants come out to their doors and often form up in
the streets to see the *ijin-sang* (foreigners) go past. Each
tries to get a good view as we drive through, and we
see youthful messengers sent off in all directions to bring
absent relations, in order that no one may miss the extraordinary sight of a pale-faced man riding in a *jinriki-sha* ;
for even now the sight appears to be a novel one in most
parts of Japan.

" Leaving the town, we pass on through scenery which
varies in picturesqueness in proportion to the nearness or
distance of the hill country. At times the road crosses
swiftly-flowing streams. In them we may sometimes notice
a system of breakwaters or groins much used in Japan. In
places where the bank is soft and is exposed to the swirl
and rush of the river, you may see a series of these, formed
of large stones or flints inclosed in wicker baskets, which

are by no means unsightly, and yet most effectual in their operation. Shinto temples are passed every now and then, but as we have visited one already we will confine ourselves to taking a peep at a typical Buddhist temple. In the place of the *torii* of the Shinto temple, we here pass through a kind of monster lych-gate with a huge overhanging roof built of small pieces of bark, immediately below which the wood is profusely carved after the fashion of Chinese buildings. The central part of this building is taken up by the gateway itself, but on either side of this stand the colossal demons which guard so many temples in Japan. To say that they are absolutely hideous would be decided flattery. One is red, the other green; they both are in striking, ferocious attitudes, and their faces are distorted with demoniac fury. They are immensely muscular, and altogether seem hardly an inviting pair to put at the entrance to a place of worship. It is reassuring to notice, however, that a thick wire netting is fixed between us and these unpleasant champions of religion. This netting is, we find, more for their protection than ours, as it is to prevent the too easy exercise of a form of religion entirely new to us, which consists of ejecting from the mouth small pellets of well-damped paper at the bodies of these gaily painted fiends. If the pellet sticks on the figure the marksman is in favour with the gods, and is likely to fare well in the future; but if it refuses to stick, it is a sign that either his principles or his practices are at fault, and need careful consideration.

"Passing through by the paved way, we find ourselves before a building resembling in its general features the temple of the other religion, but we have only to glance into the interior to discover that there is a marked difference. In the place of the simple mirror and paper *gohei* of the Shinto temple, we here find a glittering image of Buddha, encased in a shrine no less brilliant than the god himself; on right and left shine attendant deities, who, in their gilded brightness, stand out from the sombre shadow cast by the temple roof. Here, too, we find the lotus in profusion, a beautiful emblem of the Buddhist faith. Lacquered rails inclose a large space around the shrine, which is unapproachable to any but the priests, who sit, or rather kneel, on right and left, with their quaint robes and shaven heads. Worshippers come and go. They kneel before the rails, pray, and retire, but the priests take no notice whatever, as they are simply in attendance on the shrine. Here, also, small coin are thrown as offerings to the god, just as they were in the Shinto temple. Beyond the shrine on both sides there hang portraits of the founder of the temple, and other ecclesiastics who have had some connection with it at some time or another, and round behind the shrine we shall probably find many old relics associated in some way with the past history of the place. Temples, of course, vary like everything else, but the differences are only minor ones, so that every Buddhist temple in the country preserves that element of gaudiness and decoration which contrasts so strongly with the plain and unpretentious style of the Shinto temples.

" In passing on through the country one is struck by the scarcity of birds and animals. Hawks and eagles are, perhaps, the most frequently seen, and crows also are fairly numerous ; but with the exception of these, the 'fowls of the air ' are but poorly represented. Cranes are to be seen, but they are not nearly so common as one would expect, considering the part they play in Japanese art of all kinds. Wild ducks and wild geese are much more abundant, especially in the castle moats, where the shooting of them is prohibited. Domestic animals are scarce, and are but poor specimens when one does see them. The dogs are either of a type closely resembling the Constantinople " pariah," brethren both in appearance and habits, or else they are those balls of fluffy hair with little pug-noses which are known in England as Japanese dogs. The cats are shorn of their tails, and it is probably owing to this that their bashfulness keeps them almost always out of sight. The Japanese horse is small and shaggy. His mane stands on end, and his tail is rough and long. His legs and body are well built for the uses he is usually put to, but as a riding horse his general appearance could hardly be termed elegant. In some parts of Japan, on the Tokaido, for instance, one may already pass occasionally a thoroughly European excursion van drawn by one or two horses, and filled with country people, who look perfectly at home in what they, a few years ago, regarded as a barbarous monstrosity."

RINTO, OR DRAGON LANTERN, KOFUKUJI.

CHAPTER II.

Our first month in Japan was spent in the city of Tokio and its vicinity. The courtesy shown us was from the beginning very great, most of the ministers and principal officials taking an early opportunity of calling, and welcoming us to their hospitable land. One of the members of the government, General Kuroda, who was absent in the distant northern island of Yezo, the government of which is part of his duty as colonial minister, telegraphed a friendly message, and invited us, notwithstanding his absence, to visit his department in the capital, following up our visit there by presents of sea-otter skins from the Kurile Islands, and other specimens of the products of the northern provinces of Japan. The other heads of state departments acted with similar promptness, and gave us invitations, many of which we were unable to accept until after our return from our visit to the interior.

An early opportunity was afforded us of making the

personal acquaintance of the leading personages of the country, under the more festive circumstances of a dinner party, held at the house of Admiral Kawamura. On this occasion there were present, besides our host and hostess, their imperial highnesses the Prince and Princess Arisugawa, who occupy the stations nearest to the throne. To the services of the prince in the suppression of the Satsuma rebellion, and the distinctions conferred upon him by the emperor at its conclusion, I have already referred. There were also present the imperial Prince and Princess Higashi Fushimi, who come next in nearness to the emperor. The party likewise comprised the prime minister, Sanjo; the vice minister, Iwakura; Mr. Okuma, the minister of finance; Mr. Terashima, the foreign minister, and his wife; Mr. Ito, the home minister; General Saigo, minister at war; Mr. Enouyé, minister of public works, with his wife and adopted daughter; Mr. Oki, the minister of justice; General Yamagata, the commander-in-chief of the army; and several other ladies and gentlemen. The dinner was served in European fashion, but with several pretty accompaniments unknown at home, among which may be mentioned the serving of a pie out of which, when presented to me, there flew a number of small birds with written sentiments of welcome attached to their legs. All the gentlemen on the occasion wore European dress, but most of the ladies were in the picturesque native costume, some of them having the teeth blackened and the eyebrows shaved off, with artificial indications of others in colour higher up, after the ancient style of the country. The two princesses were not so adorned, or dis-adorned, as the case may be, but were dressed in robes of scarlet (the imperial colour), and had their hair wrought, so to speak, halo-fashion, as shown in the portraits of the empress. This mode of dressing the hair is materially different from that common among Japanese ladies, and appears to be special to members of the Mikado's family. I am afraid that neither my son nor myself were at all worthy of our privileges on this occasion, as neither of us could address a word in their own language to either of the imperial and noble ladies between whom we respectively had the honour to sit. The course of the dinner, however (served in a manner wholly unknown, apparently, to the ladies of the court), furnished opportunities, we may hope, for those little attentions which are often quite as pleasant, and far more useful, than any words. At the conclusion of the dinner, after toasting the Emperor and our Queen, his excellency the prime minister proposed the health of the guest, doing me the honour to make the most gratifying references to the ships which had been constructed for the imperial government under my care, and intimating that it was the wish of his majesty the emperor, no less than that of himself and his colleagues in the government, that my son and I should be made heartily welcome to Japan, and have the fullest opportunities afforded us of seeing, without veil or hindrance, anything and everything that might be of interest to us—a wish that was most courteously and completely carried out, doubtless as a compliment to our country, and to the parliament of which I was a member, much more than to ourselves alone. After what has been recounted in former chapters, I need not say that the princes and ministers who attended this banquet were men of the most representative character, and were in large part the authors as well as the witnesses of the immense changes that have passed over Japan. We have seen the parts they played, and it is unnecessary further to advert to them here.

The city of Tokio, now the eastern capital of the country, was founded, as we have seen, nearly three centuries ago by Iyéyasu, the founder likewise of the quasi-royal dynasty of the Tokugawa Shoguns, more commonly known, perhaps, as the Tycoons (or Tai-Kuns) of Japan.* Its great feature was, and still is, its castle, the word being here employed in its comprehensive sense, inclusive of all the grounds and

---

* "Tai-Kun" was an unauthorised title sometimes assumed by the Shoguns, signifying great or exalted ruler. The Shogun Iyémitsu officially (but unlawfully) employed it, and the term was employed in transactions with foreigners of late years. Under the form "Tycoon" it has often been used, but Shogun is the proper and authorised designation.

buildings comprised within its outer moats. The origin of
this castle was noted in the chapter on Iyéyasu; it grew
from time to time, until at length it had no less than eight-
and-forty gates. The moat winds in a sort of huge distorted
spiral round the centre, in approaching which from any
direction the water would have to be crossed (were that practicable) at least twice, and often, according to the direction
of approach, four times. The outermost limb of the water
spiral, so to speak, is formed by the lower part of the
largest of the rivers. The principal palaces have been
destroyed by fires occurring at different times, and at
present none but garden houses and other minor buildings
exist in the interior, or what may be called the imperial
parts of the castle inclosure.

Another feature of the modern capital, Tokio, is the great
temple district of Shiba, near to which Admiral Kawamura,
with whom we stayed, resides, and through which we often
had occasion to drive. It is a beautiful spot, in large part
adorned with fine old trees, and here and there rising into
wooded slopes and hills. Within its picturesque inclosures
are the splendid tomb-temples of the Tokugawas—those of
them which remain, fire having devoured the finest of them.
These groves of Shiba were once secluded and sacred; they
are now largely opened up to public traffic and utility.
Some regret the change, others glory in it. The shrines
that remain are striking examples of ecclesiastical art and
decoration as applied in Buddhist temples under the patronage
of the rich and powerful. Another beautiful spot of like
associations, but made far less beautiful than aforetime by
both battle and fire, is Wooyeno, or Uyeno, on the opposite
side of the city. I have elsewhere mentioned the struggle
that occurred there after the recent imperial restoration;
suffice it here to say that its elevated grounds furnish a
beautiful prospect over the widespread city; that the old and
the new there exist side by side in strange contrast, an old
colossal image of Buddha, with its lanterns and other sacred
accessories, looking down upon the entrance to a modern
restaurant, where travellers, Japanese and foreigners,

refresh themselves in European fashion in a way (as we more than once had opportunities of experiencing) not unworthy, say, of the Café Cascade in the Bois. In the springtime, when the cherry and the plum break into blossom, the heights and groves and temple paths of Woo-yeno, peopled with the picturesque and happy Japanese, form quite a paradise. There are Tokugawa temples here too, bright but now neglected memorials of a family which the exigencies of the period have made it necessary to repress, but which, as I think, when the story of Japan comes to be written a century or two hence, will take a high place among those who gave peace to the land, and encouraged the pursuit of those arts and studies which are the allies of innocence and healthful pleasures.*

Although Tokio is in the main still a Japanese city, exhibiting everywhere the life, the customs, and the costumes of the Japanese people, it bears many manifest and obtrusive evidences of European interposition. The railway, with its European station and equipments, is the first great contrast with the native architecture and appliances which strikes one. Not far from it is the foreign settlement, where many of the houses are of European type; and in looking over the city from an eminence, one sees bank buildings, schools, and occasional residences of foreign pattern rising up above the less elevated Japanese buildings—less elevated save as regards the temples alone, which here and there stand up high above all other Japanese constructions. Most of the great educational establishments, such as the University, the College of Engineering, the Military College, and the Naval College, are of European style; as are also some of the barracks, and likewise some of the manufacturing establishments. In fact, buildings of this style, with which alone

---

* In saying this I am not unmindful of the many evils of the Tokugawa rule, or regretful because it has passed away. Judging it by our European standards, it was bad enough: but judging it by comparison with that of the Ashikagas, which went before it—and history will in part so judge it—it well merits the favourable recognition of impartial persons.

we are familiar at home, but which were perfectly unknown in Tokio a few years ago, are now very frequent and conspicuous objects in the bird's-eye view of the city.

The business streets and the shops of Tokio are, with few or no exceptions, purely Japanese, the number of foreign residents being so few in proportion to the million of its inhabitants as in no degree to interfere with the native aspect of the place as one walks or drives along its thorough-fares. The interest felt as we move about among the people, looking into the stores and places of business, never flags. Such is the native taste for artistic forms and groupings of objects, that even the commonest shops first arrest the eye with masses of brightness and colour, and then amuse the mind with curious and fanciful details. An ordinary Japanese china shop is as entertaining an "arrangement in blue and white" as óne of the cabinets of Governor Pope Hennessy at Hong Kong, or of Sir Henry Thompson in Wimpole Street. And the leisurely shopkeepers, male or female, or both, inhaling frequent whiffs of tobacco with philosophic calmness, and yet always alert, and always courteous to the visitor, add to the pleasing attractiveness of the place, contrasting with the eager money-grasping habits that one gets too much accustomed to in other lands.

One of our earliest visits of inspection in Tokio was to the temple of Asakusa, a notable place of its kind, and full of interest to the stranger. It may be regarded as the principal Buddhist temple of Tokio, and is dedicated to Kwannon, sometimes god and sometimes goddess, to whose Indian origin, multiplied incarnations, and Japanese popu-larity I have elsewhere adverted. Asakusa was once an outlying village near Yedo; the city of Tokio may now be said not only to embrace it, but to have endowed it with an essentially metropolitan character. It is in many senses the most popular and frequented temple in the capital, and attracts crowds continually to its shrines, and larger crowds more continually to its precincts. But let no one imagine for a moment that the attractions of this temple bear any sort of relation to the attractions which draw the crowd

either to the Abbey of Westminster or to the Surrey
Tabernacle or to the Pro-Cathedral of Kensington. Different as are the influences which invite our people to these
churches respectively, and to those of which these are
types, and to the many other churches which attract by
forces existing in none of these, the Buddhist temples of
Japan are entirely out of relation to all of them. Nor,
so far as one can see, are they in any more relation to the
animating principles of the faith on which they are founded.
There is but little indeed in the thronged Asakusa to
remind one of the " grey-haired saint " Asita, whose ears,

> " Long closed to earthly things, caught heavenly sounds,
> And heard at prayer beneath his peepul-tree
> The Devas singing songs at Buddha's birth."

And quite as little is there to remind one of the after
musings of " Lord Buddha " himself, when in sylvan soli-
tudes he forgot himself in

> " The woes of men,
> The ways of fate, the doctrines of the books,
> The lessons of the creatures of the brake,
> The secrets of the silence whence all comes,
> The secrets of the gloom whereto all go,
> The life which lies between, like that arch flung
> From cloud to cloud across the sky, which hath
> Mists for its masonry and vapoury piers,
> Melting to void again which was so fair
> With sapphire hues, garnet, and chrysoprase." *

The attractions of Asakusa are those of a fair rather
than those of a temple. The approach is by a long stone-
paved avenue of shops and stalls, and the sides and back
of the temple are surrounded by tea-houses, waxwork exhibitions, archery rooms, monkey shows, and other entertainments. In the immediate neighbourhood singing girls
make merry the hearts of citizens and pilgrims, filling
their ears with joyous music, and their eyes with dancing
pictures. " There is nothing strange to the Japanese mind

---

* For these and the lines immediately preceding, see Edwin Arnold's
' Light of Asia.'

in this association of temples and toy-shops. The good
bonzes in their sermons declare, as the result of their
exegesis and meditations, that husbands are bound to love
their wives, and show it by allowing them plenty of pin-
money and hair-pins, and to be not bitter against them
by denying them neat dresses and handsome girdles. The
farmer who comes to town with his daughter turns from
prayer to the purchase of pomatum or a mirror " (Griffis).

Before the temple of Asakusa stands, as is usual with
the Buddhist temples of Japan, the gateway (Niomon), in
this case a huge construction, within which, one on either
side, scowl the grim giant gatekeepers (Nio), carved and
coloured with cruel art into triumphs of the hideous and
the demoniacal. One, coloured red, is said to represent the
Yo or male principle of the Chinese philosophy ; the other,
coloured green, is said to represent the female principle.*
The temple itself swarms with gods and shrines and
emblems and votive gifts, and is a very busy place indeed.
A large bronze censer fronts you as you enter, surmounted
by a rampant animal that seems in strange contrast with
what one would fain conceive of as the sacredness of the
place. Before the high-altar is a huge box or coffer to
receive the money gifts of the people. The altar itself
is screened with an open fabric of wire. The methods
of worship are various. Besides the bowing and the
rubbing of the hands which compose one method, and
the use of strings of beads like those employed by Roman

---

* " Ni-wo-son (Two Honoured
Kings), the guardians of the right and
left. These are always placed under
the gateway, as may be seen at
Asakusa, and formerly at Shiba.
The most celebrated are at Shiba-
yama-mura, in Kadzusa. The idols
are erect figures with flowing robes ;
that on the right, facing the temple,
is red, has its mouth open, and represents the *Yo* or male principle of
Chinese philosophy. That on the
left is green ; the mouth is firmly
closed, indicative of silence, the female *In* principle. Small prints of
these, pasted on the beams over the
entrances of houses, protect them
from burglars and thieves. Travellers on foot present large straw
sandals, and hang them at these
places. They also burn *sen ko* (incense), and pray for pedestrian
strength to perform their journey."
—Pfoundes, ' Fu so Mimi Bukuro.'—
See engraving facing p. 92, vol. i.

Catholics which form another, there are two equally curious, but obviously of very unequal efficiency. Of these the first—which is addressed to a god of moderate size and accessible position, and which appears only applicable to bodily ailments or imperfections—consists in rubbing that part of the body of the idol which corresponds with the defective limb or organ of the devotee, and then rubbing that limb or organ itself with corresponding energy. "Idols may be seen, well worn by devotees rubbing the figure and then the corresponding portions of their own bodies ; this god is called Binzuru Senja, and represents the servant of the disciples of Shaka (Buddha), noted for his energy and untiring perseverance in attending to his duties" (Pfoundes). Binzuru of Asakusa is a well-worn idol, undergoing slow but very certain mutilation. The features of his face are sadly reduced, not to say gone, and his original comeliness of form, which may still be inferred from what is left of him, has already disappeared. Nor is this to be wondered at considering the energy with which he is sometimes worshipped. On one occasion I observed a woman, who scarcely seemed to need much physical improvement judging from her outward figure, vigorously extracting virtue from many parts of the submissive image, and as zealously applying it, so that it was difficult to discover if she had any soundness whatever to let alone. I am inclined to believe that this lady was too religious in her way, not to say fanatical, for all the healing and active powers of poor Binzuru failed to satisfy her, and she went from god to god, and from shrine to shrine, with a steadiness and impartiality of devotion that were most unusual. Like some other devotees that one has known, however, while extracting all the blessings and benefits that her faith could secure for her, she shied (if I may so speak) at the sight of the coffers, and gave nothing in the way of financial aid to the temple of her choice. This conduct on her part is the more remarkable as she gave no indication of having come in any degree under the "civilising" influences now at work in the country; and selfishness does not seem to be a natural characteristic of the Japanese people.

The other peculiar form of worship to which I have adverted, and which flourishes in this and in similar temples, consists in chewing pellets of paper and "shying" them at the idol. If they stick, the fact is taken as a sign that the prayer is heard; if they fall off, it is a sign that it is not heard. The Buddhist gods are often elaborately decorated with these emblems of piety, and it is reasonable, perhaps, to infer that the more there are of them the greater is the beneficence of the god.

This may be the proper place for referring to yet a third mode of worship, which is to be found in Japan as well as in India, and which consists in praying by machinery. I did not observe a praying-machine within the temple of Asakusa, but there is one outside of it. It is neither more nor less than a wheel mounted in a stone post. An account of a similar wheel at Hakodadi is given with a sketch * in the official record of Commodore

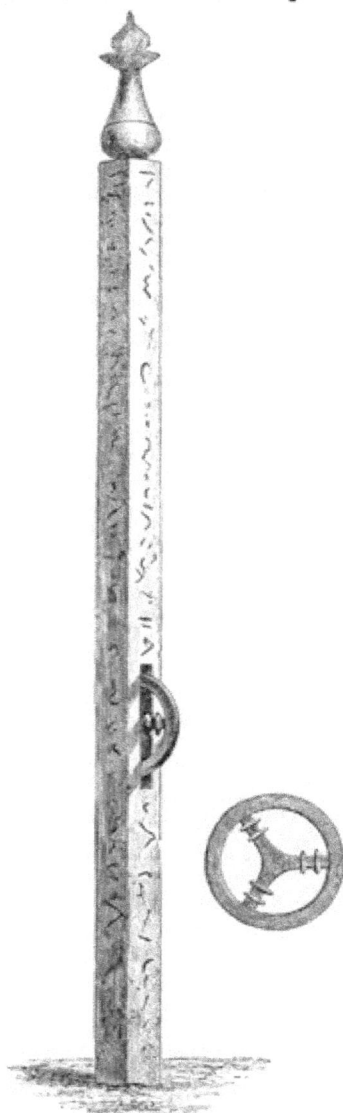

PRAYING-WHEEL

---

* From which the engraving which I give is roughly taken.

Perry's American Expedition to Japan. It consisted of a tall post, having an iron wheel inserted in a mortice upon an axle. The wheel had three spokes, with two loose iron rings upon each. The jingle of these rings calls the attention of the god when the passer-by turns the wheel. Every one who turns the wheel is supposed to obtain credit for prayers proportioned to the number of the wheel's revolutions. The four sides of the post are covered with Buddhistic inscriptions, of which the compiler of the record referred to gives the translations which I repeat in a footnote.* The compiler also refers to the praying-mills of Thibet, to some of which water-power has been applied, and suggests to the Japanese the desirability of improving upon this by employing steam-power for the purpose— a suggestion which the modern Japanese will know how to estimate at its just value, let us hope.

Other forms of devotion common in this temple and throughout Japan are those of writing prayers on slips of paper and attaching them to the shrine of the god to

---

* "The great round mirror of knowledge says, ' Wise men and fools are embarked in the same boat ': whether prospered or afflicted, both are rowing over the deep lake; the gay sails lightly hang to catch the autumnal breeze; then away they straight enter the lustrous clouds, and become partakers of heaven's knowledge."

"The believing man, Hanyo Shenkaman, who no longer grows old."

"The believing woman, once called Yuenning : happy was the day she left."

"Multitudes fill the graves."

"To enable to enter the abodes of the perfect, and to sympathise fully with the men of the world, belongs to Buddha. It is only by this one vehicle, the coffin, we can enter Hades. There is nought like Buddha, nothing at all."

"We of the human race, with hearts, minds, and understandings, when we read the volumes of Buddha enjoy great advantages."

"He whose prescience detects knowledge says: As the floating grass is blown by the gentle breeze, or the glancing ripples of autumn disappear when the sun goes down, or as the ship returns home to her old shore, so is life, it is a smoke, a morning tide."

"Buddha himself earnestly desires to hear the name of this person (who is buried), and wishes he may go to life."

"He who has left humanity is now perfected by Buddha's name, as the withered moss is by the dew."

"The canon of Buddha says, All who reach the blissful land will become so that they cannot be made to transmigrate (or change for the worse)."

be moved, and of suspending votive pictures and other
objects, after the fashion of many Roman Catholic churches.
Some of these are memorials of gratitude for favours and
beneficent interventions in the past; others are emblems
of prayer and propitiation for future benefits. All the
accidents, mischances, miracles, hopes, ambitions, and long-
ings of life are represented here; and one is at a loss —when
looking, for example, at a framed and glazed picture of the
Pacific Mail Steamship Company's ships which is hung up
here—to wonder whether one of the great metropolitan
temples of Japan is not being brought down to the
miserable level of our own towns and cities, in which the
advertiser is allowed to push from sight and sense everything but his own monstrous impertinence, and the things
on behalf of which that is employed. " Beyond the great
space devoted to the public are the various altars and gilt
images of the deities, sages, and saints of the Buddhist
Pantheon and Calendar. Candles burn, incense floats,
and the sacred books repose here. The privileged faithful
can, for a fee to the fat priests who sit behind their account-
books, come within the iron wire screen, and, kneeling on
the clean matting in front of the great altar, may pray,
or read or chant sacred books, canonical or liturgical, or,
having a vow to a particular deity, or wishing to invoke
the intercession of a special saint, may enter, to kneel
remote from the crowd " (Griffis).

It is unnecessary to recount here our visits to other
temples in Tokio, either Buddhist or Shinto, as in recording
our journey through the interior I shall have many occasions to make mention of such. It was necessary to take
notice of that of Akasuka, owing to its unique celebrity,
and to the prominent place which it occupies in the present
life of the city. But as it has been described in detail
by others, I have been content to sketch its leading
characteristics.

Several days of our first month in Tokio were instructively
spent in acquainting ourselves with the methods pursued in
the production of the beautiful Japanese works of art in

lacquer and bronze. Every process and detail were laid open to our leisurely inspection, and delightful it was to observe and watch the operations of the art-labourers. These manufactures are carried on in small detached rooms and workshops, which bear no resemblance whatever to the great factories with which we are familiar at home, and after many visits to them, both in the capital and in the interior towns, I can cordially say with Dr. Dresser, who visited Japan to study the subject, that "while the art processes of Japan are such as render the production of quantity impossible if excellence is to be obtained, they yet secure the highest degree of art merit." I can likewise say with him : " I have watched the poor artisan labouring at his work with an earnestness and love such as I never beheld out of Japan, and the very features of the workmen testify to their happiness, and to the love with which they perform their painstaking labour. No thought of gain appears to enter their minds, and no touch is spared which will make the work more lovely ; this is how the beautiful works which we delight to look upon are produced." It is also true, as has been said,[*] that "in the Japanese workman there is first an intense love of nature ; he is a student of nature, and loves birds, flowers, and insects, and he carries out this love in his work. But the great point is that he thinks, so to speak, through the material in which he works. In all my experience and examination of Japanese objects I have failed to find any evidence that the workman has ever thought of imitating any other material, method, or process than that in which and for which he was working."

From the earliest days the production of lacquer-work has been a specialty of Japan, and one in which it has never been equalled. It is considered by some that it attained its greatest artistic perfection in Japan about five hundred years ago, of which and of former periods there are many specimens extant, while the manufacturing skill lavished upon it was greater from one to three centuries ago than at

---

[*] By Mr. George Wallis.

any other period. It is satisfactory to know, however, more especially as the old lacquer of Japan is now becoming exceedingly rare and precious in the country,* that although large quantities of common lacquer-work is now produced in the country, the art of producing the best work, in both a manufacturing and artistic sense, is still fully preserved and practised, although the value of labour has greatly increased, of course, in the country since the days either of Taka Uji or of Iyéyasu. The exhibition of Paris in 1878 furnished the world with abundant proofs of this statement. This and former European and American exhibitions, while amply recompensing the Japanese exhibitors, have created so great a further demand for their products that it is not easy to sustain a proportionate supply. The difficulty lies in the fact that the characteristic refinements and delicacies of the best art have been handed down from age to age, from father to son, and cannot be learnt from books or in schools of apprenticeship.

I have said that this production of choice lacquer-work in Japan comes down from very remote times. A book said to have been written nearly two centuries before the Christian era speaks of articles of lacquer being employed at the court; and we ourselves saw in the temple of Todaiji, in the ancient capital of Nara, lacquer boxes for containing prayer-books which appear to have been made in the third century of our era, which are much admired by connoisseurs, and are held to prove that the art had attained great excellence even in those ancient days. In the year 380 A.D. a minister of state published a work† in which red and gold lacquers are mentioned. In 410 an officer (Minamoto-no-Juin) published another work,‡ in which he speaks of lacquers of gold, and likewise of other lacquers known as *nashiji*, which are of orange colour sown with sparks of gold,

---

* " For a box about six inches square I was asked in Japan £100 sterling, and Lady Parkes told me that fine specimens were, in Tokio, bringing their weight in gold."—Dr.

C. Dresser, at the Society of Arts. My own experience corroborates this.

† 'Engishiki,' by the Sa-Dai-jin.

‡ 'Utsubo Monogatari.'

and the makers of which he speaks of as "very celebrated."
In 480 a lady, who achieved literary renown, in one of her
works * speaks of a novel description of lacquer incrusted
with pearl. Further progress cannot be traced up to the
tenth century, early in which the country obtained rest
from centuries of political and military strife, and the
peaceful arts began once again to exhibit vigour. In an
official compilation published at the last Paris Exhibition it
is stated that at the beginning of that century the artistic
taste of Japan awakened, and its art-workmen applied themselves with devotion to the production of articles which
should be distinguished alike by the utmost solidity and
the greatest beauty, in order to keep pace with their neighbours. The objects then produced unite these two qualities
in the highest degree, their creators having spared neither
time nor pains in the effort to produce works which should
carry their names down to posterity. The productions of
the Japanese lacquer-workers from the year 910 to 1650,
known as *Jidai mono*, are very highly esteemed. In the
long peace enjoyed subsequently under the Tokugawas the
taste for works of art extended, and the rich and noble
families came to consider articles in lacquer as indispensable
adornments of their palaces, and their production consequently was greatly increased. But this and all other
branches of art and manufacture in Japan were dependent
upon local demands down to our own time, and only obtained
the stimulus of a foreign demand when in 1859 the port of
Yokohama was thrown open—or shall we say forced open?—
to foreign commerce. Lacquer has since become one of the
chief articles of exportation. In the Vienna Exhibition of
1873 a great falling off in the quality of the Japanese exhibits of lacquer-work was observed. The government of
the country thereupon addressed themselves to the revival
of the art, and with so much success that it is doubtful if
the vast Exhibition of Paris in 1878 contained anything
more strikingly beautiful and admirable in every respect

---

* ' Genji Monogatari,' by Mura-saki Shikibu.

than the lacquer exhibits of the Japanese section. It is
thought by some authorities that the finest specimens of
ancient work were then surpassed both in form and in
colour.   The manufacture is carried on in several provinces,
but its best workmen and most perfect works are to be
found, it is said, in the three great cities—Tokio, Kioto, and
Osaka.

The Japanese lacquer is laid usually upon articles of wood,
and not upon articles of papier-maché, as many suppose.   It
is produced from the sap of the *rhus vernicifera*, which is
taken in its natural state into a large wooden tub or vat,
and there stirred in the sun with a large spatula until its
excess of water is evaporated.   In some cases the varnish so
produced undergoes careful straining; in others it is mixed
with sulphate of iron, and in others with vermilion, or red
oxide of iron, or indigo.   Oil is sometimes employed, and
powdered stone likewise.   Into some inferior varnishes a sort
of paste, made of rice, enters in a considerable proportion.
There are a dozen methods of employing the various varnishes,
differing according to the nature of the object to be produced.
In the best lacquer numerous coatings are applied, dried,
and polished successively.   The first polishings are done
with a stone named *tsushimada* (suitable for hones), the later
by means of water and charcoal, made from the *Andromeda
ovalifolia*, and the last with pulverised stag's horn.   All the
polishings are effected by the hand.   The laying on of the
successive layers of varnish is often a matter of great skill,
care, and patience, especially where highly raised surfaces are
required by the conditions of the finished design; and those
who examine some of the best specimens of Japanese lacquer
little imagine how much of these qualities have been expended upon them.   In his recent work on the 'Art and Art
Industries of Japan,' Sir Rutherford Alcock says: " Mr.
Audsley speaks of one cabinet in the collection of Mr. James
L. Bowes in which he thinks he can distinguish nine different
species of lacquers, and twenty-four different modes of artistic
treatment, together with sixteen different modes of applying
and decorating gold-work, and seven ways of treating various

metals. . . . There is infinite variety in the value which the Japanese themselves attach to specimens, according to the fineness of the varnish employed, and the time that has elapsed since the work was completed, as the varnish acquires by age a vitreous hardness.   Of course the quality of the design and artistic treatment enters also largely into the question of value."

In the passage which I have omitted from this quotation occurs this sentence : " Gold and other metals and colouring matters are sometimes mingled with, and at others applied on, the surface, as the designs are elaborated, *but all, I believe, in a liquid state.*" *   As Sir Rutherford has himself seen, as he states, the production of Japanese lacquer-work, it is hard to call in question the statement of fact which he reports ; but it is certainly an error to say that gold, for example, is applied to Japanese lacquer in a liquid state. In the case of smooth-surface lacquers, where the gold is not to be in relief, the course pursued is as follows.   The design to be produced is traced upon a leaf of paper, which is then reversed, and has repeated upon the opposite side of it the outlines and other features of the design, in a mixture of varnish and vermilion softened over a mild fire.   This side of the paper is then applied to the lacquer to be decorated, and the paper is rubbed and pressed upon it by means of a small spatula of bamboo.   The transfer of the pattern from the paper to the lacquered surface is further assisted by gently beating the paper down with a small silk bag containing powdered stone.   The paper is then peeled off, and can be used again if desired.   The slight relief of the pattern so produced upon the lacquer is rubbed down with carbon polish, and the design, and that alone, is then lightly covered with a thin layer of quickly drying varnish.   Gold in powder is then applied to the moist surface—by means of a camel's-hair pencil if the gold-powder be fine, and by means of a small tube if it be comparatively coarse and heavy.   The article is then dried for a day in a warm closet, such as is

---

* The italics are mine.

used for drying the ordinary lacquer varnish. The design is next lightly coated with a very thin layer of varnish, applied by means of paper steeped in it, and passed very delicately over the object, which is then re-dried in the closet. The object receives several further extremely light coatings of varnish and subsequent polishings before it is completed. Silver is applied in powder in the same manner.

When either gold or silver has to be applied to designs in relief, the details of the process vary considerably from the foregoing, but the application of the metals is effected in substantially the same manner. When leaf-gold, and silver in leaf, have to be applied, they are laid upon the varnished surface prepared to receive them, and dealt with in the usual manner, the varnish acting as a "size" for the metal leaf. When mother-of-pearl has to be employed as an incrustation for lacquer, it is laid on during the varnishing processes, earlier if it be thick than if it be thin, and the final polishing is proceeded with until the pearl is brought to the surface.

The production of articles in cast metal, like that of articles in lacquer, began so early in Japan that all trace of its origin is lost. As far back as the middle of the seventh century of our era the discovery of antique copper bells beneath the ground commenced (while levelling the site of the temple of So-fuku-ji in Omi), and has continued at intervals down to recent times. It was hastily considered that these were relics of ancient Buddhist temples, but Buddhism had but so recently made its way into Japan, when the bell above-named was discovered, that the true explanation of the existence of these buried castings has yet to be sought. It is certain, however, that these bells, and all other cast articles of very early periods, containing copper, were either the productions of other countries, or were produced from imported metals, for native copper was not discovered in Japan until the eighth century of our era. In view of this fact it is highly probable that the art of casting in bronze, as well as cast articles, was introduced into Japan from Korea or China. But "if the Japanese have borrowed from the Chinese in bronze-casting, of which there is no proof," bluntly says Sir Rutherford Alcock in the work already quoted in this chapter, " they seem to have nothing to learn from us. They not only give all the delicate moulding of the lotus-leaf by some process unknown, but produce relief ornamentation by cutting the surrounding metal away, as Mr. Audsley has rightly pointed out. Such relieved work they further enrich with the burin or damascene with gold and silver. . . . They are much in the habit of graving diaper and other patterns on bronzes and filling them up with silver wire, with which they cover large surfaces in salvers or vases with good effect, and very original designs on patterns."

The Japanese method of producing bronze articles is to commence by modelling in wax (mixed with resin, etc.) the object to be produced, and then most carefully to cover the wax model with clay or *argile*. By submitting the whole to the action of heat the wax is melted from the interior of the clay, and a mould is thus left, into which the molten bronze is poured. The process seems simple enough when thus described ; but it is often worked out with such marvellous skill and elaboration as to excite both wonder and admiration when the finished result is beheld. In forming the model, the wax is used chiefly for the more delicate parts, blocks of wood being employed for the more solid parts. Care is taken, of course, to so form and proportion these blocks that they can be withdrawn from the mould before the casting takes place. In forming the mould around the model of wood and wax, a succession of liquid or semi-liquid argillaceous coatings are laid on with a brush, the quantity of sand being increased in the successive coatings, and each coating dried to receive the next. When the delicate model has thus been substantially protected, and had its finer interstices filled in, the whole is covered in with dry sand, which is pressed into the cavities and depressions, and formed into a rough exterior suitable for the further operations. The mould is then placed in the furnace, which is of a sufficient heat to melt the wax, which is largely absorbed by the sand, and converted into escaping gas. Care has to be exercised before the pouring in of the bronze, to bring the mould to a proper temperature, in order to secure a free flow of the metal, unchilled, throughout the finer parts of the mould.

The European mode of casting ornamental objects, such as birds, flowers, etc., in very high relief as decoration of larger bronze objects, is to employ " piece moulds" produced in the following manner. After moulding the pattern in wax or clay, and taking a plaster cast from it, you from this again take a cast in an alloy of tin and lead. This is then sharply chased and divided into a number of pieces, and is then used as the pattern from which the bronze or other article produced is moulded. The process is, of course, an expensive one, and it is not resorted to by the Japanese. They never employ piece-moulds, and yet such is their skill that they produce complex flower-forms as perfect as simpler castings, and more perfect than we ever, as a matter of fact, do produce by aid of our piece-moulds. It follows from their plan that whereas with the piece-mould system a succession of articles can be produced from the same mould, the Japanese require to remodel every article. As Dr. Dresser says: " If a thousand articles had to be cast, each with a flower in relief on the side, and if each vase was to be of precisely the same pattern, a separate model would yet be prepared for the casting of each, and the same labour would be expended in producing every one that was expended on the production of the first."

The idea of producing a thousand ornamental articles precisely alike is entirely foreign to the Japanese. I have never yet seen a pair of bronzes alike in all respects, and one of the great charms of their productions lies in the certainty that each is a separate and more or less independent work of art. That they produce articles in pairs is known to everybody, but while there are general resemblances between the two articles composing the pair, there are also marked differences between them. I have, for example, a splendid pair of bronze vases (measuring 26 inches high and 14 inches across) which represent, in my judgment, the most perfect work now executed in Japan.* They are a pair in form and general features, the conventional peacocks which form bracket-handles and the conventional nameless creatures which surround the base, being also alike in both. The general disposition of the ornamental work upon them is likewise the same in both. But beyond this the resemblances of the two vases do not go, for every detail of the flowers, birds, fans, and other decorative ornaments is different; where the same flower is repeated, it is presented in another form, with a different arrangement of stalk, leaves, and buds. The main ornament on one side of each vase is a figure group, but the figures are different, and differently disposed; that of the other side is a group of flowers, sprays, and birds, but the grouping of the two bear little resemblance. These vases furnish a striking example of the success with which the Japanese artist contrives to cover a very large portion of the object with decoration, and yet to avoid any such crowding of objects as to suggest excess. They also furnish an equally striking example of the variety of artistic interest given by them to individual objects. They are adorned with objects in relief, others in intaglio, and others in plain insertion. Various precious metals are employed in all of these ways, gold being most commonly used in *in relievo*. There are forty-five figures in gold in a single group of birds and flowers, exclusive of many scattered blossom-specklings in the same metal. But it is unnecessary to dwell upon the beauty of the Japanese bronzes, for it has been freely recognised by all who have studied the subject.

The method of producing coloured pictures in metals, known as *syakfdo*, has been justly pronounced by Mr. Audsley† as perhaps the most characteristic of all the

---

* They were presented to me by the imperial government in token of the satisfaction which his majesty the emperor was pleased to express with the three armour-plated vessels of war which I had the honour to design and superintend for him.

† One of the authors of 'Keramaic Art of Japan,' by Messrs. Audsley & Bowes, of Liverpool.

metallurgical works of Japan. " In this," he says, "numerous metals and alloys are associated, the designs being produced in colours through the agency of the various coloured metals; white being represented by silver, yellow by gold, black by platina, all shades of dull red by copper and its alloys, brown by bronze, and blue by steel. Gold, silver, and polished steel, of course, represent themselves in design as well as abstract colours. A red garment, embroidered with gold and clasped with silver, would be executed in red-coloured copper, inlaid with gold, and furnished with a silver brooch. The sword in the hand of the warrior would be unpolished steel, and, if bloody, would have red copper laid in it. I have seen many beautiful specimens of *syakfdo*, and can bear witness to their faultless execution." Of *repoussé* work Sir Rutherford Alcock says it " is said to be known and practised by them, but I cannot say I have ever seen any clearly marked specimen." But it is a fact that this class of metal work is produced in Japan, as I can state from observation there. It is sometimes produced by beating the metal into a steel mould, sunk and engraved for the purpose; at other times it is produced by simply hammering, with or without a mandril. The artists sometimes make a point of putting no ornament that would obliterate the traces of the hammering. This branch of metal work, however, is much less common in Japan than that of casting.

Before concluding these remarks on bronzes, I ought to note that by an act of courtesy on the part of the governor of Tokio we were privileged to see, and to study repeatedly and leisurely, what all the Japanese who saw it pronounced the very finest specimen of bronze-casting that had ever been executed in Japan. This splendid specimen of the national art—a man's figure engaged with a dragon—was sent to Admiral Kawamura's house by the governor soon after our arrival, and was allowed to remain there throughout our visit. I feel quite incapable of putting into words any such description of it as would convey to the reader even an approximate idea, either of its beauty as a work of art, or of its wonderfulness as a mechanical production.

One exceedingly pleasant and interesting day of our first month was spent in visiting the paper mills of Ogi, a short drive from the city, under the guidance of their excellencies the minister of finance (in whose department part of them are) and the minister of public works. The art of paper-making is one in which the Japanese have long excelled, some of their paper productions surpassing in strength, and others in parchment-like qualities, those of every other country, even down to the present time. My esteemed friend Sir Sydney Waterlow advised me before I went to Japan to note with particular interest this branch of manufacture, observing that there existed in this country demands for some very special classes of paper which could only be supplied from there. In pursuance of this suggestion, I lost no opportunity of looking closely into the subject, although I cannot profess to have discovered any secrets relating to it. By the kindness of the government I was able to bring away with me assorted specimens of the productions of Ogi and of other mills, and so beautiful are some of these that I was not surprised to find the Ogi factory executing large orders from the French and Russian governments, and from several private firms in Europe, the quality most in request being a beautiful fine-surfaced paper of excessive toughness, which is found very valuable as a material for military maps, and for other purposes in which great durability and power of sustaining much wear and tear without injury are objects of first importance.

It is impossible to trace the history of the paper-manufacture in Japan back to its commencement. Specimens produced at the beginning of the eighth century after Christ still exist, and show that the art of paper-making was then highly developed. In the *Nihonki* mention is made of the matter in the year 590 A.D., and the words " Paper is manufactured " are there recorded; but this was probably suggested by the introduction of some improvement from Korea rather than by the invention of paper-making, as it is known that books were already in existence. In the year 900 A.D. three descriptions of paper were produced in Japan : 1. *Mashi,* made from hempen rag pulp ; 2. *Hishi,* made from such plants as *gampi* (*Wickstroemia canescens*) ; 3. *Kokushi,* made from *kozo* (*Broussonetia papyrifera*), which was like the paper now in common use in the country.

Excepting paper made from rags, for the production of which large European factories have been erected at Ogi, Japanese paper is produced from a small number of materials, the chief of which have just been named. The first in importance of these is *kozo*, the plant named last in the preceding paragraph. It is the fourth order of the twenty-first class of the Linnaean system, and is a small shrub reaching to about six feet in height, with branches springing directly from the earth, and grows in nearly all the provinces of Japan. It is a deciduous plant, bearing its new dark-green leaves in springtime. The leaves are " ovate in form, with a sinuous or serrated margin, and very rough upon the upper surface." There are two kinds of this shrub, pistilliferous and staminiferous.* They are propagated either by layering (*marcottage*) or by root-slipping. The mode of treating them for paper-making purposes is as follows : They are cut into 3-feet lengths and steamed in a large boiler containing a little boiling water. The bark is then peeled off, steeped in water, and has the dark outer rind or pellicle scraped off with a knife, the scrapings being used for producing inferior paper. The bark thus scraped and cleansed is next carefully washed in running water, and then exposed to the sun until bleached sufficiently white. After this it is boiled in a lye, formed with buckwheat ash, to remove gummy and resinous substances from it.

---

* " The staminiferous blossom about the middle of May ; the inflorescence is axillary, and supported on a peduncle of a little more than an inch in length ; the corolla is monopetalous, divided into four lobes at the limb, and is of a dark purple colour. These blossoms are tetrandrous. The inflorescence of the pistilliferous plant is also supported on a peduncle, and consists of a number of flowers arranged together in a head ; from each blossom a long pistil projects ; their colour is dark purple."—Mr. Sakakibara Yosino, in Exhibit on Japanese Education of 1876.

The fibres are then readily separated. After cutting out knots of excessive hardness, the workman now beats the fibre into a pulp with wooden mallets upon blocks of stone. This pulp is mixed in tubs or vats with the needful quantity of water, to which is added a milky substance prepared with rice flour and a gummy decoction from the bark of the *Nori noki* (*Hydrangea paniculata*) or from the root of the *tororo*.* When the steeping in this mixture has proceeded sufficiently long, the pulp is spread out into sheets by means of fine sieves of bamboo and silk. After draining, the sheets are transferred by means of brushes to drying-boards.

Similar processes are employed for producing paper from *gampi*. This plant (*Wickstroemia canescens*) is the fourth order of the eighth class of Linnaeus, and is a small shrub growing sometimes ten feet in height, with leaves arranged alternately on the stem, the under surface of each leaf being covered with soft hair. Its blossoms, coming about the middle of June, are of a pale yellow colour. The flowers are octandrous, with one pistil. The paper made from this shrub is very fine and supple, and is therefore very suitable for taking transfer copies. It has also the advantage of not becoming worm-eaten. Paper is also made from the *mitsu mata* plant (*Edgworthia papyrifera*), the first order of the eighth class, a deciduous shrub growing to seven or eight feet in height. At the close of autumn many buds spring on the ends of the branches and arrange themselves in a cluster, " hanging down like a wild bee's nest," and blossoming when the spring comes round. The branches are so

---

* " *Tororo Hibiscus.* The seventh order of the sixteenth class of Linnaeus, a genus of *Malvaceae* of De Candolle. This is an herbaceous plant, the seeds of which are sown in spring. It grows to the height of one or two feet, and is of a hairy nature. The leaves are palmate, having five or seven lobes, and are arranged alternately on the stem. During the hot season flowers spring from the ends and axils of the branches. The corolla has five petals, and is more than two inches in diameter; it is of a pale-yellow colour, with a dark-purple blotch at the bottom of each petal, and is ephemeral. These flowers are monodelphous and polyandrous. The pod is five-celled, each cell containing many seeds. The root is conical, and abounds with viscous juice."—*Mr. Yosino.*

pliant that they will not break when knotted.* The corolla
of the flower is white outside and yellow inside. The leaves
appear after the blossom has fallen.

The Ogi mills comprise one which belongs to a company,
and which is fitted up throughout with English machinery,
first for preparing the materials by sorting, cutting, dusting,
boiling, washing, bleaching, beating, and colouring; and
secondly for converting the prepared material into finished
sheets of paper, by the processes of straining, knotting (the
separation of knots, impurities, or of matted fibre which has
formed into strings, or is insufficiently ground), making,
pressing, drying, glazing, cutting, sorting, polishing, and
packing. The machinery was supplied by Messrs. Easton
and Anderson, of London and Erith, and is among the best
that can be produced, embodying nearly every modern improvement. This machinery was ordered in August 1873,
and was shipped to Japan in June 1874 ; by August 1875 it
was at work, having been erected and fitted under a skilled
European overseer, but entirely by the labour of Japanese
artisans. The English officer, Mr. Frank Cheeseman, who
superintended the work at Ogi, has stated that he was
favourably impressed by the intelligence and skill of the
Japanese workmen, and by the high character of the native
gentlemen who own the mill. The mill is capable of producing from fifteen to twenty tons of paper per week.

The uses to which paper is put in Japan are almost as
numerous as those to which bamboo is applied in that and
other eastern countries, and those who have travelled in such
countries know how very diversified are the uses of that
invaluable plant. Besides its application to all the common
purposes with which we are familiar at home, paper is
employed in Japan in place of glass in the sliding walls of
the houses, for pocket-handkerchiefs, napkins, in lieu of
string, etc., and I have brought to England with me table-
cloths made of paper, and even waistcoats and other such

---

* " Its stem and branches are tri-
chotomous. . . . The flowers are like
those of the *Daphne odora*, having
four slender petals. . . . The flower
is enneandrous, and has one pistil."
—*Mr. Yosino.*

articles of wearing apparel. I am disposed to believe that when the Japanese table-cloths and napkins become well known in this country they will come into very large demand. And the same appears to me to be highly probable with regard to stationery, and more particularly to envelopes, which, although wholly formed of paper, are much superior in strength and toughness to many of the linen-lined envelopes employed by us for business purposes. The leather-like wall-papers of Japan are exceedingly beautiful and very cheap. There has nevertheless sprung up in Japan, since the European invasion, a considerable demand for some descriptions of paper which we use, but which were previously unknown there, and I am informed that there are five factories now in Tokio engaged in manufacturing paper to meet this want.

The language and literature, the arts of drawing and painting, the colleges and schools, the public services, the museums and other institutions of the country and of the capital, likewise engaged more or less of our attention during our first month in Japan ; but the results of our observations must be reserved for later chapters, as this is already of unusual length. I will only add the following notes on the " Fu " of Tokio, which a high official was so obliging as to furnish in response to a request which I made to him.

" The Tokio Fu-Cho is an office of the local government having for its management the protection of the persons and property in Tokio, the capital of the whole empire, and is thus a branch of the central government. The extent of its jurisdiction is 7 *ris* (17 miles) from east to west, and the same from north to south. (Its limits are New Tone River on the east, Tanashi postal station on the west, Rojugo River on the south, and Ara River on the north; the first being the boundary between the provinces of Musashi and Shimofusa, and the three last being in the province of Musashi.) Its boundary line is 30 *ris* long (73·5 miles); under its jurisdiction are what are called the seven isles of Idsu, but as they are wholly separated from the land they are now omitted here, and the whole Fu is divided into 15 *kus* (formerly called Fu Proper) and 6 *guns* or *koris* (formerly called Fu Exterior).

" The 15 *kus* are the following: Kojimachi, Kanada, Nihonbashi, Kiobushi, Shiba, Azabu, Akasata, Yotsuya, Ushigomé, Hongo,

Koishikawa, Shitaya, Asakusa, Honjo, and Fukagawa. The district included under these names was in the days of the Tokugawa Shogunate called Yedo, and was under the jurisdiction of the north and south *yakushos*, or offices. After the revolution of 1868 its name was changed into Tokio.

" Not only is it a great metropolis, but it is a seat of the imperial palace, of the chief posts of the army and navy, of the various *kwans* and *shos*, the source of all laws and institutions, and place of the foreign legations; where the traders and artisans crowd from all quarters of the empire, where the key of the foreign commerce is kept; nay, it is the centre of all business, political, civil, commercial, industrial, agricultural, literary, and artistic. It is indeed the greatest city of the whole empire, and must not be considered as equalled by other *fus* and *kens.*

" As to the 6 *guns* or *koris*, they are the following : Yebara, East Tama, South Tashima, North Tashima, South Adachi, and South Kadzushika. These consist mainly of extensive fields, and are inhabited by farmers, almost all of whom subsist by cultivation, thus separating the *guns* from the fifteen *kus*, or the Fu proper. Every *ku* has its *kucho*, and every *gun* its *guncho*, who are respectively the president of each *ku* and *gun* office, and there are *kuchos* in the *mura* into which the *guns* are divided.

" These officers are all under the superintendence of the Fu Cho, and are ordered to manage the affairs of the local executive government under their respective jurisdictions. The *kuchos* and *gunchos* are appointed by the Fuchiji, or the governor, and the *kochos* are chosen by the people of the *mura.* Besides there are the representatives from every *ku* and *gun*, who are chosen by the people, and are summoned periodically or occasionally to the Fucho to discuss the local interests and benefits. They compose what is called Fu Kai, or the Fu Parliament. There are also Ku Kais and Cho-Son Kais (or the *ku* and *mura* assemblies), consisting of the deputies elected by the people to discuss the economy of their own districts.

" The administration of affairs under Tokio Fu differs in several respects from that of other local governments. For instance, in other local governments the police affairs are under the direction of the governors, but in Tokio they are superintended by Daikeishi, who is the head of Keishi Honsho, wholly separate from Tokio Fu, and established by Keishi Kioku, a department of Naimu Sho in the central government. Thus the execution of all regulations concerning the persons and property must be subject to the approval of Daikeishi before they are carried into effect.

" The situation of the office of Tokio Fu is No. 1 Sichi Saiwai cho Tokio, occupying seven thousand *tsubo* (5·7 acres). It is divided into many departments, and has under its jurisdiction the fifteen *kus* and six *guns* before mentioned.   Its affairs are very multitudinous. The following is a brief summary :—

" The investigation of the census.

" The education of the people.

" The development of industry, agricultural, manufactural, and commercial.

" The inspection of the franchised market-place (Tsukiji).

" The gathering of taxes.

" The management of rivers, dykes, aqueducts, and banks.

" The construction and repairing of roads and bridges.

" The supply of water for city use.

" The drainage and the prevention of plague.

" The control of sanitary affairs in general.

" The payment of yearly pensions to the decoration-wearers and pension-holders of Kuwazokus, Shizoku, and of Heimin.

" The making of awards to virtuous people, obedient children, and faithful wives and servants.

" The superintendence of the Shinto and Buddhist priests.

" The helping of the poor widows and widowers, orphans, childless old men, maimed persons, and paupers.

" The establishment of the means of giving medicines to, and curing the diseases of, the poor and helpless.

" Besides, it manages the affairs concerning the appeals of the people.   But in all cases of importance it needs the direction from the central government, or every *sho*, concerning the affair.   Every *sho* is subject to the control and guidance of the central government, and has for its management the department of the navy and army, the home and state affairs, the finance and justice, the public works and education.

" A brief account of the landed property and the number of houses and population is as follows.   The area of Tokio Fu is estimated at 33 square *ris* (197·5 sq. miles), and the landed property is more than 100,000,000 *tsubo* (82,101·8 acres), of which 7,000,000 *tsubo* (5747·1 acres) belong to the government, and 93,000,000 *tsubo* (76,354·7 acres) belong to the people.   The number of houses is 25,830, and population is 1,000,000; the length of public roads is more than 87 *ris* (212·8 miles); the number of rivers is 32, bridges 350, ships 18,000, carriages more than 44,000, temples both Shinto and Buddhist nearly 2000 each, colleges and schools 890, hospitals 30, and banks and other companies more than 100."

CHAPTER III.

LANGUAGE AND LITERATURE.

Early Japanese an unwritten language—Transmission of records by word of mouth—The Indian Vedas—A colossal system of mnemonics—Ancient language of Japan—The Loo-choo dialect—Japanese a Turanian tongue—Mr. Hyde Clarke's theory of an ancient Turano-African empire—Intercourse with Korea—Influence of Chinese literature—"Letters of the god-age"—The alphabet—Spoken and written language—Difficulties of exploring Japanese literature—Diary of the old court noble—A Japanese classic—Japanese poetry—Poetry of the gods—A verse by the god Susanoö—Chant of the goddess Uzumé—A "No"—Specimens of native poetry—Remarkable influence of women upon literature—Interchange of prose and poetry between a Chinaman and a Japanese—Captain Brinkley on the Japanese language—Mr. Hyde Clarke on his Turano-African theory.

A MODERN official Japanese treatise says, "In the earliest times the Japanese language had no written characters," an opinion which is based upon the results of the researches of the most learned men of the country. There are those who hold a contrary opinion, but the authority which I have quoted affirms that the grounds for their belief are the "mere forgeries of literary impostors." The point is, of course, one of great importance, for a nation which commences its career with a written language usually carries with it much more direct demonstrations, or at least indications, of its origin than a nation that grows up, on its historic ground, from a condition so little developed as to be devoid of written characters.

In the chapter on the God-period I have had occasion to refer to the circumstances under which the sacred book *Kojiki* assumed its known form by being taken down from the dictation of Hiyetano Aré, by whom it had been committed to memory; and although this occurred as late as the year 711 of our period, while we know that Confucian books were introduced into Japan in the third century, still it is an illustration of the fact that there, as in other countries, the transmission of traditions, etc., by word of mouth was a national practice. And but few people know to how great an extent this practice prevailed in some nations, even long after the introduction of written languages. However strange it may seem to say so, it is a fact that the most ancient of all the sacred books in which we ourselves, as part of the Aryan world, are interested, viz. the Rig-Veda, has been transmitted orally down to our own day, and has had its sacred text first published in a complete form by a scholar who is still alive, and still illuminating his age by his genius. The Rig-Veda has in some sense been the Bible of millions upon millions of our fellow-creatures for thousands of years, but it was Mr. Max Müller who brought out "the first complete edition of that sacred text, together with the most authoritative commentary of Hindu theologians." * There, no doubt, have long existed manuscripts of the Veda, but Mr. Max Müller himself states that but few MSS. in India are older than one thousand years after Christ, and there is no evidence that the art of writing was known in India much before the beginning of Buddhism— the last remark being one which may be applied to Japan likewise, bearing in mind that Buddhism only reached Japan a thousand years after the life and death of Buddha—

> "Prince Siddartha styled on earth—
> In earth and heavens and hells incomparable."

The sacred traditions were handed down from generation to generation by disciplined and practised memory alone. "As far back as we know anything of India, we find that the years which we spend at school and at university were spent by the sons of the three higher classes in learning from the mouth of a teacher their sacred literature. This

---

* The Commentary of Sayana Akarya.

was a sacred duty, the neglect of which entailed social degradation, and the most minute rules were laid down as to the mnemonic system that had to be followed. Before the invention of writing, there was no other way of preserving literature, whether sacred or profane, and in consequence every precaution was taken against accidents."* Stranger still is the fact that those Brahmans who may be considered the especial guardians of the sacred traditions of India in our own day do not employ either the written or the printed texts in learning and transmitting their holy lore : "They learn it, as their ancestors learnt it thousands of years ago, from the mouth of a teacher, so that the Vedic succession should never be broken," and so well do they perform the duty, and so accurately do they transmit the text, that "there is hardly a various reading, in the proper sense of the word, or even an uncertain accent, in the whole of the Rig-Veda," which consists of more than a thousand hymns averaging ten verses, and contains more than one hundred and fifty thousand words.†

These glimpses into the system of transmitting literature by oral teaching and by the training of the memory are valuable, as serving to account for the extreme elaboration which written characters underwent in Japan after their invention and adoption. Educated as we now are, and living as we do, it is difficult to think with toleration of any language, whether spoken or written, which cannot be fairly mastered in a year or two, and it is with impatience that we read of Japan that "at the lowest estimate a schoolboy was required to learn one thousand different characters;" that "in the government elementary schools of the present time, about three thousand characters are taught ;" and that "a man laying any claim to scholarship knows eight or ten thousand characters, while those who

---

* The Hibbert Lectures, 1878.

† In a postscript to his third Hibbert Lecture Mr. Max Müller cites very interesting passages from an ancient work showing in detail how the oral teaching of the Vedas was carried on at least 500 B.C., and adds statements from the pens of two native scholars to show how it is maintained at the present day.

pass for men of great learning are expected to be acquainted with many tens of thousands." * While looking into this matter, in Tokio, I requested my friend, Captain F. Brinkley, R.A. (perhaps the greatest master of the Japanese language among foreigners), to favour me with his views upon it, and this he was kind enough to do. The memorandum with which he accordingly furnished me is so valuable and instructive that I append it without alteration to this chapter. It will be seen from it that some twelve or thirteen thousand characters in all must be " stored away in the memory, beyond the reach of time and the necessity of revision," before a young Japanese can fairly start in pursuit of science ! But it is easy to see that this colossal system of mnemonics grew naturally enough out of that far earlier system under which, before the invention of writing, memory was the only library, and the toil of long years the only means there were of storing it. Now that Japan has entered upon the modern period, she must, so far, discard her ancient forms of language as to furnish her sons with readier means of acquiring knowledge.

The ancient language of Japan—by which I mean the language spoken before the opening of her communications with Korea and China—appears to have stood alone. It had some degree of affinity with that of Korea, less (according to the highest authorities) in the roots of words than in grammatical form and structure. There is, however, but one language outside of Japan itself which can be considered as having many words in common with Japanese, and that is the language of the Loo-choo Islands. This appears to so far resemble the Japanese that Mr. Satow, who examined a Loo-chooan vocabulary, says that it differs very little from it ; and adds that some members of the Loo-chooan embassy to Yedo spoke Japanese with perfect correctness. This correctness must, however, be regarded as an accomplishment, and not as a proof of identity between the two languages,

---

* Dr. David Murray, late Superintendent of Education in Japan, in the Philadelphia Exhibit on Education.

because interpreters are, as a matter of fact, often employed to facilitate communications between natives of the respective countries. It will be correct to assume, with Mr. Aston, that the Loo-chooan tongue is an offshoot from the Japanese—a mere Japanese dialect, in fact. The relation between the languages of Japan and Korea is doubtless a wholly different one, and one of far greater historic significance, but it is quite beyond my power to throw any light upon it. All I can do in the matter is to express surprise that, as far as I know, this early philologic relationship between Japan and the Korean peninsula has been so little studied.

It is to the absence of any living or known languages allied to that of Japan and Loo-choo that we must primarily attribute the little progress that has been made by comparative philologists in their investigations respecting it. It has not yet received even a definite place among the great families of tongues, some writers, at least, placing it, with the Korean, among languages that are of doubtful origin.* Authority on the whole, however, certainly excludes it from the Aryan and Semitic classes, and includes it in the Turanian group of tongues, although it is not to be found in the long genealogical tables of that family of languages which are given by Mr. Max Müller at the end of his 'Lectures on the Science of Language.' Mr. James Fergusson, in his most interesting Ethnological Appendix to his 'History of Architecture,' boldly says: "In the old world the typical Turanians were the Egyptians; in the modern the Chinese and Japanese." Mr. W. G. Aston, who has acquired a masterly acquaintance with Japanese, and has written grammars both of the spoken and of the written language—which differ greatly—says that it possesses all the characteristics of the Turanian family, being agglutinative (i.e. maintaining its "roots" in their integrity), without

---

* The author of the article "Philology" in the 1878 edition of 'Chambers' Encyclopaedia,' for example, who, under the heading "Monosyllabic or Isolating," places 1, the Chinese, 2, the Tibetan, and 3, the Siamese, Anamese, and Burman, adding, "Japanese and the language of Korea are doubtful."

formative prefixes, poor in conjunctions, and copious in the use of participles. He adds : "The Japanese language is further an example of the rule common to all languages of this family, that every word which serves to define another word invariably precedes it ; thus the adjective precedes the noun, the adverb the verb, the genitive the word which governs it, the objective case the verb, and the word governed by a preposition the preposition." In a paper read at the Asiatic Society of Japan in 1874, Mr. Aston nevertheless — following up Mr. Edkin's theory, that the Chinese language had remote relations with the Aryan family — himself points out some resemblances between Japanese and that family, and gives numerous examples of apparent identity between Japanese and Aryan roots. He lays no great stress on the matter, and adduces the difficulty which I have already mentioned, viz. the absence of cognate languages, as the great obstacle to the pursuit of inquiries of this kind.

My learned friend Mr. Hyde Clarke, whose ethnological and philological researches are well known, has long had his attention drawn to the Japanese language, and after many labours has discovered relations between that and the languages of Ashantee and western Africa. His expectations of finding a solution of the main problem were discouraged by the vast ethnological differences between the peoples ; but having, on ethnological grounds, "to distinguish a white race earlier on the field of history than the Aryans," he has, in accordance with his readings of history, looked for this race in High Africa — "regions as healthy as those of High Asia, from which the Aryan migrations are held to have proceeded." Pursuing this line of inquiry, he has arrived at the opinion that it is in an ancient Turano-African empire that the origin of the Japanese should be sought. This view is so novel and so far-reaching that I have appended to this chapter the memorandum upon it with which Mr. Hyde Clarke has been so obliging as to furnish me.

It was very early in our era, as will have already been seen, that Japan began to have intercourse with Korea, and to derive thence aid and instruction which greatly facilitated the progress both of the fine and of the industrial arts; and few things are more striking even among the many striking things which may now be observed in Japan, than the complete and handsome manner in which her present scholars, historians and officers, recognise this ancient indebtedness to the people of the neighbouring peninsula. The Japanese have plenty of native pride, no doubt, but they appear to be without the false pride which deters some people from acknowledging the advantages which they have derived from others. A recent native writer says that in the earliest times the use of alphabetical characters was unknown in his country, and that it was introduced when intercourse with foreign countries was first opened. Characters are said to have been so introduced by natives of Minama (part of Korea) who visited Japan during the reigns of Kaikua and Sujin (157–30 b.c.). Books were first seen in Japan when the warrior-empress, Jingu Kogo, carried away from Korea as many of them as she could lay hands on, with everything else that was at once valuable and portable, after her successful invasion of that country. In the third century (a.d.) the son of the emperor Ojin was, as we have seen, taught to read Chinese works, and from that time forward Chinese language and literature exerted a strong influence upon those of Japan.* Prior to this, there is reason to suppose,

---

* It is reasonable to ascribe to this cause the circumstance that in Japan as in China "writing" has always signified so very much more than with ourselves. Our alphabet is little or nothing more than a mechanical system of communication; but in China there is a divine authority and beauty about their written characters. Some of them came from the scales of the turtle or dragon-horse that Toh-he found in the river bed. These he expanded to the great lines of the universe. The starry curves of the heavens, the undulations of mountains, the winding of rivers—in these were the elements of writing, and these elements shared the divinity of creation. Obviously a system of writing thus begun, or thus developed, would greatly favour that fanciful interweaving of meanings which it is impossible, as one so often finds, to render in a language like ours, or indeed in any foreign language whatever. I may have occasion to make mention again of the difficulty in the chapter on Proverbs and Phrases.

1. Yositune riding on the Tengu to take his Fencing Lessons at Kurama Yama.
2. Taibo: a fabulous bird: the Japanese "Roc."

From Hokusai. Reproduced for this Work by a Japanese Engraver.

To face page 54, Vol II.

the writing of letters was never practised, but epistolary correspondence soon became practicable after the introduction of Confucian books, and with them the commencement of the study of the literary art. Nothing like Chinese composition was, however, practicable in Japan until the sixth century, when the introduction of Buddhism and Buddhist writings gave a strong and lasting impulse to the spread of Chinese literature, and now the number of Chinese words in the Japanese language greatly exceeds the number of native words. They are for the most part easily distinguishable, it is said, although in some cases Japanese words have undergone changes which make it difficult to recognise them. It must not be inferred from this that a knowledge of the Chinese language is absolutely necessary for students of Japanese. "What is really essential," says Mr. Aston, "is an acquaintance with the meaning and Japanese pronunciation of the Chinese character. A familiarity with Chinese constructions and forms of expression is not without value to the student of the later form of Japanese, but it is quite possible to have a knowledge of the language sufficient for all practical purposes without being able to construe a single sentence of a Chinese book." He adds that a knowledge of one of the spoken dialects of China is of no use whatever to the student of Japanese.

Whence came the earliest written characters ever employed in Japan is a question that has excited much controversy. Came they from the gods? Were they the invention of the sages? Or were they introduced from Korea? Each of these questions is answered in the affirmative by some scholars, and denied by others. They are known as *Shinji*, "letters of the god age," and the priests of the old Shinto faith, with such modern Japanese scholars as Hirata Atsutane, deem them to be the oldest written characters known in Japan, and of purely Japanese origin, dating, in fact, from the divine age. Others, who modestly refrain from asserting the immediate descent of the Japanese from the gods, maintain that these characters

were the invention of those later and lesser gods, the sages,
and contend, as stoutly as the others, for their purely
Japanese character. The third theory—that they were
derived from the Korean Rito system of writing, and were
in substance brought over from Korea by the Japanese
army of invasion on its return home—is maintained by
Buddhist writers, and has many other supporters. Mr.
Aston thinks it the correct one, and says that the *Shinji*
have, at any rate, left no traces in the existing alphabets,
" nor have they been the vehicle for transmitting to our
day any literary remains of the age to which they belong." *

The differences between the spoken and written dialects
of Japan are very remarkable. The grammars of the two
are so different that Mr. Aston has published a separate
work upon each, so that merchants and others who wish
to acquire a knowledge of the colloquial tongue may proceed directly to their object. So broad is the distinction
between the two that foreign residents in the country
sometimes become familiarly acquainted with the colloquial
language, and yet remain incapable of reading a newspaper
article, a book, or a letter addressed to them; while, on the

---

* It is no part of my plan to attempt to give any detailed descrip-tion of the language of Japan, which must be sought in the grammars of Mr. Aston and in the writings of other scholars; but it may be inte-resting to some readers to say that in the Japanese language there are forty-seven syllables, by the combina-tion of which, and of a supplementary character corresponding to *n* placed at the end of the syllable, all the words of the language may be repre-sented. The equivalents of these syllables, with a few supplementary ones, are given in the table below, ex-pressed in Roman characters, and in reading them the English sounds should be given to the consonants and the Italian sounds to the vowels. The table should be read down the verti-cal columns, and from right to left :—

wa	ra	ya	ma	ha	na	ta	sa	ka	a
wi	ri	yi	mi	hi	ni	tsi	shi	ki	i
wu	ru	yu	mu	fu	nu	tsu	su	ku	u
we	ro	ye	me	he	ne	te	se	ke	e
wo	ro	yo	mo	ho	no	to	so	ko	o

other hand, a foreigner may acquire in his own country a good knowledge of the written language, and have caught the accent of Japanese, and yet be unable on visiting the country to carry on a conversation with a native. There is, of course, a notable distinction between the spoken and written styles in most countries—there certainly is in our own; but the difference is far greater in the case of Japan than in that of ours or any other well-known language of Europe.

Although the literature of Japan is a mine which has scarcely yet been opened, and it is but natural to expect that it may hereafter be worked with great interest and advantage, those who have hitherto sunk their shafts and opened up workings in it seem to have found it less rich than they had hoped. This arises from two causes: first, most of the literature that has come down to us from the period when the language was at its best and purest was composed for the very limited objects which the Mikado and the court had in view in those days; and, secondly, all Japanese writers appear to have hung one narrative or story so much upon another that it is often difficult to select one complete in itself. Other causes are the abundance of verbal artifices, which cannot be translated, and the circumstance that the habits of thought and life of the Japanese people have been so wholly unlike our own that we could not permit ourselves to publish much of that which has been most characteristic and telling among themselves.

In the chapter on the Shinto Religion I have referred to, and quoted from, the diary of an old court noble who lived a thousand years ago, and I would again advert to it here as a highly interesting example of old Japanese literature, giving many bright glimpses into the life of the country at that period. Mr. Aston, who describes and translates it, calls it an Ancient Japanese Classic. It was entitled by its author *Tosa Nikki*, or "Tosa Diary." This old fellow, named Tsurayuki, who proudly traced his direct descent from one of the Mikados, had been for four years prefect at Tosa, and wrote the diary when on his way back to the imperial city.

He was a poet of eminence, and author of another work, which has been pronounced the most perfect extant composition of the native style. In mingled jollity and grief—jollity from hob-nobbing, including verse-making, with his successor, and grief for that he left behind him a girl-daughter who had died there—he set sail from Tosa. The new prefect's brother making his appearance on a neighbouring cape, Tsurayuki landed on the beach, drank, and composed verses with the brother, until the captain summoned him back on board. The *saké* was all gone, and the verses had been bad—for, says he, it required the united efforts of two of the party to make one bad verse, and he compares the verse-makers to two fishermen labouring along with a heavy net upon their shoulders—and he was nothing loth to rejoin his vessel. Detained afterwards at Ominato for ten days, many presents were sent to our Lucullus, one of them being a pheasant, which, according to an old Japanese custom, was attached to a blossoming plum-branch. With some of the gifts came verses; here is a specimen:—

> "Louder than the clamour of the white surges on your onward path will be the cry of me, weeping that I am left behind."

"If that were really so, he must have a very loud voice," says our old friend, who must be excused the scoff on the ground of the impatience which delay would naturally beget. At length they were under weigh again; and passing a grove of ancient firs growing near the sea, with storks flying about among their tops, he wrote the verse:—

> "Casting my glance over the sea; on each fir-tree top a stork has his dwelling; they have been comrades for a thousand years"—

a verse not a whit truer or more poetical, that I can see, than that at which he scoffed before. But who that remembers the early passages of literary arms between a Bulwer and a Tennyson, the 'New Timon' and 'Alcibiades,' who

> "Hated each other for a song,
> And did their little best to bite"

shall wonder at these old *saké*-steeped versifiers on the sea-beach of Japan a thousand years ago saying a smart thing or two at each other's expense!

In those days, and in very small vessels, impelled mainly by oars, as was this boat of Tsurayuki, the mariners cast their small anchors for the night; and here (always quoting Mr. Aston's graceful translation) is our poet's description of the nightfall: " Whilst we rowed along gazing on this scene, the mountains and the sea became all dark, the night deepened, and east and west could not be seen, so we entrusted all our thought of the weather to the mind of the master of our ship. Even the men, who were not accustomed to the sea, became very sad, and still more the women, who rested their heads on the bottom of the ship and did nothing but weep. The sailors, however, seemed to think nothing of it, and sang the following boat-song." He gives a few lines of it, and then proceeds: " There was a great deal more of this kind of stuff, but I do not write it down. Listening to the laughter at these verses, our hearts became somewhat calmed, in spite of the raging of the sea. It was quite dark when we at length reached our anchorage for the night." Three days more brought them to Murotsu (close to the easternmost of the southern peninsula of Shikoku), and there they landed and took a bath. The diarist tells us, in this day's entry, that no one wore scarlet or other rich colours in the vessel lest they should incur the anger of the gods of the sea. After five days they sailed again, very early in the morning, with the moon shining over a waveless ocean, which reflected the sky so perfectly that the two could not be distinguished. Then he wrote this stanza :—

" What is this that strikes against my oar as the boat is rowed along over the moon of the sea-depths? Is it the bush of the man in the moon?"

At another time, when sailing in company with a large number of other junks, he wrote, to my mind more prettily—

"It is spring, but it seems as if over the sea the leaves of autumn are being scattered."

I pass over much of the narrative, pausing to observe that
at one place, where there were many beautiful shells upon
the beach, Tsurayuki composed these lines in allusion to a
shell which the Japanese call the *wasuré-gai*, or "shell of
forgetfulness" :—

> "I would descend from my ship to gather the shell of
> forgetfulness of one for whom I am filled with sorrowful
> longing. Do ye, O ye advancing surges, drive it forward
> to the strand."

He afterwards says, pathetically enough, that the true
wish of his heart was not to forget her whom he had lost, but
only to give such respite to his sorrow that it might afterwards gain greater strength. Then follows the passage
about the propitiation of the sea-god, first with *nusa* and
then with his mirror, which I quoted in a former chapter.
After many storms and delays they entered the Osaka river.
All the passengers, men, women, and children, were over-
joyed at reaching this point of their voyage, and clasped
their foreheads with their hands in ecstasies of delight.
Landing at Yamazaki, our old aristocratic friend sent for his
bullock-cart from Kioto, as befitted a man of his rank, and on
its arrival started for the capital. He noticed the shops as
he went along, looking exactly as when he went away, and
wondered whether he would find as little change in the
hearts of his friends. By his own arrangement, he arrived
at his home by night :—

> "The moon was shining brightly when I reached my
> house and entered the gate, so that its condition was plainly
> to be seen. It was decayed and ruined beyond all description
> —worse even than I had been told. The heart of the man in
> whose charge I had left it was in an equally dilapidated
> condition. The fence between the two houses had been
> broken down, so that both seemed but one, and he appeared
> to have fulfilled his charge by looking in through the gaps.
> And yet I had supplied him by every opportunity with the
> means of keeping it in repair. To-night, however, I would
> not allow him to be told this in an angry tone, but in spite of

my vexation offered him an acknowledgment for his trouble. There was in one place something like a pond where water had collected in a hollow, by the side of which grew a fir-tree. It had lost half its branches, and looked as if a thousand years had passed during the five or six years of my absence. Younger trees had grown up round it, and the whole place was in a most neglected condition, so that every one said that it was pitiful to see. Among other sad thoughts that rose spontaneously to my mind was the memory—ah, how sorrowful!—of one who was born in this house, but who did not return here along with me. My fellow-passengers were chatting merrily with their children in their arms, but I meanwhile, still unable to contain my grief, privately repeated these lines to one who knew my heart. . . . I cannot write down all my many regrets and memories ; be it for good or evil, here I will fling away my pen."

So endeth the quaint and pleasant narrative of this charming old *littérateur.* His story is quoted by Mr. Aston as a notable example of the truth of Buffon's dictum that " style is everything." Containing no striking adventures, wise maxims, or novel information, possessing only the merit of describing in simple yet elegant language the ordinary life of a traveller in Japan in his day, its literary qualities have gained it a high rank among the classics of his country, and insured its being handed down to our own day as a most esteemed model for composition in the native Japanese style. Indeed, it established, conjointly with the author's other writings, a new style of composition, known as *Nikki* and *Kiko* (literally, diaries and travels).

We have seen that in Tsurayuki's day people spent much of their spare time in composing poetical stanzas, and this amusement is practised down to our own day. I have brought with me from Japan numerous examples of short compositions of this kind, executed for us by those with whom we had the pleasure to associate in that country. The governor of the ancient (now western) capital of Kioto, for example, Mr. Makimura Masinao, wrote us two upon large sheets of Kioto silk. One was written in connection with a most delightful day spent in the midst of romantic scenery, and, being translated, runs thus :—

> "Greeting a good guest with spring wine, mountains and rivers all seem to participate in our delight ; "

which, in English verse, might perhaps thus be rendered :—

> "Greeting a welcome guest in spring with wine,
> Mountains and rivers share the joy divine."

The other was designed to celebrate the mutual delight and good-fellowship which men might feel though belonging to separate and distant nations, and was thus translated :—

> "Let friends not stand upon ceremony among each other, but have joy, with the nations of the world, sitting as it were together, and breathing the winds of spring."

Poetry, or what is known in Japan as such, has been composed there from the earliest days. It was originally supposed to be delivered with clear intoned cadence, but since the middle ages of Japan there have been two kinds, one to be read and the other to be sung. The former kind underwent great development. Verses were usually either of five or of seven syllables in length, but others, of six and of eight syllables, were sometimes composed. The length of the stanza was not fixed, but it most frequently consisted in later times of thirty-one syllables. Poetry first became a distinct art in Japan about the year 1000 A.D. The various styles of poetry have been classed according to six periods, but their respective characteristics could not be explained without a greater assignment of space to the subject than I can afford. Suffice it to say that Japanese poetry does not depend for its merits upon resemblances in sound, nor upon quantity, nor upon rhyme. Its characteristic is *metre*, and, as already intimated, its lines are alternately of five and seven syllables in length ; all departures from this are irregular, and in singing such departures are eliminated.

Specimens of Japanese poetry have been handed down from very early periods indeed. In the 'Philadelphia

Exhibit ' (so frequently adverted to by me) is given a brief poem by a personage of the greatest dignity and antiquity —no other than the god Susanoö, the unruly brother of the sun-goddess. He had built a palace in Idzumo for himself and wife to retire into after their marriage, and upon the clouds gathering thickly about it he composed the following lines: it will be observed that they consist of five, seven, five, seven, and seven syllables respectively :—

> " Ya kumo ta tsu :
>   Idzumo ya-ye-gaki ;
> Tsuma-gomi ni
>   Ya-ye-gaki tsukuru :
>   Sono ya-ye-gaki wo! "

Of these lines Mr. Pfoundes gives the following translation:—

> " Countless piling clouds
>   Idzumo's rocky heights envelop ;
>   My spouse there have I placed,
>   A fence around her raised,
>   My strong arm protects her."

This is doubtless a very free translation, especially in the last line. Mr. Aston gives the following, which is probably a much more literal, although a less valorous, one :—

> " Many clouds arise :
>   The clouds which come forth are a manifold fence :
>   For the husband and wife to retire within,
>   They have formed a manifold fence :
>   O that manifold fence! "

Whatever degree of faithfulness there may be in either translation, it is satisfactory to find that Susanoö, however badly he may have behaved to his sister, was a domestic personage after all, or he would not have broken out into poetry on finding himself so thoroughly shut in by cloud-fencings with his wife Kushinada-himé.

Another very brief and much more curious poem has come down from the divine age. This is the " six-syllable song or charm of numbers " which I have adverted to in the chapter on the God-period as having been sung by the goddess Uzumé during the enticement of the sun-goddess from her cave. Printed in Roman letters it runs thus :—

> " Hito futa miyo
> Itsu muyu nana
> Ya koko-no tari
> Momo chi yorodzu."

With a single exception, these words correspond exactly with the Japanese words for the numbers one to ten, one hundred, one thousand, and ten thousand, the exception being *tari* for ten, instead of *toro*, the word actually used.[*] But Mr. Satow points out that the words may be interpreted in quite a different manner, which is probably the correct one, the words employed being subsequently taken to stand for numbers. The first line, interpreted according to its sense, is, " Men ! look at the lid ! " which is equivalent for "Gods ! look at the cavern door!" the second is equivalent to " Majesty appears ! hurrah ! " the third is readable as " Our hearts are quite satisfied," and the fourth as " Behold my bosom and my limbs ! "[†] In the chapter before referred to it is said, the reader will remember, that Uzumé got so excited with her singing and dancing as to let her robe fall, and it is this incident that is here alluded to. The whole verse, therefore, runs thus :—

> " Gods ! look at the cavern door !
> Majesty appears ! hurrah !
> Our hearts are fully satisfied.
> Behold my bosom and limbs ! "

There is extant a collection of Japanese poems, called *Manyoshiu*, dating from before the tenth century A.D., in which, although Chinese characters are employed, the Japanese sounds are rendered, the foreign characters being

---

* Thus :—

Hito-tsu .	.	. one	Nana tsu .	.	seven
Futa ,, .	.	. two	Ya ,,	. .	eight
Mi ,, .	.	. three	Kokono ,,	. .	nine
Yo ,, .	.	. four	Momo-chi .	.	one hundred
Itsu ,, .		. five	Chi-dji .	. .	one thousand
Mu ,, .		. six	Yorodzu	. .	ten ,,

† Literally " thighs."

used phonetically only. Mr Aston gives the following translation of one of these :—

> " By the palace of Futagi,
> Where our great king
> And divine lord
> Holds high rule,
>
> Gentle is the rise of the hills,
> Bearing hundreds of trees,
> Pleasant is the murmur of the rapids,
> As downward they rush.
>
> So long as in the springtime,
> (When the nightingale comes and sings)
> On the rocks
> Brocade-like flowers blossom,
> Brightening the mountain foot ;
>
> So long as in the autumn
> (When the stag calls to his mate)
> The red leaves fall hither and thither,
> Wounded by the showers—
> The heaven be-clouding,
>
> For many thousand years
> May his life be prolonged
> To rule over all under heaven
> In the great palace
> Destined to remain unchanged
> For hundreds of ages."

Those who are accustomed to reflect upon the subtle delicacies of language in which much of the charm of true poetry consists will know how impossible it is to convey in a tongue so alien as is ours to the Japanese the qualities that delight the native reader. The thought which a verse or a poem expresses may doubtless be translated, but the subtle sentiment and formless music of the original clings to it, and is not susceptible of separation. This should not be forgotten in reading such translations as I have quoted, or may yet quote. And yet one cannot peruse lines like the following translation by Mr. Aston of a dramatic passage from a Japanese *No* (short dramatic sketch) without detecting something of the charm of the original. The principal personage of the piece having announced that he has been

commissioned by the emperor of China to spy out the
intelligence of the inhabitants of Japan, the chorus strikes
in and thus describes the voyage:—

> "Oaring forth his ship,
>   He would visit the land
>   Of the quarter
>   Of the rising sun,
>   Of the rising sun.
>   As she sails,
>   As she sails
>   Far over the wave-path
>   Of the eastern sea,
>   Behind her sets the sun,
>   O'er her is the void of heaven,
>   Where the cloud-banners
>   Are still bright with his radiance—
>   And now the moon comes forth;
>   On the same quarter
>   Mountains are first descried;
>   Ere long
>   Even at the land of Japan
>   He hath arrived,
>   He hath arrived."

It must be acknowledged that this description is vigorously and nobly wrought.

Having requested Captain Brinkley to be so kind as to
favour me with translations of a brief specimen or two of
Japanese poetry, with the view of myself transforming
them into English verse, he was so obliging as to give
me the following seven short pieces. The gallant translator
has performed his part so well, and invested the citations
with so much grace and beauty, that it would be sinfully
presumptuous in me to touch them. I therefore—although
without his permission, I regret to say—give them as they
came from his pen:—

> "Destined at last to become part of the mighty ocean,
>   The valley runlet creeps yet a moment under the drooping
>   leaflets."

> "To him that seeks the path of virtue with sincerity,
>   The guardianship of the gods comes unsolicited."

" Rain and rime, snow and hail, distinguish them ever so wisely,
   Fallen, do they not all become the self-same river of the
     valley ? "

" The storm that shreds the blossom tells the story of our lives;
   Inexorable towards all steals the season of decay."

" Fair as the blossom's softly falling snowflakes
   Is the quiet decay of a ripe old age."

" A peerless sage was wine to the sages of old,
   Clearing from life the clouds of sorrow and dejection.
   A draught loosed the tongue of converse and merriment,
   A second wakened thoughts of the days that were no more,
   And a third stirred the chords of poesy and song.
   But now with the lust of liquor come dissension,
   Ignorance, crime, and neglect of all time's duties,
   Making of life a dissolute sterility.
   Blame we then the wine or the heart of the drinker ? "

" Types of our children are the tiny grasses,
   Tender and fragile in the ample moorland :
   We know not to what fragrance their infant sprouts may
     blossom,
   Nor wist to what sweetness their unborn fruits may ripen,
   But hoping ever wait till autumn tells their story.
   Oh ! cherished children, may ye never perish,
     Flowerless, fruitless, in the early springtime,
   Nor like this petal trampled by the wayside,
     Fall in the fuller promise of your prime."

These extracts are ample to show that the native literature of Japan contains much that is poetic in the true
sense of the word. Taking together the passages which I
have quoted, we have proof that it is notable for the combination of manly power with feminine delicacy and beauty.
Nor is this surprising, for while literature is in the main
the profession of men in Japan, women have in various ages
achieved great distinction in it. Indeed, during the long
and repeated periods of civil war, when the men of Japan
were devoting themselves to mutual slaughter under am-
bitious leaders—as men have been too ready to do in other
ages and in other countries as well as in Japan—the women
of the land, to their enduring glory be it said, not only
sustained the literary art, but exalted it to a greater

eminence than that to which men had ever raised it. It is considered by some, it will be remembered, that Hiyetano Aré, who committed the sacred *Kojiki* to memory, and handed it down to all time, was a woman, and it was certainly during the reign and under the active patronage of a woman that the work was accomplished. Speaking of the time of Tsurayuki (our old friend the ex-governor of Tosa a thousand years ago), Mr. Aston bears this most remarkable testimony: "The learned were at this time devoted to the study of Chinese, and rarely composed in any other language, whilst the cultivation of the Japanese language was in a great measure abandoned to women. It is honourable to the women of Japan that they nobly discharged the task which devolved upon them of maintaining the credit of their native literature. I believe no parallel is to be found in the history of European letters to the remarkable fact that a very large proportion of the best writings of the best age of Japanese literature was the work of women. The *Genji Monogatari*, the acknowledged standard of the language of the period to which it belongs, and the parent of the Japanese novel, was written by a woman, as were also the *Isé Monogatari*, the *Makura Zoshi*, and much of the poetry of the time." It is to these facts, probably, that we must look for the origin of that delicacy of sentiment and expression, in a literary sense, which softens and adorns nearly all that flows to us from classic Japanese literature through the channels of translation. Nor are we without testimony to its beauty from those who are familiar with it in the original. "It would be hard," said Mr. Chamberlain in a discussion at the Asiatic Society, "in the mellifluous classical language of Japan, to find one word which is less euphonious than another: in that tongue, so different from the semi-Chinese jargon of the present day, every syllable is a delight to listen to."

The gentleman just quoted, in an able paper read before the society referred to, explained some curious elements in Japanese literature which have been called "pillow-words." These he considers to be, after the cadence of the alternat-

ing five- and seven-syllable lines, the chief characteristic of
the classical poetry of Japan.   The pillow-words appear to be
words which once had a meaning, but which, having fallen
out of significance, are used for the succeeding significative
word to " rest its head " upon, so to speak.   The " pillow "
for the verb *to yearn*, for example, is a word signifying " in
the manner of a weeping infant."   The subject is too ab-
struse, however, to pursue here, although two native authors
record as many as six hundred and sixty-seven pillow-words,
and explain their use.   Of examples of punning, or playing
upon words, which is also a common literary device in
Japan, Mr. Chamberlain gives, among others, this—

> " Matsu ga né no,
> Matsu koto tohomi," etc.,

which is nearly literally rendered into English, pun and
all, by

> " Like to the *pine*-trees, I must stand and *pine*."

Desiring to furnish my readers with a specimen of modern
Japanese modes of thought and expression, but dating from
before the invasion of our civilisation, I have searched for
a suitable example, and have found it in the records of Commodore Perry's expedition.   A Chinaman, having embarked
from China in the American squadron when about to leave
for Japan, kept and afterwards published a journal of his
visit.   While lying off Yokohama, a learned Japanese, among
others, visited the squadron, and inquired respecting the
troubles then existing in China.   The Chinaman showed
him an account of the Chinese insurrection which he had
drawn up, and a book on the principles of good government.
These the Japanese gentleman borrowed, and afterwards returned, together with a letter expressing his own opinion.
From that letter I take the following translated extracts,
observing that they were written at a time when the
country was, and had been for two centuries and a half
at least, completely closed to foreigners (excepting the
distant port of Nagasaki).   The Japanese writes :—

" As I have shut up your volume my feelings have found vent in
sighs. . . . The essential evil of such a state as China may be described

in a single phrase—it is the desire of gain. Now, the desire of gain is common to all men, and is the pregnant womb of all evil. Confucius seldom spoke of gain, wishing to check the lust of it in its source. This, also, was the reason why my ancestors cut off all intercourse of foreign nations with Japan, because the desire of gain led astray the ignorant people, and wonderful arts in the investigation of principles deceived the perverse, so that they got striving together, seeking gain and hurrying after what was wonderful, till filial duty, modesty, and the sense of shame were all forgotten. To a man who has reached this stage of evil, neither his father nor his sovereign is anything."

He goes on :—

" The ways of Heaven are great. It nourishes all things in the universe. Even among the dark countries who dwell by the icy sea, there is not an individual who is not a child of Heaven and Earth— not one who is not made to love his fellows, and be friendly with them. On this account the sages embraced all men with a common benevolence, without distinction of one from another. The principles for mutual intercourse, all over the globe, are the same—propriety, complaisance, good faith, and righteousness. By the observance of these a noble harmony is diffused, and the heart of Heaven and Earth is abundantly displayed.

" If, on the contrary, commerce is conducted merely with a view to gain, quarrels and litigations will spring from it, and it will prove a curse instead of a blessing. Against such a result my ancestors were profoundly anxious. Looking thus at the subject, the one topic of intercourse, it is the means by which the people exchange the commodities which they have abundantly for those which they have not, and one nation succours the distress of another; its propriety is plainly indicated by Providence, and peace, harmony, and good feeling are its true result. Yet if gain—gain—be what is sought for by it, it will only develop the lusts and angry passions of men, and there will be a melancholy termination to what may be begun under good auspices. It is but a hair's-breadth which separates those different results; for give selfishness the reins, and righteousness is instantly merged in the desire of gain. . . . God, by his spiritual pervasion, however, sees, with a parent's heart, how his children impose on and strive with one another. Must he not be grieved? Must he not be moved to pity? "

Fine sentiments these ; often heard even in England—in pulpits and on platforms; but what know we of them on 'Change or in the market-place ? Are these the principles of our trade at Hong Kong, at Yokohama ? Let the benighted Japanese dream on to his conclusion :—

" But the world may be compared to a chess-board, and every nation also. There cannot be wanting worthy princes and heroic lords. Who is he that shall go before his fellows, whip in hand, to execute the laws of Heaven? [How Carlylean a philosopher have we here!] Now great changes are occurring. It is a time of revolution, when every prince should set his heart to act in obedience to providence, and labour for the good of his people. You now live in a steamship of the United States, and you wander over the seas. Have you seen such a man as I indicate? If you have not, I pray you, wherever you go, to inculcate the principles I have stated on every sovereign and ruler; so shall the wishes of Confucius and Mencius, so many centuries after their time, be made to shine conspicuously in the whole world."

This man is, it seems to me, a fair specimen of the people whom we insisted upon civilising!

The Chinese passenger who elicited the above statement of principles from the Japanese gentleman tells us in his journal that he was kept very busy in writing verses and sentiments, upon fans chiefly, as souvenirs for his Japanese acquaintances, they in return often presenting him with like mementoes. One officer gave him an ode which he had written on New Year's morn. It ran thus :—

> " The bear begins his course again ;
> To me the world seems cold and vain.
> Tsing Hok's high aim my soul inspires ;
> But not in me are Woo-how's fires.
> With poet's pencil in my hand,
> And wine-cup near me on the stand,
> I hear the willow rustling at my eaves,
> And watch the opening of its eye-like leaves."

The sad and modest contemplativeness of these lines must strike the most prosaic of minds—if any such should venture into this chapter. Another officer presented some lines on spring :—

> " Last night among the flowers I walked and sang,
> This morn again my voice in green woods rang.
> Beyond men's ken the way of God above,
> But this spring greenery well proves his love."

In response to this our Chinese friend felt impelled to

produce "something of the same kind," and wrote some lines commencing

> "O face of spring, that now revisitest
>   The earth, my soul is stirred by thee to song,"

and ending as an English poet on the Thames would probably have ended—

> "Where shall I go to taste the inspiring cup?
>   I'll row my boat to yonder clump of trees."

One other extract from this Chinese eye-witness of Japan in its pre-civilised days: "The people are all Buddhists. All about, on the hillsides and by the sea-shore, are images of Buddha, and on most of their tombstones are engraven some words from the ' Water-lily ' classic. At the temple of 'Great Repose' I saw people worshipping Buddha, without either incense or lighted candles. When they had finished, they put some money in a box, calling it ' let-go-life ' money, with reference to the Buddhist doctrine which forbids the killing of animals. There were two priests in the place, who asked me to write some characters for them, on which, struck by the scenery around, I wrote 'Encircling peaks, girdling waters.' They in return described their position in the following lines :—

> "'Here in our little cells we sit,
>   Round our inkstones the white clouds meet.
>   Mere dust to us is gold so rare,
>   The future gives us not a care.'

" While I was sitting with them, there came a woman to the temple to worship. The sight of her beauty greatly stirred me :—

> "'Her lips vermilion red, her teeth were white,
>   Her hair in clouds rose o'er her eyebrows bright.
>   In glittering headdress starlike was her sheen,
>   Or like the moon through plum-tree branches seen.'"

The following is the very important memorandum upon the Japanese language by my friend Captain Brinkley, R.A., of Tokio, which I promised to append to this chapter :—

" It may be roughly said that a Japanese must devote at least ten years' persistent and earnest study to the acquisition of his own language if he desires to possess a knowledge of it sufficient for the purposes of an educated man. The chief difficulty he has to encounter is the caligraphy.

"There are three varieties of character used in writing: the square (Kaisho), the running (Giyosho), and the free (Sosho).

"The Kaisho may be called the parent character. It is the same as that used in China, and though perfect familiarity with it will generally render the Giyosho comprehensible, the same cannot be said of the Sosho, which is a form so very rudimentary and incomplete that it requires a separate and even more attentive study than either of its *confrères*.

"Assuming then five thousand as the number of these perplexing hieroglyphics necessary for reading and writing, it will be seen that without attaching unjust difficulty to the differences of the three forms, some twelve or thirteen thousand characters in all must be stored away in the memory beyond the reach of time and the necessity of revision, before a Japanese can take his first untrammelled step in pursuit of science.

"Formerly in teaching these characters no attempt was ever made to appeal to the pupil's reason. For years his studies were confined to a sort of 'singing at sight' process, and it was not until constant repetition and recitation of the notes uttered by his instructor had enabled him to express the sounds of all the hieroglyphics in the 'Bible of obedience' and certain other Chinese classics that the explanation of what he read began to form a factor in his education. It may easily be imagined how little the reflective, and how largely the mechanical, faculty was developed by this process, and indeed it has been always found that the Japanese student's acquisition of western science is not a little impeded by too minute efforts of memory, and such a bigoted worship of formula and rule that originality and self-reliance cease to be serviceable items in his intellectual *répertoire*.

"The system pursued in the modern schools is in this respect considerably improved. The 'Kana,' or Japanese syllabary, is first taught. Of this there are two sorts: the 'Katakana,' consisting of 48 symbols, and used only in conjunction with the square character for explanatory purposes or to express grammatical terminations; and the 'Hiragana,' also consisting of 48 primary characters, but numbering nearly 150, if varieties of form be included. The latter is very extensively used. With the addition of some 500 'free' or 'grass' characters, it forms the syllabary employed by women, and in novels, children's books, and all publications intended for circulation among the illiterate classes it is used alone when sufficient, or with the square character added where confusion of homonyms has to be

avoided. After he has mustered these syllabaries the child is trained
to recognise and write such easy and common words as are expressed
by single characters, the meaning as well as the sound being taught,
and subsequently he is introduced to books compiled on a progressive
system. No doubt the student's difficulties are considerably smoothed
by this improvement of method, but still the fact remains that at the
age of thirteen or fourteen, when he has completed his curriculum at
a preparatory school, he must still devote at least five years to the
study of his own language before he can be qualified for any official
employment, or before he can aspire to even passable proficiency in
writing and composition.

" It has been suggested that the characters might be more accessible
if acquired through the medium of the ' radicals,' of which there are
246, classified according to the number of strokes (from 1 to 17)
employed in writing them. Every character is built up with one or
more radicals, and it certainly seems a more rational and thorough
method to make these the gradient of ascent to the characters than to
attack the latter in their unbroken entirety. Europeans have always
followed a system based upon this reasoning, but there might be a
little presumption in an attempt to substitute the analysis of any
novice, however scientific, for the experience of centuries.

" The possibility of dispensing with the square character altogether,
and using only the Japanese syllabary, has often been discussed, and of
course there can be no second opinion as to the immense mental relief
such a change would afford the nation. But the question is one of
considerable difficulty. The ' Kana' would be amply sufficient to
express the *sounds* of the various words, but its unaided employment
would necessarily entail much confusion of homonyms, of which there
are a great number in the language. Cases where the context might
suffice to establish distinctions would also be rarer than in a European
language, for the character of the written style of Japan, as compared
with the spoken, is that in the former grammatical inflections and
syntactic particles are for the most part omitted, the result being a
sort of skeleton structure scarcely intelligible without the aid of the
eye as well as the ear. Thus the abolition of the Chinese symbols
would not only produce perplexity in particular instances, but also
entail a considerable general change in the construction of the language
for literary purposes. Nevertheless the attendant advantages seem
completely to outweigh the objections, and it may be confidently
predicted that until the burden of these multiform hieroglyphics shall
have been completely cast aside, Japan must ever be a laggard in the
pursuit of science. Probably she has already recognised this fact
herself, though the conviction is not yet strong enough to extinguish
her reverential love for those quaint monstrosities, in every one of
whose complicated strokes she discovers evidence of cultivated re-

finement, and whose perfect forms are in her eyes the most consummate creations of educated art.

"For the rest, the language is by no means deficient in terseness or power of expression. It has in Chinese a source upon which it can always draw for supplement or addition—a source quite as fertile as the ancient classics are to our own language, and more accessible. Thus it is generally possible by the aid of Chinese roots to construct precise and compact equivalents for the terms employed in western science, and since the restoration (1868) not only has a very large number of such words been added to the vocabulary, but also the classical tendency of public taste has brought into use a variety of pithy and elegant forms of expression that would not have been obtainable from Japanese proper. The want of a relative pronoun occasionally produces involved and somewhat clumsy constructions, and the liberality of the nation's moral code is marked by a paucity, or at times complete absence, of terms expressing the subtler distinctions of western metaphysics; but on the whole, if only the terrible blemish of its complex caligraphy were removed, there is no reason why the language should not rank with the most euphonic and not the least complete of our European tongues."

The following is the memorandum of Mr. Hyde Clarke upon the relations between the Japanese and African tongues :—

"One reason why the comparative philology of the Japanese and Loo-choo languages has given so much trouble to investigators is that there are no longer any allied languages in the neighbouring regions. The subject long since attracted my attention, but successive endeavours to obtain a solution were baffled. At an early period of these researches I was aware of resemblances to the Dravidian languages of India and to the Basque, but they afforded no decided results. The first real step made by me was the discovery of relations between the languages of the Japanese region and the Ashantee and others of Western Africa. Such a connection seemed, however, very unpromising, because the ethnological differences between the Japanese and the Western Africans are so very decided. It was, however, my duty to register the results, awaiting the explanation. Although other investigations have occupied me, so that it has not been possible to work out fully the Japanese problem, the area of observation is now determined for the language, the mythology, and even the ethnology.

"These investigations are given in more detail in papers which have been this year given to the Anthropological Institute, the Philological Society, and the Royal Historical Society, and which are in continuation of my books and papers on Prehistoric and Protohistoric Comparative Philology and Mythology and on Krita-Peruvian. These labours have been directed to the explanation of the position of the races of early culture, the Abkad-Babylonians, the Egyptians, Lydians, Etruscans, the founders of the Chinese and Japanese empires, and also those of the North American mounds and monuments of the civilisation of Mexico and Peru.

" In carrying out this undertaking it was necessary for me on ethnological grounds to distinguish a white race earlier in the field of history than the Aryans. Lately it has seemed most consistent with the course of historical events, and in conformity with all the incidents, to look for the seat of this Turanian white race in High Africa, in regions as healthy as those of High Asia, from which the Aryan migrations are held to have proceeded.

" The first conquests of these Turano-Africans were evidently made in Central Africa, because the languages of all the leading states and nations, Pulo, Bornu, Mandenga, etc., afford to this day the identical words of the early dead languages, as well as of those living languages that are considered to be allied with them. Thus the Abkad words in the vocabularies of M. Lenormant will be found, and also the Ugro-Altaic illustrations.

" It was also from the West African regions that migrations were made to North, Central, and South America, in continuation of earlier migrations. So to this standard are brought the languages and mythology of America. If a linguistic map be made down of this Atlantic hemisphere, then the languages of America will be found to converge towards West Africa, and from that point the living and dead languages spread out again. As to the mythology and also language, a monograph will be found in my memoir on Siva and Serpent-worship, founded on the Bribri and other languages of Central America.

" That the Egyptian language and civilisation had the same origin is evident from the fact that the Egyptian and Coptic words (and also those of the allied language of the Ude of the Caucasus *) are found on the same area. This has been long looked for on the supposition that the Egyptians propagated culture in Africa, whereas the reverse was the case. The researches have not, however, borne full fruit, as they were not rightly directed. Leo Reinisch,† in attempting to establish a Tibbu or Teda origin, has supplied a mass of matter on the relations between Egyptian and the languages of West, Central, and South Africa. Professor Owen is decidedly of opinion that the early ruling race in Egypt was of a high type.

" The tide of migration and conquest flowed to Babylonia. As

---

* See my ' Comparative Philology of Egyptian, Coptic, and Ude ' (London, Trübner).

† ' Der einheitliche Ursprung der Sprachen der Altenwelt ' (Wien, 1873).

already stated, the language is of the Turano-African class. The same is to be said for the early occupants of Asia Minor, Syria, Greece, Italy, and Spain.

"With regard to India, the Naga languages now spoken by inferior hill-tribes belong to the class cited, and in sequence to them are the Kolarian languages and the Dravidian. So close does the Kolarian come to one African type that the Mundala dialect of the Kol has been traced by me word for word with the Houssa of Africa to a great extent.

"The fall of these Turano-African empires in succession, and over a long epoch, completely altered the condition of mankind. The dawn of history shows us the Semites first, and the Aryans afterwards, engaged in this task. Syria and Babylonia were conquered by the Semites, while the Aryans became masters of Greece, Italy, and Spain at a later period, and then of Asia Minor and Greece, and afterwards of India.

"The Egyptians, profiting by the weakness of their masters, established their own government. Ethiopia lingered, but the African states must early have fallen into the possession of the black natives, however long white dynasties continued to reign.

"The knowledge of ascertained historical events and of actual facts prepares us to apply this knowledge to the case of the Japanese. The conquerors of the islands were of the same class as the other conquerors, and they found a local population of one or more races. At that distance from their centre, and consisting of bands of seamen and soldiers, gradually recruited, they would have few women of their own kin, and would intermarry with the natives. In time the ruling caste would cease to be separate from the main body of the people.

"What the conquerors and founders of the Japanese language and mythology were will be found from the comparative table of words herewith given.* These are far from complete, as the labours imposed by the main inquiry have not allowed me to devote a special attention to the Japanese branch.

"Whoever will take the trouble to look at these records philosophically and statistically will find guiding facts. He cannot fail to discern that there are resemblances and identities in the African column. He will further find that these are not casual, as the same names of African dialects constantly recur.

"With regard to the illustrations from Indian and other languages, they are less striking, and for this reason, that the languages are better and more copiously preserved in Africa than elsewhere. For instance, in Northern India the Aryans have established their languages among the main populations, and driven the non-Aryan-speaking tribes to the hills.

---

* See Appendix.

" The incidence of language like that of mythology is altogether apart from that of race, and we have white, brown, and black men speaking allied languages, just as we find white, brown, and black Christians and Mussulmans.

" With regard to the relationship of the languages, it is to be explained that in the Turano-African class it is very different from the Indo-European. What we call Indo-European languages are very much alike in words and grammar. It is true that some words are not of the same stock, but still any two languages are very much alike.

" This is by no means so in Turano-African. Indeed an example, which belongs to this class, shows it. The Ugro-Altaic languages are placed together by philologists, and their grammatical characters have the strongest resemblance, but the Magyar and the Turk, for instance, have little community of words. When a comparison is made of Abkad with Ugro-Altaic, the words will mostly agree with the Ugrian portion, and not with the others. Nevertheless Abkad is not Ugrian.

" We have to contemplate a class of languages consisting of various groups, say A, B, C, D. If we take a language, say Japanese, and compare it with A, we shall find only a partial resemblance, and so with B, C, and D, but it is equal to A, B, C, D, and so with Abkad or Coptic. There are similar variations of grammatical forms. Our comparison has to be made with the whole class in order to determine the classification. On being put to this test, Japanese is distinctly Turano-African.

" It consequently belongs to the epoch of early culture, earlier than that which we understand as the Babylonian, and in which language, characters, mythology, astronomy, geology, and it may be said geography, were determined.

" With regard to the ethnology of the Japanese populations, it is more obscure. The language of the Ainos is not indigenous, but is to be traced to the general stock of languages, and its analogies are to be found in Africa.

" In Africa, more distinctly than anywhere else, is to be found the ethnological characteristic of short races. These short races are in linguistic communion with other short races. The language of the Great Andaman Islanders has been positively identified by me as having African affinities.

" The best explanation that can at present be proposed is that the Japanese islands were occupied by the migrations of the short races. These were subjected by a subsequent migration of the white Turano-Africans, who intermarried with the native women. This would produce a mixed race, differing again from the races of shorter aborigines. Thus the new dominating Japanese race would maintain and propagate their dialect of the language and their sect of the religion, and, being in more favourable conditions, would displace the pure natives.

" When the Pacific route to America was closed by the weakness of the Turano-Africans, and the rising of cannibals and other savages, the Japanese would be isolated on their east. On their west, the Turano-African dynasties in China and Korea fell, and were replaced by natives, the same kind or series of events taking place as in Egypt, and again in Peru and Mexico.

" Japan was isolated from the other states, and in time various ethnological, mythological, and political conditions were established, making the distinctions successively more marked.

" The Japanese language, however, appears to have been less affected by these changes than Egyptian or Chinese.

" The tables given in an Appendix show some comparisons of Japanese with African languages, and with others, chiefly of the Indian region."

JAPANESE JUNKS.

CHAPTER IV.

DRAWING AND PAINTING.

Our opportunities of studying Japanese art—Temple art treasures—Studies
in Kioto—Artistic *séances*—Foreign derivation of the art—Government
patronage—Early artists of distinction—Kano and his school—The
Tobo school—Okio and the Shiyo Riu—Hokusai, the Japanese Hogarth
—The "schools" of Japan—Professor Anderson upon Japanese design,
composition, drawing, perspective, chiaroscuro, and colour—The beauty
of the human form not duly appreciated in Japan—Sir Rutherford
Alcock on Japanese art—Frequent recurrence of pictorial subjects—
Legend of the cuckoo and the moon—Anticipated progress of the
Japanese in European art styles—Their technical mastery.

IF the inspection of Japanese drawings and paintings of
every age and every description qualified one for writing
upon this subject, or even if adding to this inspection the
repeated expositions of those who have studied it, and frequent witnessings of the exercise of the art, fitted one to
speak with confidence upon it, then might I enter upon this
chapter with a very considerable amount of assurance. For
in the three months spent in the country we had extraordinary and multiplied facilities for examining examples of the
works of every age since drawing and painting began to be
practised in Japan, and saw many works of eminent artists
produced in the capitals and other places. In addition to
our visits to the most ancient temples, in some of which the
very earliest works are preserved, we had repeated opportunities of leisurely inspecting the old temple treasuries of
art, usually kept in the priests' residences, in which some of
the choicest products of thirteen hundred years of art-
production are kept with sacred care. On one occasion
during our stay in the western capital (Kioto) we were so

fortunate as to be taken to the store-rooms of an art-exhibition then in course of formation, and there inspected a collection of drawings and paintings brought together from the principal temples throughout the land. In addition to a large number of most precious Japanese works, we had the advantage on that occasion of seeing many ancient paintings brought from China by the Buddhist clergy of various periods. Besides these choice possessions of the temples, we likewise saw the imperial palaces at Kioto and Nagoya, where are some of the most perfect and characteristic paintings ever produced in the country—in addition to carved work, which, I may say incidentally, at Nagoya far surpassed any that I elsewhere came across, and which was inferior in no respect, I believe, to the work of Grinling Gibbons, while to a European eye the subjects were often quaint and novel to the last degree. Further, we had opportunities of inspecting valuable private collections; and as the habit of frequently changing the *kakemono* * prevails in Japan, a large number of the best examples that could be put before us passed under our view. Our host, Admiral Kawamura, was particularly thoughtful and obliging in this way, having the walls not only of his reception rooms, but of our private apartments likewise, hung with a constant succession of works of the highest class, sometimes ancient and sometimes modern. The governor of Kioto was equally kind, having the walls of the temple-residence in which we stayed hung almost daily with a succession of the finest examples of art which that ancient city contains. Nor was this the case as regards *kakemono* only in Kioto, for the same thing took place with respect to the screens which are so largely used in Japan, and which were continually changed, choice and fresh drawings, paintings, brocades, and embroideries on silk thus passing daily under our eyes. The like attention and complimentary care were shown also by the courteous governor in respect of other works of art,

---

* Hanging pictures mounted on rollers—the almost universal form of wall-pictures in Japan.

including *gakumono*,* lacquers, bronzes, ivory carvings, *cloisonné* ware, fans, silks, and other of the best productions of the long-sacred but now busily commercial city.   But we had yet another and very valuable opportunity of studying both ancient and modern Japanese pictures, one afforded to us by Professor Anderson, the director of the Medical College at Tokio, who has made a close study of this branch of art during his residence in that city.   Professor Anderson has collected there a number of highly characteristic drawings and paintings, and was engaged in preparing a paper —and if I remember rightly a book—upon the subject. Besides showing us his collection, and explaining the various merits and demerits of the pictures, he was good enough to furnish me with some historic and critical notes, of which, with his permission, I propose to avail myself freely in what follows.†

The above opportunities, numerous and invaluable as they were, were not, however, our only means of studying the art of Japan as now practised.   By the kindness of Admiral Kawamura and his friends, we were favoured with repeated *séances* with eminent living artists, and witnessed the drawing and painting of many pictures, not a few of which were subsequently presented to me.   These *séances* occurred both in the capital and in country cities and towns, as we found leisure in travelling through the interior.   It would be difficult to exaggerate the interest and pleasure of these occasions, the artists ranging from sketches of the boldest character executed in the most rapid manner, to works of minute and painstaking detail, growing up under the hand of the artist with all the sincerity and much of the beauty of natural objects.   Nor did we fail to see a large amount of amateur drawing performed, skill with the brush being no uncommon

---

* Pictures mounted on rolls to be viewed in detail as they are unrolled by hand.

† By the courtesy of Professor Anderson I came into possession of an excellent copy of Hokusai's celebrated sketches in many volumes, from which the great bulk of all European illustrations of Japanese drawing has been derived.   This work is now becoming rare, and difficult to obtain.

accomplishment among both the ladies and gentlemen of this "nation of artists."

Although the rise of the pictorial arts of Japan is lost in the distance of tradition, and although it is not solely a mere imitation of the art of China or Korea, it is not denied that it was originally derived from foreigners. So long ago as the year 463 A.D. the emperor Yariaku, who did so much in the way of bringing skilled and instructed foreigners into Japan, likewise brought over from Kudara, in Korea, a band of artists among whom was one whose name, Inshiraga, has been preserved. Others followed from time to time; and although it is not possible to affirm with certainty that any of their works have descended to us, there is great reason to believe that certain portraits, etc., which were shown to us in the ancient temple of Horiuji (between Osaka and Nara) were the productions of the famous Prince Shotoku-taishi, or at least of his age, he being the son of the empress Suiko, who reigned at the end of the sixth and the beginning of the seventh century.* It is recorded that during the reign of this empress, one Doncho, a very learned priest and a painter of great merit, was sent by the state of Koma, in Korea, to promote the interests of the Buddhist faith, then making its conquest of Japan. The art had so far progressed at the opening of the eighth century that the government had established a painting department, comprising several artists, and as many as sixty secondary artists or sketchers. Early in the ninth century this department was merged in the architectural department, and the work of the artists and their staff was probably purely that of decorating the imperial palace, etc. Religious art, so to speak, was at this time, however, firmly established, and many pictures were brought over from China by the priest

---

* The native authority says: "*Les œuvres de cette époque* [fifth century] *ne sont pas parvenues jusqu'à nous, et le plus ancien tableau que nous possédions représente le prince Shó-toku-taishi. Ce tableau,* *exécuté sous le règne de l'impératrice Suiko, au commencement du* VIIe *siècle, est précieusement conservé dans le temple de Horiuji, situé dans la province de Yamato.*"

Kukai (Kobodaishi), to whose learning and services I have
before referred in the chapter on Buddhism. Kobodaishi is
said to have painted many Buddhist pictures, together with
a portrait of himself. But the first Japanese *artist* well
worthy of the name was Kosé no Kanaoké, a court noble,
who flourished during the second half of this century (the
ninth). He was a pupil of a Chinese (Gokiyoshi), of whom
we know nothing but his name. Kanaoké, whose name is
a household word in educated Japan, painted landscapes,
animals, portraits, and Buddhist pictures with remarkable
skill, and is the subject of many curious legends. Some of
his works are still in existence, and are thought to justify
the esteem in which he is held; one, a portrait of the
Buddhist deity Fudo,* is to be seen in the temple of Daiyo-
ji, Tokio. It is distinguished by great ease and vigour of
outline, and compares favourably with some of the efforts
of the early Italian masters. The descendants of Kanaoké
maintained his reputation for several generations at the
court of Kioto.

Toba Sojo, a high-rank priest of the Tendai sect of Buddhists, distinguished himself as an original and skilful artist
in the eleventh century. Toba was a humourist, and his
sketches gave the name to all later caricatures, which are
still called *Tobayé*. The productions of his successors and
imitators are too ill-drawn to deserve serious artistic criticism, besides which the wit which has inspired them is too
Rabelaisian to allow their reproduction in the present age.
Other names that have lived became distinguished in the
next century or two; among them several members of the
otherwise renowned Fujiwara family. There were Fujiwara
Mototsuné, Fujiwara Nobuzané, and Fujiwara Tsunétaku, the
grandson of Fujiwara Takayoshi. Tsunétaku, in addition to

---

* Mr. Pfoundes says that this idol
is generally seated, and always
surrounded with flames, holding a
naked sword in the right hand,
with which to punish wicked and
terrified humanity into obedience.
and in the left a coil of rope to tie up
the guilty. He would therefore have
been a suitable illustration of the
theology of some so-called Christians
not very many years ago.

becoming celebrated as a court painter, became vice-governor of the province of Tosa, and his descendants therefore adopted Tosa as the family name. The first to adopt it was Fujiwara Mitsunobu (the fourth in descent from Tsunétaku), who is looked upon as the real founder of what is known as the Tosa School, or *Tosa Riu*. This branch of art was employed to delineate the nobles of the court in their ceremonial dresses, and other like subjects. It was a less vigorous style than that which went before it, but was not deficient of a certain sort of beauty, and was particularly noted for the fineness of its strokes. The school has lasted for five hundred years; but in 1662, Hiromochi, one of the descendants of Tosa, changed the family name to Sumiyoshi, and under that name the Tosa family of artists have continued down to our own day.

A native writer says: "During the middle ages, from 1305 to 1349, Kao, Meicho, Josetsu, Shiubun, and others appeared, who studied the style of the Chinese dynasties of So and Gen. This style is noted for its sketchy character, confining itself to making, by means of a few hasty strokes, a mere approximate outline of the object delineated." Professor Anderson puts the case somewhat differently in his notes. He says: "In the fourteenth century, a period of art decadence was terminated by a priest named Josetsu, a native of Korea (he is claimed by some authorities, however, as Japanese), who founded a school which boasted among its *alumni* three of the great names of the art history of Japan, Sesshiu, Shiubun, and Kano Masanobu. Little or nothing is known however of Josetsu himself. Chodensu, a monk, the most distinguished representative of religious art, was a contemporary of his. Sesshiu completed his education in China," where, during the Min dynasty, he is said to have attained great fame, "and on his return painted many remarkable landscapes, chiefly depicting views in the Celestial Land. Some of his most valued works were produced after the age of eighty. Several of his pupils gained great renown."

Kano Masanobu, whose name Professor Anderson mentions

above, and who was of the province of Sagami, had a son,
Kano Motonobu, who achieved great fame as an artist, and
holds probably the first place in the estimation of native
connoisseurs. He founded the most prolific school of Japanese
art, and his descendants, like those of Sumiyoshi, continue
to practise the profession at the present day. I have in my
possession several pictures painted by a member of the Kano
family during my visit to Japan, and presented to me by
Admiral Kawamura. No one could fail to discern in them
merit of a very high order, or to derive great pleasure from
them.[*] Professor Anderson says of the pictures of Motonobu,
the founder of the Kano School : "Even to the eye of a
foreigner the vigour of design and the complete mastery
of the brush displayed in his paintings of landscape and
figures appear very extraordinary." Of his descendants the
best known are Kano Tanyu (sixteenth century) and Tsuné-
nobu (seventeenth century). Towards the end of the sixteenth century, Iwasa Matabé took up the Tosa style, and
delineated the customs of his age.

In the latter part of the seventeenth century a pupil of
the Kano family, named Hanabusa Icho, distinguished himself by displaying much original genius. Casting aside the
traditions of his youth and training, he struck out a new
line for himself, and took scenes of ordinary street life,
and more especially such as were humorous, as the subjects
of his art. "His drawings show little attention to details
of form or colour, but are novel in design and forcible in
outline" (Anderson). His most noted follower was Ippo.
Between 1688 and 1703, Hishagawa Moronobu, of Yedo,[†]
did much to render the Matabé style popular. Professor
Anderson says "he is considered the inventor of the *Ukiyo-yé*,"
(or "social pictures"), "but in reality the credit should be

---

* A native writer said last year
(1878) : "*Les familles de Kano et de
Tosa existent encore aujourd'hui, et
comptent dans leurs rangs des peintres
de mérite.*"

† Mr. Yosino speaks of him as of
Yedo ; Professor Anderson calls him

"a native of Kioto." While the
latter authority speaks of him, as
the text shows, as the inventor of
the Ukiyo-yé, a native authority
speaks of him as the founder of the
Utagawa style.

shared with Icho." Mr. Yosino and other native authorities, however, state of Matabé, who was earlier by a century, that "his productions are generally known as *Ukiyo-yé*," and say that Hishagawa Moronobu's distinction is that of rendering popular the style of Matabé, as I have already said.   Torii Kiyomitsu, Okuda Masanobu, and other artists also distinguished themselves in the practice of this style.

Early in the eighteenth century (about 1720) a celebrated Chinese painter, named Chin-nam-ping, went to Nagasaki, acquired a great reputation, and taught many pupils. Other countrymen of his followed (Chinumei, Shabuson, and others), and Chinese painting again became the fashion, and spread itself throughout the country. But towards the end of that (the last) century, two contemporary Japanese painters exhibited so much originality and power as to give a fresh start to Japanese art, and upon a direction tending farther than ever from the traditions of the schools. These were Maruyama Okio and Katzushika Hokusai. These great artists indulged in more direct reference to nature than any of their predecessors. Of Okio Professor Anderson says he only partially carried out his principles; and although the Shiyo Riu, founded by him,[*] has had many followers, it has not succeeded in diminishing the influence of the Chinese style and its modifications. Of Hokusai, who did not emerge from obscurity till rather late in life, he says that he was the first *heimin* (commoner) of Japan who made for himself a name in art, and this his genius enabled him to do in spite of the neglect and professed contempt of those who considered themselves the best judges; "but he alone understood the *Ukiyo-yé*, and the multitude of admirers he found in his own class consoled him, if he needed consolation, for his seclusion from the select artistic circles." Hokusai has

---

[*] " His most noted pupil was Genki. In more recent times, an offshoot of the school, named Hikuchi Yosai, rose into notice, but the art-critics did not know whether or not to admire his free unconventional outlines, which, although expressing admirably the intentions of the artist, were at variance with all the revered examples of past ages. The *Zenken-no-jitsu*, in twenty volumes, gives the best example of his style."—Anderson's MS. notes.

left but few of his drawings behind him, owing to the fact
that he devoted himself mainly to sketching on wood for
the engraver; but his thirty well-filled volumes of engraved
sketches are a worthy memorial of his powers.   He excelled
in drawings illustrative of the life of people in the field and
street, giving the comic more often than the tragic, or the
neutral, aspect of things ; but he sometimes applied himself
with success to historical and religious subjects.   His works
have been so often copied by strangers that it is chiefly
from them that foreigners have derived their ideas of
Japanese pictorial art.   Hokusai had both rivals and pupils,
but none who has eclipsed his name and fame.   A hundred
other names of note in Japanese art might be given—names
more readily recognised by the average Japanese than those
of Reynolds and Hogarth by the average Englishman ; but
the above will suffice for my purpose.

I have said that it is largely from such sketches as those
of Hokusai that foreigners have derived their ideas of
Japanese pictorial art, and in this fact I have virtually
stated that their ideas of that art are extremely narrow
and mistaken.   The style copied is no doubt both original
and characteristic in a high degree, as was that of John
Leech, for example, among ourselves; but no one would
think of judging English art by the works of Leech, and no
one should think of judging that of Japan by the works
of Hokusai.   The historical sketch that I have given above
shows that the *Ukiyo-yé*, or popular art, is comparatively in
point of time, and essentially in point of form, modern, and
no sort of justice to Japanese art can be done by those
who limit their attention to its delineations.   For this reason
works like that of Sir Rutherford Alcock ('Art and Art
Industries of Japan '), in which nearly all the illustrations
of pictorial art are derived from the one source, must not
for a moment be considered to present a fair general view
of the characteristics of Japanese drawing and painting.*

---

* I am told that a similar remark
would apply to Mr. Jarves's American book, 'A Glimpse at the Art of
Japan,' but that work I myself have
not seen.

Nor, if that were otherwise, is any sort of justice usually done in such works by the English engravers to the delicacy and beauty of the Japanese originals which they profess to copy. I have compared many such professed copies with Hokusai's original engravings, and am obliged to say that they can only be considered as coarse and rude reminiscences of the work that left the hands of the Japanese artists. The meaning of the sketches is also, I am told, often misinterpreted. I have had a few engravings copied by Japanese engravers from Hokusai for this work.

The schools or styles of Japanese pictorial art may be summarised as follows: 1. *Korai Riu*, or Korean School, which was the first introduced into Japan, as we have seen, and which resembles the Chinese School in all essential particulars. 2. *Kara Riu*, or Chinese School proper, which has been subdivided into periods from the To * (in Chinese, Tang) to the Sei (Tsing) dynasty, and into three styles which may be compared in execution to the square, cursive, and intermediate characters in caligraphy. This *Kara Riu* is, beyond doubt, the true parent of Japanese pictorial art, the Korean School, although arriving first in the country, being but an offshoot from the Chinese. The *Kara Riu* was largely taught — chiefly during the Sung and Min dynasties—by Chinese immigrants, and by Japanese who had been to China to study art. " Until the time of Okio, at the end of the last century, Japanese painters adhered so closely to the rules framed by the Chinese schools, and commonly even to the subjects in vogue with Chinese artists, that Japanese art was entitled only to rank as a branch of the other school ; the only exceptions are found in the works of Icho and Hishigawa Moronobu, and even their productions scarcely merit the name of original art " (Anderson). Desirous as I am to do justice to the Japanese, I am bound to say that injustice is often done to the Chinese in works upon Japanese art by foreign writers. The

---

* To (Tang) is the name of the dynasty which governed China from 618 to 906 of our era; but the word To has come to be generally used in Japan for China and the Chinese. To-jin is a Chinaman.

Japanese themselves, as I have elsewhere remarked, are
always ready to bear the fullest testimony to the advantages
derived by Japan from China and Korea through many
centuries, and in many branches of art and industry. But
foreigners who visit Japan appear to fall so completely under
the spell of the land and of the people—and fascinating both
certainly are—that they fail to see what is original and what
is derivative in that which they behold. But in fairness to
China it must be acknowledged, and by the Japanese is
acknowledged, that much of that " grace of outline, freedom
of stroke, and delicacy of colouring" which characterise
Japanese art, and constitute no small part of its charm, is
drawn from the art of China. I have had, as stated earlier
in this chapter, rare opportunities for comparing Chinese
paintings of the Min period still preserved in Japan with
those of various Japanese masters, and I greatly doubt if
Sir Rutherford Alcock or Mr. Jarves, or any other writer
who may have exhibited a tendency to undervalue the art of
China, would be able to separate them with certainty into
their respective schools. 3. *Kanaoka Riu*, founded in the
ninth century by Kosé no Kanaoka, as previously stated,
and continued by his family for many generations. 4.
Takuma Riu. This was an adaptation in the early part of
the thirteenth century of the existing rules of Chinese art
to the representation of Japanese court ceremonials, etc., and
although exhibiting skill in its way was devoid of any
great artistic merits. 5. *Toba-yé*, originated as already
described in this chapter. All roughly drawn caricatures
are still known as Toba-yé, but Toba Sojo does not appear
to have been succeeded by artists at all comparable with
himself. A later form of caricature, originated by Iwasa
Mitabé, and first sold at the ancient city of Otsu, derived its
name from that place, and became known as, 6, *Otsu-yé*.*
Of 7, *Josetsu Riu*, nothing need be added to what has already
been said, but of the school founded by Josetsu's pupil Ses-

---

* " No artists of note contributed to   present found in Kioto, Osaka, and
maintain the reputation made by the   other places are scarcely worthy of
founder, and the ' Otsu-yé' as at   notice."—*Anderson.*

shiu, 8. *Sesshiu Riu*, I must quote a few words : " Sesshiu, after studying in China, became one of the greatest artists of Japan. His most noted pupils were Shingetsu and Sesson, but many well-known painters belonged to his school. The Sesshiu Rin so closely resembled the Kara Riu, that it was probably only the celebrity of Sesshiu that gave the school a distinctive title. One of his descendants living in the last century maintained that the Japanese art of his period was as much Kara-yé as that of modern Chinese painters, both being drawn from the same source, and more or less modified by individual artists " (Anderson). Of 9, *Tosa Riu*, it is needless to add to what has been said, beyond observing that, while it afforded considerable display for colouring, its merit inclined to decorative rather than to imaginative or truthful art. 10. *Kano Riu*, the best-known and most influential of all the native schools, and coming down, as we have seen, from the fifteenth century to our own day. 11. *Icho Riu*, and 12, *Ukiyo yé*, already described. The latter name I have rendered as " social pictures "; by others it is sometimes rendered " worldly pictures." It literally means, I am told, " floating world," and implies that the subjects are taken from actual life, in distinction from the favourite Buddhistic and legendary motives of the older schools. " The *Ukiyo-yé* may be divided into two sections, an order to which belong Hishigawa Moronobu and his followers, and a modern phase of which Hokusai is the presiding genius." The pictures of Hishigawa Moronobu, not unlike those of the Tosa Riu in style, represent a less characteristic phase of· Japanese life than those of Hokusai, and are less spirited and truthful. The later *Ukiyo-yé* is best exemplified in the Hokusai *Mangua*, and the *Ukiyo Guafu* by Keisai Hiroshigé. More may be learned of the true nature of the Japanese masses from a study of these marvellous collections of sketches than from a library of the descriptions of the country found in Europe, but it is necessary that every page should be explained by a Japanese, and perhaps by a Japanese *heimin*, one of the class for whom the work was composed " (Anderson).

13. *Shiyo Riu.* This school was founded, as previously stated, by Okio, and was characterised by a more direct and loyal resort to nature than his predecessors had allowed themselves; but the influence of Chinese principles and methods were too strong even for him, and he was not successful in inspiring his pupils even with the same amount of devotion to nature as animated himself. 14. *Butsu-yé*, or Buddhist paintings. The first paintings known in Japan were of this kind, and, although the style was imported from Korea, it is probably of Indian rather than of Chinese origin. This branch of art bears close and curious analogies to the early religious art of Europe, both being practised chiefly by monks, and both exhibiting much bright and decorative colouring, with a free use of gold in the display of saintly forms and glorifications. Lastly, *Bunyi-ré*, an unimportant but common style of painting, employed for the illustration of poetry, most frequently by noble amateurs.

The practice of painting in Chinese (or "Indian") ink is exceedingly common in Japan, and this form of art is designated *Sumie*. Originally this prevailed only among poets and literary persons, and had, says a native writer, "pour caractère distinctif le bon goût." He goes on to say: "Les peintres qui ont ensuite imité ce genre de peinture ont quelquefois voulu représenter sous une forme légère une idée sérieuse, et ont suppléé parfois aux imperfections de l'esquisse par des strophes de poésie. Les règles relatives à ce genre sont peu nombreuses et vagues; mais, bien que les traits en soient vigoureux et hardis, on y retrouve pourtant certains petits détails. Les sujets favoris des peintres de ce genre sont les sites pittoresques, les montagnes abruptes, les rochers escarpés, etc.; ils transportent, pour ainsi dire, par l'imagination, le spectateur sur les lieux mêmes." One would scarcely have supposed that these last observations were specially applicable to Indian-ink drawings; but there they are, in an official record, and they must be taken as the expression of the opinion of the native writer.

Anticipating that my own opinion of Japanese art would

carry but little weight with it, and nevertheless desiring to include in this work some statement of its characteristics that would be valuable to my readers, I obtained from my friend, upon whose kindness I have already so frequently drawn in this chapter, Professor Anderson, the following summary of his conclusions :—

"*Originality of design.*—Not strongly marked until within the last two hundred years, most of the older pictures being variations of Chinese models. Wit of a high form is perceptible even to the foreign eye in many drawings of the Toba-yé and Ukiyo-yé.

"*Composition.*—Nearly always good, the grouping of figures and accessories contributing as far as possible to tell the tale and to please the eye.

"*Drawing.*—Almost invariably conventional. Excellent in birds, flowers, monkeys, fishes, and insect life. Defective as regards anatomy in the human figure and in most animals, but successful in conveying impressions of action, and usually correct in the proportional relations of different parts of a figure.

"*Perspective.*—False. In a few modern pictures more or less successful efforts to realise distance by fixing vanishing and distance points have been made, but in these cases the artist has received education from Europeans. Any painting in which the laws of perspective are observed is *not a specimen of Japanese art.* Of the false perspective there are two kinds, one in which lines parallel in nature are made to diverge as they recede, another in which they are drawn parallel without any convergence towards a distance point or point of sight. The impression of distance is obtained by an absurd elevation of the horizontal line in the Chinese School and its modifications, and by the interposition of conventional clouds to separate nearer from more remote objects.

"*Chiaroscuro.*—Absent. A false chiaroscuro is often practised, and this by Mr. Jarves and Sir R. Alcock has been accepted as the genuine element. Figures in silhouette against a moonlit sky are often drawn by the Ukiyo-yé artist (*vide* frontispiece in Alcock), but the overstrained imaginative descriptions of such efforts are mere literary decoration.

"There are no shadows in any true Japanese pictures.

"*Colour*.—From a decorative point of view the colour is mostly to be highly praised, as the better Japanese painters are masters of harmonies and contrasts; but the absence of all the variety of tint produced by shadows, and direct and reflected lights, prevents criticism from higher ground.

"The older Japanese painting is chiefly caligraphic; the modern chiefly decorative. Caligraphy and painting were in old times esteemed as equally important branches of the fine arts, and in both China and Japan a single character written by a noted caligrapher would often command a higher price than the finest specimen of pictorial art.

"The designs for metal work, ivory and wood carvings, and porcelain and lacquer decoration, were almost invariably supplied by noted painters of the Chinese, Kano, Tosa, or Popular Schools; hence all the important qualities of Japanese art must be sought in its pictorial manifestations."

It may not be deemed altogether presumptuous for me to express concurrence in the above opinions, and to add to them the following remarks: First, as regards design, it appears to me that the absence of novelty and power in the exercise of this branch of pictorial art in the earlier schools was due less to the absence of the necessary faculty than to the rigid traditions and rules under which the life of Japan was conducted for so many centuries. With a religion founded on the worship of ancestors, and all the offices of the state and of the church, so to speak, descending in families, the evil effects of what we have known in our past as patronage must have pressed heavily indeed upon all rising artistic faculty in ancient and mediæval Japan, for the whole public life of the country was a system of patronage in a highly organised, and therefore in a very oppressive, form. In the sphere of literature, concerning which we have naturally got to know more than of that of painting, evidences of this restraining influence abound. Even under Iyéyasu and the succeeding Shoguns of his family—and under him and them the genius of the country appears first to have begun to expand freely—the labours of the greatest intellects were pursued under more or less burdensome conditions, the military and civil supremacy of the Tokugawas being of course the primary consideration. When greater freedom became possible, fertility of design appeared with it in a remarkable degree, and in this fact, it seems to me, the capability of the Japanese became vindicated. It was said by Opie that but for the Greeks even beauty in nature itself would perhaps have remained undiscovered until now, or so far misunderstood that we might have preferred the artificially crippled form of the Chinese, or the rank and vulgar redundance of a Flemish female, say, to the Venus of the Tribuna. And if we for a moment restrict the phrase "beauty in nature" in the manner to which his illustration points, viz. to beauty of the human form, no opposition to his remark could be drawn from Japanese art, for certainly human beauty has not been at all worthily appreciated or illustrated in Japan. Nor indeed could it be illustrated until quite recently (however much it might be appreciated), for the principles of anatomy were unknown in Japan a century ago.* In point of fact,

---

* In a paper on the early study of Dutch in Japan, read at the Asiatic Society there by K. Mitsukuri, a native gentleman, the author gives a very quaint and interesting account of the introduction of anatomical study at Nagasaki. It is derived chiefly from the posthumous work of a physician named Sugita Fusai, who is referred to in the following extract as the author. Mr. Mitsukuri writes: "Another friend of the author, Nakagara Kiowan, also a physician, serving under the same Daimio as himself, being interested in the products of different countries, was a constant visitor at the quarters of the Dutch whenever they appeared in Yedo. It was in 1771, one day, the interpreter showed him two Dutch books on anatomy which were for sale. He took them home, and among those who saw them was our author. Sugita could not, of course, read a word, but was struck by the fact that the illustrations of bones and organs represented them to be very different from what he had believed them to be. He wished to buy the books, but was too poor. Fortunately, however, he succeeded in persuading a karo (councillor), who by his influence had the price paid from the public treasury of the Daimio. Ever after this, Sugita longed for the opportu-

the beauty of the human form has not hitherto made any
worthy impression on Japanese art. Woman has been kept
in an inferior position; even her face has for the most part
been defaced by the shaving of the eyebrows and the black-
ening of the teeth; her gait has been ruined by the clumsy

---

nity to test which of the theories
was correct. He had not to wait
very long. As good luck would have
it, he was invited, shortly afterward,
to a dissection which was to take
place in the execution grounds of
Kozukappara. Such a thing was of
rare occurrence at that time, and
Sugita was not the man to enjoy it
by himself. He knew that several
of his friends, among others Nakagawa Kiowan and Mayéda Riotaku,
would be very glad to avail themselves of such an opportunity. He
must let them know, by all means;
so he wrote to them, though it was
somewhat difficult to do this, and
appointed a place to meet next
morning. The anxiously expected
day came, and all were promptly at
the rendezvous. Mayéda had with
him a Dutch book on anatomy, which
he had bought in Nagasaki some
time before, and when they came to
examine it, it proved to be the same
as one of those which Sugita had
been fortunate enough to procure
lately. They were soon in Kozukappara, the famous execution grounds
near Asakusa. The hour for which
they had longed had actually come.
They were about to know whether
the things they and their fathers
had believed in were right or wrong.
I can imagine how their hearts
must have beat. The dissection was
performed by an old executioner, an
eta who had had some experience in
this line. The result is soon told.
They of course found that their theory
was entirely mistaken, and the way
in which the illustrations in their

new book coincided with real objects
raised their admiration to a high
degree. On their way back, Mayéda,
Nakagawa, and Sugita were together.
The events which had taken place
of late must have seemed to them as
if they had been prearranged. How
fortunate that Nakagawa should
happen to see those books, that
Sugita should be able to buy them,
that they should have a chance to
test their doubts! And what a
coincidence that Mayéda should possess the same book! As they walked
home they talked earnestly. Shame
that they should have lived all their
lives as physicians, and not know,
till now, the construction of the
human body, on which the science
of medicine was necessarily founded!
If they could understand the true
principle of anatomy from the real
objects they had just seen, if they
could translate this book which they
had obtained so luckily, they would
do an immense service to the country,
and would not have lived in this
world in vain. So they went on,
and when they separated for the
night they had come to the agree-
ment that they would try their best
to master the strange language, and
that as such things were the better
the sooner begun, they would commence the very next day. They
had set before them a hard task,
but they were determined to accom-
plish it. As they parted, their hearts
were perhaps too full to speak, but
they must have shaken hands most
heartily, if such a thing had been
known then."

clogs she has had to wear, and by the artificial system of turning the toes inward; and the wonder is that so much grace and charm, and beauty too, have survived so many ages of depression and injury. For that many are beautiful, and very beautiful, cannot be doubted by any one who has seen much of the people. Still, the art of Japan has yet to develop sympathy with that strength and symmetry and beauty of the human form which gave to the arts of Greece their highest and most enduring glory. But when we employ the phrase "beauty in nature" in its broader and more lawful sense, we have to say that without the aid of Greece—even in the indirect and dubious way of transit through Indian and Chinese art—Japan has developed a genuine and intense love of natural objects, and in connection with them a power of design both eminent and attractive. Not only in its drawings and paintings, but in other branches of art, the Japanese have evinced a wonderful power of arranging natural objects in such relations to each other as to give grace and charm to the whole; and the same thing is true when we pass beyond the *design* of their works to the *composition*. And perhaps of all the divisions of art none furnishes a truer or better test of sound artistic feeling than this. No design, no drawing, no colouring, nor any other quality can redeem a work of art if it be badly composed. "The composition," as has been said, "should appear the true efflux of a mind so heated and full of the subject as to lose all regard and attention to everything foreign;" and although some may suppose that this fulness and fervour of the mind can only be occasioned by striking scenes or circumstances, they really are the provocations of the true artist to the accomplishment of whatever object he sets before himself. The composition of Japanese pictures is usually notable for its pleasing effects.

What has been said of design is equally true of *drawing*, as regards the absence of success in dealing with the human form, and indeed with all the higher animal forms; and likewise as regards the true and great success with which birds, flowers, and other such natural objects are rendered.

It is a real pleasure, and not a small one, to find oneself
among a group of Japanese artists, and witness the happy
mastery which they have acquired over the brush. At the
same time it is melancholy to consider within what limits
their arts even now move, and we cannot help hoping that
Art like Woman will in Japan speedily lay aside its conventional aspect and movements, and proudly and joyously
display its nobler qualities.

But to be more technical : Professor Anderson's remarks
upon Japanese perspective are in the main true, and those
who read them, and fancy they have observed indications of a
juster knowledge of perspective than seems compatible with
them, must bear in mind his admission respecting the effects
of European teaching in some cases. To me it seems likely
that those writers are correct who fancy they discern the
effects of Dutch influence in the Japanese pictures of the last
century or two. I agree with Sir Rutherford Alcock in
thinking that the curious example of perspective given in
Hokusai (and repeated by Sir Rutherford in his 'Art and
Art Industries of Japan') is probably derived from some
Dutch source. The following sentences of Sir Rutherford's
are also worthy of careful consideration : " If they learned
nothing from the Dutch, the question arises, Did the
Jesuit fathers [who, as we have seen, carried their ideas and
practice of Christianity into Japan] teach drawing in their
schools, or occupy themselves with the arts, as some of those
at the court of Pekin, in the reign of Kanghi, unquestionably
did ? The latter introduced, for instance, as we know, the
use of vignette medallions on the best China ware, never
prior to that adopted in the ornamentation of Chinese
porcelain. Then, again, some of the caricatures and illustrations of popular customs, in all their grotesqueness and
coarseness, powerfully recall the Dutch paintings and
engravings of similar subjects in the sixteenth and seventeenth centuries, in the Höllen, Ostade, and Teniers style.
The Japanese themselves do not admit any tuition from either
of these sources, whether in perspective or the treatment of
subjects for the pencil. But when we reflect on the aptitude

they have shown to adopt foreign ideas, and imitate European arts and customs in the present day, we cannot help seeing the possibility of their having borrowed something in the way of art." Answers, and clear and conclusive ones, to the questions here raised can doubtless be obtained from a careful chronological study of Japanese pictorial works, and it is possible that Professor Anderson's book now in preparation may furnish us with them. But whatever may be the truth of this matter, and whether the power be native or derived, it must be acknowledged that although Japanese perspective is usually more or less false, it often comes wonderfully near the truth, especially as regards aërial perspective.

The statement that "there are no shadows in any true Japanese picture" is a very strong one, even when one throws out of the category of Japanese pictures all those modern productions which are manifestly influenced by European teaching or example. It is nevertheless perfectly true, at least to this extent, that the rules upon which *chiaroscuro* is produced by European artists are entirely unknown to the artists of Japan. They have known absolutely nothing of such rules; while, I need hardly say, such developments of chiaroscuro as Leonardo's principle of central radiance is even farther from the scope of Japanese conception. Still, I cannot but feel that it would be incorrect to say either of Japanese or of Chinese art proper that light and shade are absolutely unknown to it. This has often been freely alleged, and was generally accepted as true until recent times; but the late Mr. Wornum, who appears to have seen but little more of Chinese art than an exhibition at Hyde Park Corner, nevertheless contradicted some of the academy professors on the point, and said the Chinese had made "considerable progress in light and shade." As a general rule, however, the chiaroscuro of Europe has no parallel in the art of Japan.

As regards *colour*, Professor Anderson's statement of the case seems to me to be perfectly correct. All those changes of tint and tone which result from gradations of light and shade are wanting; and as a consequence it is chiefly for its

decorative merit that the Japanese employment of colour is
valuable and instructive. But it cannot be denied that,
subject to the above limitations, Japanese artists are great
masters of the art of colouring, and masters after a fashion
mostly, if not wholly, their own. Mr. J. Leighton (quoted
by Alcock) has borne ample tribute to this great merit of
theirs, claiming for the Japanese a subdued and refined style
superior to that of the Chinese. " I do not wish you to
understand," he says, " that the Japanese artists do not use
bright colours, for few men know their value better ; but
what I desire to convey is that they use them judiciously,
and in comparatively small proportions, cleverly supporting
and contrasting them with their secondaries, and other
compound colours, which they use in grounds and large
masses generally." Sir Rutherford Alcock, I am pleased to
see, does ready justice to the fine Japanese sense of harmony
and tone in colours, himself evidently enjoying equally in
their way both the splendour and the quieter beauty of their
effects. Sir Rutherford, like myself, delights in bright
colours, and is not ashamed to own it. " A relative arrangement of tints will do much to produce harmony," he
says, " but will scarcely satisfy a colourist who loves masses
of the brightest hues, such as in a sunny clime are a perpetual feast to the eye, and a delight to the sense which
revels in profusion. The Roman scarf, or the handkerchief
of the *contadina*, the bright coloured sash of the Andalusian,
and the glowing scarlets and gold of the Indian bazaars, are
all living evidences of an innate sense of the beauty of bright
and pure colours. We have not in England the sun of these
southern and eastern climes, which gives to the skies and
mountains, to trees, birds, and flowers, a glory of such
brightness that colour of the most vivid and brilliant hues
forms, by daily and hourly association, a needful element in
the life of the people."

Some objects are continually recurring in the pictorial as
in the other arts of Japan. Among natural objects are the
blossoms of the plum, the cherry, the peach, and the apricot ;
the pine-tree ; the *Paulownia Imperialis*, a straight-growing

tree with large leaves (as an emblem of rectitude) ; the flowering peony, the bamboo, the willow, the maple, and the chrysanthemum ; also various birds, most frequently the stork, the
wild duck, and the eagle ; and, perhaps more commonly than
anything else, the glorious and sacred mountain of Fuji-san,
or Fuji-yama.   Numerous striking historical characters and
incidents likewise are often repeated by artists.   Some
objects frequently recur in association, the following examples of which I take from Mr. Pfoundes's collection of
notes entitled 'Fu so Mimi Bukuro.'   The pine-tree and
stork ; both are emblems of longevity : this design is very
frequently used in the embroidery of robes presented to
new-born babes.   The peony and Chinese Lion ; the peony
is usually sketched on large articles, such as screens at the
entrances of temples, on panels, ceilings, etc.   The bamboo
and sparrow, both being of a mild and gentle nature—
a design often seen in embroidery, and on fans and
screens.   The willow and marten (or swallow) ; the willow
waves in the breeze, and the swallow sways to and fro—a
favourite design for fans, etc.   The cherry and pheasant ; the
cherry, cultivated solely for its bloom, is jointly named with
the " gorgeously plumed pheasant."   The plum-tree (in Japan
" the poet's favourite tree ") is associated with the Japanese
nightingale (the *uguisu*).   This combination is a very common
design, the plum-tree having, from a verse written by Wani in
honour of the ancient and popular emperor Kintoku, become
associated with poetry, and the *uguisu* being the poet of the
woods.   " ' Send forth your fragrance upon the eastern winds,
O flowers of the plum-tree ! and do not forget the spring,
because of the absence of the sun,' cries a native poet.   Not
unfrequently does one see the plum-tree stand all leafless in
the snow, but adorned with white blossoms, like a bride before
the altar.   It bursts into clouds of fragrance and beauty in
February, the leaves appearing later " (Griffis).

Another frequent design is that of a bird flying across the
crescent moon.   This is " the moon and the cuckoo," and
springs from a legend of the twelfth century.   About 1153 A.D.
the Mikado fell sick, being nightly stricken with a horrible

nightmare. It was discovered that a dark cloud moved from over a grove of trees and rested upon the imperial residence, two fiery orbs shining out from it. The priests failing by their prayers to drive away the brooding demon, one Yorimasa undertook to slay it, and after successive watching at lengths breathed a prayer to the great god Hachiman, and added to his prayer (what the orthodox priests had omitted) a heavy arrow from his well-bent bow. The arrow, or the prayer, or both, brought the monster down, and Yorimasa made his work complete by nine plunges of his sword, each time to the hilt. The demon thus slain was formidable enough to account for its brooding dangerously even over the breast of an emperor, for it had an ape-like head, the body and claws of a tiger, and a tail that was itself a huge and venomous serpent. It was called *Nuye*, from its cry resembling that of a bird of this name. The emperor, wishing to reward Yorimasa, gave him a celebrated sword called *Shishi no O* (the king of wild boars). Besides, knowing that he secretly loved Ayame * no Maye, and that the love was returned, he bestowed her on Yorimasa. The noble who was appointed to present the sword to Yorimasa, knowing his reputation as a poet as well as a brave man, bethought him of trying a verse after the *Zo-to* style, and just at the moment a *hototogisu* (cuckoo) was heard, giving him the "key-note" of his verse, the *kami no ku* of three lines of five, seven, and five syllables.

> *Ho-to-to-gi-su*
> *Na-o mo ku-mo i ni*
> *I-gu-ru kuna,*

and immediately Yorimasa answered him with the following *shimo no ku* of two lines of seven syllables each—

> *Yumi ha-ri tsu-ki no*
> *A-ru ni ma-ku-se-te*

---

* Ayame, the blossom of the *Calamus aromaticus*, or flowering sweet flag. Female names were usually derived from flowers. *Maye* is the ancient affix to female names. *Hime* was only used for the daughters of men of rank.—See Pfoundes's 'Fu so Mimi Bukuro,' from which, as I have previously said, these illustrations are taken.

—making the complete *honka* of thirty-one syllables. And his readiness and wit increased his reputation as a scholar and a soldier. In this way the moon (*tsuki*) became associated for ever with the cuckoo. But in order to fully understand the connection, the qualified reader must note the double meaning of the verse, which it is impossible to render into English. It reads one way—

> " The *hototogisu*
> Above the clouds—
> How does it mount?
>
> The waning moon
> Sets not at will."

But as it alludes to Yorimasa's elevation to imperial favour, there is the concealed meaning—

> " Like the cuckoo
> So high to soar,
> How is it so?
> Only my bow I bent,
> That only sent the shaft."*

Geese and rushes are often coupled together, it being believed that wild geese, on making long flights, carry in their beaks rushes which they drop upon water, and then alight upon them to rest. The chrysanthemum and the fox are drawn together in reference to one of the many fox-myths which abound in Japan. The story goes that a royal prince was bewitched by a fox in the shape of a damsel, who became his mistress. One day she fell asleep in a bed of chrysanthemums, resuming her normal shape, and while thus lying was shot at by her lover, whose arrow smote the creature in the forehead. On afterwards finding his sweet-heart with a wound in the temple, he discovered her true

---

* " The play on words in the first portion is only alluding to the soaring of the bird and comparing it to Yorimasa's elevation, the real comparison and readily improvised verse inciting the native admiration. In the second portion, the allusion to the bow-like shape of the waning moon and its setting, the play is on the word *tsuki no*, moon, or one's own will—on *Yumi hari*, to bend a bow —the shape of the waning moon— and *Aru*, to set (as the moon sets)— or to send a shaft."—*J'foundes.*

character. The bamboo and the tiger are united, because the tiger fears the elephant, and therefore hides in the bamboo jungle. Peach-trees and oxen are often coupled ; there is a Chinese saying, "Turn the horse loose on the flower-covered mountain, and the ox into the peach orchard." A dragon is often shown crossing the summit of Fuji-yama on the clouds, a small snake having become the dragon ; so an abject person sometimes becomes an exalted one, rising to a great height, and easily surmounting the greatest obstacles : the design is therefore an emblem of success in life.

I must conclude this chapter by expressing my conviction that under the new order of things now prevailing in Japan, and more especially on account of the great intercourse between their country and Europe, Japanese artists will make extraordinary strides in the mastery of European art, and will combine with it elements of power and beauty peculiar to themselves. Mr. Jarves and Sir Rutherford Alcock concur, apparently, in thinking that at present Japanese artists "have a technical mastery of other means, not known to genre and landscape painters in Europe, by which they produce effects that place a scene before the eyes in a way to fill the imagination with a vision of things only suggested by the pencil." I agree with them, for I find no other explanation of the extraordinary pleasure which one experiences alike in seeing the Japanese artist dashing his wondrously effective strokes upon his paper or silk, and in turning over the pages of a book embodying the results of his labour. I have seen the French Tissot, the Neapolitan Martino, the Russian Aivasovsky, and some of our own artists wielding their cunning pencils with swift and startling effect ; but no European that I know rivals the native of Japan in artistic legerdemain. From the blending of his traditional and mystic skill with the art familiar to ourselves, we may justly expect to gather rich results hereafter.

THE ASCENDING DRAGON.

To face page 104, *Vol. II.*

CHAPTER V.

Many proverbs and proverbial sayings—Expressions for what is impossible
—Injunctions for avoiding the appearance of evil.

THE proverbs and phrases current among a people reflect
their character and modes of thought, and in so reflecting
them tend to increase their permanence. Mr. Pfoundes, in
his 'Notes,' Herr Knobloch, in the 'Transactions of the
German Society of Japan,' and Mr. Griffis, have all helped
to bring a number of Japanese proverbs and sayings into
an accessible form, and from their collections I select the
following, observing that in many of them there is in the
original a play upon words which cannot be translated, but
which sharpens the point of the phrase to the native.

Impossibility is a good reason.

Open lips make cold teeth.

The mouth is the door of mischief.

An ugly woman avoids the looking-glass.

The fox who borrows strength of the tiger.

To water your own field.

Life is a light in the wind.

To number the years of a dead child; *i.e.* probably, to do
something that is quite useless.

Illnesses come through the mouth.

To give a sail to ability; *i.e.* to assist talent.

Even the monkey falls from the tree.

To cut a stick after the fight.

Of whom we speak, his is the shadow; *i.e.* he of whom we speak throws his shadow upon us.

Willow twigs dig no snow.

Daughters-in-law become mothers-in-law; *i.e.* probably, the young and agreeable become old and disagreeable.

Prophets know nothing about themselves.

Covetous about one *mori* (a small coin), and neglectful of a hundred.

Flowers on a dead tree.

The devil's "Help, O holy Buddha!" *i.e.* like the devil crying to Buddha for help.

To blow away the hair and find a wound.

Like trying to seize a *tai* (a sort of perch); *i.e.* trying to seize an eel.

Indolence is a powerful enemy.

To give something more to a thief; *i.e.* to give your cloak to the stealer of your coat.

To adapt the sermon to the hearers.

Like going into the fire with an armful of bamboos.

To submit is victory.

A fallen blossom does not return to the twig.

Sufficient dust will make a mountain.

Even the fool has his art.

The magnet can attract iron but not stone.

Adapt yourself to the place you are in.

Too much courtesy is discourtesy.

He who holds a tiger brings trouble on himself.

The bat of a village without birds; as we say, in the company of the blind the one-eyed are kings.

The sea-eagle has hatched a falcon.

Many captains, and the ship goes on to the rocks.

Even two leaves of the spendan give forth perfume.

The heart is the same at sixty as at three.

The snakes know the paths of the *dsha* (a large species of snake).

No fish in clear water.

One crane's voice is better than (the chirping of) a thousand sparrows.

A drunkard cannot deny (conceal) his real character.

Like pushing a stone with an egg.

The heart is better than a beautiful face; *i.e.* to have a heart is better than to have a beautiful face.

Rubbing salt into a wound; *i.e.* adding insult to injury.

Listening to a child you fall over a precipice; *i.e.* attending to trifles and neglecting more important matters.

Tears even in the devil's eyes.

Poking out the eye with an insignificant twig.

Overcome in words, in truth victorious.

Pinch yourself and know how others feel.

The dog bites the hand that caresses it.

To reach the cub you must enter the tiger's den.

The stomach will not allow itself to change places with the back.

Burnt cheeks do not fear the sun.

No door can be made for the mouth.

Beware of beautiful women as you would of red pepper.

The crows laugh at tales that are three years old; *i.e.* they are foolish enough to be amused with anything.

To fall seven times, to stand the eighth.

In evil times the hero appears.

To buy misfortune at market.

A firebrand is easily kindled.

The frog in the well knows nothing of the high seas.

Too much done is nothing done.

Like sitting a child alone on a well.

To look at the heavens through a cane tube; *i.e.* to take a limited view of great things.

Like a fox on horseback.

No standing in the world without stooping.

No art against deceit.

He who touches vermilion becomes red.

He who breaks through a thicket disturbs the snakes.

Poke a cane-brake, and a snake will slip out.

The absent get farther off every day.

Unpolished jewels do not shine.

To be thirsty and dig a well; *i.e.* huge exertions to satisfy a trifling want.

Bearing wood to the flames.

The blind man does not fear a snake.

Like a wolf in priest's clothing.

To steal a bell with your ears covered; *i.e.* to affect to dislike something whilst taking it.

To give wings to a tiger.

On the road a horse would eat a marsh-mallow; *i.e.* too hungry to be dainty.

Ice comes from water, but is colder than water.

Egg-plants do not grow from melon-seeds.

A deserter is terrified even by the *tzuszuké* ears (a kind of long grass).

To talk to the crows of the white heron (white animals are often held sacred in Japan).

For travelling, a companion; for the world, kindness.

Hairs even on a bald head.

Poverty cannot outrun industry.

Lanterns and bells; may perhaps be read as meaning two different means to the same end, namely, the warning travellers that a vehicle is approaching.   Both articles are employed thus in Japan.

No escape from the nets of heaven.

To give honey to eat; to flatter; or possibly equivalent to " sending you ruffles when wanting a shirt."

The bird that flies upwards does not ruffle the water.

People that are hated strut about the world.

Use the stick soon and save a fall.

Like seeking for fish on a tree.

After three years even an evil becomes a necessity ; *i.e.* habit is everything.

Habit has more weight than instruction.

Eagerness is loss; *i.e.* most haste worst speed.

A novice does not at once become a superior.

Poverty leads to theft.

Good medicine tastes bitter.

Dumplings are better than flowers.

Even a new shoe will not make a hat; *i.e.* no use to try improper means.

Great words little deeds.

A friend at hand is better than relatives at a distance.

A devil in the heart (an evil conscience) torments the body.

The hand goes to the itching spot.

A clever falcon hides his talons.

When the tiger is dead, spare his skin.

Pleasure is the germ of sorrow.

To hide the sword with a smile.

If dogs go about they must expect the stick.

Before argument, proof.

Hated children fear not the world.

Thankless labour brings fatigue.

To speak loud, and then purse the lips. (It is useless to shut the mouth after shouting out.)

Moral people beget many children; probably honest bodies get the heaviest loads thrown upon them by the cunning.

Money thrown after thieves; equivalent to throwing good money after bad.

Emerald and crystal are known by their sheen.

Old people led by their children.

For a broken pot a mended lid; or nothing is so bad that there is not some use for it. Even an unprepossessing woman finds her mate.

Lepers envious of those with sores.

The first-born comes with most difficulty.

Be careful to be careful.

Crying faces wasps sting; or, misfortune seldom comes singly.

After pleasure there is grief.

If falsehood takes the road, truth hides.

Truth cometh out of falsehood; or, truth comes to the surface.

Do you know how to boil potatoes? Used in addressing stupid or clumsy people when they commit some foolish mistake.

After the swallowing the scalding is forgotten; it might be paraphrased, danger past is laughed at.

A demon with a club. Doubly frightful.

Cheaply bought, money lost.

To wish to send a letter, but not being a writer. When one wishes to excuse oneself on the ground of inability or want of opportunity.

Children are a burden on one's shoulders, past, present, and future.

To my own experience hoist the sail, meaning " to ride one's own hobby."

The master's favourite red cap. (The great man's will must be humoured.)

To hide the head but not hide the tail.

Hearing of Paradise and seeing Hades.

Carelessness is great danger; literally, oil exhausted, a great danger.

Ignorance bliss.

Providence is a strange thing; apparently in the sense of " Chance brings together queer couples."

The poor have no leisure.

Those who know the ropes do most hauling.

Kio no yume, Osaka no yume—" A dream of Kioto a dream of Osaka." Building castles in the air.

Child-bearing is easier than child-tending.

If in haste go round.

The spawn of frogs will become but frogs.

By searching the old, learn the new.

More words, less sense.

Clever preacher, short sermon.

Who steals money is killed, who steals a country is a king.

Like learning to swim in a field.

The gods sit on the brow of the just.

Send abroad (or from you) the child you love most.

Making an idol does not give it a soul.

Live under your own hat.

A (wife's) tongue, three inches long, can kill a man six feet high.

The heron rises from the stream without stirring up the mud.

If you curse any one, look out for two graves. " Curses, like chickens, come home to roost."

There is no teacher of Japanese poetry. (*Poeta nascitur, non fit.*)

Good doctrine needs no miracle.

Regard an old man as thy father.

Expressions for what is impossible : —

To build a bridge to the clouds.

To throw a stone at the sun.

To disperse a fog with a fan.

To bale the ocean with the hand.

Injunctions for avoiding the appearance of evil : —

Don't wipe your shoes in a melon patch.

Don't handle your cap when passing under a pear-tree.

Don't stay long when the husband is not at home.

ANCIENT BURIAL-PLACE OF AN EMPEROR.

CHAPTER VI.

THE INLAND SEA AND NAGASAKI.

HAVING spent, and well and busily spent, nearly a month in
the capital of Japan, it was next arranged for us to make a
trip through the most important parts of the country, and on
Wednesday, February 5, soon after midday, we left Tokio
for Yokohama, and before three had embarked on board the
twin-screw steamship *Meiji Maru*, belonging to the lighthouse department of the Japanese government. The departure of this commodious and fast government steamer
upon lighthouse duty in the Inland Sea and on the west and
south coasts, with Mr. McRitchie, the government engineer-
in-chief of the department, on board, was a convenient
opportunity for facilitating our visit to the interior, and
a more satisfactory one to me than the appropriation of a
special steamer for the purpose, which had been contemplated. By taking passage in this vessel, when engaged
upon her periodical visit to the lighthouses, I was enabled to

view the coast more minutely, both outside in the Pacific, and in the Inland and Japan Seas; to visit some of the lighthouses and acquaint myself with their construction and working arrangements, in company with the superintending engineer; and at the same time to visit Kobé, Hiogo, Miramar, Miyajima, Shimonoséki, and Nagasaki without much expenditure of time, owing to the high speed of the *Meiji Maru.* It was arranged for his excellency Admiral Kawamura also to make this inland journey, as he had public business to transact at several of the ports and other places which lay on our route. His excellency Enouyé (then minister of public works), whom the lighthouse department was under, was good enough to see us comfortably berthed on board the *Meiji,* and after he had taken leave of us, at three o'clock, we steamed down the Bay of Yedo, passing on our way the P. and O. steamer *China,* just arriving from Hong Kong, carrying the English and Continental mail into Japan. The *Meiji* is commanded by an accomplished English officer, Captain Peters, whom I had had the pleasure of knowing a little in England, and who by his intimate acquaintance with the coast, the tides, set of sea, etc., was able to spare us in the first night and throughout our trip with him much of that inconvenience which better sailors than I can pretend to be confess to experiencing when their ship is very uncertain how to keep upright, and very violent in its endeavours to do so.* The first lighthouse to be visited was

---

* Owing perhaps to a little perversity of my own, and also to a trap being laid for me by the unwisdom of a servant (and how much more we all suffer from want of sense in others than from any intended wrongs!), I nevertheless contrived to get an ugly fall during the first night. Having persisted in selecting an upper bunk to sleep in, and vaulted into it with as much agility as was available, a servant heedlessly threw a fur-lined coat over the rail of the bunk below; consequently, in alighting afterwards from my elevation, my foot slipped over the fur as soon as my weight came upon it, and I fell upon the edge of the upper bunk, and thence to the deck. The fall was apparently a trifling one, and made no mark, but I became very sick and ill for a time, and a rib must have been badly bruised, as I felt so much pain afterwards that I had to take medical advice at Nagasaki, and as I write these lines, seven weeks after the fall, I still feel the effects.

that situated on the eastern point of the island of Oosima, off
the peninsula of Kii. The island is spelt Oshima on the
map of Mr. Brunton (who preceded Mr. McRitchie in his
office), and Oosima in the Nautical Pocket Manual published
in Shanghai, the name of the light being given in the latter
as Kashinosaki. It is a white catoptric light, of the second
order, revolving every half-minute, and is visible for eighteen
miles. There is nothing to be said of our passage to Oosima,
except that the evening after our departure was fair; that
the sacred Mount Fuji was a splendid and impressive feature
in the shifting picture; that after we had cleared the Bay of
Tokio and the Sagami Sea we had nothing but the sea
between us and Australia; and that we reached our anchorage inside the island we were bound for soon after midday
of the 6th. The day was singularly fine and warm, and we
landed, at a very difficult landing-place, upon an isle so
pleasant that one began to think of the " Lotus-eaters "—

> "In the afternoon they came unto a land,
> In which it seemed always afternoon."

It was curious to observe that in anticipation of earthquakes the lighting machinery of the lighthouse was all
supported upon a bed-plate resting on three spheres, partly
to allow the upper portion to slide or roll upon the lower,
and partly on the same principle as that which induced Sir
Joseph Whitworth to support upon three points his "true
planes," and his own billiard table which he has in his
Manchester residence, viz. the mathematical principle that a
plane surface can be passed through *any* three points in
space, and therefore when a plane surface rests upon three
points only either or all of those points can change its position
without distorting the surface. The arrangement as adapted
to the English-built lighthouse at Oosima is perfectly sound
in principle, but even in Japan earthquakes of sufficient
violence to upset lighthouse apparatus are so unfrequent
that I strongly suspect the bed would usually be found
resting upon the additional supports which are intended for
use when men are moving about the light-machinery for

cleaning and other purposes. Still when a violent earthquake does come, and they *do* come at these parts of the
country as we have seen, it will be well if the light is found
poised on its spheres.[*]

I have elsewhere spoken of earthquakes at some length,
but this is a suitable place for mentioning what happened
twenty-five years ago near this spot—off the peninsula of
Idzu, which was passed on the previous evening. On a bay
at the end of that peninsula, and inside Rock Island, is the
town of Shimoda, which had been opened as a foreign port.
A great earthquake came, and with it tidal waves and sub-
sidiary waves of such a nature that the Russian frigate
Diana, which was lying there, was spun round forty-three
times in thirty minutes, as previously stated, and was thrown
high and dry, a useless wreck, at the end of the revolutionary
period! This was in 1854, and we are informed that this
same earthquake shook and injured the country for some
hundreds of miles along this south-eastern part of Japan.
It was in the next year that the great earthquake at Yedo

---

[*] Since writing the above I have
consulted a paper on "the Japan
lights" read at the Institution of
Civil Engineers by Mr. Brunton, C.E.,
by whom many of them were established, and find that he does not
think altogether favourably of the
plan adopted. He finds that while
the free motion of the upper over the
lower part of a structure may neutral-
ise the effects of an earthquake
shock, it at other times has incon-
venient results. A person stepping
on one of the "aseismatic" tables, for
the purpose of trimming or cleaning
the lamps, causes the upper part to
roll to such an extent that the lamps
become deranged, and in the case of
revolving lights the regular motion
of the clock-work is interfered with.
To remedy these defects Messrs.
Stevenson introduced an arrangement
of vertical springs, but it was only
partially successful. In the paper
referred to Mr. Brunton discusses—
as he and others had previously done
at the Asiatic Society in Japan—the
best mode of constructing buildings
to resist earthquakes; and gives a
full and most interesting account of
the lighthouse system of Japan—one
of the best in the world, and continually undergoing extension. An important discussion followed, in which
Messrs. Stevenson gave an instance of
considerable damage being done by
an earthquake to the Sagami (Japan)
lights in consequence of their aseismatic arrangement being put out of
working order. The apparatus appears to have been caught by the
earthquake in exactly the state in
which, as stated in the text, I
anticipated on the spot (at Oshima)
it would be found.—See Proceedings
of the Institution of Civil Engineers,
vol. xlvii. Session 1876-77, pt. 1.

(now Tokio) took place; and in fourteen months of 1854-55 no less than eight hundred and seventeen shocks were experienced.

We left Oosima before three, steaming out at the western end of the island, and passing a remarkable series of rocks running a mile out from the shore, and forming an almost continuous natural breakwater. We now rounded the southernmost point of the province of Kii, passing the high light of Siwomi-saki, which is a fine fixed light of the first order, and steamed up between Kii and Awa, through the Isumi Strait, past the island of Tomagashima, on the western extremity of which is another fixed white light (third order), extremely well placed. We anchored before midnight in the harbour of Kobé. Rain had come on at sunset, and the night had continued wet, but next morning clear, warm sunshine streamed over the pretty European-looking town of Kobé (one of the places open to foreign trade), and over the hills beyond. Hiogo, which is a genuine old Japanese town, practically adjoins Kobé, and is continuous with it, the road leading through them having to surmount one of those river beds which are embanked considerably above the level of the adjacent country, and of which we afterwards saw so many. At anchor in Kobé, besides a large number of merchant craft, was the large iron-belted Japanese corvette *Hi-yei*, which I had the honour to design and see built in England for his majesty the Mikado: and likewise H.M. surveying ship *Sylvia* and gun-vessel *Lily*. The captain of the *Hi-yei* came to fetch us, and we proceeded to his ship, which had just returned from Korea, and which was minutely inspected by his excellency the minister of marine. H.M.S. *Sylvia* is commanded by Captain Aldrich, who so much distinguished himself in the sledging work of our recent North Pole Expedition. I was unable, from want of time, to visit his ship (which I myself had had fitted at Woolwich as a surveying vessel many years ago), but I had the pleasure of calling on Captain and Mrs. Aldrich on shore later in the day. During the forenoon we drove to the famous waterfalls two or three miles out of the town, or rather to the base of the hills down which they drop, having then a delightful climb through lovely scenery of hill, wood, and stream to the falls themselves.

All the way up are scattered tea-houses, with one more or less pretty girl at least to each. Nor is the place wanting in the conveniences of worship, for there are little temples and gods and shrines sufficient in number for all reasonable people. We stopped at one of these on the way down, where the goddess Kwannon was surrounded by small gilt figures, just as the Virgin is surrounded by angels of music in Fra Angelica's famous picture in the Uffizi Palace, Kwannon's angels and the Virgin's being of about the same size. There were other gods about this building, and we happened to be present at the time when numerous cups of rice were being offered upon the altar by an old woman attendant. There was a box for voluntary subscriptions. I could not quite understand this temple, as no priests were visible, and there was a business-like money-making look about the arrangements which gave the whole thing the appearance of a purely commercial speculation. There were several Japanese gentlemen with us, but none of them seemed to understand any more about it than I did; one of them suggested, however, that the proprietors were probably priests, and that may have been the true explanation of the matter. At any rate there were the gods and the opportunities for worshipping and subscribing all complete.

In the afternoon we visited the great Shinto temple of this place, and took a drive through and about Hiogo, this being the first purely Japanese country town of large size that we had yet visited. In the evening after dinner, by the kindness of Mr. McRitchie, we were introduced to the club, where was an abundance of English newspapers, and an excellent billiard-room with several good billiard-tables. At 11 P.M. we re-embarked in the *Meiji Maru* by means of the *Hi-yei's* boats, and at midnight the anchor was weighed and we were under steam again for the Harima Nada, which may be called the second part of the Inland Sea going westward, the first part being the Idzumi Nada, upon which Kobé and

Hiogo are situated.   The two are separated by the island of
Awaji, north and south of which are connecting straits.

By breakfast time next morning we had passed through the
Harima Sea, and were well in among the beautiful clusters
of islands which lie thickly spread in an east and west direction for nearly two hundred miles.   After spending some
hours at anchor at the light of Nabéshima (a small picturesque island close to the southern extremity of the
northern shore) we proceeded again through lovely lakelike
scenery, with multitudinous islands, all much less bright
and green and flowery at this season than in the summer of
course.   About noon we reached, and cast anchor in, the small
Bay of Mihara or Mirawa, which has been spoken of as a
suitable situation for a great protected naval establishment.
I need hardly say that the approaches to this place, and
its naval and defensive capabilities, were carefully noted,
with results that it would be too wearying to the reader to
enter upon here.   We landed, after luncheon, at the nearest
village, and proceeded in *jinriki-shas* to the old castle of
Mihara, where some time was occupied in the inspection of
the harbourage, the artificial river banks, and so forth, and
likewise, and not least interestingly, in going over the old
palace and outbuildings of the castle proper, with its ancient
spears, bows and arrows, matchlocks, pictures, screens, etc.

The following day, Sunday, 9th of February, we rose soon
after six, to see the ship start, and in order that we might
observe the character of the western approaches to Mihara,
and enjoy the island scenery we were to pass through.   And
well was one repaid for rising early, by witnessing the
strange fantastic beauty of the dawn.   In the north-west
was a vast dense zone of snow-cloud, deeply fringed with
red at the top, and lowering over a vast dark amphitheatre
of glorious hills and mountains.   The picture was grand
and sombre; but presently the amphitheatre, being already
full of dawnlight, began to fill with daylight, and then
again with direct sunlight, until at length it brimmed
and ran over with vivid glory, and, says my note-book,
" seemed to invite, not admiration, but festive enjoyment."

It was what Shakespeare calls "jocund day," that filled the world.

There were official reasons for going up to view the town of Takahara or Takéwara, which lies in a pleasant situation in a valley, with the sea coming up to and flowing past it, through a pretty channel that admits of the passage of boats and junks. We were under way again before eight o'clock, steaming between the beautiful scattered islands, with their sides terraced for cultivation, like the Rhine-side vineyards, broken at intervals with cataracts of green vegetation streaming down to the sea, and relieved by the shining sails of innumerable junks given to the morning winds that wander, literally wander, among the countless islands of these inland waters. At 9.30 we struck northwards, or north-westwards, from the main route to Shimonoséki, in order to visit the ancient and extraordinary temples of Miyajima, which but very few Europeans have seen.

These temples are situated upon the island of Itsuku (impregnable), off the mainland of the province of Woa, and in view of the large town of Heroshima, lying ten miles to the east. Approaching their site from the south, as visitors do, and on the outside of the island, one comes to a stone lantern standing out of the sea off the corner of the island, as a receptacle for a night-lamp for the guidance of local boats ; and passing this, next appears the unusual sight of a large *torii* standing in and rising out of the sea ; and inside of this again open up as you advance a crowd of temples, and a town at the foot of hills. These hills are high, have obviously once been thickly wooded, and are in many places thickly wooded still. It was on these hillsides that the sacred deer and the sacred monkeys of Miyajima once flourished, and it is at their feet that their few remaining representatives still linger.* The first thing we did on

* "The mistake," says Mr. Max Müller, "which is made by most writers on early religions, is that they imagine there can be but one motive for each custom that has to be explained.

Generally, however, there are many. Sometimes the souls of the departed are believed to dwell in certain animals. . . . Monkeys are looked upon as men slightly damaged at the

landing was to spend a trifle on the food prepared at little
stalls for the purpose, and to feed therewith whatever of
sacredness still animated the forlorn-looking deer that
followed us to obtain it. Emerson somewhere speaks of
those divine days in which even the cattle in the fields seem
to have great and tranquil thought ; and if these surviving
sacred animals have any great thought, or even any thought
at all, they probably employ it, like good old-fashioned
Tories at home, in deploring the loss of " the days that are
no more." I am much afraid, however, that their sacredness has nearly disappeared from Itsuku ; and as to the
monkeys, they seem to have almost all gone away in
company with their sacredness, for in all Miyajima I could
find but one. I was assured that there are two in one of
the temples, but although I looked carefully about it I
could see only the one, leaping lazily from rafter to rafter
overhead, stopping occasionally to let a glance fall upon our
party. I am sure that he was a sacred one, however, by
the coolness and indifference with which he did this, for
even among ourselves we always find that the more we are
disposed to treat people with respect and reverence, the
more sure they are to treat us with contempt in return.
But I have been too anxious, I find, to give attention to
these awe-inspiring beings, and have spoken of them too
soon. I leave them to that slow-descending but certain
doom which awaits them.

Numerous skiffs came off to land us, but we took a boat
of the *Meiji*, and were advised that we could pass under
the *torii* and land at the temple itself. This we attempted,
but unsuccessfully, the tide falling fast, and our boat
drawing too much water. We therefore landed at the town,
and strolled round to the Shinto shrines. The *torii* which
we passed under twice is of wood. A large one in stone to

Creation : sometimes also as men thus
punished for their sins. They are in
some places believed to be able to
speak, but to sham dumbness in order
to escape labour. Hence, it may be,
a reluctance arose to kill them, like
other animals, and from this there
would be but a small step to ascrib-
ing to them certain sacro-sanctity."—
' Hibbert Lectures,' 1878.

replace it has been presented by some wealthy personage,
and huge granite blocks, already trimmed to size and shape,
have been brought to the spot for erection. But for some
reason or other,—perhaps the whirling of the revolutionary
tornado—they have not been erected, and are lying there on
the shore, with the sea rising over them each tide. The
older parts of these Shinto shrines of Miyajima date from
the year 589 A.D., the later parts being about seven hundred
years old. Outside there are huge stone and bronze lanterns,
some of them of great size and fine workmanship, to say
nothing of a pair of large bronze animals, three hundred
years old, which some people call lions, but which others
might without much offence, I should think, call by any
other of a score of names. At high tide the water flows
around and under the outer platforms of the temple. The
temples are hung with portraits of a hundred poets of all
ages, many of them belonging to the imperial family
(which is not surprising, seeing the sacred character of
the sovereigns, and the leisure enforced upon them and
theirs); and there are also to be seen a large number of
votive writings, drawings, and paintings, some of them such
as no one would covet, and some few of them of a very high
class of art indeed, and of great value—more, I should
think, than their custodians are aware of. There are also
here some treasures and curiosities, among them the
immense bow of the hero Yaguro, and a sword which
belonged to the prince of Noto, the scabbard of which I
found to measure $7\frac{1}{2}$ feet in length, and the handle $3\frac{1}{4}$ feet.
There is also, standing about 15 feet in length above
ground, and 18 feet round, part of a tree planted by the
emperor Takakura (1169–80), and therefore at least seven
hundred years old.

And now I will detail to my readers a few facts about the
origin of this temple, which were communicated to me by
the authorities on the spot, and in perfect good faith, so
that no one need doubt them unless he pleases. The
goddess of this temple is Mihashirano-himé-o-kami, who was
the daughter of Susanoö-no-mikoto, whom we know so

much about, from what has gone before. The sun-goddess, Amaterasu, ordered *our* goddess (as we will for the moment call her of this temple) to come down from heaven and abide here. She came down, but for a long time no residence was provided for her. In point of fact this goddess must have been wandering, neglected and homeless, for an immense period, for it was only in the reign of the empress Suiko (593–629 A.D.) that she had the temple built for her. Now as she probably came down long before Jimmu-Tenno began to reign, and as his reign commenced 660 B.C., it would seem that thirteen hundred years would be much within the term of her wanderings. However, these came to an end at last, and in the following remarkable way. It appears that a man named Saekino-Kuramoto, living near the island of Itsuku, was out in a boat fishing "with another old fellow" (so runs the narrative), and when they had gone as far as Okanoshima they observed coming towards them a boat with a red sail set on her. This boat closed upon them and at length came up to them, and who should they see on board of her but our goddess, who told Kuramoto to ask the Mikado (at that time an empress) to build a temple for her in Miyajima (Itsuku-shima), and promised to protect the Mikado's government for ever. Kuramoto forthwith made his way up to Kioto, and recounted to the government what he had seen, and the instructions he had received. It happened that there was some sort of mischief or trouble on foot at the time in Kioto, and the government, discerning in this a proof of our goddess's anger at the neglect shown to her, at once gave orders for the building of her abode. Kuramoto came back with his order for the temple—delighted enough, no doubt!—and applied himself to finding out the best place for it. While engaged in this, down from the top of the mountain flew a bird, and went right ahead of the boat in which Kuramoto was making his exploration. Kuramoto— as we must see by this time—was far too wise "an old fellow" to neglect a chance like this; he followed the bird till it stopped, and it stopped at the site of the present temple, upon the building of which Kuramoto at once set to work, continuing with such energy that he got it completed in November of the same year. I am sorry to say there is another account; got up, I should conjecture, by some one who grudged Kuramoto his fame and honour : this says that the goddess was placed on the island as long ago as the time of the emperor Sujin-Tenno, who was reigning when Christ was born, and reigned twenty-nine years afterwards. I cannot determine which account is correct, and for a reason which will appear from the following quotation from a written communication made to me in English on the subject. " There was a fighting between the one called Minamotono-Hironari, who kept all valuable writing about Miyajima, and Ochi-Yoshitaka; and the former was totally defeated, and his house was all burnt down; therefore we lost all valuable writings about Miyajima in that time. However, when Haishiyogoku Kiyomori was the prince of Akinokuni, the buildings were made much larger, and it became almost the finest temple in Japan."

There is also at Miyajima, superbly situated on a hill, a Buddhist temple of a thousand " mats "; and likewise a pagoda. The town and vicinity are celebrated for their beauty in the season of blossoms, and have admirable tea-houses and gardens. One such place in particular, which we visited, known, I believe, as the Maple tea-house and garden, must be a charming place in spring and summer.

Before turning from this very delightful spot, I must repeat an interesting story about the " fighting " that occurred here nearly three and a half centuries ago, the record of which Mr. Satow has quite recently published in connection with a history of the Christian church at Yamaguchi, in Suwo, next to Choshiu.* The characters concerned are Yoshitaka, governing prince of the district, Harukata (who was known previously as Takafusa), his most powerful vassal, and Motonari, a neighbouring magnate and general. The first act (if I may so far assume the dramatic style) reveals

---

* Transactions of the Royal Asiatic Society of Japan, vol. vii. pt. 2, 1879.

Yoshitaka at a banquet given by himself in his castle of Yamaguchi in honour of envoys from the Shogun and the ruler of the province of Bungo : an alarm is given, Harukata being discovered marching on the town with an armed host. Yoshitaka sends for his uncle and cousin, but they prove disloyal, and do not come ; his officers propose to send and slay them ; but Yoshitaka refuses, still hoping them loyal ; his more courageous friends offer to march out and meet the enemy, but he hesitates and wavers. At last a traitor induces him to abandon the castle, and he flies with three thousand followers to a neighbouring Buddhist monastery. In the night most of these followers desert him ; in the morning he is surrounded by the enemy, with five times his own numbers. He offers terms ; but all conditions are refused. Night comes on, and he slips away to the sea-shore to cross the Inland Sea to Chikuzen, but the wind is against him, and he cannot pass ; he creeps to another monastery, and is there discovered and again surrounded, and finally commits *hara-kiri* (disembowels himself) as the last resource, in those days, of a noble (Japanese) mind. This happens September 30, 1551. But before applying the knife, Yoshitaka wrote a letter to Motonari, entrusting to him the task of avenging his death. Motonari wept on reading it, and vowed to punish Harukata's treason, but prudently resolved to wait for a more favourable opportunity. In 1553 he began to lay his plans for attacking Harukata, obtained from the Imperial court a commission for the punishment of the traitor, and summoned supporters from near and far. In June 1554 Motonari and his sons put their forces into motion, captured several of the enemy's strong places, and were victorious in a first engagement with a detachment of Harukata's troops. But Harukata brings together 30,000 men, while Motonari has but 5000, and the latter therefore proceeds to make up by stratagem what he is deficient of in numbers. This brings us to the second act. Motonari begins to fortify this sacred island of Miyajima (Miya-shima), raises fortresses and redoubts on the main-land hard by, and on the little island of Niho (completed

June 1585), and affects to regret having wasted time in fortifying a place still so easily to be taken. Harukata marches into the trap, goes off with 20,000 men to Ihakuni, which is near to the island, ferries them over in junks, captures the island (to the horror, doubtless, of the sacred deer and monkeys), and sends off his defiances to Motonari. This is in October. Now comes the third and last act, premising that in the interval Motonari hastens down to Kusatsu, on the mainland close by Miyajima, thus cutting off Harukata's retreat ; and that, although most of the *samurai* of the province thought Motonari's defeat was certain, and consequently held off, he had 300 fighting vessels placed at his disposal from the province of Iyo, in Shikoku, and Providence sent him a fine night-tempest to aid in covering his operations. This enabled him to fall like a storm-god upon his foe. During the tempestuous night (the last of the month), Harukata's army sleeps ; no sentries are posted, the storm being a sufficient guard, they think ; but the troops of Motonari are more than awake, they are thirsting for slaughter ; they embark ; they stand over to the sacred, or rather say desecrated, island ; they silently land. As the day breaks, their battle conches sound the assault ; they rush upon the fortifications ; the too-numerous defenders get in each other's way ; the Motonari men storm over them ; the defences are carried. In vain Harukata endeavours to rally his men ; they break away from him in terror ; they rush to their junks ; they drown by thousands in attempting to crowd on board of them. Poor Harukata himself, though a hero, is a stout and there-fore a slow one ; as well as he can he pants and presses and sways his way to the shore ; but boat there is none, and like his lord against whom he turned, he too has only the one road of death along which he can now travel : he com-mits *hara-kiri*. In such straits the French, they tell us, take their courage in both hands ; but the Japanese of the now bygone time used to take his courage in one hand and his cowardice in the other, and so put an end to himself ; not an altogether admirable ending for anybody at any time.

A delightful run southward of a few hours among the islands brought us in the evening again into the route for Shimonoséki, and at 11 P.M. we sighted the Hesaki light, at the eastern entrance of these remarkably narrow straits. This light is near the northern extremity of the great island of Kiushiu, which is separated by these straits of Shimono-séki from the mainland of Japan, or, strictly speaking, from the great island of Honshiu, which is by far the largest of the four great islands of which Japan is chiefly composed. Mr. McRitchie and his lighthouse staff, and the *Meiji Maru* with her captain and crew, were busily at work at an early hour in the morning upon the changing of buoys, the supplying of stores, and other duties of their department; but it was not until a later hour that I found myself on deck, admiring and enjoying the beautiful shore scenery. The place was not without interest to an Englishman, as these are the waters into which steamed, in 1863, the squadron of Christian England (composed of nine war-ships, carrying 100 guns, and leagued with three French, four Dutch, and one American ship, carrying together more than another hundred guns), to blaze away at the lives and batteries of the subjects of the prince of Nagato—Nagato being a small county 60 miles long and about 15 miles broad for the greater part of its length, and 40 miles at its very broadest point. The first crime to be punished was the warning off from forbidden waters (June 25, 1863) of the American steamer *Pembroke* by a blank discharge, and the attacking of her by two local men-of-war on the following day because she refused to move away, but so attacking her that she sustained no injury. An American writer whom I often quote in this work * says: "As a matter of international law, the Japanese had a perfect right to close the Straits of Shimono-séki, since the right to use it was not stipulated by treaty, and each nation has a right to a league of marine territory along its shores, and to the straits and water-passages commanded by cannon-shot. . . . The *Pembroke* had no right

---

* Mr. W. E. Griffis, M.A., in 'The Mikado's Empire.'

where she was. She disregarded the warning of blank cartridges." However, America, like ourselves, recognising some other principles as much higher and more commanding than mere "right" and "justice," her envoy sent down the *Wyoming* to take retribution, and on the 16th of July she had a sharp engagement with the two Choshiu ships and the shore batteries, blowing up one of the vessels and sinking the other. His own ship was much knocked about also, having five men killed and six wounded. At about the same time some French and Dutch ships were also warned off by blank fire, and therefore some French and Dutch men-of-war went and blazed away at the Shimonoséki batteries with shell-guns. "Ample vengeance was thus taken," says Mr. Griffis, "by Dutch, French, and Americans. No British vessel was injured." But this was an affair of a sort such as England could not of course be kept out of, and although "orders from H. M. Government forbidding British participation in the needless and wicked act of war arrived after the squadron had sailed, and Sir R. Alcock was then recalled to explain the situation" (Griffis), in went the English ships on the 5th of September 1864, and with Americans, French, and Dutchmen bombarded the batteries, landed men to silence them, and removed the guns. In the next month the representatives of the same four powers decided that it would be a good thing to add to this bombardment a demand for *three million dollars*, as "indemnities and expenses for the hostile acts of the prince of Nagato," and they insisted on the money being paid; and it has been paid, the last instalment having been handed over in 1875. It is the present government of the Mikado, struggling bravely along the path of civilisation and progress which England, France, and America have pressed them to pursue, that has had to provide the money, and that too at a time when its chief difficulty in pursuing the new course has been a financial one.

> "O wad some power the giftie gie us,
>   To see oursels as ithers see us."

This is the spot where the bombarding fleets lay; there

were the batteries that we overthrew; and here, at my side,
as I look at both, is a Choshiu officer, now of the Japanese
navy, who was on shore there doing the best he could to
resist the Christians. He smiles when the words Christian
and Shimonoséki get by any chance thrown together, or near
each other, in conversation. Mr. Griffis says " the total expenses incurred by the United States in this expedition were
less than 25,000 dollars," and gives 785,000 dollars as the
share of the indemnity which it claimed and took. Worthy
sons of a noble sire! In looking at the spot where lie the
English dead killed in the engagement referred to I could
but regret their loss.*

The Straits of Shimonoséki are very narrow, less than half
a mile broad at one part, and as they connect the Inland Sea
with the Sea of Japan, a strong and swift tide oscillates
through them. The town, of 10,000 inhabitants, lies along
the northern bank near the eastern end of the strait, and is,
I should think, quite two miles in length. We landed at
1 P.M., to look through the town and its temple, while the
Meiji Maru proceeded with her work at what is fast becoming
known as the Rokuren lighthouse, from some misprinting of
the name. It is really situated on the island of Mutsuré,
and marks the western entrance of the straits. I observe,
however, that even the lighthouse department now sometimes adopt the erroneous name of Rokuren. Our first visit
on landing at Shimonoséki was to the Shinto temple, which
is situated at some little height up the hillside, but has its
torii standing close to the sea's edge. There is an interesting legend—but why should I call it a legend? why not a
history?—connected with the establishment of this temple.

---

* I have purposely touched but
lightly in this work upon the conduct
of ourselves and others in connection
with the bombardments and pecu-
niary extortions of both the Kago-
shima and the Shimonoséki affairs,
as it is neither necessary nor desirable to revive the controversies that
grew out of them. I ask my readers
to believe, however, that the feeling
of aversion with which I regard
those acts has not been lightly
entertained, but is the result of a
careful perusal of despatches and
other documents and publications.
The Shimonoséki demand was entirely unjustifiable, and the money
taken ought to be returned.

I could not obtain full particulars of it ; all I could learn was
that the strong current of the straits was so persistent in
carrying away the stones which were to form part of its
foundation that it became necessary to appease the offended
powers by the sacrifice of a life, and some beautiful and
devoted woman, offering herself, was lashed to one of the
stones before it was lowered into the rushing waters.   The
offering was accepted, the difficulty was thus got over, and
the noble martyr has a shrine, which she well deserves,
devoted to her memory.   I am sorry that I cannot help to
immortalise her, in however small a degree, by recording
her name here.

Our subsequent stroll through the town was very interesting, as we had leisure to look carefully into the shops, and
note the articles of trade and manufacture special to a Japanese sea-side town, which, down to the meanest and poorest
things, were curious and interesting to us strangers.   Nor
could one forget that Shimonoséki has its historic interest.
Hither, nearly seven hundred years ago, the Taira men were
driven by the victories of Yoshitsuné, and here the two
armies prepared for a further struggle, to take place this
time upon the water.   The Taira men are said to have had
five hundred junks, and to have embarked in them not merely
their wives and families and aged persons, but court ladies,
including the dowager-empress with the dethroned child-
Mikado and the sacred ball and sword (the duplicate).   The
Minamoto men, unincumbered with women and children,
manned seven hundred junks.   The battle was heroically
fought, at first going in favour of the Taira men ; then by
acts of personal prowess Yoshitsuné turned it in his favour,
and in the end utterly overwhelmed his enemies.   Warriors,
old people, children, ladies, alike perished.   The grandmother
of the child-Mikado, in presence of the mother, leaped with
the child into the sea, and both were drowned with the
others.*   The sacred emblems were recovered—as they were

---

* For a fuller account of the overthrow of the Taira at Shimonoséki,
see vol. i. p. 150.

quite certain to be. If the history of Japan were as well
known in Europe as that of Greece and Rome, the Shimonoséki waters would perhaps become as celebrated, and for
the same cause, as those of Syracuse and Actium.

By 3.15 P.M. the *Meiji* was again at hand to receive us,
and we were soon passing along the western branch of the
straits, on a lovely afternoon, observing the little shrines
and temples which are to be seen in picturesque places along
the shore opposite to Shimonoséki; and beyond, on both
shores, and up the wooded hillsides, the beacons which
assist in marking the channel, and which carry small lights
at night. Villages nestled in every sheltered bay, with
their picturesque junks and boats clustered in front of
them; and as we got round on the western side of the land,
where the ship-channel curves away northwards, we came
upon the broad shining surface of the smooth sea, that doubtless overspread many a once beautiful landscape, of which
only the mountain-tops, in the form of islands, are now visible.
But even as we looked over this smooth sea, shining with more
than rainbow promise of a calm passage round to Nagasaki,
whither we now were bound, a breeze began to stir the distant surface and travel towards us. Scarcely had it reached
us before this breeze got broken into gusts, which separately
smote the sea, and made it foam wherever they struck it.
Meanwhile the atmosphere began to thicken, the mists to
gather into clouds, and the clouds to cluster into stormy
masses; and before we had taken the lighthouse passengers
on board at Mutsuré (Rokuren) it was obvious that we were
in for a roughish night of it. And this, I am told, we had;
but I can say nothing of it from personal knowledge, for I
went early to my shelf, and only awoke to find our ship at
anchor on a fine morning in the lovely harbour of Nagasaki
—second to none perhaps in loveliness. On landing, some
of us became the guests of a gentleman * well famed for
years past in Japan, and whose residence, Iponmats (One
Pine-tree House, the one pine-tree growing up through the

---

* Mr. Glover.

roof of the conservatory into the sunshine), has the finest
view obtainable in this neighbourhood of fine views. As the
grounds of Iponmats include a lawn-tennis ground, and as
Nagasaki has some remarkably pleasant ladies resident in it
(the gentlemen are duly complimented, I hope, in that statement—at least their good taste is recognised), we found
ourselves under fortunate conditions for the four days, all
too short, which we remained in it.

Our first day in Nagasaki was notable for the firing of an
imperial salute at noon, with foreign men-of-war dressed in
flags for the occasion, and on inquiry I was informed that
this was a celebration in honour of the coronation of the first
Mikado, Jimmu-Tenno, and that all the men-of-war of Japan
in other ports were at the same time saluting this imperial
and divine personage. Now there is a doubt among learned
men whether Jimmu-Tenno ever was a veritable man, and
perhaps the doubt may have some sort of justification considering that he is reputed to be only fifth in descent from
the sun-goddess, that his parents alighted from heaven upon
a mountain top, and that he himself is said to have been
guided in his invasion of Yamashino by a demigod in the
form of a gigantic black crow. Still, he is set down in all
the official histories of Japan now published as the first
Mikado. As the date of the commencement of his reign is
given (660 B.C.), and as his exploits are recounted at great
length and with great particularity, we will not, here at
least, be so impolite as to question his historical existence
or distinction. But taking these for granted, and nevertheless remembering that for many ages past he has been deified
and worshipped, it certainly was a little startling to find
guns thundering at midday in a commercial port in his
honour, and foreign war-vessels hoisting joyous colours in
sympathy with the celebration.

Our stay of four days in Nagasaki was made available for
visiting the government (Japanese) and some private establishments there, and also for inspecting the island coal-mines
of Takashima. In the latter, by the courtesy of the proprietor and managers, we had a luxurious luncheon laid out

200 feet below the ground—or, possibly, below the sea, for these mines run under the sea in places. Tiffin was spread in a chamber hewn out of two very thick strata of coal, one 10 feet and one 8 feet thick, with but 2 feet of earth between. The chamber was connected with the ventilators, whitewashed of course, and lighted with safety-lamps. After luncheon, in order to verify the nature of the chamber, a man was brought in with tools, and opened up the coal in several places.* While waiting for the steamer, I climbed the hill near the pit, passing among the houses of the pitmen and pitwomen, both of whom work in the mine all but naked, and on my way down I met a man occasionally who seemed to consider that coal-dust alone was a sufficient attire for a philosopher. On the hilltop was a little churchyard, affording scores of proofs that among even these poor miners a few flowers or a bit of green or a little something in a cup or a vase could be found and carried to the hilltop as a tribute to some dear one dead.

As what I have to say about the government establishments upon the shores of Nagasaki harbour is somewhat technical, I cheerfully consign it to a footnote.† I ought to notice,

---

* We are indebted to Mr. Glover and Mr. Martin for much kindness and courtesy on the occasion of this visit.

† The following are a few particulars of the government establishments in Nagasaki which are connected with the manufacturing section of the public works department. The engine works, which are situated at Akunoura, in a sheltered position on the west side of the harbour, about a mile and a half from the entrance, were established about twenty-three years ago, and were chiefly constructed and conducted for some years under the superintendence of Dutch engineers. These works cover about six acres of ground, and have during the last four and a half years been entirely reconstructed. The machine and erecting shop is a building 150 feet long by 80 feet wide, in three bays. The centre bay, being 40 feet wide by 30 feet high, will be fitted with a 10-ton travelling crane. The side bays are each 20 feet wide by 14 feet high. The boiler shop is 130 feet long by 70 feet wide, in two bays, one 50 feet wide by 25 feet high, and one 20 feet wide by 14 feet high. In this shop at the time of my visit they were fitting up a hydraulic rivetter and a 16-ton crane, over which the roof is 40 feet high. The rivetter and crane will be worked by the same accumulator, and when these are complete they will be able to construct both land and marine boilers of any size up to 13 feet 6 inches diameter, and of plates 1¼ inch thick. The foundry is 130 feet long

however, here in the text, the very large stone graving-dock, one of the finest in the world, which the Japanese government are building, and which is now rapidly approaching completion. At Nagasaki I had the pleasure of again meeting the Rev. Mr. Andrews, of the Church of

---

by 40 feet wide by 21 feet high, supplied with two cupolas, four brass furnaces, one 10- and one 5-ton crane. The forge is 130 feet long by 50 feet wide by 18 feet high, and contains sixteen blacksmith's fires, one 5-cwt. and one 2-ton steam hammer, with suitable furnace and cranes. The coppersmith's shop is 50 feet long by 25 feet wide, with a small galvanising shop attached. The store, which is 270 feet long by 25 feet wide, is well stocked with all necessary materials. The office, gate-houses, two landing places, and the sea-walls are also new. On the wharf there is a pair of sheer-legs capable of lifting 40 tons. In front of the wharf there is about 18 feet of water at low tide, and it can easily be increased to 25 feet if necessary. The works employ 475 men at present, not including officers, clerks, etc., or contractors' men employed on improvements. The principal work done in the factory up to the present has been repairs to steamers, at an average of about two per month. With regard to new work, during the last four years and a half they have constructed thirty marine and land boilers, one or two pairs of small marine engines, two pairs of hauling engines, with pumps, etc., for mines. They had in February, when I saw the works, orders for two pairs of hauling engines, four special pumps, a pair of simple marine engines of 500 indicated horse-power, and a pair of compound of 1000 indicated horse-power, with boilers, etc. In connection with this department the government are constructing at

Tatagami the large dry dock mentioned in the text, under the superintendence of Mr. Vincent Florent, who was kind enough to show us over it. The dock was commenced about twelve years ago, but very little was done until Mr. Florent was engaged to complete it six years ago. The dock is 460 feet long by 89 feet wide at the top, with 29 feet of water on the sill. The caisson was sent out from England in pieces, and is being built up in the dock. The pumping machinery, which consists of four 13-inch centrifugal pumps driven by two horizontal engines, was made at Akunoura. I was sorry to see this dock so completely cut off from the engineering establishment; a better site existed close to the latter. Opposite the dock, on the other side of the harbour, at Koski, there is a patent hauling-up slip, also belonging to the government, which is capable of taking on vessels of 1600 tons (gross tonnage). It was built about eleven or twelve years ago by Mr. T. B. Glover of Nagasaki, but was afterwards bought over by the government. At the slip they had orders for building two small coasting steamers for private owners, and one large steamer for the mining department. These three departments are under the control of one director, Mr. Watanabi, and the head office is at Akunoura. The government appeared to me to have a very valuable young officer in the person of Mr. F. R. Storie, the superintending engineer.

England Missionary Society, who, with Mrs. Andrews, came out in the same ship as ourselves from Suez. They were good enough to show us the little new church and schools in which they hope to labour for years to come in educating, in more ways than one, such of the resident Japanese adults and children as may be willing to receive their instructions and ministrations. It would be well if missionary authorities could always obtain such services as theirs, which, I feel confident, will be conducted with a wise regard to the excep-tional, and often trying, conditions under which they have to work. Their church buildings and residence are situated on the western side of the old Dutch settlement of Deshima (where I am afraid the Dutch did not always set a very Christian example), commanding a beautiful view down the harbour, between the blooming hills on either side of it. Fortunately Pappenberg, down the steep sides of which the Japanese Christians were hurled into the sea by thousands two hundred and fifty years ago, is not within their home-view, and I hope they will not remember too often that it was at Nagasaki that Christians were before their time crucified. May they and their present work prosper !

We embarked at Nagasaki at midnight on Friday, 14th of February, in the *Tokio Maru*, one of the fine steamers of the Japanese company known as the Mitsu Bishi Steamship Company. The accommodation in these steamers, the largest of which run between Yokohama and Shanghai through the Inland Sea, is excellent, and the speed of the *Tokio Maru* was most satisfactory. Leaving the harbour at 1 A.M. on the 15th, we were at Shimonoséki by two o'clock the following afternoon, and at Kobé at noon next day, learning, as we passed on to the anchorage, that the pro-jecting land which shelters the bay of Hiogo and Kobé is artificial, having been formed six hundred years ago. We also had a good opportunity, on this bright day of warm sunshine, of observing the fortifications and the lighthouse. Soon after two o'clock we were in a railway train *en route* for the ancient and historic castled city of Osaka—great for both its military and its commercial importance.

Osaka is one of the three largest cities of Japan, having a population of over 600,000 persons. By the courtesy of the governor, Mr. Watanabé, I was able to observe the growth of this city from its foundation up to the present time in a series of maps which have been preserved, and lately reproduced. It is said to have been near the site of Osaka that the first and, as many suppose, the mythic Mikado Jimmu-Tenno landed on his progress eastward, and near here also that he was defeated and induced to reconsider his purposes. By means of suitable consultations and ceremonies, he ascertained that the sun-goddess was displeased with his continual advances eastward, instead of moving, like the sun, the other way, and he prudently turned in a different direction. It was here that Nobunaga, towards the close of the sixteenth century, not only besieged his Buddhist enemies in their strongly defended temple, but gave to the sword some thousands of people, of both sexes and all ages, and sent a boatload of their ears and noses as a caution to the remaining defenders, who ultimately gave way to him. Upon the improvement of this city, as upon that of Kioto, the great Taiko (Hideyoshi) afterwards set to work, deepening the river, digging canals, and building the immense castle which has long been so famous, and the strengthening of which is said to have engaged his last thoughts. It was in this castle that Iyéyasu, the first of the Tokugawa Shoguns, besieged the Taiko's son, Hidéyori, in the year 1615, burning the citadel, and slaying Hidéyori and thousands of his supporters. It was from Osaka, in January 1868, that the last Tycoon, Keiki, started for the great battles near Kioto which determined the fate of the empire and assured to Japan its present form of government, and it was to Osaka Castle that his beaten and shattered army retreated for dear life, only, however, to burn its citadel and to finally flee from it before the victorious forces of the Mikado.

架之圖式

鷹の鷹家にも率多く長くて画家すも習多く大切な住量
ろきものなり

釰鯏

挂高廿五尺斗

架埀絹

大総

A FALCON.

Engraved for this Work by a Japanese Engraver.

To face page 156 Vol. II.

CHAPTER VII.

THE CITY OF OSAKA.

Approach to the city—Well-managed railways—The imperial reception-house—Governor Watanabé—A nursery garden—Views over the city—Kozu, the temple of deified emperors—Another Shinto temple—An ancient Buddhist temple—Reminiscences of Prince Shotoku-taishi—The temple of the sea-gods—A musical service therein—A prehistoric boat—Divine jewels (*magatama*)—A Japanese fair—The castle of Osaka—Its modern arsenal—Immense monoliths—A ceiling of arrows—A gilded roof—The castle keep—Inspections of barracks—Studious soldiers—A private Japanese dinner—A public dinner—Japanese music and dances—A speech by the President of the Chamber of Commerce—A pretty compliment—Dramatic performances—A purchasing expedition—The power of art—Presents—The imperial mint—The new coinage—Output of the mint.

On leaving Kobé, and before coming in view of Osaka, the neighbourhood of a great commercial city was made manifest by the presence on the distant bay of from two to three hundred junks of all sizes, including many of obviously sea-going character. The district through which the train bore us was no less significant of agricultural activity, for although much of the land was but poor, consisting indeed of little more than sand washed freely down from the neighbouring hills, yet every foot of it was carefully culti-vated, and the road swarmed with villages. We passed through several tea-plantations on our way, and we were informed that the district is a notable one for the dis-tillation of the best description of *saké*, the native wine. It was a lovely sunny afternoon as we rolled through this land of industry and peace, and it was with pleasure that we presently saw the high white castle walls of Osaka shine brightly forth. On this short railway journey, and on our arrival at the Osaka station, we had renewed evidences of the efficient business-like manner in which the Japanese have taken to railway management, and likewise to the English police system, nothing being wanting to the orderly and rapid despatch of trains and passengers, and the stations being such as would improve the credit of many English towns if transferred to them.

Upon the bank of the main river, and at no great distance from the famous castle, are the European buildings of the great government mint, including a handsome residence known as the imperial reception house, which on one or two occasions has accommodated the emperor during his visits,* and is available for the general use of the state. There not being yet a European hotel in Osaka—at least we saw and heard of none—we were courteously received in this official house, a distinction doubtless due to our association with his excellency the minister of marine. Here were our headquarters for more than a week, during which, however, we made our excursion to the ancient capital of Nara, and were besides so hospitably treated by the governor, the military authorities, and the leading merchants of the city, that we seldom found ourselves within the walls of our residence save at night.

The day succeeding our arrival was spent in company of the governor, Mr. Watanabé, who, like the governors of Kioto and Tokio, holds his appointment from the crown. The kindness of this gentleman to us was equal to the high reputation which he bears, and he is a man who has rendered

---

* "His imperial majesty the Tenno visited Yamato province. to offer personal worship to Jimmu Tei, on the second month of this year, 1877, and on his return from that province his majesty made a short stay at Osaka, and on the fourteenth day of the second month, the Sempukuwan (imperial reception house) of the mint was converted into the 'Anzaisho' (temporary residence of the Mikado'. On the 15th his majesty condescended to inspect the mint, and before retiring ordered presents to be made to the officials, foreign and Japanese, according to their ranks. On the 16th his majesty the Tenno left the 'Anzaisho' (Sempukuwan) at 9.40 A.M., and returned to Saikei Kioto) by train."
—'Mint Report.'

signal service to the state. Besides handsome presents, exhibiting the productions of the city in artificial flowers and other specialties, he on one occasion took me into the sword room of his residence, and bade me choose from among at least a score of swords, most of which had associations that gave them special value to him, any one I preferred. As politely as I could I declined the privilege, but on getting back to Kioto a few weeks afterwards I found awaiting me as a present from him a splendid sword by one of the first makers, Yoshikagé of Bizen, valued in the official certificate that accompanied it at one hundred and thirty pieces of gold. I mention this as an illustration of the thoroughness of the generous attentions which were shown to us, even in the provinces, and far from the capital.

The first place to which the governor conducted us was a famous nursery garden and tea-house, where we saw to the best advantage possible at the season of the year (February 17) the characteristic plants of Japan—miniature evergreens, blossoming miniature plum shrubs, miniature pine-trees, small sage palms, small red-berry plants, drooping shrubs grown in pots, Chinese and Japanese bamboo-plants, curious grasses and ferns, camellias and camellia creepers, plants curiously grown into circular and serpentine forms, strange cacti, etc. Visiting a small tower, we gained a splendid view over the city—that city, the reader may remember, over which the ancient emperor Nintoku looked when he realised the distress of his people, and the revival of which he regarded as evidence of his own prosperity. Osaka was not then, however, as it now is, a city of nearly one hundred thousand houses and more than three hundred thousand people, neglecting suburbs and the towns that all but adjoin it. At a later period of the day we ascended the spot on which Nintoku stood, upon which a temple now stands, where he is worshipped, and from which the view over the city and plains beyond is superb. Nintoku reigned fifteen centuries and a half ago, and I was shown a plan of the city at that period; beyond a few temples there was but

little city to speak of. In a map made seven hundred to
eight hundred years ago, which also we saw, vessels were
shown floating where the centre of the city now is. From
the elevation of which I have spoken the Venetian character
of the modern city was very visible, but not so manifest as
one sees it to be on driving about the streets. It is everywhere intersected with rivers and canals, spanned by innumerable bridges, and alive with countless vessels and boats
gliding hither and thither.

The first temple visited—that just before referred to—
was the Shinto temple of Kozu, where several gods (*kami*)
are worshipped, and thirty six poets are celebrated. The
chief *kami* are the emperors Nintoku, Chuai, Ojin, Jingu
(empress), and Richiu, their worship commencing a thousand
years ago, in the reign of Seiwa-Tenno.

The next temple visited was likewise of the Shinto type,
and known as that of Ikudama (in Higashi nari gori). The
gods worshipped here are two in number, viz. 1. Ikukuni
dama, and 2. Tarukuni dama. These gods were first
adored in the forty-ninth year of Jimmu-Tenno's reign, and
have therefore been worshipped for nearly twenty-five centuries. This temple is also very ancient, having been
originally founded on what is now the site of the castle, in
the third year of the reign of Ojin-Tenno (273 A.D.), and
subsequently removed to its present site in the year 1585.
At this temple also we were met by the priests, who took
great interest in our visit, and explained the uses, or rather
services, of the *gohei* and "mirror" to us.

We were next conducted to the ancient and celebrated
Buddhist temple of Korujo, in Tennoji. This temple was
founded in the very early days of Buddhism, at the request
of the famous prince Shotoku-taishi, of whom I have written
much in former chapters. It was so founded in the year
589 A.D., but was removed to its present site ten years later.
It has existed, therefore, for nearly thirteen hundred years,
and includes among its treasures, which were obligingly
shown to us, several sacred books brought over from Korea
in those early days; an arrow used in the struggle against

Buddhism ; Shotoku-taishi's sword ; a history of the foundation of the temple written by him, and bearing the impress
of his hand ; his image of Buddha ; a ceremonial gown of
his ; a manuscript seventeen hundred years old ; an image
of Kwannon thirteen hundred years old ; a brass globe one
thousand years old ; and several other interesting antiquities.
One need hardly say that this temple and its memorials
cover almost the entire period of the existence of the religion
of Buddha in Japan   A curious scholar, learned in Buddhistic and Japanese literature, might possibly draw some
interesting parallels between the Indian prince Sidarrtha
(Buddha) and his ardent Japanese disciple Prince Tiyoto
(Shotoku).

The last temple visited this day was the most famous
among mariners in all Japan—that of Sumiyoshi (in Nishinari
Yori Setsu).   It is a Shinto temple, and we were met at the
entrance by the priests, in mauve dresses with black caps.
Four gods are worshipped here.   It is a very ancient temple,
dating from the eleventh year of the reign of the warrior-
empress Jingu Kogo (212 A.D), to whom it is dedicated as
the patron *kami* of all who travel by sea   It, therefore, has
existed for nearly seventeen centuries. The three gods of
the temple were first worshipped in the first reign of that
empress.   They are—

1. Soko-tsutsu, God of the Sea Bottom.
2. Naka-tsutsu, God of the Middle Sea.
3. Uwa-tsutsu, God of the Sea Surface, and Wave Con-
   troller.

As a fourth, the empress Jingu is herself here worshipped
under her own name of Oki-naga-Tarashi-himé.   The priests
could not tell me when she was first worshipped.   The name
of the temple, Sumiyoshi, signifies Fortunate Residence
of the Four Incorporated Gods.   This is the famous temple
referred to in the chapter on the Shinto religion as that of the
god whom the old ex-governor of Tosa vainly sought to pro-
pitiate a thousand years ago by throwing *nusa* into the sea,
but who was only appeased by the sacrifice of his excellency's

mirror. Its present aspect is a very prosperous one, the
temple itself having been lately rebuilt apparently, and its
precincts adorned with magnificent lanterns in bronze and
marble, with a large number of others of inferior magnitude
and character, but many of them very fine indeed. The
vessels of *saké* presented to the gods at the shrine were
freely served, and certainly it was not the fault of the
Japanese or of their priests if the bottom, the middle, and
the surface of the sea were not all as peaceful as the soul of
the veriest landsman could possibly desire. Not only were
the temple and its accessories such as I have described, but
to add to the interest and impressiveness of the place, the
head priest was so courteous as to have a musical service
performed before us by the ministers, the musicians, and
the virgin priestesses of the temple. This took place, not
in the main building, but in a separate and smaller one,
hung with votive pictures. The arrangements and proceedings were so much like those which we afterwards witnessed
at the still more sacred shrines of Isé that I need not here
attempt any description.

From the temples we took a stroll to the river-side, over
one of the steeply-curved bridges that few but experts can
surmount, and thence were taken a long and swift run in
our *jinriki-shas* to the museum of Osaka, a small institution,
modelled upon the European type. Among the many interesting antiquities there seen was one of a remarkable
character. This was a very ancient boat, wrought out of
solid timber, and dug up from a depth of 30 feet below the
present level of the soil of the city. The portion of this
boat which was recovered was 36 feet long and 5 feet
broad, and was formed in two pieces, joined together by a
scarph 5½ feet long near the centre of the boat. It was made
before metal was known or brought into use, and had no
other fastenings but those which resulted from the ingenious
scarphing of the parts, from the tie of a longitudinal keelson
piece which overran the scarph, and from the manner in
which the thwarts were worked. Some sort of mastic was
probably employed to help in making the scarph water-

tight.   Although formed probably with flint implements,
before the iron and bronze ages, it was well built, and now
bears distinct traces of what appears to be an ornamental
moulding worked upon the outside of the gunwale.   It was
difficult to determine of what wood it was built, but it was
considered by the Japanese to be either of camphor wood or
mulberry-tree.   How many things have happened, in Japan
as elsewhere, since the hands that wrought her have ceased
to ply their trade—possibly the expedition of Jimmu-Tenno
to Osaka among other things !

There was also shown us in the museum a small but very
good collection, as I think, of *magatama* jewels, which are
beautifully wrought carved pieces of hard stone, perforated
at the end.   They are very ancient and rare, coming down,
it is supposed, from the Divine Period, being occasionally
dug out of the soil, and not otherwise obtainable—except in
counterfeit or imitation.   After taking tea in a little secluded
garden tea-house—tea made of the powdered leaf, by an accomplished master of the art of mixing it, whose deliberation
and ceremony in carrying out each stage of the process was
the more amusing as it exhibited what young ladies are
taught as a high accomplishment—and after following up
the tea with a parting glass of champagne, drunk in an
elevated summer-house with the governor, we took our leave
of him, and drove in our *jinrikis* to a sort of fair.   There,
entering a series of booths in succession, we saw men and
women walking over half a dozen yards of burning logs
with naked feet, a dwarf, a lady with a face of horrible
deformity, a series of very well-made wax figures, a tiger, and,
better than all, the common people in crowds amusing
themselves with admirable good humour, and behaviour
orderly in the extreme.   It was now time to return to our
home in the mint, which we did at a speed that made
jinriki men running tandem more respected and pitied
than ever.

Our next day was spent in visiting the fine old castle of
Osaka, with its large moats, grand gateways, huge monoliths,
and ruined palaces and keep ; also, within its outer limits,

the modern arsenal and arms manufactory, which have been established in European fashion, and appear to be working with much efficiency. During the recent rebellion in Satsuma great demands were thrown upon this arsenal, and a large quantity of arms underwent repair and renovation there. Much of work of the same kind was still proceeding, together with the manufacture of ammunition for small arms. The buildings were solid and good, rock foundations being easily obtainable for most buildings near to Osaka Castle; the machinery was likewise good, and in good condition. I did not observe a single European, officer or man, throughout these works. As it rained heavily during our visit, we were unable to make a close inspection of the large new buildings now constructing as a factory for great guns, but they were obviously of a very substantial kind, and the erection of a great-gun manufactory in Japan may be noted as a sign of the times.

An officer sent by the general commanding the troops in the Osaka district next conducted us over the castle bridge, through the great gateway, up the long flight of broad steps to the level of the old palace and of the existing official buildings. It would be difficult to exaggerate the combined beauty and grandeur of this fine old castle, with its lofty walls of stone, its curved outlines, its picturesque white buildings at the corners, its massive tower, its broad moat, and its huge blocks of granite of unexampled size and weight. The whole or most of the walls are notable for these very large blocks of granite, which vie with the largest of those built into the great pyramid of Cheops, near Cairo, in Egypt; but as the main entrance to the castle proper is approached, one sees block after block of the most astonishing proportions, until at and opposite to the entrance itself are single stones of such immense size that one is almost driven to doubt whether his senses are not deceiving him. It is so difficult to understand how such huge masses can have been quarried, transported, raised to such a height, and there worked into walls. I could not conveniently measure the largest stones, but I feel sure that some of them must be over twenty feet in height, nearly twice that in length, and several feet thick, and must weigh three hundred to four hundred tons. In reply to questions it was stated by some of the officers quartered at the castle that these stones were probably brought from quarries by the Inland Sea, situated near Mihara, more than one hundred miles from Osaka, but that some thought it probable that they were obtained from the hill on which the castle stands. It was positively asserted that the castle, with its stupendous walls, was built within fifteen months, a statement which appears to me incredible, however great a command of labour the builder may have possessed.

Our visit to this historic castle was a very pleasant one, in spite of the weather, which was damp, with occasional showers. We were received by the general and other officers of the garrison, and taken to an elevated tower-room, from which a good view of the castle and city around could be obtained. The history of the castle was briefly stated, and plans of Osaka in very early times and at subsequent periods after the building of the castle were inspected. The general was so obliging as to give me a tracing of the castle and present buildings, with some statistical information of much interest. Another of the officers was good enough to present us with some very old gold-bound arrows, which had formed part of a ceiling formed of arrows in the old castle of Kanazawa, in the province of Kaga, together with a tile bearing the crest of the Daimio brought from the same castle, and an ancient tile from another castle the roof of which was once covered with gold, the tile in question still bearing traces of gold upon its surface.

After taking light refreshments we went to the old castle keep, which, although the upper stories are gone, still stands high above everything else, overlooking the whole city and the country round to the mountain limits. We then returned to the castle gate, there taking leave of the general, and proceeding to visit the infantry barracks, the artillery barracks and stables, and other military places of interest. What most struck me in these barracks, and in other military barracks in Japan, was the multiplicity of books and appliances for reading and study. Every common soldier appears to furnish himself, or to be furnished, with quite a small library all to himself—a circumstance that may, perhaps, be traced to the pre-revolution period of Japan, when the *samurai* class were at once the soldiers and the scholars of the country. Perhaps with the pay of British troops steadily increasing as it is, and with so many facilities for study and recreation as they are now furnished with, the time may not be far distant when our own soldiers will occupy, as they well might, a comparatively high position in the social scale, and when the army will attract to it the surplus members of the civil community of all grades that are respectable and well instructed.

The evening of this day was devoted to our first dinner, taken after the fashion of the country. In Tokio we had taken lunch in native style occasionally in a tea-house, and had made our first acquaintance (at a meal) with the floor as a table, chopsticks as dining implements, and dancing girls and *geishas* as our table attendants. But we had not before dined in this fashion, and now at the invitation of Mr. Godai Tomo-Atsu (colloquially Mr. Godai), president of the Osaka chamber of commerce, we were to test the system. I am free to confess that neither on this nor on any future occasion did I flatter myself that so far as I was concerned the experiment was a success. The rigidity of forty years and an octave, with the restraints of European dress, are unfavourable to the commencement of floor gymnastics, and as my chopstick hand happened to be crushed a few years ago, to the destruction of some of the muscles, I found the chopsticks almost as difficult to play as the piano. But the only defects on the occasion were with myself. After a brief sojourn in the "poetry room" of my host, and another in the ceremonial tea-room, where Madame Godai presided as some Japanese ladies can—which is very perfectly, let me assure the reader, as Madame Godai will not read this—and after indulging our eyes with wonders of lacquer work, bronze, and painting, we dined, and learnt how Japanese do dine, when they have a mind. All I will say further on the matter here is that on every possible occasion thereafter I was much more than content to dine Japanese fashion, " in spite of all temptations " of the best European cooks to be found in the country.

On Wednesday the 17th of February we started on a visit to the ancient and sacred city of Nara, which was the capital of old Japan in the time of the famous empresses of the seventh and eighth centuries. But the story of that visit I must tell, however hastily and imperfectly, in a separate chapter, and here pass on to our rearrival in Osaka. In the Nara chapter I shall bring the narrative down to the entertainment of which I now proceed to speak, and which took place immediately on our return from Nara. This banquet was a highly characteristic one in many ways. It was, I understood, the first ever given by the merchants of the city of Osaka to any foreign visitor; it was attended by one of the ministers of state, Admiral Kawamura; it was given on a scale of great splendour, in a purely Japanese style in every respect; national music, singing, and dancing of the very highest class were performed during the evening; and the hosts were the president, vice-presidents, and members of council of the chamber of commerce and the stock exchange of Osaka,* who in conveying their invita-

---

* The following list of our principal entertainers was handed to me—I give it without alteration : Godai Tomo-Atsu, President of Commercial Chamber, and originator of Stock Exchange, Osaka. Nakano Goichi, Vice-President of Commercial Chamber, Osaka. Hirose Sekei, do. Kato Yo-ichi, Manager of Chamber of Commerce, Osaka. Shibakawa Matakei, do., and Inspector of Bai-shio-kwaishio (where is transacted the business for rice). The above gentlemen are voted and intrusted to their office by the people of Osaka. The Commercial Chamber is constructed by the many thousand very different parties of the merchants of Osaka, and the representatives are voted more or less according to the number of the parties. There are now two hundred and thirty representatives in the Commercial Chamber, and they desired the above gentlemen to receive you as their substitute. Nakayama Nobu-aki, President of Stock Exchange, Osaka. Konoike Zenyemon, originator of Stock Exchange, Osaka. Mitsai Motonoshe, do. Sumitomo Kichiza-yemon, do. Kasano Kumakichi, do., and owner of Kow-giyo-kwaishio (where is transacted the business for exportation). Hirase Kamenoske, originator of

tions adverted to their representative character, acted in the name of their fellow-citizens, and received us with great cordiality. The scene on entering the dining-chamber was singular and beautiful ; excepting a few handsome screens and works of art near the walls, the room had no other furniture than silk cushions to sit upon, *hibachis* (small portable square bowls containing charcoal fire) for giving warmth, and smaller fire-bowls for lighting the small Japanese pipes, cigarettes, or cigars. But although still not far from the middle of February, the evening air was mild, and one side of the room was thrown entirely open to an unusually large garden, with a fine sheet of artificial water winding about it. The verandah and the garden and water beyond were illuminated with hundreds of Japanese lanterns, richly coloured, many of which were kept moving throughout the evening. We sat down about twenty in number, and the banquet commenced by a few girls, quietly but prettily attired, coming into the room, advancing and falling upon their knees in front of us, placing handsome lacquer trays with cups of tea and slices of sweet cake before us, and bowing the head to the ground before rising and retiring. This kind of proceeding, I may say shortly, went on for several hours, the lacquered trays bearing in succession soups, meats, fish, game, and all sorts of vegetables daintily prepared, and served in a form that enabled me to deal with them by means of chopsticks only— not, I am bound to say, without the liberal use of the teeth in aid thereof. There were doubtless many articles served to which we in England are strangers, but sea-weed and bamboo-shoots—both very palatable indeed—are all of them that I can now call to mind. The universal strong drink of the country, known as *saké*,* drunk both cold and hot, was served, together with European wines, and English ale and stout as desired. At an early stage of the dinner poured in a stream of

---

Stock Exchange, Osaka. Yamaguchi, Kichirobey, do. Eno-kuchi Shin-zabro, do. Kumagai Tatstaro, do.

* This *saké*, brewed from rice, has been made and drunk in Japan for sixteen centuries. It is not usually what the English would consider very strong.

dancing girls arrayed in Japanese crapes and silks of the brightest and most diversified colouring and pattern, with hair dressed into wonders of an art that reaches its climax perhaps in Osaka, and with faces and necks powdered, eyebrows deepened, eyelids tinted, and lips polished with vermilion enamel. There were at least five-and-twenty of these pretty creations of imperial Osaka who were unquestionably very choice works of art, and I am afraid they cannot be considered at present as very much more. It appeared on this and other occasions to be their function, not merely to dance when called upon, but to sit about among the diners, assist them to anything they might require, and make themselves generally useful; and as they did this very nicely and successfully, I have perhaps shown in this sentence that I did them some injustice in my last, for which I apologise. In addition to these brilliant little beings, there were numerous singing and music girls, or *geishas*, and behind the screen some singing men besides. It is difficult—it is indeed impossible for a stranger to fully appreciate such musical performances as theirs, because much of their merit must be due to elaborate cultivation of taste. Still it was impossible to listen to such instrumental and vocal music as was heard on this occasion without observing qualities which must be the result of combined natural endowment and high training. Beyond this, however, it is impossible for me to go, and I can only assert the very eminent merits of the artists upon the authority of my informants. The instruments used were the *koto*, the *kogu*, and the *samisen*.

I cannot even give the names of the several dances, nor can I presume to describe them; suffice it to say here (as I have mentioned the Japanese dances elsewhere) that they began with two very young girls performing a dance in masks; that the second was a dance in which the parasol played a considerable part; that the third was performed by one of the very young girls, who successively made use of a branch of blossoms and of two fans, which were handled with a dexterity that was marvellous in so young a child.

The remainder were more general, most of the dancers joining in them, usually with the accompaniment of hand-clapping. Notwithstanding the extreme monotony of the music, some of these dances were maintained for a long time, and with wonderful spirit, the younger hosts and guests joining more or less in them. In the course of the evening, something very analogous to the drinking of healths set in for a short time, but happily was not prolonged as it is at home. It will be interesting to quote the following translation of a brief abstract of the speech of the President, Mr. Godai, the president of the chamber of commerce, who was likewise the originator of the Osaka stock exchange.

He said : " When our harbours were hardly opened, foreign civilisation was unknown to us; but after friendly relations, we were gradually brought to the light, and are now making progress so much that we have succeeded in the formation of this Chamber, and the meeting of the people. Just on the completion, I am happy to say, you gratify us, Mr. Reed, with your visit, leading us to a new idea by gathering ourselves to this meeting to welcome and entertain you, which was never done before to any of our past foreign guests. In showing you our appreciation of your visit, we also give you a sight of our progress, which I am glad and proud of. One thing remains in my mind, and a word I must say: when his Royal Highness your Prince [the Duke of Edinburgh] was on his visit to this empire, our people were not at all well informed, and were ignorant of the way how his Royal Highness should be welcomed and entertained, and were consequently unable to afford the same attentions as now. Finding ourselves now more quali-fied, and having once started, I am in hope that we will be able to give to all our future foreign guests of rank or distinction an equal reception with that we give to you."

I ought not to forget to mention one of the attentions shown at this dinner, as it was both interesting in itself and indicative of the amount of consideration which these merchants of Osaka were pleased to show to us. Towards the end of the dinner there was brought in and placed in

front of me a stand about 2½ feet broad and 4½ feet long,
on which was modelled a beautifully coloured representation
of a golden pheasant, a pine-tree, some very fine large
flowers, with numerous small bouquets of Osaka artificial
flowers.   This is, I was informed by one of my interpreters, a compliment only paid at weddings, and on
occasions of very pronounced welcome and consideration
to guests.   The Osaka flowers were distributed among the
company, most of them finding their way sooner or later
to the vain little heads of the pretty *geishas* and dancing-
girls.   A curious feature of the arrangement was, however,
the material of the golden pheasant and the larger flowers,
which were all cut out of fresh turnips, or of some similar
vegetable, and were so beautifully formed and coloured as
to present a more natural appearance than many permanent
works of art.   The party was broken up about eleven o'clock
by our departure, the run home in *jinrikis* being made at
an astonishing speed, which was very agreeable to those
of us who had already ridden in them during the day
some thirty miles or more.

It is needless to prolong this account of our visit to Osaka
much more, although many a page might readily be filled
with the story of it.   There are, however, a few facts and
incidents which must not be omitted.   Among these must
be named another banquet, given to us this time by
Governor Watanabé.   This was served in European style,
and was wonderfully well done ; but the principal charms
of the occasion, in addition to the perpetual charm of joyous
hospitality, were its Japanese features—the mottoes on the
wall, each a compliment and a poem ; the illuminated
garden ; the writings in silk from the hands of the rebel
Saigo and the martyr Okubo ; the many swords of the host,
each with its own story told, or that could be told ; and
above all, the dramatic performances which followed the
banquet.   For on this occasion the governor had arranged
for the performance of a series of dramatic pieces, mostly
comedies, and for the first time we became acquainted
with a branch of Japanese art which, however ancient in

itself, had not even in rumour reached us. Whether the drama did or did not originate in pantomimic performances, as some suppose, I know not, but certainly in the Japanese drama such performances still retain a most important and prominent part. I must not, however, enter upon the subject here. Whether, when I come to see more of these dramatic exhibitions, I shall be able to give any intelligible account of them I cannot say; but on the present occasion I must pass them over all but in silence, full of extraordinary characteristics as they were. The wife of our host, and an interesting child or two of theirs, were present, besides the invited guests, so that one really assisted at a family party as well as at a dramatic display.

Another interesting feature of our stay at Osaka was our purchasing expedition. In this we were most fortunate, having for our guide and friend Mr. Ohno Norichika, of the imperial mint, who, in the absence of the senior officer, acted as our host, and performed the duty handsomely. We revelled for hours in curiosities of all descriptions (with buyers' appetites but imperfectly indulged), but the greatest delight of all was among the pictures—*kakemono*, *gakumono*, screens, pictures for screens, and volumes upon volumes of artists' work of every description. What a gift it is, that of an artist! What a power it is which he possesses! by a few swift touches of ink or colour to create—or is it not truer to say to revive?—in us the image of a bird, a flower, a landscape, a sea, a storm!

> " 'Tis the privilege of Art
>   Thus to play its cheerful part,
>   Man in earth to acclimate,
>   And bend the exile to his fate;
>   And, moulded of one element
>   With the days and firmament,
>   Teach him on these as stairs to climb,
>   And live on even terms with Time;
>   Whilst upper life the slender rill
>   Of human sense doth overfill."—*Emerson.*

And after purchasing came the still more pleasant task—in some respects, but not in all—of receiving presents. The governor's liberality I have already spoken of. Mr. Ohno gave us sets of the old gold and silver coins of rectangular form, which make pretty necklaces for daughters. Mr. Kasano Kumakichi, one of the merchant princes, from whom we received many kindnesses, brought a beautiful specimen of the large oval coins of gold, also of the olden time. Mr. Godai sent one of my daughters a splendid glove-box of the finest ancient lacquer-work; and so forth.

But I must not conclude this account of Osaka without a word of appreciation of the fine buildings and beautiful machinery of the imperial mint. Most of the machinery was imported, of course, from Europe, and erected and originally worked under European care; but the number of Europeans now remaining is limited, I believe, to one or two, and the smaller machines now required are manufactured in the country. The skill with which the various departments are carried on by natives is very remarkable, some of the duties in which special dexterity and quickness of eye are necessary being performed in a manner which could hardly, if at all, be matched by any other people. The trial of the pyx is carried out as with us, and the results checked in some foreign countries. The modern coins are very handsomely designed. The national traditions oppose the stamping of the image of the divinely descended Mikado upon them, and some time will probably yet elapse before this is brought about. His majesty's imperial and family crests or badges, the *kiku* and *kiri*, with wreaths and tassels and bannerets bearing the sun and the moon, adorn one side of the gold coins, which are five in number; the other side being decorated with a splendid dragon and legend round. The silver coins bear a similar dragon and legend on one side, and the *kiku* crest with wreaths and tassels, and the coin's denomination on the other. All but the smallest coins in gold and silver have milled edges. The new silver " trade dollar " does not greatly differ in appearance, nor in size and weight, from the " one yen " piece, the *yen* being the Japanese dollar. It has lately been notified that the trade dollar, which was

originally coined for the convenience of commerce at the
open ports, and was current only at those ports, will henceforth be made universally current, and may therefore be
used in making and receiving payments of taxes and in all
other public and private transactions, both internal as well
as external. The bronze coins do not differ materially in
design from those of silver, but none of their edges are
milled. The following are the coins struck at the mint,
viz. :—

Gold.	Silver.	Copper.
20 Yen	1 Yen	2 Sen
10 Yen	Trade	1 Sen
5 Yen	50 Sen	½ Sen
2 Yen	20 Sen	1 Rin
1 Yen	10 Sen	
	5 Sen	

Up to the middle of last year (1878) there had been
coined at the Osaka mint nearly 3,000,000 ounces of gold,
23,000,000 ounces of silver, and 91,000,000 of copper coins,
of a total value of about 83,000,000 dollars, or nearly
£17,000,000 sterling. The weight and number of gold,
silver, and bronze coins struck during last year (ending
June 30, 1878) were as follows :—

Denomination.	Weight. Troy oz.	Number.
Gold 20 Yen	32·15	30
„ 10 Yen	19·83	37
„ 5 Yen	19,080·55	71,216
„ 2 Yen	19·20	179
„ 1 Yen	9·12	170
Silver Trade Dollar	382,103·14	436,673
„ 50 Sen	79,927·67	184,440
„ 20 Sen	1,235,448·20	7,127,562
„ 10 Sen	1,177,548·05	13,586,479
„ 5 Sen	622,548·78	14,365,849
Copper 2 Sen	13,322,015·60	29,080,239
„ 1 Sen	5,597,486·60	24,422,948
„ ½ Sen	3,060,440·40	26,709,834
„ Rin	670·80	23,000

CHAPTER VIII.

THE SACRED CITY OF NARA.

It was in consequence of a strong desire of my own to visit Nara that our trip to that ancient city was undertaken. Knowing that it had been the capital city of Japan more than one thousand years ago, that it still contained the celebrated monster image of the great Buddha, that its temples, shrines, and ecclesiastical treasures were of high antiquity, and that it could be reached in a few hours from Osaka, I suggested that it would be a mistake to pass it by unobserved. The suggestion was immediately taken up by my friends, who at once set about the necessary arrangements. I should have been quite satisfied to take the chance of such accommodation as might be found there, but the auspices under which I was seeing the country put this out of the question. My first idea was to start very early in the morning, and return the same day, employing relays of *jinriki* men; but this was considered to be, if not im-

practicable, at least very undesirable, especially as the days
were still short and the weather uncertain. It was therefore resolved to start about ten o'clock on Wednesday, 21st
of February, proceeding by the roundabout route through
Sakai on account of that being much less hilly than the
direct route, and therefore preferable for the draught-men,
though of greater length. Sakai was only about seven and
a half English miles from our residence in Osaka, but it
was arranged for us to visit a carpet-manufactory and to
take tiffin at the house of a gentleman there, with the
mayor of Sakai, performing the rest of the journey before
our evening dinner.

It was a lovely morning when we started, with a warm
spring sun shining, and even the men who had to drag us
the twenty-seven miles to Nara—for they themselves objected to the employment of relays—were merry and glad
as we rattled out of the imperial mint compound, a party of
about twelve *jinriki-shas*, some of the younger and smaller men
riding double, with three men to each *jinriki*, except where
the loads were light and where two sufficed. The greater
part of the city of Osaka had to be traversed, and a very
large city it proved to be. In crossing the space between
its southern boundary and Sakai, including many suburban
places, we seemed to be passing through an almost continuous town, until we reached the boundary bridge of
Sakai, where the secretary of the governor of the district,
and the head of the district police, met us, and undertook
the conduct of the party for the rest of the journey. The
whole town of Sakai appeared to have heard of the visit, and
to have turned out along the line of route to inspect and, let
us hope, to admire us—a circumstance which gave us the
great advantage of returning the compliment by observing
and admiring them. It was an excellent opportunity, as it
proved—this trip to Nara, during which I saw no European
face whatever, except my son's—to see the people of the
country as they daily live and move among themselves. We
noticed in Sakai, as we had already done in Osaka, that the
notion of the Japanese being almost universally a small race

of men and women is altogether an erroneous one, the
majority being of fair average height, and many of them
men of a size and height which were much above the average
European standard. I think the women were, however, on
the whole, smaller in proportion to the size of the men than
would be usual among ourselves. The most picturesque and
amusing beings, however, in Japan, are not the men nor the
women, but the children, owing to the bright colouring and
the infinite variety of pattern of the stuff of which their
dresses are made, and the quaint old-fashioned look which
the dress gives them as they toddle about (especially, I
presume, in the winter season, when they wear more clothes),
with their little shaved heads, chubby faces, and jet-black
eyes. These youngsters, during their earliest years, are
always, apparently, mounted upon somebody else, either in
front or behind, usually slung when very young with hands
and face snugly nestled in the open bosoms of their mothers,
sometimes similarly but less warmly suspended upon their
fathers. A little later on in life they take to the backs of
their fathers and mothers, and more often still to those of
their little brothers and sisters, this form of family affection
being carried to such an extent that the two brats—the
rider and the ridden—are so near of an age that one sometimes fancies they must be taking it in turns, and carrying
one another. I may say in passing that I have but one
very strong objection to these little life-visitors to the sun-
rise-land, and that is that they do not, as a rule, get their
little noses attended to nearly often enough, though even
in that matter they are, perhaps, "more sinned against than
sinning." In visiting the carpet-factory, where a considerable manufacture of carpets and rugs for export is springing
up, and taking an excellent mixed tiffin of Japanese and
European dishes as the guest of the mayor, Mr. Saisho—a
pleasant, meditative gentleman, in whom the spirit of
antiquity seemed to live still, and who kindly exhibited to
us some exceeding old bronzes and other objects of interest
—we took our final departure for Nara at a quarter past one,
facing eastward for the hills. Our road lay at first up a

short hill and over an open plain, which presented a peculiar appearance, from the number of *shadoofs* (levers for raising water from pits and distributing it over the land), which stood up like light masts by hundreds; the ground here being above the river levels, and therefore requiring special means for its irrigation. As the level of the land crossed became lower, these *shadoofs* became fewer in number, and before long altogether disappeared. The ranges of hills in front of us were extremely picturesque; the landscape between them and us was liberally supplied with trees; occasionally there stood up out of the plain large artificial mounds, surmounted with clumps of pine-trees, and surrounded with moats; rivers and sheets of water brightened the land; *torii* and temple roofs attracted the eye to many a village and shrine; the people, catching sight of our advancing procession of *jinriki-shas* (and perhaps apprised by the local police, who evidently expected us, of the passage of some Europeans—to them a very unusual sight), swarmed in the village streets, or hurried across the fields from all quarters, to catch sight of us as we passed; and over all the pretty moving scene, a sun, warm as that of our English summer, poured down its refulgence, animating and cheering the hearts of all. The raised mounds which I have mentioned, and of which we saw many on the road to Nara, and in its neighbourhood, are the burial-places of deceased Mikados, and are, as a matter of course, I presume, made the sites of Shinto shrines. One of them, concerning which I happened to inquire particularly, was the tomb of Inkiyo, the twentieth Mikado of the present dynasty, who reigned in the beginning of the fifth century (A.D.), and another, that of the twenty-second of the line, who reigned in the same century. In a wood seen on our right hand was the burial-place of the war-god, Ojin-Tenno, one of the most famous of the still earlier Mikados, the sixteenth of the dynasty. In accordance with Japanese practice, this Mikado, who reigned in the third century, A.D. like the others, became worshipped as a god after his death, but the deification appears to have been founded in his case upon very substantial deeds and services. He was, as before stated, the son of the warrior-queen Jingu Kogo, who conquered Korea with such important results to her own country. "Through this peninsula, and not directly from China," says Mr. Griffis,* "flowed the influences whose confluence with the elements of Japanese life produced the civilisation which for twelve centuries has run its course in the island empire. . . . To a woman is awarded the glory of the conquest of Korea, whence came letters, religion, and civilisation to Japan. In all Japanese traditions or history there is no greater female character than the empress Jingu (god-like exploit). Her name was Okinaga Tarashihimé; but she is better known by her posthumous title of Jingu Kogo, or Jingu, the wife or spouse of the Mikado. She was equally renowned for her beauty, piety, intelligence, energy, and martial valour. She was not only very obedient to the gods, but they delighted to honour her with their inspiration. She feared neither the waves of the sea, the arrows of the battle-field, nor the difficulties that wait on all great enterprises. Great as she was in her own person, she is greater in the Japanese eyes as the mother of the god of war [Ojin Tenno]." A good deal of the miraculous is mixed up in their recorded history of Jingu and her great son Ojin; they are taken by Japanese scholars, nevertheless, to be undoubtedly historical characters, and are worshipped in many temples in Japan, the empress-mother as "Kashii dai mio jin," and the son as the god of war himself. "Down through the centuries," continues the author just quoted, "he has been worshipped by all classes of the people, especially by soldiers, who offer their prayers, pay their vows, and raise their votive offerings to him. Many of the troops, before taking steamer for Formosa, in 1874, implored his protection. In his honour some of the most magnificent temples in Japan have been erected, and almost every town and village, as well as many a rural grove and hill, has its shrine erected to the Japanese Mars. He is usually repre-

---

* In 'The Mikado's Empire.'

sented in his images as of a frightful, scowling countenance, holding, with arms akimbo, a broad two-edged sword. One of the favourite subjects of Japanese artists of all periods is the group of figures consisting of the snowy-bearded Také-nouchi, in civil dress, holding the infant of Jingu Kogo in his arms, the mother standing by in martial robes. . . . The Buddhists have canonised him, Ojin, as Hachiman Dai Bosatsu,* or the Incarnation of Buddha of the Eight Banners. Hence, among the devotees of the India faith, this god of war and patron of warriors is called Hachiman. . . . Hachi-man (*hachi*, eight; *man*, banners) is the Chinese form of Yawata (*ya*, eight; *wata*, banners)."

On this trip to Nara, as on some former occasions, we crossed several rivers the beds of which have in the course of centuries been raised considerably above the level of the adjacent country, the banks being raised, of course, still higher. In some cases the high road now passes under the river bed by a level tunnel.

At 2.30 P.M. we passed from the open plain, through orchards of peach-trees and orange-trees, into the hilly district, where the country became more picturesque and beautiful than before. By the roadside, and entirely open to road and field, were little village burial-places, with tomb-stones, usually of low and small square columns of granite, but sometimes of unshaped or roughly-shaped slabs of stone with figures sculptured on one side. On the hill-sides, often embedded in the woods, were small temples and shrines, which certainly lent themselves freely to the pic-turesque and the artistic, whatever may be thought of them as instruments of religion.

At 2.45 we stopped at the village of Kokubu, to rest the *jinriki* men, and to refresh ourselves with cups of Japanese tea, speedily resuming our journey, our course leading us through as pretty a hill-country as can be desired, with a swift river rushing past the road. On this river were extremely shallow boats (carrying land-produce and other

---

* See footnote, vol. i. p. 264.

goods), propelled sometimes by sails aided by pushing-poles, sometimes by the latter alone, and almost as frequently by the still more primitive method of the boatmen walking up the stream and dragging their boat with them. Much of this river traffic was in charcoal, and in wood cut in the neighbouring forests, prepared for conversion into charcoal. Our road afterwards stretched across a beautiful valley, from which one could at intervals catch distant glimpses of what proved afterwards to be Nara, while away on the right, on a lofty mountain summit, a white village gleamed like a group of silver shrines. The road lay through many more villages, the inhabitants of which were inferior to none in the interest they took in our long and rapid and noisy procession, led by our Sakai chief of police, Nara being situated in the Sakai district.

At the village of Tatsuta we turned off to visit the famous and ancient Buddhist temples of Horiuji, where we were most courteously received by the two principal priests and other officials, who hospitably entertained us with tea and cakes. This group of temples, with a pagoda, were all twelve hundred years old, and bore the marks of their age both externally and internally.* They possessed some wonderful treasures—after the fashion of many of our Christian temples in Europe—the most precious of all being a piece—an extremely small piece, but still a piece—of the very bone of Buddha himself! I am not quite sure, but I have some reason to think that this most precious relic, which our unworthy eyes were permitted to behold, is no other than that which was held in the clenched hand of Prince Shoto-ku-taishi when he was born, and was revealed when at the age of two years he turned to the east, invoked Buddha, and displayed this very wonderful proof of heavenly favour. The valuable and wonder-working relic was inclosed in a small crystal globe, within which you could both see and hear it as the globe was shaken, the sacred crystal sphere being supported on a stand of crystal, and surmounted with

---

* For mention of the founding of these temples, see vol. i. p. 79.

a crystal crown-piece. Every day at twelve o'clock the people were permitted to see and bow before this unquestionable evidence of the greatest verity of Buddhism, the mission of Buddha himself to the earth! As shown to us, this treasure was set out upon a splendid silk cloth, thickly embroidered with gold, and adorned with cords and tassels, which may have had a significance too profound for me. Another very valuable treasure, which the priests generously allowed us to examine closely, in the inmost centre of the shrine itself, and with a candle to illuminate it, was an image in wood of the son of the famous Shotoku-taishi, carved by the hand of that great personage himself. There were also numerous wooden idols of ancient date, some of them reminding one of the very old Egyptian gods, carved in wood and with painted eyes, etc., with which Mariette Bey has enriched the museum at Boulak, near Cairo. Chief of all was the celebrated image of Buddha, on the back of which is the ancient and unreadable Chinese inscription mentioned in the previous chapter on the God-period.* There were those likewise which Shotoku-taishi is said to have carved and borne upon his head after the army when a youth.

In a separate temple, which appeared to have been specially patronised by the grateful classes, and which was probably dedicated (although I was not so informed) to the great god Ojin, whom I just now referred to, were countless swords, bows, mirrors, lanterns, gimlets, or something of that sort, and other articles which faithful Buddhists had thought it well to present and leave behind in this place. It was impossible at the time, and is as impossible now, to do justice to the treasures of these temples, from which we had to hurry away Nara-wards. Our way lay through a beautiful valley, with lofty hills falling behind us, and loftier ranges in front of us, and villages scattered freely throughout its extent. I take from my note-book the following remark, jotted down at this point: "Along the near side and at the foot of yonder hills are so many towns

---

* See footnote, vol. i. p. 21.

or villages that they seem to be almost continuous for many miles. It must be in this lovely valley—lovely as we advance, lovely as we look back—that Nara lies, and I do not doubt that one or other of the clusters of buildings that we see is it." This proved afterwards to be so, Nara being the largest town then visible on the left or north of the landscape, but still several miles distant. Unlike those of most Japanese villages that I had previously seen, the houses in this part of the country, and chiefly in and near Nara itself, are made white, and are consequently much more visible at long distances, and in certain lights, than they would otherwise be.

All along the route thus far pursued the country had been remarkable for the care and closeness of the cultivation, and we subsequently found that this continued all the way to the old city which we were seeking, and doubtless is a characteristic of Japanese agriculture, at least near the lines of the great high roads. It may be confidently said that the whole of the low ground, and most of the hillside, where not wooded, was cultivated as thoroughly as an English kitchen garden, throughout the journey from Osaka, by Sakai, to Nara.

The sun disappeared behind the hills before half past five, and it was already nearly dark when we passed through the large and important town of Koriyama; but again the good people of the place lined the streets for our inspection. The air began to get decidedly cold, and when we were still two or three miles from our destination rain began to fall, and continued to the end of our journey. To cheer their flagging energies the *jinriki-sha* men multiplied their responsive noises among themselves, and quickened the pace withal. At length we passed between two large illuminated stone lanterns, which proved to be the beginning of the present town of Nara, the whole length of which had, however, to be travelled, as we were bound to Tonain, the temple-residence of the chief priest of Nara, Tsuzaka Senkai, which is situated within the gate of the great temple of Dai-butsu. Chilled and hungry, we gladly stepped at last

from our *jinrikis*, and entered a beautiful residence of pure
Japanese type, in one of the principal rooms of which we
saw framed and hung an inscription written by the hand of
the present Mikado, signifying "residence of the pure," or
something of that kind. It appears that this house had
been occupied by his majesty during his visit to Nara some
little time ago. All those parts of the house which we saw
were very new, and elegantly furnished, and probably owed
much of their superiority in these respects to the fact of his
majesty having sojourned in it. However that may be, it
was an extremely pleasant retreat for our present party,
and made the more so by the speedy serving of an excellent
dinner. It was not at a very late hour that we made a
further retreat to our beds (on the floor, of course), there, in
my own case at least, to sleep the sleep of the grateful.

A cup of tea at seven o'clock, with a breeze of fresh
morning air let in from the hills, were the pleasant be-
ginnings of the next day at Nara, which proved so delightful that we shall never quite forget it, I hope. The rain
had gone, and the sun was shining brightly and warmly
as I stepped out upon the verandah and looked abroad.
A pretty Japanese garden, with winding water, artistically
trained trees and shrubs—the more cherished ones just
opening their fragrant blossoms here and there—and gravel
paths raked into ornamental patterns, with a background
of green and of wooded mountain slopes rising high above all,
composed the pleasant picture we looked upon, and from
which, refreshed with sleep, one gladly drew further refreshment still. We had already decided to devote the whole
day to Nara, returning the following day, but nevertheless
there was no time to lose; therefore, breakfast over, we
started on our tour of the temples, guided by experienced
officers, and attended by a pleasant set of Japanese companions and interpreters. Besides a few European coats
upon some of our conductors, there was nothing to break
in upon the aspect which this part of the old city had worn
for more than a thousand years.

On leaving the grounds of our temporary residence, we

stepped at once into the shadow of that huge structure the
great gate of the temple of Dai-butsu—an immense and
imposing pile, containing two of the colossal carved gatekeepers or kings previously described, of very forbidding
aspect and attitude, but who were less hideous than others
of the kind. This great gateway was on our left; on our
right, at a distance of three to four hundred yards, was
another gateway to the great temple, the broad road between
the two gateways having wide grassy spaces on either side,
from which spring many ancient and lofty old trees. The
space between the two gates is therefore a broad and beautiful promenade for the greater part of the year. Our first
visit was to the famous temple of the Great Buddha. As
usual in approaches to Japanese temples, there are several
shops near to the temple itself. In the centre of the large
open space between the lesser gateway and the temple is an
immense and very old bronze lantern, large enough for a
man to stand in. This lantern was presented to the temple
by the renowned hero and statesman Yoritomo, who died in
the year 1199, and is seven hundred years old. It is in
daily use still. This temple was originally founded and the
immense image made by the Mikado Shomu, the forty-sixth
of the present line of emperors, and the third of Nara, who
died 748 A.D. The temple was destroyed seven hundred years
ago, in the terrible civil wars of the twelfth century, and
again seriously injured, so that the head of the god had to be
recast, in the seventeenth century. The great gateway, however, with most of the other buildings of this great temple,
have escaped such injuries, and although constructed of wood
have stood as they now stand for more than eleven centuries.

The interest of this place centres, of course, in the great
god of bronze and gold, who (subject to the mischances just
mentioned) has been the wonder of Japan for so many ages
past. It has been positively stated by some that a considerable amount of gold entered into his composition, but those
on the spot seem to be uncertain as to whether the gold
employed in making him was mixed with the bronze of
which he is cast, or applied superficially to him. That much

has been applied in the latter way there can be no doubt, and in places in which the gold is visible, and which I closely examined, it seemed to me that it conformed to an external line of ornament in each case, which would indicate that it was superficial only. The dimensions of this god are truly colossal. His height from the base of the sacred lotus-flower on which he sits to the top of his head is 63½ feet, and above this rises a halo 14 feet wide, above which again rises for several feet the flame-like glory which arches in the whole figure. The face proper is 16 feet long, its width 9½ feet. The eyes are 3 feet 9 inches long, the eyebrows 5½ feet, the ears 8½ feet. The chest is 20 feet in depth. Its middle finger is 5 feet long. Around the head, shoulders, and sides of the god, in front of the halo, are sixteen sitting figures, said to be 8 feet long. The leaves of the immense lotus on which he sits are each 10 feet long and 6 feet wide, and there are fifty-six of them.* The casting must have been wonderfully well executed, although the fineness of the leaf-edges, and other parts which we were able to examine, and the elaborate engraving which can be traced upon the lotus-leaves in the uninjured parts, leave no doubt that the founder's art was elaborately supplemented by the file and graver. The countenance of the god is less mild and calm

---

* " This idol was first cast in the year 743. It was twice destroyed during the time of wars in its neighbourhood, and the idol which at present exists was erected about seven hundred years ago. The casting of this idol was tried seven successive times before it was successively accomplished, and about 3000 tons of charcoal were used in the operation. The total weight of metal is about 450 tons, and it consists of the following ingredients:—

Gold . .	500 lbs. avoirdupois.	
Tin . .	16,827 „	„
Mercury .	1,954 „	„
Copper .	986,080 „	„

1,005,361 lbs.

" It is cast in pieces, and these pieces are joined together by a kind of solder called *handaroo*, and which answers its purpose very satisfactorily. . . . The various pieces composing the image are not fitted together in a very finished manner, but the cement keeps the joints perfectly tight and close. The whole construction is one which shows great skill and original genius in the mixture of metals, and in the methods of casting them, and it is further one which will, no doubt, be a source of pride and gratification to the Japanese people for many centuries to come."—R. H. Brunton Esq., C.E., on 'Constructive Art in Japan,' in 'Transactions' of Asiatic Society of Japan.

of expression than is usual in images of Buddha.   The right hand is open and raised upwards, the left rests on the lap.

The surroundings of this enormous image are interesting, some of them very beautiful.   On his right hand is a very large image of Kokuzo, and on his left one of the goddess Kwannon, who here seems to occupy a more pronounced and immediate association with Buddha than usual.   In this temple of Dai-butsu, as in many others, there are magnificent bronze vases, some plain and some richly gilded, and many bronze lanterns of equal merit and value.   There are also many treasures of antiquity, which we had an excellent opportunity of inspecting as fully as time permitted, as they were arranged in order around the temple in anticipation of an exhibition shortly to be held.   Among them were writings of the ancient Mikados defined and preserved by the engraving of the surrounding parts; some of the weapons used in the invasion of Korea by the empress Jingu Kogo, including a large and powerful bow, said to have been that of the empress herself.   There was also the imperial standard of the Mikado Go-Daigo, of the fourteenth century, and the door from the Mikado's palace on which the famous patriot Nanko, or Kusunoki Masashigé, inscribed with the point of an arrow some parting words expressive of his apprehension that he would not return from the war to which he was going, of his devotion to the Mikado, and of his hope that his name would live long in the history of his country.   The characters of this inscription are well preserved and perfectly legible.   I obtained from the priests what is known to many as a " rub " of this inscription.   On a later day, going from Osaka to Kioto, the governor of Osaka was good enough to point out to me a pine-tree in the village of Sakurai as the spot on which this warrior, Nanko, took leave of his son before he went

"Far down to that great battle in the west,"

near to Hiogo, where, his counsels being rejected, he was grievously defeated.   He gave to his son, a boy of thirteen, the sword presented to him by the Mikado, desired him to fight for the Mikado as he had done, and was about to do,

he believed for the last time, and urged him to avenge his
death when he was gone.   After his defeat he put an end to
his life by committing *hara-kiri*, and a large number of his
followers imitated his example, as previously stated.   It is
said that the son desired to do the same, but being prevented
by his mother became a soldier a few years afterwards, and,
like his father, fought and died for his sovereign.[*]

But I must hasten over these treasures, some of which
were very remarkable indeed.   There was, for example (and
if I mix up the historic and the fabulous in my summary,
the Nara priests must be responsible for the incongruity),—
there was a sacred stone with a deep indentation of the very
foot of Buddha himself—a very large foot, and that of an
extremely weighty personage, judging by the impression made
in the granite.   There were also no less than four pieces of
the bones of Buddha, and some of the eating vessels, incense
burners, and other articles employed by him when on earth;
and a few articles likewise that had belonged to his apostles.
There was a wooden image of Kwannon, and a bronze shrine
of hers, of the date of the thirty-third emperor, who reigned
in the sixth century, and therefore before the introduction
of Buddhism into Japan.   This shrine, thirteen hundred
years old, was beautifully adorned with engraved figures,
and otherwise.   There was an old bell or sounding plate,
giving out different sounds when struck in different places,
and five metallic mirrors over one thousand years old.
There was an ancient tray, upon which had been written,
between one thousand and eleven hundred years ago, what
is pronounced by specialists to be the most perfect writing
in Japan—although what standards the specialists set up I
am at a loss to imagine.   It is the production of Kobo
Daishi, a very eminent scholar and priest, who went to
Korea and China to study there the knowledge and religion
of that period, and brought back an eminent zeal for the
Buddhist faith, afterwards founding in Japan the sect known
as that of Shin Gon, as previously related.   He was the

* See vol. i. chap. viii., on "The Hojo Domination."

author of a Japanese alphabet, which he introduced very early in the ninth century of our era.* There was also an extremely vigorous contemporary drawing illustrating the rebuilding of this great temple, the principal subject being the transport of an immense log of timber, which was carried upon a four-wheeled truck, and drawn by a large crowd of men. Instead of a whip wherewith to lash the hauling crowd—as in the clever picture, and no less clever imitation, by Mr. Tenniel of ' The Israelites in Egypt '—the principal character in the picture was armed only with a *gohei*,† *goheis* being, in fact, so far as I could see, the only stimulants brought to bear upon the labourers. There were also some large and magnificent wood carvings, among them being one of the martyred scholar and prime minister Sugawara Michizané, whose banishment was brought about by intrigue in 903 A.D. Here again was a box in which a prince imperial had been put six hundred years ago, and covered with sacred Buddhist writings, and thus smuggled out of the power of his enemies ; here one of a million little turned models of a quasi-pagoda which were distributed twelve hundred years ago at the founding of the neighbouring temple of Horiuji (already spoken of), each containing a passage from the Buddhist scriptures ; here the model of the pagoda of that temple of the same date, made before the pagoda itself was erected, and here boxes of MS. Buddhist scriptures thirteen hundred years old, inscribed in gold on

---

* " There is another arrangement of the Japanese syllabary, said to have been invented by the priest Kobodaishi, who was one of the most celebrated Japanese scholars. It was contrived for the purpose of facilitating the memorising of the syllabary. Being divided into words, the whole composes the following celebrated stanza :—

' I-ro-ha ni-ho-he-to chi-ri-nu-ru-wo
Wa-ga-yo ta-re-so tsu-ne-ra-u
Wi-no-o-ku ya-ma ke-fu-ko-ye-te
A-sa-ki yu-me mi-shi e-hi-se-su.'

From the first three letters in this arrangement the syllabary is commonly called the I-ro-ha, just as the English word *alphabet* has been derived from the first two Greek letters."

—' Outline History of Education in Japan ' (Philadelphia Exhibit).

† A Japanese religious emblem, as elsewhere explained.

blue paper. The imperial family, in addition to its distinction as a dynasty lasting through so many centuries, and to its many other claims to notice, has distinguished itself apparently by producing a wonderful member of the house, who became a hermit, and acquired the remarkable power of eating a certain kind of fish, and then breathing out images of Buddha from his holy lips. An image of this sainted personage is to be seen here. More historical possibly are the fragments of clothes worn at Nara when it was the capital of the empire eleven hundred years ago. It struck me as a noteworthy fact that the modern spirit has penetrated Japan so thoroughly that an exhibition of modern works and educational appliances was to be held not only in this odd, out-of-the-world city, in the centre of the country, but in the very temple which for more than one thousand years had been signalised for the colossal character of the idol which there was worshipped.

Leaving the great temple of Dai-butsu, we ascended a very long flight of steps, and proceeded to see and hear the large bell, weighing over thirty tons, of the same date as the temple. It was slung too low, owing to an error in the building, and, consequently, was struck below the boss intended to receive the blow, and from this cause possibly, although the sound was mellow and prolonged, it was not pure.

We next visited the temples of Nigetsu, dedicated to the goddess Kwannon, who appears under various conditions in her temples. The first temple on this spot was the shrine of an image found eleven hundred and twenty-eight years ago, but the building was burnt down and rebuilt one hundred years ago. The approaches to and grounds about this temple were remarkable, even among those of similar shrines in Japan, for the extraordinary number, variety, and beauty of their *toro* (fixed lanterns), in stone and bronze. It is not possible to convey readily in words a true idea of the extent to which this system of presenting lanterns to temples is here carried, or a true impression of the beauty of many of them,

THE GREAT TEMPLE OF DAI-BUTSU, AT NARA.

especially those in bronze. It really would almost appear
that the ingenuity of man, moving within certain conventional limits of size and form, had exhausted itself in
giving variety to them. Even those of stone exhibit great
differences of design, and are often beautifully ornamented
with carving and engraving.

I must observe in passing that the landscape view from
the hillsides on which these temples stand is peculiarly
fine, and it was refreshing—both at Nara and elsewhere,
while visiting a succession of temples, and observing the
infinite pains men have taken to get away from the simple
elements of religious feeling and worship, and to indulge
the rudest and wildest fancies in setting up their own
emblems of what is divine—to step occasionally into the
open air, in view of some beautiful stretch of scenery, and
there, lit with the sun and blown on by the breeze, to be
thankful that the power of enjoying the world and works
of God is still continued to us. Under such conditions,
even the distant temples and pagodas—being distant—
seemed scarcely to hurt the beauty and purity of nature.

One of this group of Kwannon temples is quite a chamber
of the gods. The building is nearly eleven hundred and
fifty years old, never having been burnt down, as so many
such edifices have been. Of all the gods and goddesses
here accommodated I will only mention one, but that
shall be a very remarkable one—the Kwannon of a thousand hands. In strict truth this sacred lady had not, I
believe, so many arms and hands as a thousand: I looked
well at her, and although I do not suppose that I saw them
all, I could not count many, if any, more than fifty. These
were all in use, however, holding cups, lotus-flowers,
mirrors, swords, croziers, infant hands, small gods, and
many other necessary articles. Another Kwannon goddess
here has three eyes.

Our next visit was to the Shinto temple of Hachiman
of Tamoki, in connection with which is an ancient building
used as a safe-house for the temple. It is eleven hundred
years old, and is built almost exactly like the log-houses of

modern Russian villages, but is raised well above the ground. The temple was built in the reign of the empress Kokei, in the middle of the eighth century.

We now visited a tea-house a little farther up the hill, from which a very fine view of the valley was obtainable, and where we made the acquaintance of a charming girl, the daughter of the house, who spoke a little English, and who, with her chaperone, completed the tour of the temples with us, adding brightness to the day's brightness. The view from the house was superb, commanding the whole valley in which Nara lies. The only building in the whole city that reminded one in the least degree of Europe was seen near the great pagoda, a mile away, and this building we found to be one of those normal schools which the present enlightened and progressive government of Japan has established throughout the country.

The Shinto temple of Kasuga came next on our route, with its sacred deer wandering about in the grounds, the gods of the temple having brought them there originally from Kashima. Four gods and goddesses have their shrines in this temple, which was built about two hundred years after the temple of Dai-butsu. The four shrines have, however, to be rebuilt every twenty years. It will be worth while to give the names, as they were given to me on the spot, of those to whom these shrines are dedicated, although they will hardly be intelligible to some of my readers. Each shall have a line to itself.

1. Takemikadotchinokami.
2. Futsunushinokami.
3. Amatsukoyanenokami.
4. Himeokami (daughter of the last-named).

I believe I shall not be far wrong, however, in identifying these deities as follows. It will be remembered that in the chapter on the Shinto Religion I had occasion to mention the gods who descended from heaven to conquer the country for Ninigi-no-Mikoto, and I gave the names as

Take-mika-dzuchi, and
Futsu-nushi,

the honorific affix "no kami" being omitted in both cases. Now the second of these names is precisely the same as that given me here at Nara, if we omit the same affix; and the first is so nearly like the other as to leave little or no doubt about their identity likewise. No direct identification of the third god has occurred to me, but I remember that in some accounts it is said that the god who was associated with Take-mika-dzuchi on his mission from heaven to Japan was Ame-no-tori-fune, and that the latter was despatched by the former to summon back the god Koto-shiro-nushi from hunting and fishing to say if he would surrender the country. It is possible, and even probable, that this may be the third god worshipped here—a supposition which at least has the merit of associating the four gods consistently together; but whether my conjecture as to the third god be correct or not, only probably Japanese scholars can say. It is, however, beyond doubt that the gods still worshipped in this temple of Nara are those who are supposed to have surrendered the country to the present dynasty at the demand of messengers from heaven.

At this temple again we found lanterns literally by the thousand—three thousand of them; no less than six hundred are lighted every night. I hope the priests who were good enough to meet us at this temple and conduct us through it —as, indeed, did the priests of the Buddhist temples already mentioned, usually giving us tea, cakes, and cigarettes wherewithal to refresh ourselves—will forgive me for saying that this very impressive temple derived, in my opinion, most of its nobleness from the truly magnificent old *sugi* and other trees which everywhere abounded within its precincts, and from the noble avenues by which it was approached. Older or finer trees than many included within the *torii* of this temple are seldom to be found.

The important Shinto shrine of Wakamiya, which we had yet to see before leaving these eastern groups of temples, was made very interesting to us by the circumstance that the priests were good enough to have a religious dance performed for our instruction. The dancers were three

young virgins dressed in red crape, with white robes over,
and adorned with two large bunches of artificial flowers
standing out like floral horns from their foreheads, balanced
by two gilt ornaments projecting backwards from the neck.
Three surpliced young men, gifted with a great power of
remaining steady for a long time upon one note, led the
dance with vocal and instrumental music. Like all Japanese
dances, the present one was entirely unlike everything that
passes for dancing in Europe, consisting rather of posturing,
attitudinising, advancing and retreating, and other such
movements, usually conducted very slowly. In the course
of the dance the girls each made use of a bunch of bells
with silk bands depending from it, as usual in the Shinto
dances—in imitation, doubtless, of the goddess Uzumé, who,
according to tradition, employed in her dancing small bells
suspended from a bamboo cane. The dance was in some
respects pretty, as all graceful movements of well-trained
young girls are sure to be ; but I hope it had in it some
profounder religious significance than I could discern, for in
other respects it was not to be considered inspiriting. They
were unfeigned thanks, however, which we tendered to the
chief priest for his courtesy in showing me so interesting a
spectacle—the first temple-dance we had seen in Japan.

We now took our *jinrikis* and drove to a batch of temples,
all Buddhist, near the great pagoda of Nara, situated near
the centre of the present town, in what has now been its
public garden for the last seven years, under the new *régime*.
These temples are all over one thousand years old, and in some
of them we find again the Kwannon of one thousand arms,
and also one of six arms. It would be tedious here to dwell
upon the details of these places of worship, although they
were extremely interesting for many reasons. Suffice it to
say that in one of them I was presented with a little carved
god of wood as a souvenir, and I am strongly inclined to
believe that if he should prove to do me little or no good, he
will most assuredly not work me any sort of mischief—which
cannot as a rule be confidently said of either gods or men.
Before returning to tiffin, we looked at the celebrated

Haneno-Matz, or flowering pine, a tree which, if it be not itself over eleven hundred years old, is at least in the direct succession of a line of pine-trees that have occupied the same spot continuously throughout that period. This inspection over, we lost no time in seeking our refreshments, after which we gave the afternoon to hunting the old curiosity shops, of which there are a few at Nara which I can strongly recommend to those who desire to possess themselves of some of the remaining antiquities of Japan. It is quite a mistake to suppose that all the old and curious and valuable things have been bought up; there are many remaining, and to those who care for them the twenty-six miles' run from Osaka in a *jinriki* will be well repaid by a few days spent in this ancient, historic, and most charming city of Nara.

Our return trip was a delightful one. Up at seven in the morning, we were soon sunning ourselves in the delicious brightness and warmth, with a pretty and curious garden before us, and old temples, old woods, and old hills all around us, and a sky above us far older than all of them, and yet wrought of material as unsubstantial and evanescent as a dream. The attendant girls, more numerous even than on the previous evening, took leave of us with regards as lingering as if we had known and loved them all our lives, and we were ourselves loth to leave beings so engaging and pleasant as we had found them. But away we went, taking another view of the old home of Dai-butsu among the hills that had sheltered the spot long before he made it sacred—

> " Long ere great Buddha strode
>   Upon his calm, colossal, godlike way
>   O'er the broad rolling rivers of Cathay,
>   By the Korean road,
>
> And stepping stormy seas
>   Hither, to mount the golden lotus throne
>   Of Nara, there to rule and muse alone,
>   Through lingering centuries."

Passing once more the grim gatekeepers, away we rolled, merrily through the merry morning, past the old temples and

pagodas; among the staring people; between the huge
lanterns of the portal, and on to the westward-spreading
plain over which eleven hundred years ago the imperial
sacred city shone. On our right lay large mounds, the tombs
of emperors and empresses, each one of whom has been a god
for ages past. Over their tombs spread clumps of pine-trees,
and beneath the pines stand their shrines, to which a people
reverent, and with cause, of their ancestral gods resort to
breathe forth their simple prayers. About a mile and a half
from the present boundary we reached a village, at which the
road turned right and left, and it was to this point that the
ancient capital extended. Three fourths of a mile on the
southern road stands a pagoda, and this, in those old days,
marked the southern boundary of the city. The limits are
fixed by the names of the roads and villages which indicate the
avenues, boulevards, and streets of a city. The temples and
pagodas, by the nature of their designations, serve to
complete the desired record. The pagoda referred to stands
in a village the name of which signifies the Western
Temples, and is known to have formed the western limit of the
capital, the temples round the Dai-butsu being the Eastern
Temples, and forming, as they did then and do now, the
eastern limit. The plain over which the city stretched is
now cultivated to the last inch of it, but after crossing it, it
was easy on looking back, with the aid of a stimulated and
sympathetic imagination, to restore the former greatness
and glory of the place, the distant parts (those which we had
recently left) standing up in the morning light and shining
in it precisely as they had done when reality and not imagination made the display. The road-scenes, the village-scenes,
the wood-scenes, the mountain-scenes, the river-scenes, of the
return journey took their places in the brilliant panorama as
we spun along; and as it was hard to write, even to the extent
of jotting down notes, in the leaping and jumping *jinriki-sha*,
I utilised the circumstances (as on similar occasions) by composing verses, into which I will hope some of the beauty and
the spirit of the time found its way. At a quarter past one
we emerged from the gorges of the hills, and at half past

one the white walls of Osaka Castle again glittered in the distance.

Before reaching Sakai we turned off to the south, in order to pass through a fine group of Shinto temples and shrines, covering, I should think, thirty to forty acres. Some of the small shrines were so picturesque, both in themselves and in their surroundings, that one was strongly tempted to linger among them, and to sketch, however roughly, the prettiest of them. But this our time did not allow, and we were able only for a moment to witness the sun-goddess lavishing her light upon the shrines and symbols reared in her honour. On entering Sakai, once more the whole population turned out along the line of route, thus politely offering themselves again for inspection. Alighting at the house of a private gentleman of wealth, who was unfortunately too ill to appear, we were received in the kindest manner by the mayor, with whom we were delighted to see his excellency Minister Kawamura, who had recovered from an indisposition which prevented him from visiting Nara. We found ourselves once more in a purely Japanese residence of a high class, one of its features being a small fish-pond, with very large gold and other fish, embedded in the centre of the house. The house was beautifully built and decorated, and the mayor—who is fond of antiquities, as we saw on our previous visit—had brought for our inspection a fine collection of old Japanese coins, jewels, mirrors, jars, and other articles of very great age. Luncheon was served European fashion for our convenience, but most of the dishes were Japanese, and tea was subsequently made and served by the daughters of the house, in that elaborate and ceremonial style which shows with what care and delicacy even the simplest operations of domestic life may be performed when people can afford the time for studying them. The two richly dressed girls, with their pure Japanese faces, hair curiously cut and contrived after the fashion of the country, kneeling at their tea-service, and attended by kneeling servants in the background, formed as pretty a picture as you could anywhere find even among the exquisite and varied arts of Japan. But like the pictures of the sun-

goddess which we had just passed, it was one over which we
could not linger, for we had arrived late, the hour of four
was getting near, we were still from one and a half to two
hours' distance from our residence in Osaka, and we had to
dress for a great dinner, with which the day, as we saw in the
last chapter, concluded.

THE COLOSSAL DAI-BUTSU OF KAMAKURA.

CHAPTER IX.

On Wednesday the 24th of February we left Osaka for Kioto, the former capital of Japan. When Yedo was made the seat of government, and had its name changed to Tokio, or Eastern Capital, the name of Kioto was officially changed to Saikio, or Western Capital. In the former case Tokio has everywhere superseded Yedo, but except in government documents its old name, Kioto, clings to the western city still.

Several of our Osaka friends came to see our party off by the train, Governor Watanabé and Mr. Godai giving us the honour and pleasure of their company on the short railway journey. The route lies through the "cockpit" of Japan, where many a hard and prolonged contest has been fought, the last of which was the deadly four days' struggle between the troops of the Mikado and those of the Shogun, early in 1868, which resulted victoriously for the young Mikado, and gave him that undisputed power which he has since worthily exercised.

On reaching the railway station at Kioto, we were met by the carriages of the governor, and driven at once to the Buddhist temple of Kenninji, where quarters had been prepared for us, with careful regard to our European habits, and to the impediments they would meet with in a house adapted only to the habits of Japanese. European tables, chairs, beds, and other similar furniture had been provided, the manufactures of Kioto being richly illustrated by an abundance of beautiful rugs, embroidered silk table covers, *cloisonné* cigar-boxes, and porcelain services. The walls were hung with *kakemonos* of rare merit, and in every room were folding-screens of great beauty, some of them displaying the best obtainable specimens of that embossing and embroidering with silk in which the Japanese are excelled by none. The rooms were made still more beautiful and interesting by bronzes, porcelain figures, and lacquer work of the best kind. These latter, together with the pictures, were changed daily during our stay in Kioto (as elsewhere mentioned), to increase the attractions of the residence. The house has beautiful gardens, upon one of which our rooms gave, and in sunny hours, of which we had many, was a miniature paradise—without the embarrassments of an Eve in this case.

After taking some tea, we sauntered forth to the mineral baths at Maruyama, where we climbed a tower and obtained a splendid view of the old historic city, with the crested summit of Mount Atago in front of us westward, and ranges of hills in every other direction. For eleven centuries this city, lying there below us, had been the capital of this extraordinary country, the government of which had always, throughout that long period, been of such a nature as to make the capital the centre of its influence. Beyond the city, in the south, lay the ground on which the great and decisive struggles for the dominion of the country had over and over again taken place, the last so recently as 1868, when the troops of the Shogun, who was seeking to obtain possession of the person of the Mikado, were defeated and routed by the loyal troops, whose valour, displayed through three days of fighting, secured for Japan the freedom, the enlightened administration, and the growing constitutionalism which she now enjoys.

After witnessing the beautiful and touching prospect for a time—having each his own thoughts, probably, about the fleeting fates of cities and nations, and the comparative permanence of the old hills and the immeasurably older sun that was then steeping all the scene in warmth and lustre—we strolled to the large and splendid Buddhist temples of Higashi-Otani and Chionin. In a quaint and very brief little guidebook of the city Mr. Yamamoto says of the former: " Higashi-Otani was constructed about the year 1690 after the Christian era, and its idol was Midabuds, which was thought to be very sacred to the people. For this reason the structure was completed much more grandly than any others. I think it may be called one of the most distinguished places, for it grants a delightful sight of Kiyoto. It has a comely gate called Karamon, and before you enter the gate you will find a very nice road with shady trees on both sides." This is rather meagre information, so I will add that Higashi-Otani is really the cemetery belonging to the great temple of Higashi-Honganji (of which I shall have occasion to speak hereafter), and is under the same control. It is famous as containing the grave of Shinran Shonin, the founder of the great Shinshu sect of Buddhists, as stated in the chapter on Buddhism. There is a noted stone upon the grave, known from its shape as Toraishi (Tiger-stone), which was at the spot where Shinran Shonin died, but was taken in Hideyoshi's time to the castle of Fushimi, and brought thence afterwards to its present place. The buildings are about one hundred and ninety years old. The name Otani—which, as we shall afterwards see, is the family name of the heads of the Shinshu sect—

was derived from the ground first appropriated as the grave-
place of Shinran Shonin, upon which now stands the great
temple of Chionin, to which we next proceeded.   Higashi
Otani is famous also for the beauty of its display of blossoms
in springtime.

Of the other temple, Chionin, Mr. Yamamoto says:
" Chionin, where the prior exhibition of last spring [1872]
took place, is a large and most magnificent temple in Kiyoto.
It was erected by Genkuwu, a successful priest of the
Buddhist religion, for the purpose of spreading the religion
through this country, about the year 1202 after the Christian era.   The present edifice, which is a wonderfully large
and splendid building, was built by the illustrious carpenter
Hidari Jingoro.   There is also a great bell that is 18 feet
high from the top to the bottom, and 10 inches thick.   It
is on the hill to the south-east of the edifice."

On the following morning we commenced our serious
survey of the city, and first visited the palace of his
majesty the Mikado, entering by the " Gate of the Sun."
This palace and grounds are of great interest historically,
as they exhibit the conditions under which the Mikado
existed before the late revolution of 1868, until which
time he had been secluded as a sacred personage, whose foot
must not touch the ground, and who was to the great bulk
of his subjects, and indeed to all, even less approachable
than any other of their gods.   It was in this palace that
the emperor-god dwelt: here he was enthroned, here married,
here lived, here died.   When he walked in these gardens,
mats were laid before him as he stepped, to keep his foot
from touching earth, and when he left them, as he rarely
did, he was conveyed in a large carriage closed in by screens,
and, as he passed along, the people stopped and worshipped.
Any eye that saw his sacred form would, the people believed,
be blinded by the sight.   Here he somehow had to lead his
life, with none of the duties of government left to him, and
finding it difficult no doubt to wear the hours away, being a
monarch and yet a prisoner, a god and yet a slave !

The palace buildings differ externally in no way that an

untrained eye can discover from the residences of ordinary
nobles, or from the ordinary forms of Buddhist temples and
temple buildings.   It certainly is not superior, or even
equal, in construction to many of the temples of Kioto.   In
the square in front of the throne-room (Shishindeen) were
on the one hand a cherry-tree and on the other an orange-
tree, which the Mikado Jito planted in the seventh century ;
or rather let us say, the present trees had come down in a
direct and unbroken line of succession from those planted on
the same spots by Jito.   The Shishindeen was but little
more than a large open room, with a small throne-chamber
partitioned off opposite to the central entrance.   This
chamber contained a chair (in lieu of the throne) and a
pair of bronze Korean dogs, whose presence at the foot of
the Mikado's throne was an emblem, I presume, of the
conquest of Korea by the empress Jingu Kogo sixteen
hundred years ago.   On the wall were very good portraits
of the present emperor and empress, painted in European
style, and lower down representations of thirty-two of the
wise men of China.   We next went to the ceremonial
chamber, outside of which were two bamboo bushes, the
object of which was said by my informant to have been to
collect birds whose songs and twitterings would wake the
Mikado early, at the time when his sleeping-chamber was in
this building.   After passing through the reception-rooms of
the residential part of the palace, we came to a beautiful
garden, with winding waters, stepping-stone paths, stone and
wooden bridges, and trees trained and distributed after the
picturesque fashion of the country.   Giving upon this garden
was the Mikado's study, decorated with some of the prettiest
and most chaste paintings anywhere to be seen.   Passing
on through other rooms of residence, looking over, or rather
into, other gardens—for seclusion seemed to have been the
ruling object with which the gardens had been composed,*—
we came to his majesty's bedroom, an inner room remark-

---

* I say composed, for a Japanese garden is essentially an artistic
composition, and to be appreciated
should be regarded as a picture, but
as a picture with many points of
view.

able chiefly from the circumstance that its walls were throughout adorned with fine and spirited paintings of wild beasts, very evil-looking beasts most of them. I remarked that this seemed a strange class of decoration for a bedchamber, but was told—it is not for me to conjecture with what correctness—that the object was to scare demons from the imperial and divine presence! Adjoining the bedchamber, with its guard of painted wild beasts, is a small but splendid room, in which his majesty used to keep his valuables, or, as I rather think, the sacred stone or jewel, and the copies of the other sacred symbols of the Shinto religion—the sword and the mirror, of which the originals are at the famous shrines of Isé and Atsuta. Then came a spring room and a summer room, of which the former is adorned with paintings of one hundred animals, while the latter looks upon another exceedingly pretty garden. There were likewise the usual small room for ceremonial tea-taking, a flower-room, and other apartments. The passages of temples and palaces of this kind are usually decorated by paintings upon the natural wood, which often have a very pleasant and effective appearance; but in this instance I observed that the walls of the long passages connecting the apartments of the emperor and empress are altogether without paintings, and although the empress has very charming quarters, and some of the paintings upon her walls are exceedingly graceful and pretty, her rooms are on the whole much inferior to those of the emperor. Near to the quarters of the empress is the wedding-room, in which the imperial couples were married, with a gate close by for the admission of the lady who was to have the distinguished honour of becoming the mother of Mikados. In the gardens were a bridge formed of a single stone, some trees trained into curiously twisted forms, a tea-house, and withal an earthquake-house—not an uncommon provision in this country, which, as we found when in Tokio, appears at times to be floated upon earthquakes.

Departing from the palace, we proceeded in our *jinrikishas* to the great Shinto temple of Kamonnoyanoshinsha, at the village of Shimagomo, on the northern side of the city. This is one of the temples the expenses of which are provided by the government. It was built in commemoration of Tamayorihimé and Oanamuchino Mikoto, and has two shrines dedicated to them. It is one of the largest temples in or near Kioto, and has been reverenced by the Mikados— so the priests of the temple informed me—beyond all others. The date of its foundation is uncertain, but the *Kin-shaki* states that Kamo was first built in the seventh year of the reign of Sujin-Tenno (and therefore ninety-two years before Christ), and the *Kokushi* history of Japan says that in the second month of the sixth year of Temmu-Tenno (679 A.D.) Kamo was repaired by the Yamashiro district, in which it stands. My readers will be glad to learn who were the distinguished individuals to whom the two shrines were dedicated, and whose unfamiliar names I have faithfully, and I hope correctly, recorded. I know but little of them, but I am able to state that they stood to each other in the relation of father and daughter, the name beginning with O belonging to the father. The daughter, the princess Tama- yori, is said to be the first person who improved the land of Yamashiro, and, if that be true, no right-minded reader will question her claim to a shrine ; while her father Oanamuchi —well, he was the princess's father, and in Japan the father of every distinguished person is honoured even before the person himself.* But according to one history, he appears to have been personally worthy, for the *Niphon Shoki* represents that he acted as a guide to the army which Jimmu-Tenno, the first Mikado, sent against the rebellious eastern savages, and enabled it to conquer them †

This temple is approached by a long avenue of noble trees,

---

* When a person exhibits par- ticular skill in public, in the wrest- ling ring or elsewhere, the compli- mentary cry of the spectators is equivalent, I am told, to "Has he not a father?" or "Has he father?" the recognition of the father being the immediate result of individual merit.

† I have repeated in the text the information given me on the spot; but on pages 35, 36 of vol. i. will be found facts which go to show that the deities of this temple are the mother of the first emperor, Jimmu, and her father.

the ground beyond being well wooded. It is, in fact, quite a delightful open park-like place, resembling in this respect most of the great temples in this country—a beneficent circumstance for the crowded towns in and about which these temples are situated. The buildings and shrines presented the usual appearance of the larger Shinto temples, and, as the movable curiosities and antiquities of the place had been lent to a forthcoming local exhibition, there was but little to see beyond the buildings. The chief priest and his assistants were very pleasant and hospitable, and offered us tea and biscuits in abundance. As we walked back through the long avenue I could not but remember the lines (of Bryant, I believe) beginning—

> "The groves were God's *first* temples."

I suppose His last will be that

> "Temple of immortal splendour"

which holds the worlds

> "Within its arching walls of diamond light."

After crossing the bed of one branch of the Kamogawa, which here divides into two, we again committed ourselves to our man-carriages, and started for a hillside summer seat of his majesty the Mikado, called Shugakuin. This we found to be a fine wooded park, containing a large artificial lake with islands, and furnished with numerous tea- and summer-houses, some of which offered delightful views of the Kioto valley and the Atago mountains beyond. Here and there, in selected places, the summer-house tables had been spread with light refreshments, and upon the lake were boats, one of them hung with flags and gala trappings. It was a lovely scene, and one which it was impossible for innocent people not to enjoy; and we did enjoy it. We boated and strolled and moved our minds over the landscape, and let the quiet and the beauty of the place have their own way with us—and what a pleasure it is to let the quiet and the beauty of any natural scenery do that in these days of hurrying activity! I ought to mention, as part of the pleasures of the place, that the tables were furnished for the occasion with some of the choicest productions of Kioto manufacture, in the shape of embroidered silk table-covers, porcelain tea-services, cigar-holders and ash-cups of *cloissoné* work, and so forth. Before leaving, we found a substantial tiffin spread in the entrance-house of the park, and this, as well as everything else in this beautiful place, we carefully endeavoured to appreciate. Shugakuin was built about two hundred and fifty years ago by Iyémitsu, one of the great Shoguns of the Tokugawa family, whose daughter was married to the Mikado, and who played so signal a part in the history of the country that he has received fuller notice elsewhere.

On leaving the imperial grounds we visited, hard by, Mr. Schumako's large private school, which is well known in the neighbourhood. It is a mixed school of boys and girls, and the opportunity we had of observing the teaching in the various class-rooms convinced me that the instruction there given in elementary knowledge was solid and good.

We next proceeded by a pleasant country road, which was very steep and rough in places, and much of it bordered with tea-plantations, to the Buddhist temple of Ginkakuji (Silver-storied Temple), which was built more than four hundred years ago by the Shogun Ashikaga Yoshimasa, who had the best procurable things brought from all parts of Japan for its construction and ornamentation. It was originally his country seat, named Higashiyama-den (Palace of the Eastern Mountains) by Go Tsuchi Mikado Tenno, but now his (Yoshimasa's) image, carved by a clever contemporary, is one of the principal objects of worship. An image of Amita two feet high, standing in a lotus-flower, which was the object of his own worship, is also still worshipped here. Yoshimasa like many other monarchs and quasi-monarchs has become more famous from a comparatively trivial circumstance than from any of his more serious acts. He was the first person to establish, in a small room (of $4\frac{1}{2}$ "mats"), into which we went, what is known in Japan as ceremonial tea-taking, to which I have on other occasions adverted. In doing so he acted upon the advice of the

clever friend who, as just stated, carved his image, one
Sohami. This Sohami appears to have been a fellow of very
various accomplishments, for, besides his carving and his
tea-making, he did some very clever painting on a screen,
which was shown to us, and he was represented by the
priests, who were good enough to take us about the temple,
to have been a most learned man besides. We also saw some
fine old paintings by the famous artist Kano Masanobu, who,
with his son, founded the Kano School of Japanese painters.
The tea-room in the Tokindo to which I have referred is
further interesting on account of the visits which the emperor above-named (Go-Tsuchi, who reigned 1465-1501)
used to pay to Yoshimasa at this palace, and of the tea-taking
that used to be carried on by them on such occasions in this
little room. At such times these two—the sacred and the
secular monarchs of the country, as they may be roughly
called—used further to amuse and interest themselves by
the equally harmless processes of burning and smelling incense and of composing poetry. Several compositions of the
emperor, and articles liked by him, are still preserved in this
temple. Yoshimasa died in his fifty-sixth year, leaving
instructions that his seat should be converted into a temple
of the " Jen " sect, which was done, the chief priest, Hosho
Shuzai, of Shokokuji, one of the principal Jen temples then
in Japan, being appointed to govern the new one. Since
then the families of Ashikaga, Konoye, and Nijio, all noble,
have furnished the chiefs of the temple, which, until about
one hundred years ago, was very flourishing. In front of
the temple is a curious winding steep-sided mound of
sand, about four feet high, and a frustrum of a cone
of the same material somewhat higher, which have been
kept up ever since Yoshimasa's time, although they look
as if the first shower of rain would go far towards levelling them. I was told, however, that the hot sun does
much more injury to them than rain. There is also
a most lovely garden here, but one with an antique look
about it, shrubs, trees, buildings all looking very, very
old. There is an old and small separate two-storied

building likewise, which gives the name of " Silver-storied Temple" to the whole.* It has a parlour or tea-room below, and a shrine of Kwannon above, all looking, to me, neglected, and likely soon to tumble to pieces; but this may have been a mistaken impression. Within the grounds of this temple there were also some small Shinto shrines, with *torii* and everything complete. I had often before seen the temple grounds of the two religions, Buddhist and Shinto, running more or less into each other apparently; nor was this altogether surprising, seeing the efforts made by some of the early Buddhist missionaries and converts to make their own faith include the Shinto—efforts carried by some (Kobo-daishi, for instance) to the length of asserting, as previously stated, that the Shinto gods were, in fact, neither more nor less than so many manifestations of Buddha. I had not before observed, however, the presence of the shrines of the one faith entirely within the temple-precincts of the other, as here. Nor could I get any satisfactory explanation of the circumstance. What made the matter still more difficult, perhaps, was the alleged fact that these Shinto shrines dated from the foundation of the place. It was suggested by one of the attendants of the temple that probably they were erected for private worship by the founder, Yoshimasa, before the conversion of the palace into a temple; but there are difficulties in that explanation of the matter which are obvious. Ginkakuji was visited by the present empress of Japan in January 1877.

From Ginkakuji we drove to the famous Shinto temples of Yoshida, which, like the former, are situated upon the open hilly ground on the north-east of the city, but are somewhat nearer to it. These temples, which were built three hundred and sixty years ago, cover many acres of a beautiful wooded hill, with approaches from its opposite sides. They ought to be very sacred temples indeed, for they are

---

* It was the intention of Yoshimasa to adorn the walls and ceiling of this building with silver leaves; hence the name.

dedicated to no less than eight million gods, all of whom are
gods of Japan, and all of whom have separate, though slight,
consideration shown to them in this place.* There are
several shrines at different parts of the temple grounds, but
the eight millions of gods are worshipped in one main
temple, with a series of small shrines arranged around in
the open air under a tiled canopy. The way the matter is
managed is this : the deities are grouped according to
districts—returns having been made, I presume, of the
number in each district, from all parts of the country—and
the name of the district, with the assigned number of deities,
is written up in each case. I took a few of the numbers
down as they happened to run from one end, and found
them to be very variable, viz. 16, 34, 187, 6, 50, 131, 65,
71, 21, 24, 24, 50, and so forth. It would obviously take an
immense number of shrines to make up the eight millions,
at this rate, for here we have but an average of less than
sixty gods per shrine ; but I presume there are some districts very much more fortunate than others, and that if
we could have given sufficient time to the matter we should
have found some in which there were deities by thousands
and tens of thousands. More interesting to me than this
congestion of consecration, if I may so speak, were some of
the minor shrines, representing the ancient Japanese architecture. There was one such shrine in which the form of
building in vogue two thousand years ago was accurately
preserved,† and another of seven hundred years later date
showing the same style somewhat elaborated. There were
also on this hill of Yoshida the tomb of some of the Mikados,
including those of Yozei, who reigned in the ninth century
(A.D.), and Nijo, who reigned in the twelfth century, the
former living beyond the age of eighty, and the latter dying
at the early age of twenty-three.‡

Near to Yoshida is the ancient and splendid Buddhist

---

* This is not a very large number,
however, when compared with that
of the Hindu gods, of which there
are three hundred millions.

† See illustration on page 136, vol. i.

‡ These dates and figures are taken
chiefly from the Philadelphia Education Exhibit.

temple of Shiuniyodo, which is approached by a sloping avenue of extremely fine red maple-trees, and is celebrated for its beautiful flowers. This temple was founded about the year 1050 A.D., and was originally the country seat of Sanjo-in, the mother of the Mikado Ichijo, who reigned from 1017–36, dying at the age of twenty-nine. It was once burnt, and rebuilt on the same site. A three-storied pagoda is attached to it. The main shrine is dedicated to the god Amita, of whom it contains a very famous image made by a priest named Ikakudieshi. The head priest—who, with others, most kindly received and entertained us—was good enough to open the shrine, and permit us to view the god, before whom there happened to be standing at the time what I presume were cups of rice, fourteen in number. This temple contains also a very large and particularly fine specimen of Kioto silk embroidery in a picture (about twelve feet by fifteen) crowded with detailed figures exquisitely worked. It is a pictorial illustration of the description of heaven given in the sacred Buddhist books. The adornments of this temple are very rich, the canopy over the chief seat of the officiating priests being a remarkably fine work.

We had still two great temples to inspect before our day's work was over, the next being the famous Buddhist temple of Kurodani, which is one of the four great temples of the Jodo sect. This is one of those Buddhist sects which came from India through China to Japan, being established there in the thirteenth century. The great Tokugawas belonged to this sect. Kurodani stands in the same quarter (the northeast) of Kioto as the foregoing temples, but is somewhat nearer the city than they. The other name of it is Shiunzan (Purple Cloud Mountain) Konkai Komiyoji (Temple of Golden Brilliant Light). It covers about eleven acres of ground. The priests of the temple—who, like those of Shiuniyodo, received us well, and entertained us in the temple with tea and cigarettes—gave us a short account of it from a translation of which, by a Japanese gentleman of Kioto, I take the following passage :—

"In the fifth year of Shoan, or 1175 A.D., when the founder Yenko-daishi left his lovely dwelling of Kurodani in Mount Hi-yei [which rises high over Kioto in the north-east] for the purpose of introducing the Jodo sect, he saw on the way to Shiuniyodo, where he used to worship, a wonderful divine exhibition of purple cloud and brilliant light, and on the spot he erected a temple, and from the divine exhibition which he saw he named the mountain Shiun, and the temple Konkai Komiyoji."

The temple is, however, known by its founder, who in that age was called by his place of abode rather than by his name. He was known to the people of his day as Kurodani Shonin (a high title for priests), and gradually the temple has come to be known by the name of Kurodani. The temple was burnt down one hundred and four years ago, and after a few years the present structures were built by Jingo Kaurei, the head priest of the forty-fifth generation. The main shrine is that of Yenko-daishi himself; the adjoining buildings are the Amitado, the shrine of Amita; the Tenrinzo, for the holy books; the Kwando, the shrine for Kwannon; the very fine Saumon, or temple gate; the tomb of the founder; and the three-storied pagoda. There are also twenty-five dwellings for the priests of the temple. While visiting this fine temple we had the advantage of a conversation with the priests upon Buddhism, and the sects into which Buddhists are divided.

We had still the temple of Nanjenji (a little southward of Kurodani) to visit. This also is a Buddhist temple, but it belongs to a different sect, viz. the great Jen sect, of which it is the principal temple in Japan. Originally it was the pleasure palace of one of the Mikados. I have not any very clear information respecting its conversion into a temple, but an account was furnished to me, and I will give it here for what it is worth, leaving the curious language to stand in connection with the circumstances, which are quite as curious :—

"How the palace came to be a temple is on the following

accounts: In the beginning of Shoo, as often some wonderful occurrences happened in the palace, so several priests were called from Nara in order to put an end to the occurrences, but they could not execute their duty. In the fourth year of Shoo, Ninkan Jenshi, the head priest of the third generation of Toki Kuji, was called by the emperor, and he, with twenty priests accompanying him, made prayers in the palace, and then the occurrences ceased for ever, so that the emperor (now retired) became the very deep believer in Jen sect, and came to offer his palace as a temple. In the seventh month of the third year of Shitoku, in the reign of Gokomatsuin-Tenno, Yoshimitsu Shogun gave to the temple, in the name of the emperor, the first rank of the five main temples of Jen sects."

The present main gate of this building is a very large one, and was built by a great general, Todo Takatora, in commemoration of the many soldiers killed under him in battles at Osaka and elsewhere. It was built in eight months, and is a very imposing structure.

Our first hours and our first day in the sacred city having been devoted to sacred residences and temples, we gave our next, in part, to more secular subjects; and first we visited the silk-factory founded by the local government, the governor of Kioto being good enough to conduct us there and explain its basis and management. And this may be a convenient place for stating that in Kioto, as elsewhere, the government appears to have taken many measures for stimulating and aiding the productions and manufactures as well as the education of the country. Under the city government of Kioto there is an industrial department, the Kuwangiyoba, which was established in 1870 specially for the promotion of the industrial arts, and which has the following branches: 1. An experimental gardening department (Saibaishi Kenjo), commenced in 1872, for the cultivation of foreign and Japanese fruits and vegetables; 2. A shoe-manufactory (Seikuwajo), begun at the same time, for extending the manufacture of boots and shoes of European style; 3. A weaving-factory (Shokkoba), begun in 1873, where silks and other fabrics are woven, principally in foreign looms: this branch sent three workmen to Europe to learn the art of foreign weaving; 4. A physical and chemical branch (Semi-kiyoku), which has a sub-branch at Miyadju, in Tango, 80 miles distant, and which, with the assistance of two foreign workmen, is promoting and teaching the manufacture of chemicals, soap, effervescing and lemon drinks, *cloisonné* ware, porcelain, etc.; adjoining it is the Senkojo, for teaching dyeing on foreign methods; 5. The female industrial school, Jokoba, already mentioned; 6. The Bokujo, or more properly Bokuchikujo, which is an experimental farm, established in 1871 with the object of improving the breeding of cattle and of teaching agriculture, the foreign cattle and sheep being chiefly purchased in America, and the milk produced being sold in the city; a branch farm exists at Komo in Tamba, about sixteen miles from Kioto; 7. A department (Yosanba) for promoting the multiplication of silkworms; 8. A pauper industrial department (Jusansho), established in 1869, with a branch at Dosembo, in the south-eastern part of Kioto county, where agriculture and the manufacture of earthenware are the principal employments of the pauper colony; 9. A street-sweeping department (Kuwakaisho), where compost is prepared on the French method; 10. A paper-manufactory, established in 1875. There exist also separate branches for making and teaching how to prepare leather, beer, and mineral waters. A museum is in course of formation.

As before stated, we visited the Shokkoba, and saw in practice the processes of manufacturing woven fabrics of cotton and of silk, with embroidery. Much of the work produced was strikingly beautiful, more especially in the departments for silk embroidery; for producing artistic effects in cut pile fabrics (velvets, etc.) by cutting part of the pile only; and for producing pictorial effects by dyeing velvets. The factory is in a fine building, on the site of a former palace, and a beautiful Japanese garden is connected with it, with ornamental water of extreme purity and clearness, abounding with large grey and golden carp. Although I put a few questions respecting the economic results of this and other government manufacturing establishments, I shall not discuss the matter, as everything of the kind here is so new, and all the circumstances of the country and people are at present so entirely exceptional, that no broad and general inferences from the results of their working could yet be drawn.

The governor was good enough to take us next to the "Jiogakko," or female normal school, established under the auspices of the local government, and in a certain degree under the care of the imperial government. In connection with this school is the "Jiokoba," or female industrial establishment, already adverted to. The first-named institution, founded in 1871, is formed with five classes, of which the fifth is the lowest; but at present only the three lower classes have pupils. The object of this school is stated to be to make girls fit to become good mothers. They must be thirteen years of age before they can enter, and must pass through a class in six months, undergoing minor examinations monthly, and general examinations in the presence of the governor of Kioto every six months. Some of the students are taught the English language. Boarding in the school is encouraged, the charge for maintenance (food only) being one and a half *yen* per month (!), the Japanese paper *yen* being at present about three shillings in value. There is a vacation for the month of August. The subjects taught are those usual in elementary schools, with algebra, geometry, higher arithmetic; also English grammar and composition in the upper classes. But in addition to the book-learning imparted, the girls receive a very practical education in the duties of daily life. They are taught how to dress, to wait at meals, to receive, salute and entertain guests; to make tea ceremonial fashion, and to give and take it; to dispose flowers in vases; to hang pictures; to snuff the candles generally employed in all households at present; to dust rooms; to eat the larger fruits of the country (melons, etc.); to make

offerings to the gods, and so forth. In the other school, or
industrial establishment for girls, there are six classes, in
which the instruction is chiefly in the various kinds of
needle-work and weaving. In the lowest class the girls are
taught plain needle-work; in the next, plain weaving of
cotton, with advanced needle-work; in the next, the weaving
of cotton with patterns, the rearing of silkworms, and the
mode of making the broad girdles which form so striking a
part of the female costume in Japan; in the third class, the
weaving of silk with cotton, the making up of the tobacco-
pouches (which are in universal use throughout the country),
and the making of plain dresses are taught; in the second,
the weaving of silk with patterns, and the making of dolls'
dresses, foreign dresses, and silk coats; and in the first
class the girls are practised in every kind of silk-weaving,
and in the making of lace, of dancing dresses, and of ceremonial dresses. The pretty and useful art of composing
pictures of silk cut out into suitable designs, and pasted
upon a groundwork of cardboard, is also taught, and taught
very successfully, in this class.* There are at present one
hundred and nine students in the Jiogakko, and one hundred
and ninety-six in the Jiokoba.

Our visit to the normal school was very interesting.
Outside of it, as we approached, "the sweet girl-graduates"
were ranged on either side in their pretty costumes, bowing
low as the party of visitors passed in, and remaining so till
all had entered the building. Two of the pupils played to
us on the *koto* before we proceeded to the class-rooms, in
the first of which were twenty-four girls (all Japanese save
one), who are instructed in the English language by an
American lady, Mrs. Arnold, who was present, and who
invited us to hear some of them read. Several read accordingly, and all of them with considerable skill, notably Miss
Yo Tamatei and Miss M. Omori, both of them quite young
girls. In the next class-room were six young ladies com-

---

* Two pretty specimens of this class of art were presented to my son
and myself.

posing pictures of raised silk, after the manner just adverted to, with exceedingly good effects. We then passed through a room of one hundred girls, all engaged in making dresses, and in needle-work of a similar kind, and I am bound to say that they were an exceedingly pretty set of young ladies, worthy to take very high rank among the beauties of Japan, and fit to compare even with the charming Osaka girls. In the next class-room were six pupils working with sewing-machines, and in the next twenty-five, most of them weaving, the remainder engaged in brocade-work and rug-work. In the succeeding class rooms were thirty girls reading Japanese history aloud in succession, with lifted voices and pronounced emphasis, but with what amount of merit in other respects I, unhappily, could not judge. (Here, as in all other Japanese schools which I visited, the reading aloud of a passage from a book was immediately followed by explanations from the pupil, in order, I presume, to prove that the text was properly understood and appreciated—a very good system if loyally pursued—but it appeared to me, in almost every instance, that the explanations were delivered in precisely the same style and just as fluently as the text, and were therefore possibly not the spontaneous and immediate products of their own minds.) In the next class-room thirty girls were reading books written in the Chinese character and grammar, but with Japanese meaning; in the next, twenty girls were doing arithmetic with English figures; in the next, twenty-three performing embroidery, and making up pocket-books, tobacco-pouches, etc.; and finally sixteen were drawing pictures of flowers, trees, etc., in that bold, swift-handed, and dexterous style which is the charm of this branch of Japanese art. I could not help lingering in this room among the floral beauties that were springing from the fingers of these pretty Kioto girls, nor could I refrain from begging one of the pictures as a reminiscence of the pleasant scene. The whole sixteen were, however, sent afterwards for my acceptance, and with them two additional drawings on silk of perfect loveliness, as I think them, from the hand of the graceful young lady who was the teacher of the class, and over whose work, while I was present, I stood with what was probably ill-concealed, or unconcealed, admiration. I need not say how I value these treasures derived from this interesting school of three hundred girls in the heart of the once-sacred city of the once-exclusive empire of Japan. But the best treasure brought from it was, perhaps, after all, the knowledge that Japan is now governed by a monarch and ministers who appreciate, and are resolved to extend to boy and girl alike, the supreme blessing of education. Many a time has this reflection already been forced upon me in this country, but it seems a fitting place here to record it, when one is speaking more especially of what he saw in this female school of the good work being done, and done throughout Japan not for the stronger sex only, but for the weaker likewise.

> " If she be small, slight-natured, miserable,
> How shall men grow ? "

The government of Japan seems to have asked itself this question, and the answer it has given to the world may be read in schools scattered all over the country.

From the normal school we proceeded to a crape-factory, to see the manufacture of *chirimen*, a branch of industry I do not remember having seen before, and one of considerable interest in this country, where this soft and pretty material is so largely worn. In the course of this afternoon we visited no less than four silk-factories, witnessing, among other things, the production of some exquisitely figured silk velvets, and other goods of that class. These silk-factories in Kioto are on a small scale, but numerous, the choicest and finest manufactures for the Tokio market being produced in some of them. In one we saw under manufacture some exceedingly rich brocaded silk ordered by the household department of his majesty the Mikado, and I am much mistaken if these were not the identical fabrics which were at a later period presented to me by his majesty's command in the imperial palace at Tokio.

Our visits to the silk-factories were suspended at luncheon time, which was usefully and pleasantly spent at Karakuko,

a large school for young men and women established in a
splendid building which was constructed a few years ago
as the palace of a prince who has since gone elsewhere to
reside, and which was no doubt obtained at a moderate cost
for its present purpose.   This school is in some degree
assisted by the government, but is mainly a private one,
having two hundred and sixty pupils.   We passed through
the various class-rooms, hearing the pupils read and
expound what they read, and testing, so far as in us lay,
the quality of the education given.   As a rule, we found the
methods of instruction good, and the teachers combining
clearness of exposition with that patience and good temper
which are indispensable, especially in the instruction of the
very young.   There was a girls' branch to this establishment,
where we saw a large number of pupils busily engaged,
most of them on needle-work at the time of our visit.   Some
pretty little specimens of the work were handed to us as
mementoes.   In return I must do the girls of this school the
justice to say that, individually and collectively, they were
as pretty as their fellow-students of the normal school,
which is the highest compliment I can pay to the beauty
of schoolgirls in Japan.

Another deeply interesting educational establishment
which we visited the same day is a female school of
industry, where dancing-girls, *geishas*, and other such
young females can receive some elementary instruction, and
be taught the domestic arts which are necessary to wives
and mothers.   Until this kind of institution was started,
this class of girls in Japan, and especially in great cities
like Kioto, were in a very unfortunate position.   Highly
educated in the arts of dancing, singing, and waiting at
meals on men, their education in other respects was quite
neglected, and consequently the ordinary avocations of
respectable life, and especially of married life, were closed
to them, or open only under the gravest disadvantages.
They not unfrequently married well, I am told, but they
were usually very unfit for their new duties in such cases.
Under the present *régime* of Japan, and with the greater

respect which is now becoming felt not only for the women but for the men also of the trading and poorer classes, the neglect of this large class of young women and mere girls has been so much deplored that schools of industry, expressly designed to fill up their spare time with instruction in matters that wives and mothers should understand, have been established in different parts of the city, and receive the cheerful support and assistance of the government. We found a number of *geishas* and dancing-girls busily occupied, in the interval of their usual occupation, in receiving instruction in elementary knowledge, and especially in the use of the scissors and needle. The interest which is taken in these institutions by the governor, from whom the proposal to make the visit proceeded, is a good omen for their permanent success, until superseded, let us hope, by a wholly improved method of employing the maidens of Japan.

On the evening of this day we had the honour of dining at the palace of the chief priest of the Eastern Church (Buddhist, Shinshu sect), whose invitation, conveyed through his eldest son, had reached us some days previously at Osaka. Those who know the state of things that existed some years ago will alone know how to duly estimate this invitation. The chief priest (or archbishop) was himself at a distant part of his diocese, and the duty of entertaining his excellency the minister of marine and our party devolved upon his sons, who performed it with a cordiality and kindness not to be surpassed. In view of the desire I had shown to visit the temples, it was part of the programme of the afternoon or evening that we should first inspect the temple of our hosts, Higashi Honganji, where we were received by them, and conducted to an apartment in which tea and sweetmeats were served. We were then taken to the shrine-temple, and went carefully through it. It is not one of any great importance, being but a temporary edifice erected to take the place for a time of the splendid structure which was burnt down during the fighting between the troops of the Mikado and those of the Tycoon in 1868. The original temple was built by the chief priest Kionin Shonin, two hundred and seventy-six years ago. In one of the shrines is the god Amita, and in another the image of Kionin Shonin, carved by himself. In the year 1876 A.D. the high title of Kenshindaishi was given to Shinran Shonin, the founder of the Shinshu sect, of which, as I have said, our absent host is the eastern metropolitan.

To reach Kikokuté, the palace of the archbishop, we made use of our *jinriki-shas*, and after again refreshing our jaded selves with tea, strolled into a large and beautiful garden, where, gay with bright flags and curtains, lay at the bank of a lake a fine large barge, carpeted and cushioned, and provided with tea, fruit, cakes, cigars, cigarettes, and other comforts suited to our exhausted condition! Lest we should require something before actually embarking, an elegant lake-house standing out over the water was bountifully provided with similar necessities—such was the forethought and over-abundant hospitality of our entertainers. The warm atmosphere, the coloured light of the evening, the repose of the lake, the beauty of the islands in it and of the banks beyond, the alluring ease which the boat offered, and that desire to get afloat which ever besets the Englishman, all combined towards one end, and we were speedily gliding over the crystal calm. There were on the island and banks many objects to attract the eye and gently interest the mind. There was, for example, an old stone pagoda-like monument or To; it was very low down, and partly submerged, but it was to the memory of a great name, no other than that of Kawarano, Sadaijin, a minister who flourished between seven and eight hundred years ago. There were also some very curious old stone lanterns, which, with their quaint sculpturings of sun and moon and other devices, are always pleasing to look at. There were likewise fine old trees, with their roots half out of the earth, and their shining summits steeped in the coloured sun. All about the place were large bronze cranes, which, although found to be bronze on sufficient inspection, at each new appearance seemed to be on their way from somewhere to somewhere else. We landed on the island, and stood upon the site of an old tea-house,

now burnt down, but which till then had been notable for
its ceiling of spears, brought from the battle of Sedsa-
gataké, at which seven of the great Taiko's troops so much
distinguished themselves with spears.* Re-embarking, we
remained upon the lake till the sun went down behind the
hills and began deepening its colours and preparing for the
splendid end. Then we landed, and, having still a few
minutes to while away, spent them, boy-like, in racing, leaping, and other preparations for dinner. And what a dinner!
Although served on a table, it was (by particular desire)
Japanese in its character; it proved to be Japanese, too, in its
profusion. I must admit that on this occasion again I was
not happy in the use of my chop-sticks, but resolutely I played
them, to the exclusion of the knife and fork, though these
were provided. Making every allowance for the superior
enjoyment which a travelling Englishman would be sure to
experience at the table of a Buddhist archbishop in his own
palace, whatever the dinner might be, I must maintain that
we dined in a manner more than worthy of the occasion—
with all due deference to the minister present, be it said. I
could not possibly have dined better at my club in St.
James's (and I am homely enough to prefer my dinner there
to any which the *cafés* of Paris or the *traktirs* of Russia
produce), although it is true that one has at home to dis-
pense with raw fish and seaweed, and other like luxuries of
the East. But a choice and lavish banquet was not the
only source of enjoyment provided for us. A series of
musical and dramatic performances—very much more than
we mean by dances, though called by that name—were performed throughout the dinner, by performers of the highest
class known to Japan. The strange but obviously masterly
singing, instrumental music, and pantomimic action of the
various artists, coupled with the splendour and wonder of
their costumes, were to me so interesting that I frequently
found myself giving more attention to them than to my own
performances with the chop-sticks or the *saké* cup, a lapse

---

* See vol. i. p. 197.

which, I hope, was forgiven me by my hosts, and will be by my readers. The so-called dances presented were the following, which may possibly be familiar to some, viz.— 1. Motchiduki ; 2. Isigami ; 3. Suminuri ; 4. Tsutchigumo ; 5. Wtsubosaru. I confess that these names have not a familiar appearance to my own eye, but others may be more fortunate, and better versed in the drama of Japan.

During the dinner another surprise was prepared for us in the form of a brilliant illumination with coloured lanterns of the lake and gardens. A prettier sight of the kind could not well be anywhere produced. After the dinner and the dances came some of the renowned jugglers of Japan, of whom one very old, very stout, very testy, and very clever representative achieved great distinction, and received great applause. I shall only name one or two of his successes. One was the taking of a small glass globe, about four inches in diameter, and putting a little water into it, and then, without any means that we could see or divine, causing this globe first to become full, and then to play like a fountain, which rose and fell at his command, or as he played upon it with his fan. He also caused the water apparently to play upwards from the bowl through his fan, through any part of it as he pleased, and also to assume various inclined directions, and, in a word, to do whatever he desired. Another of his tricks was to produce a number of paper lanterns, complete, with candles and suspension loops, from a bowl of water, and to cause them to become lighted when he pleased after they had passed from his hand and had been hung up at a distance of several feet from him. One of them would not light, being, he said, too wet; but after a few minutes had elapsed, he commanded it to become lighted, and it instantaneously became so. At this dinner, as at that at Osaka, the great compliment of placing before an honoured guest a large stand of artificial plants and flowers was again paid. On this occasion the principal figures represented figures dressed in old Japanese costumes, and there was also a fine vase, many beautiful flowers, and other ornaments. The whole of these were cut out of the long turnips of the country, and very cleverly coloured. I find that one may always expect in such picture-models to find the pine, the bamboo, and the plum-tree represented, as they were in this instance. After rising from the table, we devoted ourselves to the examination and enjoyment of the many works of art about us, including rare books and scrolls of drawings, some of great age and rarity, and others more modern, but of marked merit. After taking leave of our liberal and courteous entertainers, we took our departure amidst a blaze of lanterns and basket-torches, and through a crowd of spectators, who were but ill-rewarded, I fear, for their patient waiting. I heard afterwards that the preparations for this afternoon and evening's proceedings were much greater than appeared even to a careful observer, including a new floor for the dances, and other works requiring time and arrangement. The whole affair was entirely novel in the palace of a Buddhist archbishop, and must certainly have been due to something lying very much beyond any claims to consideration which even generous friends may credit me with, and but for the post of honour being assigned to myself I should have concluded that Japanese archbishops pay wonderful respect to their ministers of the crown.

Our next day at the sacred city (Thursday, 27th of February) was commenced by an exceedingly pleasant little expedition to the beautiful village of Arashiyama, and by an ascent up the still more beautiful river beyond it. The hospitable governor of Kioto had caused all necessary arrangements to be made for carrying out the trip promptly, and at half past nine we started, a train of a dozen *jinriki-shas*, to the western part of the city, and beyond, through the garden— for it practically is a vast garden—which stretches away to the hills. Our road lay along a small canal, fed by the mountain streams, and floating scores of boats laden with the produce of the upper lands, chiefly consisting of wood, either in its natural state or in the form of charcoal. Owing to a police officer in a *jinriki-sha* going a little ahead of the party to clear the road—a necessity where the roads are narrow and without footpaths, and where even *jinriki-shas*

might do much mischief to children and others if no such
precautions were taken—the whole population of the city
and the villages turned out to view the transit of the travellers, and thus, here as elsewhere, afforded us an excellent
opportunity of seeing them, and observing all their differences of physical aspect, costume, relative cleanliness, and
so forth. And here I may remark that, from the same
cause, no doubt, we had continual opportunities of seeing
the people, and as our route usually lay along fresh lines of
thoroughfare, we must have had a passing glance of most of
the population of the city and suburbs. And very great
differences were observable, more particularly on this occasion, when the people of some of the villages appeared in
several respects so different from those of others as to
suggest, if not a difference of race, at least very marked
results of some form of exclusive intermarriage, either on a
small or a large scale. After a short drive—if one may
call that a drive in which there is no driving to be done,
the drawing being done by a man, and therefore in some
important respects an equal—we passed through the busy
forest-fed village of Udzumasa, and soon afterwards reached
Arashiyama, on the banks of the beautiful Oigawa, and
alighted at one of its three well-known tea-houses. From
the balconies of this house we obtained fine views of the
upper river, and of the high and richly wooded hills beyond.
The trees are chiefly cherry * and red maple, and when the
former are in flower, in April, the mountain-side is said to
present, and doubtless does present, such vast masses of
fragrant pink blossoms that the people of Kioto are attracted
out in large numbers to the place. In front of the village
the river spreads out into broad shallows, with contractions
of the bed in places, forming small rapids, down which boats
and rafts were frequently gliding, and up which the boats
were poled or punted with considerable skill. Large light
boats (formed of planks $1\frac{1}{4}$ inches thick, placed edge to edge,

---

* The Japanese cherry-tree differs
from ours, and is cultivated for the
beauty, colour, and odour of its
blossoms.

fastened by sunk nails, and caulked like the Japanese junks, with a fibre that swells in water) were prepared for us, as usual with tea, cigarettes, and other necessaries of life, and a number of local fishermen laid out their nets around a deep place, to exhibit the system of fishing there pursued. By stretching a net with sinkers across part of the stream, from the surface to the bottom, the ends being carried higher up stream than the middle, and by then stretching from these ends another such, but shorter, net, the boats and fishermen were inclosed, and the fish with them. The water being singularly pure and clear, the fish were then looked for, and when seen had a light hand-net thrown dexterously over them. Men, stripped for the purpose, then dived after the entangled fish, and brought them to the surface.

Our boat was soon afterwards taken in tow by three men, each with his own long and very light tow-line separately attached to her, a man at each end with a pole guiding our course, and away we went up the river, which almost immediately began to contract, and to pour down against us over a bed of immense rocks and boulders, and through channels so narrow that it seemed scarcely possible for our boat to pass. However, as we drew but about seven inches of water with twelve of us on board, on we went, smoothly gliding along the smoother places, and lifting up our bows and fairly climbing up the steep and rushing waters when the necessity was forced upon us. In some places the boat was but a few inches narrower than the channel, even in the steeper parts, and at others a way for boats had only been obtained by the building of a sort of loose canal wall in the stream at a boat's width from the shore. The day was fine and warm; the river pure and full of refreshing sounds; our tow-ers swift, our steersmen alert; and nothing was wanting to the success of the governor's kindly devised excursion. If any other excitement had been needed, it might have been drawn from one of the prettiest pieces of mountain sport that I have ever seen, which occurred before we turned our boat for the descent. High over our heads four red deer came bounding from the forest, and hurrying down streamwards as fast as their occasional bewilderment and hesitation would allow them. Presently, still higher above us, appeared the sportsmen, who saw their game but could not fire without running the risk of bringing down in our boat the first man of their own city, and a few others of less importance (his excellency was not with us), but still valued, doubtless, by some one or another. They therefore generously refrained for the time from what must have been a great temptation, seeing that even in England itself friends far too frequently get so eager after a partridge or a hare as to shoot each other's eyes out. The deer, however, seemed so little disposed to spoil sport that they made the best of their way toward the guns, and after a third discharge one of the herd came rolling down the hillside. It was brought to us for inspection later in the day (with the path of a bullet through its poor little innocent heart), and subsequently passed through the kitchen on its way to our table, and probably now is, more or less, a part of the brain that thinks and the hand that writes this.* The Oigawa River is as unlike the Thames as it could possibly be, but its wooded banks, or rather the wooded hills above them, are in places suggestive of the Thames at Maidenhead, only both sides of the river are equally fine, and the hills are continuous as far up as we went. The governor informed me that he frequently has to ascend the Oigawa to a place 8 miles above Arashiyama, and that it can be ascended for 20 miles from that village. On our way we passed several boats and trains of boats, shooting the rapids and sliding swiftly towards the city, and after a while our own boat was turned, and we commenced the descent in like manner. It was a repetition in miniature of the descent of the rapids on the St. Lawrence made six months before, and required as much knowledge and skill on the part of our pilots as is possessed by the old Indian who boards the Montreal boat for a like purpose, and settles

---

* This passage was written, of course, a few days afterwards.

down quietly and proudly to his task though devoid now of
his feathers and painted splendours. In many places the
thin bottom of the boat was lifted into a series of waves by
dragging over the rocks, but suffered little from it. A little
further fishing with lighter nets on a different system on
the Arashiyama bank completed our river experiences.

A mile and a half's drive after landing, along the wooded
bases of the hills, brought us to the Shinto temple of Mat-
suno Jinsha, which is one of the largest of those which the
imperial government support pecuniarily. It is a very fine
temple and beautifully situated, close to the foot of a
wooded hill. It was founded nearly twelve hundred years
ago by the order of Mommu-Tenno, who reigned from 697
A.D. to 707, but it has been thoroughly repaired four times:
the present buildings are three hundred and thirty-two
years old. It has three shrines, but only one god, Oyamaku,
and one goddess, with the interesting name of Ichikishima-
himeno-mikoto, which being interpreted means, I am told,
that she was the princess Ichikishima, and belonged to the
imperial family of the Mikado. The temple bore marks of
its association with the imperial family in the form of drapery
bearing the imperial crest, and of a pair of Korean dogs (or
lions, as some people call them, with little fear of being
proved wrong) in front of the principal altar.

Our drives and our river expedition having occupied some
hours, and stimulated us with plenty of fresh air, our
thoughts involuntarily began to turn towards our physical
refreshment, and I was not surprised to learn that this formed
the next part of the programme of our thoughtful hosts.
I *was* surprised, however, and delighted at the arrangements
which displayed themselves, when after another drive—
during which we passed a large government paper-manufactory and a macaroni-making establishment, both attracted
by the purity of the water—we alighted at Katsuranogobesso,*
the country seat of one of the members of the imperial
family, where luncheon was spread in an open room, with

---

* This palace was built by the great Taiko for the prince of Hatchijonomiya.

one of the most beautiful gardens that I have seen lying
steeped in sun and silence. The palace floor had been
covered with carpets and rugs of Kioto manufacture, and
furnished European fashion for the occasion, the table decorated with beautiful plants and flowers, while a boat hung
with flags awaited us on the lake, and in a lake-house screened
by trees a band of men-musicians discoursed the sweet strains
of Japan, so that all that man and Nature could together do
to make things pleasant had been done. Luncheon commenced, the band struck up 'Great Feast,' followed by
'Great Peace,' 'See the Conqueror marching back to his
Castle,' 'Long live the Son,' and other Japanese airs, some
of which appeared to me to approach much more nearly to
European music than any I had before heard. In 'Great
Peace' I was reminded of quiet passages in the 'Pastoral
Symphony' of Beethoven. During the tiffin, the susceptibilities of my son and myself were a little shocked by one
of the attentions shown us, which consisted in serving alive
a large fish taken in the morning, one side of it being almost
entirely carved to pieces; but the carving so done—this
being the proof of skill in the artist—that the fish was still
quite alive, and had, it seemed, a reproachful look in its
moving eye as it was handed round. I know that it is idle
to attempt so to live as

> " Never to blend our pleasure or our pride
>   With sorrow of the meanest thing that feels,"

for we are continually inflicting sorrow upon something or
somebody, and far too often upon some of the nobler " things
that feel; " but let us hope that we avoid this as often as
possible. At any rate, I was obliged to excuse myself from
sharing in the delicacy so much appreciated by some of the
party. In a little conversation which followed, I was reminded of our own mode of slaughtering calves and otherwise torturing animals, and had recalled to my recollection
the fact that until the civilising influences of Europe reached
Japan, and up to fifteen years ago, the slaughtering of oxen,
either old or young, was forbidden there, and considered to

be brutal. After luncheon, the governor did me the honour
of giving my health, and we then adjourned to the lovely
gardens, where for some time we gave close attention to the
music, and the instruments for producing it. A trip on
the lake concluded the entertainments of this very delightful
place.

We now drove to the great Toji temple, which is the chief
temple in Japan of the Shingon sect of Buddhists, founded
by the illustrious Kobo-daishi. It is sometimes known as
Kiyoo Gokokuji, and was first built ten hundred and eighty-
two years ago, by order of Kuwammu-Tenno (782–805 A.D.).
The principal buildings are as follows: 1. Sai-in, which was
originally the dwelling-house of Kobo, where hangs a likeness
of himself. It was last rebuilt five hundred years ago. Here
is Bishamon, one of the seven gods of wealth. 2. Jokido,
with a Kwannon of a thousand hands, over one thousand years
old, attended by four guardians of less age. Over this goddess there is painted on the ceiling an immense and splendid
dragon, in black and white, executed sixty years ago by an
artist, who received 200 *yen*, say £40, for drawing it. The
priest who kindly received us and showed us through the
temple smiled as he communicated this last piece of information, but whether at the munificence or insignificance of the
sum I know not. In this building, if I remember rightly, there
was a large collection of gods and lanterns, and other works
of art from other temples, and among them an exceedingly
clever group of three monkeys, one closing his eyes, another
his ears, and another his mouth, with his hands in each case,
possibly suggestive of things which so intelligent an animal
thought it well to avoid seeing, hearing, or speaking of.
We afterwards found this group to be popular and oft-
repeated in Japan. It must not be taken as unkind if I
remark that the gods do not improve in appearance or dignity
on being jumbled together in a crowd as they are here;
give one a shrine to himself, cover him with a curtain but
seldom opened, keep the people at a little distance from him,
set him in a dim religious light if seen at all, endow him
with great age, and treat him with a fair amount of reverence

and ceremony, and he must be a very poor image indeed if
he does not answer the only purpose for which, so the priest
positively assured me, he is ever intended, viz. that of reminding us of one whom we cannot see in person, and whom
it is most necessary to remember. 3. Kodo, where are to be
seen five large statues, and also a superb set of four holy
guards, the latter produced by the great Kobo-daishi himself.
It was not by any means by wood-carving that Kobo-daishi
made his reputation and became the founder of a great and
powerful sect, but these fine and vigorous works of his hands
indicate how great a force there was in the man. 4. Kondo,
wherein is another set of much smaller statues, about three
feet in height, but twelve in number, also carved by Kobo-
daishi, and indicating the same wonderful power in the man
as an artist. 5. Toba, or the Pagoda, which is 18 feet square,
and 180 feet in height. The first pagoda was burnt down
two hundred and forty-six years ago, and the present
structure rebuilt by the Shogun Iyémitsu. At present it
possesses but a poor assortment of images. There are in
these Toji temples other more remarkable gods, including two
called Bonden, each with three heads and four arms; but the
great charm of Toji to me—and it had a great charm—was
the fact of its standing, like so many other Japanese temples,
in a fine open wooded park, where the people cannot come
without benefit, and which supplies liberally that free
breathing-space which our cities and towns at home so often
need. I wonder whether the time will ever come again when
religious sects in our country will contrive to minister to the
minds and souls of the people in temples round which the
open air of heaven can freely circulate, and where in the
shade of trees, and with the conveniences of life provided,
they can be made to feel that religious worship can be associated with a noble regard for body and soul alike! At
any rate, I feel grateful to the priests and demi-gods and
Mikados and Tycoons of this country that they have not
made prisons of their temples, but have liberally secured
for the crowded people the blessings of air and light, and
all the other blessings which attend them.

I must admit, however, that life has not always been, and may not always remain, *couleur de rose* even at the Toji temples. The storms of war have ravaged them too often, and nine hundred years ago some of them were shaken down by an earthquake, together with other temples, and a few palaces in Kioto, no less than fifty precious priests being crushed into utter inutility in one temple alone.

From the Toji temples we drove by appointment to the great Shinshu temple of Nishi-Honganji, at which the archbishop of the Western Church had previously invited our party to share his hospitality. This is a famous and splendid temple, and a cordial invitation from the head of the (western) Shinshu faith to dine there was one which could not be other than welcome to a stranger like myself desirous of seeing the inner life of the country. Our reception and entertainment were in every way worthy of our host, who, with his brother, spared no pains to make us welcome and happy. At the entrance-door of the temple-palace we were received by the brother of the chief priest, who, after conducting and introducing us to his eminence, if I may so call him, and offering refreshments, conducted us through the temples, and then to a garden and a house which was formerly the summer residence of the great Taiko (Hideyoshi), with reminiscences of whom the place abounded. Here the chief priest, a man comparatively young, and of handsome presence—whose office, by-the-by, is hereditary—joined us and went with us over the place. The house was perfumed with sweet-smelling incense, and in one of the rooms the art of burning it ceremonially was shown in detail, and with various woods producing different odours, it being explained that one of the modes of amusing the guests of priests when time has to be past is to produce different scents, and set the guests guessing the wood from which it was produced—a pastime obviously requiring, for its successful pursuit, some experience of temple life and incense-burning. There was no time in the present instance to study this mode of amusement, nor even to see the ceremonial system of burning the incense fully carried out, but what we saw sufficed to show how pleasant a pastime the production of sweet-scented incense may be made. In the same room was shown another and more artistic form of pastime, a very pretty landscape with sea, formed in a tray with coloured sands, a piece of greystone that had belonged to Yoshimasa being employed as a rock or mountain in the model. In a tea-room was a letter written by the Taiko to an ancestor of our host, himself a chief priest of the sect and temple in Taiko's day. In one of the windows was Taiko's crest, formed by the mere cutting of the crest through a wood panel, showing the crest in light. We ascended a tower in this building known as Taiko's Tower, which had served as his private study, and in which he had, with great ability and ingenuity, painted a picture in gold dust, so laid on and placed with regard to the light that it was impossible for even the most privileged visitor to see it without bowing himself almost to the ground, of course in Taiko's presence.

After a long stroll through the buildings and gardens, we proceeded to the temple-palace, and there, in a very large room, sat down to dinner, a dozen of the principal guests at an upper cross table, our subordinate officers and attendants at a separate table at some distance from the others. On this occasion, as on the previous evening's entertainment, our hosts sat in the lowest seats at the main table, at two short side-wings arranged for the purpose. We dined at a table, sitting in chairs, but in all other respects the sumptuous dinner was served Japanese fashion, as I had desired, and included besides the usual luxuries some special ones, such as choice portions of whale, etc. Our hosts were most kind and considerate, occasionally leaving their seats and coming to make inquiries, or to give information respecting the dances. These were performed by the festival dancers of the temple, and accompanied by the temple band and singers—all men and boys. The dresses worn were those used at the great ceremonials of the church, and were quite wonderfully rich and imposing. The dances were also the ceremonial dances of the church, most of them being derived from India through China, but others of them being purely Japanese. Some which had been brought from China had ceased to be performed there, and can only now be seen in this temple. Although in China they were performed with songs, it was found that the songs were not suited to Japan, and consequently have never been used there. The first dance represented the movements of birds in a Buddhist temple in India; in the second, butterflies were supposed to be imitated, and this involved a certain amount of stepping and posturing movements which reminded one of European dances more than any previously seen in Japan—more especially of the preliminary movements of our ballet-dancers before the frenzy sets in. The third dance was purely Japanese, introduced seven hundred years ago, and performed in the old military costume of the country, the headdresses of which, with other parts, were the military fashion down to the time of the revolution of 1868. Outside of the banquet-hall, and visible through the far end of it, were large basket-torches blazing, as is usual when the festival dances are proceeding.

We had the very great advantage on this occasion of the presence of a highly educated priest, Akamatz, who had been to Europe to study and report on the religions of the West, and who spoke English very well, having been two and a half years in England. Ho took great pains to explain in a quiet way everything as it proceeded, slipping round from his place at the side-wing of the table for this purpose as often as it appeared to him desirable. It may be interesting to some of my readers to learn that this excellent priest, possessing a knowledge of England and the English, and also the chief priest who was our host on this occasion, find embraced in their section of the Buddhist faith all that they consider good and true in the Christian religion, and are not without hope of seeing England adopt this view, and with it the tenets and practice of their faith, which they consider most excellent.* It will be gratifying, doubtless,

---

* See a previous notice of Mr. Akamatz, with a paper from his pen, in the chapter on Buddhism (vol. i. p. 84).

to the many good people at home who look upon Buddhists as eligible for conversion to their particular views of the Christian religion (whatever they may happen to be in each case), to find their own generous and beneficent intentions so entirely reciprocated. And this may be the proper place to mention the figures given to me in connection with this, the Shinshu sect of Buddhists of Japan. The eastern branch of the Church has 10,000 temples and 4,500,000 believers; the western branch has 4500 temples, and 2,000,000 believers. What is the exact force of the word "believers" in this statement I do not know—any more than I know what is meant when I hear of millions of Christians in England. For my part I am always charmed to meet even a few people occasionally of whom it may in truth be said that they remotely approximate to one's idea of what a Christian professes and undertakes to be. But I know not where are to be found the millions of "the poor in spirit," the "meek," "they which do hunger and thirst after righteousness," the "merciful," the "pure in heart," the "peacemakers," and the others upon whom the author of Christianity pronounced his benedictions, and to whom he promised "the kingdom of heaven." However, there are perhaps many more likely to receive these rewards than some among us are willing to believe, and that is a great satisfaction.

In the course of the evening I ventured to ask the chief priest to favour me with an autograph writing from his hand—a thing very difficult indeed to obtain, as I afterwards learnt. He was good enough to comply, and wrote on ornamental paper a sentiment in favour of religious comprehensiveness.

At this banquet, as at former ones, the honour was done us of placing before us, towards the end of the dinner, a large and finely coloured model picture, wrought out of perishable materials—the large turnip, or radish, *daikon*. In this case also it was decorated additionally with flowers and other ornaments, which it was expected would be carried away by ourselves and other guests. At the conclusion some

time was spent in examining drawings, lacquer-ware, and
other works of art of a choice kind. We afterwards took our
leave, and drove away through the torches and the lanterns
and the crowd waiting outside, and by the time we reached
our lodgings we felt—and I hope my readers will admit—
that into this day, at least, a fair amount of pleasure, sight-
seeing, travelling, and excitement had been compressed.

The following day, quite early, our host of the previous
evening called at our residence to inquire after our well-
being, and to offer as a present—for the smallness of which
he made excuses—two specimens of the Kioto silk-manu-
facture: so that courtesy and kindness were carried to their
full lengths by him in this case. In return he requested
cartes de visite, and a piece of writing of my own composition,
and I accordingly wrote out for him a few verses of a poem
which I had amused myself by composing in the *jinriki-sha*
on the previous day—a long drive through a pleasant
country in a small carriage in which you necessarily sit
alone being very favourable, as already hinted, to literary
composition of the compressed kind, which poetry should of
course be. The subject of the verses, if I remember rightly,
was an attempt to reconcile the omnipotence of a god of
love with the manifold injuries done to man by the forces of
nature, and with the existence of so many creatures of prey;
for, as Tennyson says in ' Maud '—

" Nature is one with rapine, a harm no preacher can heal;
    The May-fly is torn by the swallow, the sparrow spear'd by the
      shrike,
    And the whole little wood where I sit is a world of plunder and
      prey."

Nor was the subject other than strictly appropriate to
one mixing intimately, as I then was, with the ministers
and followers of the gentle Siddartha (Buddha), whose soul
was so deeply moved by the same problem :—

" Then marked he, too,
    How lizard fed on ant, and snake on him;
    And kite on both; and how the fish-hawk robbed
    The fish-tiger of that which it had seized;

The shrike chasing the bulbul, which did chase
The jewelled butterflies; till everywhere
Each slew a slayer and in turn was slain,
Life living upon death. So the fair show
Veiled one vast, savage, grim conspiracy
Of mutual murder, from the worm to man,
Who himself kills his fellow. . . .
The Prince Siddartha sighed : ' Is this,' he said,
' That happy earth they brought me forth to see ?
How salt with sweat the peasant's bread ! How hard
The oxen's service ! In the brake how fierce
The war of weak and strong ! i' th' air what plots !
No refuge e'en in water. Go aside
A space, and let me muse on what ye show.'
So saying, the good Lord Buddha seated him
Under a jambu-tree, with ankles crossed—
As holy statues sit—and first began
To meditate this deep disease of life,
What its far source, and whence its remedy.
So vast a pity filled him, such wide love
For living things, such passion to heal pain,
That by their stress his princely spirit passed
To ecstasy." *

After the departure of his eminence we drove to an exhibition which is in course of formation at Kioto, in a palace formerly occupied by the mother of the Mikado. On our way we drove past and through the grounds of several palaces that had been abandoned by members of his majesty's family and by nobles since the transfer of the capital to Tokio. In one of these a permanent museum is to be built, and also a permanent exhibition building—illustrations of the great change which has passed and is passing over this land under the new system, of the best features of which the Mikado is the warmest supporter, I am told. There is in the part-formed exhibition at present chiefly articles of historic interest : among them, banners taken from the Koreans by the army of Taiko, dresses that had belonged to Taiko, writings on linen by the learned priest Kobo-daishi (who died ten centuries and a half ago), and articles brought by him from China, very old Japanese brocaded silks and

---

* E. Arnold's beautiful ' Light of Asia,' pp. 20–22.

embroidery, old Dutch tapestry, a cup from which an attendant of Taiko's son heroically drank a poisoned draught intended for his master,* a fan richly ornamented with pearls presented to Taiko by the king of Korea, two fans eleven hundred years old that had belonged to Shotoku-taishi, and a superb collection of old swords.

We next went to inspect in the same neighbourhood the carriage in which his majesty the Mikado used to move about on state occasions. It was a very large and heavy carriage, effectually shut in all round by close screen-work when in use, and drawn by an ox and by men together. Fortunately for the Mikado, he was not often required to avail himself of this mode of travelling, as he was so seldom allowed to leave his palace grounds. There was a similar carriage hard by. Our next visit was to a very long building containing an immense collection of old Chinese and Japanese drawings, and books brought together from the temples of Japan for permanent exhibition, including some portraits of large size brought over nearly eleven centuries ago from China. Among the books were histories and records of the greatest literary value, and the whole place appeared to me to be an immense mine of historic and artistic wealth, in which, doubtless, when it is made public, learned men will delve and toil with all that industry which they are known to bring to such work.

From these treasures we proceeded to the local government college, where the governor met us and accompanied us through the class-rooms. We spent some time in attending to the different lessons in progress, and were, with a single exception, much gratified with the tone and method with which the lessons were given, and with the obviously good relations between the teacher and pupil. This relation has always existed, I believe, in Japan, and is one of the things that one would regret to see changed. "The professors and teachers were held in the greatest reverence, and

---

* This rough old cup was purchased for five thousand dollars by a prince, who presented it to a temple and sent two servants of his own to permanently guard it.

Origin of the KAKE-MONO, or Hanging Picture.

From HOKUSAI.   Reproduced for this Work by a Japanese Engraver.

it was deemed the gravest offence for the scholars to show their impatience or their lack of interest by yawning, lounging, or moving their positions. Perhaps to this early severe training, carried on through many generations, are due that wonderful imperturbability of temper and that courtesy of manner which characterise the higher classes of Japan." *   One of the students of the college, in the second class, declaimed from memory a portion of Grattan's " Eulogy on William Pitt," with marked ability, and with but few departures from the pronunciation and accent with which a well-educated youth in England would have delivered it, while his emphasis was throughout strikingly good.†   Our next visit was to the mute and blind asylum for children, through the classes of which we went, not I trust without

---

* ' Outline History of Japanese Education,' prepared for Philadelphia Exhibition by the Japanese Department of Education.

† I requested the young gentleman to write out and send me the quotation; and I received from him, a few hours afterwards, a well-written note inclosing a clean and correct copy of the extract. His note ran : " To the Hon. Mr. Reed, M.P. Herewith please receive a copy of the extract from Grattan's Eulogy on William Pitt, Earl of Chatham, which you were so kind as to notice and request after my poor attempt at declaiming the same. I have the honour to subscribe myself, with high respect, yours sincerely, Y. Yoshioka. Kioto Chin Gakko, 28, 2, '79. P.S. —My age " (for which I had asked) " is sixteen years.—Y. Y." The first part of the piece recited was as follows; I give it for the purpose of showing that in forcibly declaiming such a strain of eloquence the student exhibited a very close acquaintance with both the solid and the rhetorical uses of our language : " The secretary stood alone. Modern degeneracy

had not reached him. Original and unaccommodating, the features of his character had the hardihood of antiquity; his august mind overawed majesty; and one of his sovereigns thought royalty so impaired in his presence, that he conspired to remove him in order to be relieved from his superiority. No state chicanery, no narrow systems of vicious politics, no idle contest for ministerial victories, sank him to the vulgar level of the great; but overbearing, persuasive, and impracticable, his object was England. Without dividing, he destroyed party; without corrupting, he made a venal age unanimous. France sank beneath him; with one hand he smote the house of Bourbon, and wielded in the other the democracy of England. The sight of his mind was infinite, and his schemes were to affect, not England, not the present age only, but Europe and posterity. Wonderful were the means by which these schemes were accomplished, always reasonable, always adequate, the suggestions of an understanding animated by ardour and enlightened by foresight."

compassion for the many little sufferers whose efforts to
reach by painful labours those elements of knowledge and of
pleasure which most of us acquired so easily were but too
pitiable.   So far as I could judge, the systems of instruction
pursued were like those employed in Europe, many of the
materials differing greatly of course from ours, owing to the
great difference in the character of the letters and other
symbols employed.   This visit concluded our morning's
round.

In the afternoon we visited some of the small porcelain
works of Kioto on the hill at the south-east of the town.
The articles produced are much admired, but as no special
orders were at the time under execution, there was little to
be seen of an exceptional kind.   Thence we proceeded on
foot to the temple of Kiyomidzu (Clear-water Temple), from
the front of which is afforded a fine view of the country
south and west of Kioto, showing the great military importance of the road stretching away to Osaka, and accounting
for the prolonged and bloody struggles that have there
taken place between armies contending for the mastery of
what then was the Mikado's capital.   It was at this temple,
and with this view before him, that the famous Taiko
Hideyoshi, whom one has so often to mention, was once
sitting, with his brain teeming with plans for the conquest
of Korea and China, and his heart sad because of the loss of
a child borne to him by his favourite wife.   But Mr. Griffis
shall tell the romantic story for us: "One day he went
out to a temple, Kiyomidzu, in Kioto, to beguile the sad
hours.   Lost in thought, in looking over the western sky
beyond the mountains, he suddenly exclaimed to his attendant, 'A great man ought to employ his army beyond ten
thousand miles, and not give way to sorrow.'   Returning to
his house, he assembled his generals, and fired their enthu-
siasm by recounting their exploits mutually achieved.   He
then promised to march to Peking, and divide the soil of
China in fiefs among them.   They unanimously agreed, and
departed to the various provinces to prepare troops and
materials.   Hideyoshi himself went to Kiushiu.   On his

way some one suggested that scholars versed in Chinese should accompany the expedition. Hideyoshi laughed, and said, 'This expedition will make the Chinese use our literature.' After worshipping at a shrine, he threw up a handful of one hundred *cash* in front of the shrine, and said, 'If I am to conquer China, let the heads show it.' The Japanese copper and iron *zeni*, or *kas*, have Chinese characters representing the chronological period of coinage on one side, and waves representing their circulation as money on the reverse. The lettered side is 'head,' the reverse is 'tail.' All the coins which the Taiko flung up came down heads. The soldiers were delighted with the omen. Maps of Korea were distributed among the commanders of the eight divisions, and the plan of the expedition and their co-operation explained." Hideyoshi's generals—for he gave up the idea of going himself—were very successful at first in Korea, killing ten thousand men in one battle, and pickling their twenty thousand ears to preserve them as trophies; but they had eventually to fall back, and to return home (as previously narrated), so that nothing came in the end of Hideyoshi's outrage upon the Koreans, and he died soon afterwards. I can hardly understand the state of mind of a man upon whom the beautiful and peaceful view from the front of the temple of Kiyomidzu can have had the effect which it had upon him; for my part, I felt as little disposed as I ever felt in my life to murder people even individually, much less by tens of thousands, when standing on the same spot, and I am very sorry Hideyoshi did not stop at home and amuse his generals with the invisible picture in his summer-house which I have previously mentioned, instead of going up there and fretting himself into a day-dream of ambition and conquest.

It is not only in front that the temple of Kiyomidzu presents a fine view, for at the back of it is a grand wooded amphitheatre, with a three-stream waterfall dropping veil-like through it. It has two pagodas, one of them small and one large. There is also a ten-leaved To, or square stone pillar cut into horizontal leaves, and good people, desiring to become better, or to get something which they want, throw stones and endeavour to make them lodge upon the To, they whose stones lodge getting what they want, or persuading themselves that they will get it, which amounts to nearly the same thing. The temple is reached by a long flight of steps, and the gate is guarded by gatekeepers, as is so frequently the case with Buddhist temples.

A descent south-westward, through a bamboo-plantation, and past the houses of some of the very poor people (small tanners, I think they were, and tanners have been held in so little esteem in Japan that in measuring road-distances the length of a town occupied by them has been omitted altogether as not existing*) brought us to the fine Shinshu temple of Nishi-Otani, which is under the control of the archbishop with whom we had dined the previous evening, and where the friendly priest Akamatz was good enough to receive us. Otani, I may say in passing, is the family name of the archbishop, and this temple contains many memorials of his ancestors. It is approached by a bridge of a peculiar construction, having two arches, each of which is a complete circle, so that it has become known as the "spectacle bridge." Nishi-Otani is allowed the privilege of employing the crest of the Mikado, which accordingly appears frequently in the construction and decoration of the temple. Besides the beauty of the temple itself, and its furnishings, there were several objects of interest; among them, some carvings of figures which had ornamented the vessels of the Taiko's Korean expedition; some very fine drawings of Japanese sea-dragons, and screens painted by Okio.

On the evening of this day the governor was so good as to arrange for our after-dinner entertainment a series of national dances, performed by a select but large number (at times) of the pretty dancers of Kioto. Before proceeding to the place of entertainment he presented me with

---

* This is also the case sometimes—or used to be—where roads traverse certain battle-fields.

an album of beautiful photographs of the once sacred city and its charming environs—a souvenir which I shall always highly value. I cannot describe, at length, the dances, although they were all more or less dramatic; but they served to illustrate and make clear many things that would be unintelligible in Japan, and especially in Japanese art, without their aid, more particularly as regards costumes and attitudes, which, while surviving in the various fine arts of the country, are now to be actually seen only in these dances. The principal compliment paid this evening was towards the end of the entertainment, when the professional dancing-girls gave way to a large number of young ladies of the place, whose parents had most kindly allowed them to attend for the purpose, and who danced with such individual and combined skill as to greatly surprise us. The orchestra consisted for the time of a dozen of these young beauties, for such they were, and fully twenty more of them advanced, not from behind the stage as with us, but from the front, along the sides of the hall. They were richly dressed in robes of the usual shape and size, but of black, red, and gold—with marked differences, therefore, from the dresses of the professional girls—and although it in some respects resembled a ballet in Europe, the decorum of the dances appeared to be quite perfect. At the conclusion, they came and ranged themselves, by special desire, in front of us, to give a nearer view of their pretty faces and dresses, and I should be glad if I had the power of preventing any part of their loveliness from decaying for many a year to come.

The remainder of our spare time in Kioto was chiefly spent in visiting silk- and *chirimen*-manufactories, dyeing-houses, shops for the sale of porcelain, bronzes, etc., and in strolling about the streets and witnessing the ways and habits of the people, so far as the weather, which was frequently wet and depressing, would admit. The perfection to which the ornamentation of silk and cut-pile fabrics is carried in Kioto, by embroidering, embossing, painting, and dyeing processes, is very remarkable, as is the low price of the many beautiful articles so produced. Some of the processes were quite novel, but they were shown to us readily, and apparently without reserve. The same remarks hold with respect to the beautiful Japanese *chirimens* and crapes. It is a trying thing even for a man, and it would be sheer torture for a lady, who has resolved not to spend much money to visit these shops and establishments in Kioto. To come away without putting yourself into possession of a good supply of these materials, which are always acceptable presents to ladies, is to develop, no doubt, a pronounced form of self-denial; but it is likewise also to subject yourself to reproach whenever afterwards you face your wife or your lady friends; ladies and their dressmakers are so clever in turning these fabrics of every colour and kind to pretty and picturesque account, and are so glad to have the opportunity of doing so. A Kioto china-shop is also an unpleasant place for John Bull, or any representative of his; the forms there given to teapots, cups, saucers, and a thousand other things are so pretty and various, and the colouring of them is so elegantly executed.

It is proper to say, however, that a part of one of these last days in Kioto was devoted to an inspection of another of those schools for instructing *geishas* and dancing-girls in needle-work and other useful matters to which I have previously adverted, and his effective support of which does the governor of Kioto so much honour. We also visited a training-school in which the national arts of music, singing, and dancing are taught. The business of this establishment seemed to be conducted with great order and system, and it was an interesting sight to pass through the little class-rooms and observe the poor elderly creatures, comparatively speaking, whose days of grace and fascination had for ever passed away from them, and who were now, as they fondly supposed, teaching younger ones how to master the mysteries of what was to themselves for evermore a lost art. Alas! the only instruction which they could possibly give must have been of the most rudimentary and formal kind; but happily for the young ones, youth, and the sagacities and instincts and inspirations of youth, could well be left to teach the rest. Wherever men were employed in teaching the young dancing-girls, they were invariably either old or blind, and generally both, and dreadful-looking into the bargain. If such a conjunction of beauty and horror is a necessity, it is certainly a very sad one.

We also visited a school where the art of ceremonial tea-making is taught. It is said that the practice of this art, which I have frequently had occasion to mention before, was originally established for the promotion of friendly relations at a time when society was much torn by factions and by war, and the spinning out of the time must certainly have been part of the scheme. Time is so precious nowadays, however, in Japan as elsewhere, that the ceremony is usually much compressed, and in this modern form it is pleasant enough. It is, however, declining, the peaceful pursuit of manufactures, commerce, and arts furnishing abundant opportunities for bringing people together in a friendly way.

There are several places and things of interest in and near Kioto which we had not time to visit. There is, for example, the great Dai-butsu, which, however, being of wood, and less ancient, is of greatly inferior interest to that of Nara. I am sorry to say that the Dai-butsu of Kioto is also a somewhat degraded personage as compared with him of Nara, for while both have been subjected to rough treatment from the powers of nature, the Kioto one has had to undergo the ill-usage of man likewise. It is sad to read· that "an earthquake took place on the fifth day fifth month second year Saiko (855), and the head of the famous Dai-butsu at Nara was thrown down;" but how much sadder to read that not only did the great earthquake of 1596 throw down Kioto's Dai-butsu, but that the great Taiko, on seeing it in ruins, became flushed with anger, and saying scornfully, "I placed you here at an immense expense, with no other purpose than that you might watch over and help the people, and you cannot even help yourself," discharged an arrow at the poor broken idol in its hour of impotence and shame. We had cause enough to be angry with Hideyoshi a few pages ago with reference to the wrongful determination which he came to when meditating in front of the temple of Kiyomidzu; but we hardly thought that a few years after he would be so rash and hot-headed as to fire an arrow at the very god whom he himself set up, and to do so, apparently, only because he had not set him up properly, or with due regard to the fact that Kioto, and indeed all Japan, as Japanese well know, rests upon the back of an immense catfish, which starts earthquakes every time it moves!

Our strolls through the streets of Kioto were highly amusing, especially when we took a turn along that street in particular which was principally devoted to the amusements of the people, and to the sale of tobacco and photographs. Here were the booths of the story-tellers; the waxwork heroes and heroines, respectively terrible and beautiful, and wonderful all; the conjurers, the tumblers, the loose-rope walkers; the working models of the unmentionable bad place, with the saws, and the augurs, and the other instruments for disintegrating the naughty, all at work by hand machinery; the curious animals, and the still more curious people that Nature sometimes makes in mistake; and perhaps more important than all, those long-tailed ancestors of ours who appear to have been made so without any mistake, and who linger superfluous on the stage now that their descendants have become as clever as my readers and I know ourselves to be. It was curious also to see, as we did here, peepshows of warlike scenes and battles in which were figuring several of the ministers, generals, and admirals whose acquaintance we had had the privilege of making in Tokio, and among them our distinguished host Admiral Kawamura, then in Kioto itself with us, but employing his time at the moment in a better way than that of peering into something even humbler than the penny peepshow of my native England. It was curious, too, to see in the photograph-shops these same ministers, generals, and admirals aforementioned, but here appearing, for the most part, not in their present

modernised and European attire, but in the quaint and
picturesque dresses and headdresses of Old Japan. On one
or two occasions I saw in the interior of Japan a photograph
of one of my own ships (as we professional men fondly, but
most improperly, call the ships we have built or designed
for others); and, after certain photographic experiences of
ours in Tokio, Nagasaki, and Nagoya, it is possible that
some of the travelling readers of this work may hereafter be
privileged to purchase the portrait of its author in the Sacred
Land for a few cents. I caution them, however, against
doing so, on the ground that Japan is a country in which
nature and art combine to produce much more pleasing
productions, and their money could therefore be better
laid out.

Then there is the village of Uji, which, if I may judge
by a photograph, is an extremely pretty riverside place.
We had arranged to visit it, but the probable condition
of the road after heavy rains deterred us. And then there
is the sacred mountain, Hiyei-zan, after which is named one
of the imperial corvettes which I had built for his majesty.
With this mountain are connected many important incidents in the history of Japan, and although we did not
ascend it, it was so conspicuous an object on our approach
to the city and during our stay in it, that I think it well
to condense into a small compass, in the following lines,
a few observations upon it from the pen of a gentleman
who went over it in 1877, notwithstanding the record in
previous chapters of the principal facts connected with the
famous temples of Enriaku-ji (here spelt Yenriyakuji) :—[*]

Ancient annals record that the first temple erected on it was founded
by Shotoku-taishi. In 788 a learned priest, Saicho, by command of
Kuwammu, the first Mikado of Kioto, built another temple, called, with
its surrounding shrines, Yenriyakuji. Saicho was sent to China to
learn the doctrines of the Buddhist sect, subsequently called Tendai,
which he introduced into Japan on his return. He brought back

[*] Condensed from 'Some Scenes
between the Ancient and the Modern
Capitals of Japan,' by W. J. Dixon.

Read before the Asiatic Society of
Japan, June 1878.

with him a thousand sacred books, and the first tea-plants ever seen in his country. Tradition further says that he transported from Mount Gotai in China the earth on which he built the first Japanese church of the Tendai sect. The new opinions prospered, and the temples on Hiyei-zan, comprehended under the name Yenriyakuji, increased to a large number, and became remarkable for wealth and magnificence. In the midst of their prosperity, and probably because of it, however, the priests began to take an active part in the feuds that distracted the country. Their temples became from their situation such strong castles that at length they defied the Mikado himself to subdue them. In the war between the emperor Go-Daijo (1319 A.D.) and the rebel Ashikaga, they, however, took the imperial side, and gave refuge to his majesty when Kioto was besieged. Their despotism over the neighbouring provinces at length became so unbearable that Ota Nobunaga resolved to take summary vengeance upon them, and this he did one dark night, burning the temples to ashes, and killing or taking captive the priests. In the time of the Shogun Iyémitsu (1623–49), however, the former splendour of these monasteries of Hiyei-zan was restored, and the spiritual power of the Tendai sect revived. Notwithstanding an attempt of the Shogun in 1627 to dispossess the priests of Yenriyakuji of their pre-eminence by transferring his favour to the new shrines at Uyeno, Yedo, they continued to flourish until the revolution of 1868, when, with other characteristic features of Old Japan, they fell into the background.

After describing his ascent to the summit of the mountain on a brilliant summer morning, Mr. Dixon says that they obtained from it a panoramic view of the sublimest description.

" On the north the whole extent of Lake Biwa, ' with promontory, creek, and bay,' lay calmly stretched for 50 miles to a dark mountain barrier. In the foreground its waters were overlooked by hills of the most luxuriant dark green, and its blue sheet was broken at intervals by white sails. To the east of these hills a shoulder of the mountain obscured a small portion of the lake, which, when it again appeared, was much narrower, and margined on the further side by a flat fertile shore, behind which the sand-downs traversed by the Tokaido rolled away to the hills in the horizon. Appearing right below us at the southern extremity of the lake were the thickly clustering houses of Otsu ; a little steamer was entering the harbour. Then to the south followed wrinkled hills, until the plain of Kioto came into view, with the city lying at full length, an oblong mass of brown varied with white in a green setting. The two tributaries of the Kamogawa could be followed until they met at the city's northern extremity and then united into one stream, the yellow channel of which formed two well-marked but unequal divisions of the area of houses. Numerous white spots indicated those buildings whose walls were plastered; one, long and horizontal, being evidently the Shogun's castle; and a space of thick wooding near the northern boundary marked what was at one time deemed the most sacred spot in all Japan, the secluded seat of the Son of Heaven. Cloud-shadows were slowly creeping over the plain which grew less and less distinct until it almost merges with the faint surface of the distant sea. To the west, hills beyond hills rolled away to the horizon like an ocean of billows. The summit of Hiyei-zan is marked with a little granite dome of from three to four feet high, and containing a stone image. The ascent from the point where we left our *jinriki-sha* took us about two hours, and the descent rather more than one hour. The height of the summit above the plain is 2700 feet, and, the latter being 300 feet above the sea-level, the total height of the mountain is 3000 feet.'

Mr. Dixon concludes : " These notes may fitly close with this panorama of the romantic region in which for so many centuries lay secluded from the world this venerable city of Japan, destined, let us hope, to be encircled in the minds of men with an even brighter halo than that which, in the days of the nation's childhood, the presence of the Son of Heaven threw around her. May the pearl become still worthier of its setting, for fair as any dream of elfinland are these sunny hills and shadowy glades." With this generous outburst of pretty but unsteady eloquence, I, too, will conclude my notes on Kioto. And yet, why should I not add that on Monday the 3rd of March I found myself so unwell, with chills and feverish symptoms alternating, that I resolved to remain indoors, and this I did the more readily as we had to commence on the following day our long journey of twelve to fifteen days in *jinriki-shas* through the interior of the country by the high road of the Tokaido, over which for so long a period the Daimios of the west and south had to wend their way every three years to Yedo (now Tokio), the capital of the Tycoons. Our friendly English-speaking priest, Akamatsu, of the Nishi-Honganji temple, came early to our residence, to present me with some poetic writing which he had been good enough to prepare at my request, and to again express the compliments and good wishes of

the archbishop and his brother.   Soon afterwards our recent
host, the brother of the archbishop of the Eastern Church,
did us the honour of calling and taking his leave, at the
same time presenting me with a fine example of his writing
on silk, together with a valuable tea-service of Kioto porcelain, the work of one of the best makers in the city.   Thus I
came into possession of friendly mementoes of my visit from
the heads of both branches of the great Shinshu body.   I
also received a visit from a priest of the great temple of
Chionin, which we had visited on the day of our arrival in
Kioto, and accepted from him a volume setting forth the
origin of the temple in the life of its founder.   Numerous
other memorials of our visit were sent in throughout the
day from friendly persons, including photographs, silks,
saké cups, etc.   I contrived to spend several hours in
writing, but was driven by illness early to bed.

TOWER OF NAGOYA CASTLE.

CHAPTER X.

THE SACRED SHRINES OF ISÉ.

RISING by six o'clock on the 4th of March, in spite of continued illness, our arrangements for starting were speedily completed, and soon after seven we commenced our lengthened journey to Tokio, intending to make the divergences necessary for visiting the temple of Ishiyamadera, and for then proceeding to the ancient and sacred shrines of Isé.* The governor of Kioto was good enough, with some members of his staff, to escort us as far as Otsu,

---

* "The temples of Isé, called by the Japanese 'Rio-dai-jin-gu, or literally the 'Two Great Divine Palaces,' are situated in the department of Watarai, at a short distance from each other. They rank first among all the Shinto temples in Japan in point of sanctity, though not the most ancient, and have in the eyes of the Japanese the same importance as the holy places of Palestine in the eyes of Greeks and Armenians, or Mecca in those of the Mahometans. Thousands of pilgrims resort thither annually, chiefly during the spring months, when the weather is most suited to travelling."—*Mr. Ernest Satow.*

on Lake Biwa, so that, with a further escort of two police
officers in front and two behind, our train of *jinriki-shas*
was fully as long as usual. It was a dull but dry morning
when we left, and soon reaching the Sanjo bridge we fairly
started upon the Tokaido, which takes its uphill way through
the eastern suburb of the city, and becomes a very fine
broad macadamised road, winding still upwards between
lovely wooded hills, as soon as the city is left behind.
After a mile of road, at the highest level, the Tokaido dips
down into a large open valley, from all sides of which the
clouds, which had been gathering there through the night,
were now rising like curtains of silken mists towards the
mountain-tops. The levels were studiously cultivated, the
hillsides liberally wooded, the road thronged with traffic,
and the sun was doing its best to shine on everything,
although under somewhat disadvantageous circumstances.

At a few minutes past eight we came upon the railway
works, which are in course of construction from Kioto to
Otsu, and which are afterwards to be carried by the lake-side
on to Tsuruga. This will open a direct railway route from
Tsuruga to Kioto and Osaka, so that the sea-borne products
of the northern part of Japan and of the great colony
of Yezo may find ready access to those great cities, and
by Osaka and Kobé to the capital, Tokio, instead of having,
as now, to make the long round by the straits of Shimonoséki.
For many classes of produce this will be a very great improvement. Before half past eight the beautiful lake of Biwa
opened before us as we descended towards the large town of
Otsu, situated at its southern extremity. Otsu is a town
of about forty thousand inhabitants, and has the appearance
of great prosperity. It contains several houses of European
aspect, several large schools, and an abundance of Shinto
temples.* The mayor of the district we were entering was
good enough to join us here, and provide us with tea and
cake at a lake-side house as pretty as any at Zurich, in

* In passing through the main   Shinto temples, although there pro-
street of Otsu I observed none but   bably are others in the town.

so far as scenery is concerned. Indeed the view down the lake is even finer than at Zurich, the hills on the right being more detached, bold, and picturesque. This is one of eight places from which the lake is supposed to be viewed with great advantage, and we were now about to proceed to another, still more celebrated. I may first mention, however, that Lake Biwa is by far the largest in Japan. It is 50 miles long, and its breadth at its greatest is 20 miles. It is therefore longer than, and more than twice the breadth of, the Lake of Geneva. It is narrowest at the southern end, which alone we saw, and contracts to a breadth of only about a mile at Katata, which is 10 miles off; but beyond that, north-eastwards, it rapidly broadens and becomes a splendid sheet of water.

The second of the points of view before-mentioned is Ishiyama-dera, the site of famous Buddhist temples, whither our friends from Kioto decided on accompanying us. The distance thither was not great, but we had to diverge from the Tokaido in order to reach the spot, and well were we repaid for doing so. Ishiyama-dera is one of the loveliest spots in Japan, or probably in any country. After ascending a long flight of steps one comes upon a natural platform, out of which stand up masses of sheer and apparently toppling black rocks, around and above which, on other rocky ledges and picturesque sites, is a crowd of temples, shrines, and pagodas, with trees springing everywhere from among them, and steps and terraces scattered about to facilitate the movements of visitors. The place is celebrated, as one can well believe, for its beauty by moonlight, offering on the one hand this picturesque massing of natural and temple scenery, and on the other a magnificent view of the lake with the Tokaido bridge crossing one of its branches. The temple is eleven hundred and fifty years old, having been built in the reign of Shomu-Tenno (724–48 A.D.), and parts of the original buildings, including a room into which we went, dated from its foundation. Ishiyama is particularly fortunate in its idol, for it has a Kwannon that—according to a paper lying at the door—is exceedingly generous in granting to people what they pray for. There is a curious legendary story connected with the founding of this temple, which I cannot profess to give with strict accuracy, but it runs somewhat in this wise. The Mikado, desiring to build a great image more than 60 feet high, with probably a temple to hold it, felt the need of money, and sent Sojio, a priest, to worship one of the Gongen gods, and inquire where gold could be found. Sojio did so, but was informed by Gongen that he would do better to worship and inquire of Kwannon. Sojio went to Lake Biwa, and consulted an old boatman whom he found fishing on the lake as to a suitable place for worship, and was informed that there was on the hill (where the temple now stands) a lotus-shaped rock very suitable for the purpose, the old fisherman disappearing after giving the information—thus proving himself to be a god. Sojio went to Kioto and obtained from the son of the great Shotoku-taishi a gold image of Kwannon 6 inches long, and conveyed it to the spot pointed out near the lake, there worshipping it, and inquiring where gold could be got. Gold was very soon after discovered in considerable quantities in the north of Japan, but unfortunately Sojio found that the gold Kwannon could not by any possible means be removed from the lotus-shaped rock, and therefore recommended the construction of a temple over the image.* The Mikado approved, the temple was built, and there it stands to the present hour; and although the Kwannon has but two hands in this case, it is, as I have said, liberal in the highest degree. The Mikado, in gratitude for the gold discovery, resolved to build a great temple in Kioto, and that, I was informed at Ishiyama-dera, is how the great Toji temple, already described, came to be built. While digging its foundations a precious ball was discovered, and Sojio made an image 20 feet high to contain

---

* A similar incident is recorded as the origin of the celebrated and splendid Vishnu Pagoda, near Trichinopoly, in India. A golden image of Vishnu was laid upon the ground by its bearer, Visbhishana, while its custodian bathed in the sacred tank, but to the dismay of all concerned the idol stoutly declined to be lifted again. A shrine had therefore to be built over it, and the shrine has grown into a temple, and the temple into a sort of sacred city.

it, and placed it with two others 8 feet high at the side
of it.   This is how the story was told to me, as a rough
translation of a printed paper which, with a portrait of the
goddess, was presented to us ; and although I cannot quite
make the dates and the Mikados of Toji and Ishiyama run
together, I have no doubt that all the substantial truth of
the matter is sufficiently embodied in the above version.
The ancient apartment already adverted to is celebrated as
the chamber in which a well-known Japanese work was
partly composed by a well-known Japanese authoress.   I
am afraid that neither the lady nor the book is as celebrated
in England as in Japan, but as I should be sorry to deprive
any large number of my readers of the pleasure of identifying
a literary celebrity whom they *may* happen to know of, and
as I should be proud to extend her present fame among my
countrymen, I will mention that the title of this work is
'Genji-monogatari,' and that the name of the authoress is
Murasaki-shikibu.*   This distinguished writer prayed to the
goddess Kwannon to aid her in the composition of her work,
and spent seven nights in the chamber spoken of in pursuance
of her task, and we must all be delighted to know that both
her piety and her industry have been rewarded in the widespread renown of her work.

But the time for lingering on this mount of mystery and
beauty is past, and we therefore descend to the level of the
common earth again, leaving the rocks and the temples and
the shrine of the goddess to another thousand years of
beauty and celebrity.   Before we re-enter our *jinriki-shas,*
our Kioto friends take leave of us, and we attempt in vain
to put in words our thanks for the kindness they have
shown to us—more especially the governor, to whose active
and personal exertions we owe so many advantageous opportunities of seeing the ancient city of Kioto.   We also took
leave with thanks of the mayor in whose district we now
were, and whose arrangements for our passage through it
were excellent and generous.   After regaining the Tokaido

* See *ante,* pp. 33 and 68.

and crossing the bridge, our course again lay through a very pretty hilly country, picturesquely wooded, and cultivated in the manner so frequently mentioned. The only remarkable feature of the road was its frequent passage across river-beds raised high above the surrounding country, and carrying the mountain torrents down to the lake. After lunching at the village of Ishibé, where some of the officers and servants of our party had already caused everything to be prepared, we pressed on through gloom and mist that thickened into rain, and preserved that form until we stopped for the evening and night at the village of Tsuchiyama, where in a native inn we found comfortable quarters prepared for us, and ate a dinner that would have satisfied every one but a *gourmet*. The only incident of the road, save the numberless small incidents of a passage through staring and amused villages, was the discovery on the top of a column by the roadside of the deaf, mute, and blind monkeys whose acquaintance on a smaller scale we had made a few days previously in the lumber chamber of the gods at the temple of Toji.

It was in heavy rain that we started next morning (Wednesday the 5th of March) to cross the Sudsuga mountain-pass in pursuance of our journey to Isé. The much too careful servants of the house began to stir about in my room at four o'clock, after which I slept no more, and before seven we were moving away in our *jinriki-shas*, the number of which had somehow increased to about eighteen. The rain had caused our *jinriki* men to don their wet weather apparel, which consisted of either sheets of oil-paper, supposed to be waterproof, or strips of matting round loins and shoulders, with straw hats of shapes and sizes so various that no two were probably even approximately alike : some were perfectly flat, others pyramidal, others parts of spheres, frustrums of pyramids, and bits of ellipsoids, while others were formed to nameless curved surfaces, or at least to surfaces which my geometry is insufficient to define with accuracy ; some were black and some were of the natural colour of the straw, some were large and some were small,

most of them were worn till we changed our men, but others
were slung up on the back of the *jinriki-shas* after the
wearer had become impatient of them, and others were
pitched to friends by the way as we passed through the
villages on our line of procession.   As to the oil-papers and
the straw mats, they got gradually dispensed with one after
another long before the rain left off; and whenever there was
a lull in the boisterous beauty of the scenery through which
we passed, one could amuse himself with observing the
competition between the soiling power of mud and the
cleansing quality of rain upon the naked forms of men from
the waist downward, as they toiled up hill and down for
hours together in a manner which it is very hard to reconcile oneself to.   Man is such a wonderful being even at his
worst, and out of the common crowd of men such marvellous
individuals come forth—ay, and what is to me far more impressive still, one sees even in the lowest classes of men, who
are put to do mere brute work, such a play of industry,
loyalty to duty, humour, intelligence, alertness, steadiness,
devotion, and many other virtues, that for my part I never
treat even the meanest of them with any asperity without
fearing lest I might have hurt the susceptibilities of some
mute inglorious being, or caused a better intellect than my
own to feel in some dumb way that—

> "Man, proud man,
> Drest in a little brief authority,
> Plays such fantastic tricks before high heaven
> As make the angels weep."

One is made to feel the force of this continually in these
Eastern lands, and nowhere more, I fear, than where we
Europeans lord it over the other races.   I was never quite
happy at Hong Kong when carried (as I admit you must at
present be there) upon the shoulders of the Chinese chair-
men; I am never quite happy here, among these poor
jinriki-sha men, dragging their fellow-men about in carriages
in all weathers, under all circumstances, often with attenuated
muscles and wasting lungs and breaking heartstrings.

After leaving Tsuchiyama we soon found ourselves among

the pilgrims: there is no mistaking them in any country where I have ever seen them, and this day they were numerous, for were we not journeying towards those most sacred, most universally reverenced, of all the shrines of Japan! In every house in Japan it is, or was, the custom to have some simple card or memorial of the gods worshipped at Isé, and here, on this occasion, were men, women, and young people from all parts of the country, with every kind of Japanese face, and every variety of Japanese costume, wending their wet and often weary way to and from these sacred spots.

After a long climb up what may fairly be called the mountain-sides of Sudsuga to the village of that name, we stopped a few minutes to change carriages, and then made the swift descent to Séki, at which place we were still on the Tokaido. This descent at Sudsuga is a most remarkable one, the main road being brought down the exceedingly steep side of the mountain by a series of greatly inclined slopes, alternating in opposite directions, the steeper portion being succeeded by a mile or two of ordinary road of unusually large gradient. The town at the foot of the descent is named Séki, and as that is the equivalent of "gate," and there was formerly a gate on this side of the steep descent just mentioned, I presume this was the site of the Sudsuga gate of the Tokaido. The scenery through all this part of the journey was not inferior to that between Coire and the Engadine, except in the absence of such very elevated mountains, none of this range of Japanese hills rising, so far as we could see, to what are known as Alpine heights. The beauty of the country could not, however, be easily exaggerated; lofty wooded hills of diversified shapes, rushing rivers, and endless changes of aspect all combining to please and interest the eye. We saw most of the scene under very unfavourable conditions, viz. in a heavy driving rain, but he must be but a poor traveller and a weak imaginer who cannot mentally sweep the rain-clouds from such a landscape, fill the valleys with sunshine, and dash the necessary sparkling lights on trees and streams. Besides, a landscape seen in rain, and especially a mountain-landscape so seen, has many and peculiar beauties of which the mere sun-worshipper knows nothing; and just as Emerson has felt exhilarated, as he somewhere tells us, in crossing a common through snow puddles, so may we feel and delight in the sombre beauty of rain-swept vales and hills, provided only we are in sympathy with it.   Early in the afternoon the weather cleared, as we left behind us the mountain ranges, and ere long the mirrored light of Owari Bay was seen in the distance, and passing through the large town of Tsu, and some of the most squalid and dirty villages that we have seen in Japan, we came at length about three o'clock into the town of Matsuzaka, and found charming apartments prepared for us within the gates of the Jodo (Buddhist) temple Jikiyoji.   Having lunched at Kobuta about noon, we had time to spare, and strolled through the town, to the great interest and amusement, apparently, of the inhabitants, and of none more than of the very young children, who in Japan seem at extremely early ages to employ their little bright black eyes in scrutinies worthy of more experienced persons.   Indeed, one wonders at what ages these little intelligences begin to be observant, for on one occasion— indeed, on the day now under review—I looked to see what was in a little bundle that a young woman was holding, and found in it a miniature man, who looked steadily at me as if surprised at my impertinence.   I was informed that this observant young person was ten days old.

In the course of the journey to Matsuzaka we stopped at a wayside shrine which has attached to it a religious legend that has points of interest in it.   Roughly speaking, it is this.   Nearly eleven hundred years ago a gentleman called Ononotakamura was banished for some disobedience to the Mikado, and his wife, who was sorry for him, wished to go into exile with him.   This, however, was denied her, and she consequently stole out of Kioto to the foot of Mount Hi-yei, where she lived for a time, and then started with a blind man by night for the sacred shrines of Isé.   Being unaccustomed to travelling, she got very weary on the way, and on reaching the spot where stands the shrine she inquired of a farming man the distance to the Isé temples. For the fun of the thing he told her that they were twenty days' journey, which was a great exaggeration, and this so discouraged the poor lady that she resorted to a device which shows that a lady could be as ingenious eleven hundred years ago as now. She decided on giving up the remainder of the journey, and praying to the gods from the spot where she then stood, either ignoring the remaining distance, or asking to have it treated for all practical purposes as non-existent. So, hanging some coins upon a young pine-tree hard by, she prayed, and submitted to the god her desires and solicitations. The god must have heard and attended to her, for by-and-by the farming man, on attempting to carry off the money that she had hung on the pine-tree, was frightened to see it turn into a fire-spitting two-headed serpent, which he dare not approach. He then inquired more particularly about the lady, and, repenting of his misleading reply to her question, himself "personally conducted" her and her blind friend to the shrines. The pine-tree was designated the "Hang-the-money-up" tree, a shrine was built on the spot, and whoever, being ill of any complaint whatever thereafter, ate a little piece of the tree, was pretty sure to get well forthwith. There is a very old-looking piece of a tree within the shrine, with some money hanging on it, but I am bound to give the Japanese credit for a very strict regard to truth in these matters. They never overdo, or much overdo, a miraculous affair of this sort. Had this occurred in Europe, in any of those churches and monasteries where I have listened to similar accounts, my informants would, I doubt not, have kept the original pine-tree in existence until now, and claimed identity with it for the withered limb or fragment displayed, and the coins likewise would have been the very coins brought by Madame Ononotakamura from Mount Hi-yei. But here, on the contrary, we were distinctly informed that the pine-tree in question died about four hundred years ago—and therefore lived less than seven hundred years!—and that it had been necessary to plant a successor in order to keep its memory green. I must acknowledge, however, that any one, Japanese or other, would naturally hesitate to propound even an exaggeration on a spot where a two-headed serpent had been known to spit fires in defence of the true and the right.

This town of Matsuzaka, where now we were, was the birthplace, in 1730, of a very eminent scholar and critic, named Motoöri Norinaga, whom I have had occasion to quote in the first volume (chap. iii.), and who, from his childhood, was remarkable for his love of learning. His father died when he was but ten years old, and his mother was left poor, so that he had to struggle with adverse circumstances in commencing his career. He was somehow sent to the capital, Kioto, to study language and medicine, and there deepened his interest in the pursuit of learning. He, however, returned to Matsuzaka, and commenced practice for the treatment of children. Another great scholar, Mabuchi, published about that time a now famous work, of which Motoöri obtained the loan ; and he afterwards was fortunate enough to meet Mabuchi himself. At this interview—it appears from Mr. Satow's writings—Motoöri spoke of his own desire to write a commentary on the *Kojiki*, the most ancient historical record (date 711) of Japan, and Mabuchi replied that he also had wished to explain the sacred writings, but in order to do this it was first necessary to get rid of the effects of the Chinese philosophy, and discover the genuine beliefs of antiquity. He advised Motoöri to direct his studies accordingly, which he did with such success that in 1764 he commenced his great work, the *Kojiki den*, which is an edition of the *Kojiki* with an elaborate commentary. It took him till 1786 to complete the first volume of the ancient book, but its success was immediate, and one of his biographers states that his fame drew to him nearly five hundred students from all parts of the country—poor fellow ! The second part was finished in 1792. He had a flourishing career, Daimios and princes competing for, the privilege of pensioning him. In 1801 he visited Kioto, where he lectured to crowds of admirers, including princes of the blood and court nobles; but the old King of Terrors ordered him back in the autumn of that year, and he has since reposed in a tomb previously prepared to his own order, in the monastery of Miôrakuji, near this place, Matsuzaka.

Our evening at Matsuzaka, being a very wet one, was spent indoors, and by degrees I was successful in bringing the conversation to bear upon the recent rebellion of General Saigo and his Satsuma men, in repressing which Admiral Kawamura took, as we know, a leading part, but concerning which he is usually silent. On this occasion his Excellency was good enough to favour me with a general account of the nature and circumstances of that lamentable rebellion, but I was afterwards told by an officer present at the operations which resulted in the overthrow of Saigo that I should have to learn from some other source how energetically and bravely the admiral himself performed his duty. This I was fortunate enough afterwards to do.

The following morning dawned with such a storm of rain and wind that it was decided to start later in the day than had been contemplated, and breakfast was deferred till nine o'clock, and our departure till after ten. By an oversight the *jinriki-shas* were later in coming, and the interval was spent in strolling through the town. Within the temple gates, however, was a building appropriated as a school for giving instruction in needle-work to girls, and a couple of dozen or so of the pretty little learners were at the gate indulging with many others their curiosity by viewing " the Chinese "; for the sight of a foreigner is so extremely rare in these parts of Japan that all foreigners pass with the inhabitants as people of the nearest foreign country, viz. China. We thought it unfair to those inhabitants to appear indifferent to the interests of Japanese girls, and accordingly turned towards the school to ask a few questions respecting it. But the beauties began " to back " at our approach, and retreated to the door, and, finding us still advancing, cast off their clogs, or pattens, or shoes, or whatever they may best be called, and spread through the house giggling and screaming with something that could not have been fear, and probably was not delight, so may perhaps have been amusement. We followed them in, and gently hunted them till we got them together, and then spent a few minutes in learning particulars of the school, which particulars I entirely forget. We soon separated from them for ever, as we have had to do from so many hundreds, ay thousands, of others, having at least shown them that "the Chinese" are not insensible to the attractions of their neighbours.

At the end of our stroll through the village, we stopped at the last tea-house to wait for our *jinriki-shas*, and there sat enjoying the surrounding light and warmth of the sun —for the day had become clear and fine—sipping tea and smoking cigarettes in the shade of a large Wistaria-tree, trained to serve as a roof to a bower, and in view of a very pretty garden, intended to attract the pilgrims, doubtless, on their way back from the sacred shrines. At length the *jinriki-shas* draw up; in we get, off we go, for eight or nine miles through sun that is hot and wind that is cold, and an atmosphere that is fresh and pure from the long rain-cleansings of the evening, night, and morning. The pilgrims thicken as we go, most of them walking or toddling, some of them riding packed in carts and little vans made gay with colours on the outside even brighter than the cheeks of the many plump and red-faced country-girls inside. The pilgrims are obviously mostly peasants, and, there being but little work for peasants at this season, they judiciously make their religious pilgrimages now. The fact of its being *their* season for the shrines, so to speak, is perhaps a reason for superior people choosing seasons at other periods. There was a good deal of shopping being done by these peasant-pilgrims, more especially by those returning, the trade done chiefly being in tobacco-pouches and straw hats—hats like those of the *jinriki* men mentioned not long ago. These broad hats, of all sorts and shapes, are such very odd adornments—notwithstanding their manifestly great utility as

screens from the sun in hot weather—that it was curious
to see people examining them and comparing them one with
another, and weighing in the delicate scales of their taste
their respective merits and beauties. But there they were,
holding them this way and that way, and viewing them with
nice discrimination, and after fixing upon and purchasing
one (I suppose for a very few coppers) carefully slinging it
in front, or behind, as Highlanders carry their shoes, to take
care of them, and then marching away complacently upon
their resumed journey homewards—home being in some cases,
probably, hundreds of miles away, beyond the mountains and
seas.   After crossing the rapid river Miyagawa in boats, with
crowds of villagers gathered picturesquely on both banks of
the river, and lining the streets of all the villages, to see the
foreigners and the party generally, and after a further short
drive, we alighted in Yamada, at the gate, or rather the *torii*,
of the outer of the ancient shrines of Isé, known as the
Geku, or Outer Palace.

Dating from many centuries before the introduction of
Buddhism into Japan, these are, of course, Shinto shrines, and
at the entrance we were met by two Shinto priests who had
been deputed to show us the sacred place. Passing under
the *torii* we were at once amidst trees of an age and magnitude not often to be equalled. This is such a country of
extremely tall, large, and ancient trees that no particular
notice is taken of even very striking examples, but I was
glad to observe that throughout these splendid temple-parks
of Yamada and Uji, in which are the most sacred religious
shrines of Japan, the finer and older trees were carefully
fenced in.   Within the temple limits we came first to a
small edifice in which was the white horse of the deity of the
place, which happened to be an artificial horse, the real one
having recently died, and another not being forthcoming at
present, for a reason which I did not learn. Soon afterwards we came to two living black horses consecrated to the
services of the temple, and more particularly for the god of
the place, Toyouké-himé-no-kami—" the god of food, clothes,
and house-living," as one authority explained it to me, or

"the god of the earth's produce," as another put it — to ride upon in the processions of the great temple ceremonials. As I could not get on the spot any clear and unvarying account of the gods worshipped at these Isé temples, I afterwards sought for additional information, but owing to the fact of their belonging to the mythologic period I could find nothing that was altogether satisfactory, especially as regards the sex of the deity of the Geku. The clearest account that I could get was that given in a translation by Mr. Satow of extracts from a compilation of myths from the most reliable sources by a native writer, Hirata Atsutane, observing that I propose to abridge the narrative for the convenience of this work, and to put it into my own language, so far as I may find desirable.

The history of the case runs thus : Amaterasu, the sun-goddess, sent Susanoö to search for a goddess named Ukémochi-no-kami in the central country of luxuriant reedy moors (Japan), and the messenger found Ukémochi, and solicited food from her. This request was responded to by Ukémochi, who produced food from her mouth and nose, and otherwise unpleasantly, thus angering the god Susanoö, who exclaimed, "Foul indeed, despicable indeed! Why feed me with foul things?" and, drawing his sword, struck Ukémochi-no-kami dead. On Susanoö reporting the matter in detail to Amaterasu, she was very angry, called Susanoö a wicked god, and remained secluded from him a day and a night.* Amaterasu afterwards sent Amékuma-no-ushi to see if Ukémochi was really dead, and the messenger found growing on the body of the goddess, in various parts, a silkworm, a mulberry-tree, rice-seeds,

---

* In Mr. Griffis's version of this legend, Susanoö (or, as he spells the name, Sosanoö) is the moon-goddess, and the punishment she received from the sun-goddess was, that she was degraded from their joint rule, and condemned to appear only at night, while the sun-goddess slept. But according to Hirata, the moon appears to be a masculine deity, for in quoting from his 'Koshi-Seibun' Mr. Satow says that while the sun-goddess was produced from the left eye of Izanagi-no-mikoto, from his right eye was produced Tsukiyomi-no-mikoto, also called Takehaya-Susanoö-no-mikoto; and adds, "this is the moon, a masculine deity."

barley, and a large and small bean, the head being changed
into a cow and a horse. On receiving these things, Amaterasu
rejoiced, saying, "These things are things which the beautiful green-human-herb eating may live," and she constituted
barley, bean-seeds, etc., of the dry fields, and rice-seeds of
the watery fields. Also she appointed lords of the villages
of heaven, and for the first time made them plant rice-seeds
in the narrow fields and the long fields of heaven, so that in
the autumn the drooping ears were abundantly luxuriant,
and ripened well. Also she planted the mulberry-trees on
the fragrant hills of heaven, and reared silkworms, and,
chewing the cocoons in her mouth, spun thread—the arts
of silkworm-rearing and weaving then commencing. As
Ukémochi-no-kami is identical with Toyouké-himé-no-kami,
the foregoing legend explains how it has happened that the
principal deity of the Geku came to be regarded as the
giver of abundant food, etc.[*]

There are secondary deities worshipped there, the chief of
whom is the adopted grandson of the sun-goddess and the
great-grandfather of the first Mikado, Jimmu-Tenno, who
commenced his reign in the Japanese year 1. According to the
legend, says Mr. Satow, the goddess wished to send her adopted
son, Oshi-ho-mimi-no-mikoto, down upon earth to subdue it,
but he put forth his own son instead as leader of the expedition.
The goddess then presented Ninigi-no-mikoto with various
treasures, amongst which—and here we touch upon the
central sacredness alike of the race of Mikados and of the
symbols of the Shinto faith—the most important were the
mirror, sword, and stone or ball (afterwards the regalia of
the Japanese sovereigns), and attached to his person the
other two inferior gods of Geku. With reference to the
mirror, she said, "Look upon this mirror as my spirit, keep

---

[*] " The principal deity worshipped
at the *Geku* is Toyouké-himé-no-
kami, called Ukémochi-no-kami in
the Nihongi, and Ogetsuhimé in the
Kojiki. *Toyo* means abundant ; *uké,*
food ; *himé,* lady ; and the whole
signifies ' abundant - food - goddess.'
Ukémochi-no-kami signifies the ' food-
preserving-god.' . . . Ogetsu-himé-no-
kami means ' goddess of food.' "—
Satow.

it in the same house and on the same floor with yourself, and worship it as if you were worshipping my actual presence."

To resume our narrative :   Passing under another *torii* (of plain unpainted timber, like all the *torii* of these Isé shrines), we came to the outer gate of the temple proper, to which alone of three successive gates we and the other pilgrims were allowed to approach. With certain extremely rare exceptions, extending only to the Mikado and commissioners of his, none but priests are allowed to pass this first gate. It was an open gate, however, with a simple white cloth or curtain hanging across it, blowing about as the wind listed. Through this open gate, or past the sides of it if you preferred to stand there, you could see the next gate, and beyond that again was a third, and then came the temple proper, which could not be seen.   This was all !   The buildings, as far as seen, were all of the plainest possible kind, not unlike substantial well-thatched farm-buildings at home. The mirror at this outer temple was not the original mirror, and the priests did not for a moment leave us to suppose that it was.   There was, in fact, no pretence of any kind about them ; but the ancient buildings and the plain white curtain were left to produce that which is perhaps the deepest and most lasting of all impressions made by religious externals, viz. that of combined simplicity and antiquity.   Of this outer temple I need only add that it is in every respect a sequel and appendage to the inner and more ancient temple presently to be mentioned, having been built by the desire of the goddess of the older Isé temple, who wished to have the deity Toyouké near her.   This, the outer and later temple, dates from the reign of the twenty-second Mikado of the present reigning dynasty, Yuriaku, in the year 479 A.D. Before her removal here at that date this goddess had been located in the village of Ma-na-i-wara, in the province of Tamba.

On completing our visit to this outer temple, the Geku, in Yamada-wara, we proceeded on through that village to a private house which had been placed at our service, situated on the highest ground of the adjacent village of Fruichi, and with extensive views across rice-fields and gardens to the mountains beyond. Here we took luncheon, and soon afterwards started for the inner temple, Naiku.* Here is kept the original sacred mirror, which is the most precious emblem of the Shinto faith, and is likewise, with the sacred sword and ball, the authenticating memorial of the imperial dynasty, regarded as all Japan regarded it for two thousand five hundred years, down to 1868, and as most of the people regard it still. This temple came to be built in the following manner. The sacred emblems of the national religion had, up to the time of the great Mikado Sujin, been kept in the imperial palace or temple; but he, as some say to increase their safety, and as others allege because he viewed a rebellion which broke out as a mark of divine disapprobation of their remaining in his custody, gave them into the charge of his daughter, in a temple dedicated to them. They were subsequently removed and carried from place to place, but at length, in the twenty-sixth year of the reign of Suinin-Tenno, and therefore in the year 3 B.C., it was resolved to fix the mirror at the village of Uji, on the river Suzugawa, and there and then the present temple was built.† The old

---

* The distance between the two temples must be between two and three miles; there are houses nearly the whole way.

† Mr. Griffis, in 'The Mikado's Empire,' states that the sacred emblems, the mirror, ball, and the sword, are in the Uji (Isé) temple; but this must be a mistake, as I was assured by the priests at Uji (Isé) that only the mirror is in their temple—the ball, they said, is in the Mikado's palace, and the sword at Atsutu, in Miya, which temple, as will be seen later on, we afterwards visited. In his paper on the 'Revival of Pure Shinto,' Mr. Satow, while silent as to the whereabouts of the sacred ball, correctly states the facts with regard to the mirror and sword, speaking of the sword as

"enshrined at Atsutu in Owari," and of the mirror as "worshipped at the Naiku in Isé as the representative of the goddess of the sun." Considering that the Isé temples are the most sacred and apparently the purest Shinto temples in Japan, it is not a little startling—and is an example of the strange difficulties that obstruct the rapid acquisition of clear information in Japan—to find Mr. Satow himself, in his paper on these shrines, saying: "It has been observed that Shinto temples often contain a mirror placed in a prominent position, and this mirror has been supposed by foreigners to be their distinguishing mark; but it is only to be found in those which have been under the influence of Buddhism. It is absent

building does not exist; on the contrary, a new temple is erected every twenty years; but each new temple is an exact repetition of the original, and therefore the present one is a perfect representation of the architecture of Japan at the time of Christ. The principal deity here worshipped is Amaterasu, the sun-goddess herself, as will have been inferred from what has been said before. Mr. Satow considers her as neither more nor less than a deification of the sun. Her chief name (for she has several) signifies literally the " From-Heaven-Shining-Great-Deity." The other deities worshipped are Ta-jikara-o-no-kami and Yorozu-hata-toyo-aki-tsu-himé-no-kami, of whom it is unnecessary to say more here.

On passing from Fruichi to Uji, which lies at the foot of the hills, embosomed in ancient woods, the river Mimosusogawa has to be crossed by a fine bridge, at either end of which is a large *torii*, indicating the approach to a temple of the Shinto religion. After crossing the bridge into the village of Uji, our *jinriki* men, guided by local municipal and police officers, turned to the right, and passing up the main street of Uji, through the interested and interesting inhabitants, and between such ranges of well-to-do shops as indicate that the pilgrims in the aggregate are pretty large purchasers, we passed under another *torii*, and into the temple precincts. A curving avenue of magnificent trees led us through a park of equally fine ones, past a building in which the priests preach to the people, past another in which reside more of the sacred horses kept for the convenience of the goddess, past another in which the religious

---

from all the pure Shinto temples." This is perfectly true, because Mr. Satow has been careful to introduce the words " placed in a prominent position," which the Isé mirror certainly is not, and from such a position it is true that the mirror is absent from the Naiku; but that a mirror is there, and is an object of worship, Mr. Satow's own words, quoted previously, properly state. It is, however, concealed from view. In pure Shinto temples there are no visible objects of worship, but at the Naiku the representation of the deity is nevertheless the hidden sacred mirror; and usually the spirit of the deity is supposed to be enshrined in some concealed object known as the " August Spirit-Substitute." or " God's-Seed. '

dances of the temple are performed, and then was reached a
flight of stone steps leading to the first gateway of the sacred
place.   Here the priests, who had met us at the entrance to
the temple grounds, kindly presented me with plans of the
two temples, and a brief written history of them, adding
such oral explanations as occurred to them, and answering
whatever questions it occurred to us to put.   The gateway
was open, and hung, like that of the other temple, with a
long white curtain, and beyond were seen another *torii* and
other gateways, but nothing could be seen of the temple
itself, and as little, of course, of the heaven-wrought mirror
within.   As we stood, however, the pilgrims continued to
come, of both sexes and of all ages, and casting upon the
ground a few coins, some wrapped in paper, stooping, clapping their hands, and uttering a few words of prayer, thus
attained and completed the object for which their journey-
ings had been undertaken.   I asked if this was all they saw
and did, and was told that it was.   I inquired if they
attended no religious service, saw no dances, heard no music,
received no advice; and found that as a rule they did not.
Was no blessing pronounced, no simple memorial of some
kind presented to them?   Nothing; but they all bought
little mementoes of the place at the stall in the grounds or
at the shops in the village.*   What was it they said during

---

* " In every Japanese house there
is kept what is called a *kami-dana*,
or 'shelf for gods,' which consists of
a miniature Shinto temple in wood,
containing paper tickets inscribed
with the names of various gods, one
of whom is invariably Tensho-ko-
daijiu, the principal deity of Isé.
This ticket, or rather paper box, is
called *o-harai*, and is supposed to
contain between two thin boards
some pieces of the wand used by the
priests at Isé at the two annual festivals in the sixth and twelfth months
of the year.   These festivals are
called *o-harai no matsuri*, and are
supposed to effect the purification of

the whole nation from sin during the
preceding half-year.   Every believer
who has one of these *o-harai* in his
kami-dana is protected thereby from
misfortune for the next six months,
at the expiration of which time he
ought to exchange the *o-harai* for a
new one, which he must fetch from
Isé in person; but in practice the
o-harai is only changed once a year,
perhaps less often.   The old ones
ought to be cast into a river or into
the sea, or may be destroyed by burning.   They are usually employed to
light the fire which boils the water
for the bath prepared for the *miko*,
or virgin priestesses, after their dance

the minute or two that they stooped before the shrine?
They no doubt asked for whatever they wanted in particular,
and generally for long life, and the means of life and happiness in the years to come.

As a pilgrim myself I desired to see and learn a little
more, and therefore I gladly fell in with the suggestion of
the priests, who proposed that we should go round to the
side of the temple inclosure and get a look at the buildings,
and especially at the shrine or temple itself, from an eminence
which afforded this.   This we did, and had a very good, and
for all practical purposes a sufficient, view of what we came
to see.   Of course we did not see, nor did we expect to see,
the mirror itself.   Years upon years roll by without the
chief priest himself seeing even the case containing it, and
the other priests are not admitted into the building
without good cause.   However, there was the temple, looking just as it had looked when Christ was born, or nearly
so, and, as already said of the outer temple, the whole
appearing not unlike a substantial set of farm buildings.*
Inside of the door we were looking at was the mirror
itself, and therefore nothing was wanting to complete the
success of our pilgrimage.

Our agreeable companions the priests, however, most
kindly suggested that we ought to see one of the ceremonial dances of the temple, and to this we gladly assented,
on learning that it would not be a repetition of what we had
seen at Osaka and at Nara, but one of the most ancient

---

in honour of the *uji-gami*, or patron
god of the locality, at his festival.
Up to the revolution in 1868, as it
was practically impossible for every
householder to fetch his own *o-harai*
from Isé, there existed a class of
persons, called *oshi*, who made it
their trade to hawk the *o-harai* about
the country, selling almanacs at the
same time.   This practice has been
lately prohibited by the Mikado's
government, and they can now be
obtained only at the temples them-

selves or at the recognised agencies."
—'The Shinto Temples of Isé,' by
Mr. Ernest Satow, read at the Asiatic
Society of Japan.   Mr. Satow's is
doubtless a much fuller and better
account of these ancient temples than
mine, but I have thought it best to
tell my own story in my own way,
without attempting to rival, in any
degree, his more scholarly and studied
account.

* See small engraving on p. 38,
vol. i.

description, handed down from generation to generation at
these Isé shrines.   The room had an altar at the end
opposite the entrance, over which was a large mirror. Round
the altar and walls were an abundance of *goheis*, and of
bands and tassels.   At the altar end of the room sat on one
side a priest, and along each of the side walls were the
musicians and dancers, all sitting on their heels.   The
musicians, who were also singers, were all men; the dancers
were quite young girls, attired in white and red, with
frontlets of brass, from each end of which depended a cord
and tassel.   On the tops of their heads were large bunches
of flowers; their back hair was in a *queue* with tassels
attached, surmounted with gilt bows and ribbons.   There
were two equally young girls in red and blue with plainer
headdresses, who in a certain way attended on the others.
The dance began by a subordinate priest or attendant coming
in by a side entrance with a wet branch of the sacred *sakaki*-
tree in his hand.   After bowing to the shrine he turned to
the visitors, and waved it a few times swiftly before them,
then disappearing. Returning again to the same entrance, he
handed in to the two blue-and-red attendants trays of herbs,
rice, and fruits in succession.   These were borne, cere-
moniously elevated, to the six priestesses, who conveyed them
in a similar manner to the altar, placing the contents of the
first two trays upon an inner altar, and those of the remaining four upon an outer one, returning the trays to their two
attendants, who passed them out of the building.

   While this was proceeding, the band sent forth what
sounded to me as wailing, imploring, importunate sounds, with
an occasional blow upon the drum for emphasis.   The priest,
who wore the ancient headdress, like that of the Mikado,
now rose, and after a few obeisances before the mirror sat
down (upon his heels) facing the altar, and intoned a prayer,
or *norito*, from a large sheet of paper held outspread before
him, the musicians and dancers and attendants all sitting with
bowed heads to its end.   Small branches of *sakaki* were now
brought to the priestesses, and the dance took place, to the
accompaniment of livelier music than before, the dance

comprising no very active movements, consisting mainly of short, slow, and grave promenadings, with occasional stately bowings, and much slow waving of the branches. This over, a boy entered dressed in the military undress robes of a *kugé* (court noble) of the olden times, and holding in his hands a branch of *sakaki*, with a pendant hoop, doubtless in lieu of a mirror. He danced, as it is called, to much louder music, but the dancing was little more than further promenading and making certain sweeping movements with the *sakaki*-branch, with an occasional high step. Of course it is a great pity for the significance, if any, of all this to be lost upon me and my readers, but nothing explanatory could be elicited from any of the Japanese present, and from the answers of the priests I infer that if the various movements of these dances ever had any great and special significance, the remembrance of it is pretty nearly or quite lost. The priest next came forward again, and, after elevating the written prayer a few times before the shrine, left the building by the side door. The process of placing the fruits, etc., upon the altar was now reversed, and everything was removed from the altars and taken away, the music the while playing loud and joyous strains. With this ended the most ancient of the dances in the most sacred of the purely national shrines of Japan.

The priests who had accompanied us round the temples were good enough to present me, in addition to the plans already mentioned, with a drawing of the dance which we had seen, and some reports of the revenues and expenditures of the temples. The priests number fifty-nine in the two temples. Later in the day they kindly sent me a drawing of the house we were staying in at Fruichi, and a Uji cup each for my son and myself, as further memorials of the place. Before leaving the grounds of this temple we obtained some of the papers such as other pilgrims take away as tokens of their pilgrimage, so that all the objects in view in our visit to the Isé shrines were now fulfilled. It was not possible, however, to leave these ancient woods, consecrated by the cares and prayers and pilgrimages of

millions upon millions of these good and kindly Japanese
people, and with such an air of antiquity about the great
broad-based, high-towering, time-worn trees, without once
more wandering a while in their solemn shade. At last we
passed out by a side road into the world of shops and follies
which had forced itself up to the very gates, and there for the
first and only time in Japan we found the touting system was
in full play. It was confined, however, to the first few shops,
and as the touters were pretty, nicely attired girls, one
soon forgave them, and entered into both the shops and the
follies like any other pilgrim. Then, betaking ourselves to
our *jinriki-shas*, we returned home to Fruichi, only stopping once to enter for a moment or two one of the many
places of amusement for pilgrims which exist near the
shrines, both in the villages and on the highway.

Some of the party who shared with us this visit to the
ancient temples of Isé seemed disappointed that we should
have had to go so far and see so little. But upon me their
effect was more impressive than anything of the kind which
I had seen in Japan. I suppose this was in part, at least, due
to the fact that we were there in undoubted contact with the
ancient life and the ancient faith of the country. However
mythical may have been the origin of the Shinto religion,
wherever the mirror may have come from, whatever the
degree in which the historic and the legendary may have
been mixed in the stories of the early Mikados, these
temples undoubtedly were for age after age, and century
after century, before Buddhism was known here, the objects
to which the thoughts of every Japanese and the steps of millions were directed. In fixing the dates which I have given, I
have followed the only records that profess, so far as I know,
to be authentic, and they are those given, I believe, although
sometimes with reserve, in all books now published on the
subject. At the same time I do not ask the reader to accept
them without some modification, and for the reason that to
make them good some of the subsequent Mikados must have
lived, as stated in a former chapter, to ages which, if not
absolutely impossible, as many will pronounce them, are

certainly improbable. Sujin-Tenno, who was the first to pass the sacred mirror out of his keeping, is said to have died at the age of one hundred and nineteen. Suinin-Tenno, who succeeded him, and ordered the building of this temple at Uji, lived to such an age that he must have been ready on entering it to exclaim with Tithonus—

> " Cold my wrinkled feet
> Upon thy glimmering thresholds, when the steam
> Floats up from those dim fields about the homes
> Of happy men that have the power to die,
> And grassy barrows of the happier dead."

He was one hundred and forty-one years old when released. His successor, Keiko-Tenno, is credited with a still longer life, dying at the age of one hundred and forty-three. Still whatever errors of chronology may have got into these early records, here at the Uji and Yamada temples we are in undoubted contact with the earliest historic embodiments of the Shinto faith, and look upon buildings exactly like those of Japan at the commencement of the Christian era. Along the roads over which we travelled, into the woods which we entered, up the hillside which we ascended, men and women had been coming and going through many generations, with this religion and shrines like these their only religion and their only shrines, just as we saw them coming and going to-day. Yes, still they come and still they go, caring, hearing, knowing nothing of all that which we at home consider to be the very essence of our faith, and without which many declare real religion to be impossible. He that runs may read the moral.

Although going late to bed on the evening of the shrine-visitations, so to speak, we had to be up and at breakfast by six the next morning, Friday the 7th of March (in order to allow the servants to pack our luggage and such articles of domestic use and provisions as were carried about for our convenience), and therefore at half past five I was aroused by the throwing open of the sliding sides of the house, and the letting in of the morning light. And how much more than mere light was let in ! So beautiful was the landscape dis-

played that even the native servants were loud in their
expressions of admiration. It was "A Study in Blue and
Gold" worthy of the name: the "gold" was the sky steeped
in the up-streaming splendour of the sun, as yet itself unseen;
the "blue" was the thin veil of vapour drawn across the
deep and branching valleys, woven of the night-mists and
the dawn. And there was very much more than the blue
and the gold: there were dark hills below the one and above
the other; there were the rice-swamps gleaming like mirrors
between the mists and us; there were trees and wooded islands
rising softly out of the mists; and there were many other
beauties, so pure, so delicate, so tender that I dare not blur
and injure them by attempting to paint them with my poor
pen. Ah me! yesterday was spent at the shrines of a
mythic relic of the sun-goddess of Japan; this day opens
with the rising of the sun-goddess herself—sun-goddess not
of Japan only, but of every land, and of many another world
besides ours! And yet no goddess she! Our sun in all its
glory is but one of the countless myriads of lights that blaze
for ever in the Temple of Immortal Splendour wherein it is
our privilege to worship. In that temple there is no shrine,
for the deity penetrates every part of it—no music, for its
silence is more impressive than any sounds—no dances, for
the mystic mazes of the starry motions are for ever unfolding
themselves—no priests, for its only devotions are the love
and the pursuit and the possession of truth. But, alas!
alas! a temple like this, always open and always present,
does not suit the multitudes of men. They must have books
and bits of paper, and singings and fifings and drum-beat-
ings, and clappings of hands, and standings up and kneel-
ings down, and bowings and facings about, and creeds and
formularies, and litanies and noritos, and a thousand other
inventions and contrivances; and what they demand in that
way there are always plenty to supply them with in this
and every country, and in this and every age.

At 7 A.M. our imposing procession of *jinriki-shas* was once
more in movement and rattling back to the Miyagawa.
Very pretty was the crossing of the river in the ferry-boats

in the early morning light, with the banks again crowded
by the cheerful country people; and very pretty also the
picture afterwards formed while we were walking for a
mile along the bank of the river—formed of our little
carriages with their brightly painted surfaces and brass
fittings, their red rugs, and their men chiefly in blue, with
a village hard by flying a few flags, and massing a little
crowd of its populace as a background for our picturesque
party.   A blue sky bent above, a bright sun shone down,
a fresh breeze blew past, and everybody present seemed to
share in the exhilaration of the hour—everybody except the
passing pilgrims going shrinewards, who, as they neared the
object of their long marchings and toilings, appeared to give
way somewhat to their weariness; so at least I fancied.   But
the pretty picture was speedily broken up when we reached
the group of *jinriki-shas*, and away we went again, to the
monotonous music of the men who dragged us along.   I
often tried to catch the words they employ in the partly
choral and partly responsive noises which they make, but
they are usually too indefinite, not to say inarticulate, for
me to be sure of them.   On the way to these Isé shrines,
however, on a wet afternoon, I was successful in distinguishing clearly the burden of their song, or rather of two of
their songs.   One was, as well as I can spell it —

> " Ew-y, tow-y, Ew-y, choss?
> Ew-y, tow-y, Ew-y, choss? "

the "choss" being spoken in a tone of emphatic inter-
rogative.   And the other was—

> " Sherry, sho-y, sherry, choss? "

which I need not write down again, as the reader can repeat
it to himself as often as he finds it amusing.   I tried to
discover if these or similar sounds mean anything in particular, but could not find that they do.   If they do, my
readers must kindly remember that I am ignorant of even
elementary Japanese, while these expressions of opinion,
feeling, inquiry, or whatever else it is that they express,

doubtless belong to the most recondite refinements of class language.

Pilgrims, still pilgrims, always pilgrims this morning, at every part of the road! I suppose it is the fine and bracing morning that draws them out and along the road to Yamada and Uji in such numbers. And how interesting it is to observe their faces as they pass! We speak of sculpture galleries, and go into artificial ecstasies over the poor expressionless stones of a Gibson (mostly, though not always, poor and expressionless, or expressive of something not worth expressing, as I think), and yet are often without the faculty of observing the wondrous sculptures of the streets. Here are people by hundreds, and even thousands, and in the cities and towns of Japan that we have already passed through we must have seen many hundreds of thousands of them, all roughly shaped at first by race, family descent, climate, soil, food, and other general influences; and with all the lighter and finer lines afterwards put in by personal habits, cares, joys, sorrows, loves, terrors, and all the thousand other industrious artists whose chisels and files are for ever toiling away upon the few square inches of the human face. To me the interest of their works is inexhaustible, and I know not whether the most interesting of all are not those faces on which ignorance, want, neglect, and squalor have wrought their evil work most deeply.

And almost as various as the faces of the pilgrims are their costumes. Some of the women and girls are almost as gaily robed as dancing-girls, with costly looking, parti-coloured dresses, flashing silk leggings, and hair dressed *à la mode.* Others shuffle past in colours not less bright, but with clothes of poorer texture, and, where the leggings are not, the gloss of nature occasionally gleams through the open robe. All alike wear open-breasted dresses, discoloration by sun being but little feared where birth has already done the bronzing which the sun alone does upon our more colourless forms. The men are even more variously dressed than the women. As regards head-preservers, I have already mentioned that at this wet season of the year even the newest of them, and those most worthy of being displayed, are usually carried in front or behind, those placed upon the head being very few in number. But among the pilgrims, as among the citizens of the country, in these days of change, one of the oddest things observable is the frequency with which the European hat of felt, in its diversified forms, is worn in connection with the native costume. This perhaps more than anything else gives to the people of Japan at the present time that sort of masquerade air of which one is sensible in moving about among them. But they are, I venture to believe, wise in their generation in favouring so much the adoption of a hat of comfortable shape and material. Excepting a chimney-pot hat which I took with me but never once required, I saw none of that description in Japan, and although there are many Japanese who have been to Europe who must possess such articles, they never apparently make use of them. I trust the use of the felt hat will have a great effect in furthering the abolition of the habit of shaving the head which is so very general in the country among the men and the children, and which in the latter case appears to be attended with so much injury and disease of the skin as to make a walk in the street of a city or village quite shocking to a European. But the pilgrims for the most part carry the straw hat only, and get up their hair either literally by combing it straight on end all over, or else, which is much more general, grow a front tuft of it pretty long, doubling and tying it down flat, with a part of the head shaved on either side of it as before described. This last is the style of the common people generally, so far as I have seen them. It is, however, a usual thing for all the side and back hair to be worn very long and hanging loosely about the neck. The travelling upper robes are worn short by the men, who either wear tight-fitting blue trousers or no trousers at all, the substitute being in that case a very scanty article in white linen, imitated from the fashion adopted by "the grand old gardener and his wife" after they became sinful, and had compromised us all so sadly. As regards protections for the feet, the pilgrim fashion was most frequently to do without them, or to wear straw soles attached to the feet by straw strings, the opportunities for purchasing which were abundant in every village. In some cases, as among the better-to-do people usually, a thick white sock was worn for household use, with a wooden clog or patten for road use. Most of the pilgrims, both men and women, carried a walking-staff in their right hand, and over the left shoulder a longer staff with a small parcel or two attached. The pilgrims returning from the shrines carry bundles of the charms and remembrances which they obtain there, slinging them round their necks. The ages of these religious people varied from those of young and blooming girls to those of the most decrepit old Tithonuses that ever shuffled one foot before the other. Poor old souls! poor young souls! After plodding their weary way, perhaps for many a hundred miles, they knelt or sat before the white veil, threw down their little coin or paper of coins, uttered their brief prayer, bought a little bit of paper and a stick or two, and wandered off back again, let us hope in every case with a sure and certain "hope" of something, if with nothing more. O ye gods of earth, how easily ye have your way with us poor mortals! But seldom indeed are ye more gentle, more merciful, more easy with us than at these shrines of Isé. Ofttimes in other lands ye sit with your monstrous brazen faces, your triple heads, your thousand hands, your grinning dragons, your glaring beasts, your demoniac gatekeepers, demanding, many of you, not sacrifices of the people's food alone, but feasts of flesh and libations of blood, and offerings of the very lives of those who worship you. But here, at these ancient aboriginal shrines of the Sunrise Land, whither these poor wretches toil, no monstrous idol, no grinning demon, no red-handed priest with sacrificial steel awaits them; but a simple mirror, hidden in the simplest of all buildings, and screened by a simple veil of white, is all that their deities, here at least, employ to represent and to impress upon them their faith. That they shall lave their hands in pure water, and throw down upon the open earth in front of the veil some coin, is expected of them ; but these are the only ceremonial and the only sacrifice that the gods impose on them, and, these fulfilled, their own hearts are left free to utter the prayer, and, better still, to inspire the prophecy which is henceforth to resound from this the most sacred spot on earth to them.

GOLD FISH OF NAGOYA CASTLE.

CHAPTER XI.

NAGOYA AND THE SHRINE OF THE SACRED SWORD.

The town of Tsu—An attack of illness in Yokkaichi—Amateur artists—
Habits of the Japanese—Mountain scenery—Sail on a river—The town
of Miya—The Atsuta shrine—The sacred sword "Cloud Cluster"—
Yamato-Daké—His expedition against the Ainos—The name of the
sword changed to "Grass-mower"—Native history of the sacred sword
—Estimation in which swords are held in Japan—Their forms and
qualities—Sword-making a profession of honour—Sword inscriptions—
Etiquette of the sword—The city of Nagoya—A banquet and an ex-
hibition of porcelain—Amateur drawings and writings—Nagoya Castle
—Its towers surmounted with golden fishes—An attempt to steal them
—History of the castle—Kato Kiyomasa, its designer—Palace of the
Shogun.

THE town of Ano, or Tsu, in the province of Isé, in the Miya
Ken, at which our first half-day's journey from Fruichi was
to end, is one of considerable importance. The number of
its houses is 5255, and that of its inhabitants 22,489,
about one thousand of whom are Shizoku, most of them
holding Roku Keng (pension bonds) from the government,
the interests of which they live on. The remainder are
merchants and labourers, the former being the greater
in number. This province was formerly owned by the
Todo-Uji (House of Todos), and here they resided with
their retainers. At that time the number of people was
great and daily increasing, so that the town was prosperous.
But after the change of the government from Han to Ken,
the lord of the province removed to Tokio, and made Kwo-
zoku of the Tokio-Fu his seat; the trade of the place then
became depressed, in consequence of the scarcity of purchases by the *samurai*, and of the decrease of the people.

By degrees the town was thus made dull, and less inviting than before. Now, however, with the founding of the government offices, judicial departments, and school for teachers (Shi hang Gakko), the place is again populated with officials and students, and the town being on the highway of the Isé Dai-jingo, or pilgrims, is constantly visited by the passers to and from, to the number of more than a hundred thousand people yearly. The people from the provinces of Amooki, Ichisi, and other places also frequently visit this town to make purchases, and fish of different sorts are brought to market here, so that Tsu is now resuming its former liveliness and prosperity. On our arrival there the mayor of the Ken was good enough to receive us, in a building facing the castle,* and on the bank of the castle moat. Here we took luncheon and a brief rest, soon resuming our journey towards Yokkaichi, where we arrived long before sundown, taking up quarters prepared for us at an inn in which the trouble had been taken to build an additional small room or two for the supply of such extra accommodation as was presumed to be essential to Europeans. Our main rooms were, however, essentially Japanese, and unfortunately I had a longer opportunity of studying them than was anticipated or de-

---

* During the years of Airoku, Hosono-Ikino-kami-Fugi-Atsi erected this castle. In the eleventh year of Airoku (1568 A.D.) a part of the province was conquered by Ota Nobunaga, Lord of the Giffu Castle, who took possession of the castle and placed Ota Kamongnosuke Tada Hiro in command of the frontier, and returned to Giffu. In the twelfth year of Airoku (1569 A.D.) Ota Kazukenosuke Nobukane succeeded Kamongnosuke. In the eighth year of Tengshoo (1580 A.D.) Nobukane erected a five-storied pagoda in the castle. In the eleventh year of Tengshoo (1583 A.D.) Tomita Shinano - no - kami Tomonobu became lord of the castle, and afterwards removed to Ji-iyo. In the thirteenth year of Kei-cho (1608 A.D.) Todo-Izumi-no-kami Takatora (from Ji-iyo) was made lord of the castle and occupied it, when repairs and alterations were made. During the years of Genna (the first year of Genna was 1615 A.D.) the moat surrounding the castle in and out were made. At that time the lord of the castle's receipt was 323,950 kokus per annum (each koku nearly five imperial bushels). In the fourth year of Meiji (1871 A.D.) the government was changed, Hang made into Keng; and the castle has since been used as barracks for the Osaka garrison.

sired.   At midnight, after writing for three or four hours, I
rose to prepare for bed, but found rising no easy matter;
whether from the long journeys in the *jinriki-shas*, or from
a violent rheumatic attack, I knew not (and even now can
only conjecture), I found myself in extreme pain in the
muscles and nerves of the back as soon as I attempted to
move.   It was impossible to help myself beyond calling for
assistance, and with that assistance I was got to bed.   On
Tuesday, the day of starting from Kioto, we had travelled in
these little jolting hand-carriages nearly forty miles; on
Wednesday about thirty-five miles; on Thursday, more than
twenty; and on this day, Friday, nearly forty miles, the
intervals of travelling being, perhaps, too much occupied
with sitting at a writing-table.   However, after having the
best that could be done for me without medical aid during
the night, doctors of experience were telegraphed for from
Tsu and from the city of Nagoya, the former, a native
gentleman, having nearly twenty miles of road to travel, and
the latter, a German professor, Dr. Roretz, an almost equal
distance.   Both were most friendly and attentive, and with
their kind personal assistance, extended over three days of
pain, I was able to start again, on Tuesday the 11th of
March, for Miya by steamer, and thence to Nagoya.

During my illness presents of fruit were sent by local
persons; most of the attendance was performed by girls,
whose cheerful presence, it was supposed, would contribute
to the pleasant passing of the idle hours; and when the
improvement of my health justified it, visitors dropped in
and amused me in various ways.   One of the officers of the
adjoining county of Aichi, Mr. Hinoki, who had come over
from Miya, next Nagoya, to further the arrangements for our
stay there, was kind enough to drop in and draw some
pretty ink pictures, occasionally executing parts of them,
for the amusement of the thing, with a brush held in his
mouth, or in his nostril, or tied to his elbow, or between
his toes, the results in all cases being good, and sometimes
excellent.

This illness of a few days in a purely Japanese inn enabled

me to see much of the mode of life in such places, one of the
oddest features of which was the pulling out of the pipe and
tobacco-pouch and the taking of a few whiffs by almost
every one who came to your room, from the native doctor
who was there to prescribe for you, to the woman who fed
your *hibachi* with charcoal, and the girl who handed you
your cup of tea.   Of course I very much regretted delaying
his excellency Admiral Kawamura for three days on the
journey homeward to the seat of government, but his patience
and kindness were inexhaustible.

We left Yokkaichi at 9 A.M., on a morning of great beauty,
judged even from our point of view, viz. that of mere men,
whose only paths lie along the surface of the earth and the
sea, subject to every variation of cloud and breeze belonging
to the mere surface, and often cut off from that splendour

> " Which o'erspreads
> All noise and tempest."

I say judged from our point of view, because a little way
up, of course, just above our low and varying clouds, the
splendour of sun-brightness and star-beauty alternately
prevail, undimmed by cloud or storm, and of this mountain
regions frequently remind one.   The streets of Yokkaichi were
lined with people, exhibiting unusual interest, it having
become known, doubtless, that our party, including a
minister and two foreigners, had been staying in the town
for several days—an unwonted event.   The mayor of the
Ken and the physician from Tsu accompanied us to the
steamer and saw us off.   We were in the centre of an
amphitheatre of mountains, with the bay and the level-lands
for the arena.   And how beautiful were the mountains!   In
the west, all the way up from Isé in the south to the
north-west of Yokkaichi, the morning light displayed their
jagged outlines and their carved slopes as clearly as if we
had held them in our hands like sea-shells, and observed thus
closely their grooved and chased surfaces.   On the north-
east, towering into the very heavens, and more snow-white
than any tent, was the mountain of Komagadaké, which we

had seen from Isé on the morning of our quitting the shrines and towns; and more to the east the snowy ranges of Ibouki, with dark peaks and bright peaks, near peaks and distant peaks, rising in such loveliness between and beyond as if the object of their author had been to sketch a picture rather than to build a world.

At noon we arrived outside of Miya, which is the port of and continuous with the great city of Nagoya, and in open boats, with sails formed of separate strips of linen, after the fashion of Japan, sailed into and about two miles up the river to the town. The river approach has obviously been preserved (from silting up by the river deposits) by artificial works laboriously carried out and renewed. After a Japanese luncheon in Miya, we drove a few hundred yards to the famous Shinto temple of Atsuta, which is supported by the government, and which is renowned as the depository of the Sacred Sword, Kusanagi-no-mitzurugi (Grass-mowing Sword), one of the three emblems of the Shinto faith. We visited it unexpectedly, but were well received by the simple-minded and modest-mannered priests, who answered such questions as we put, and gave us a written description of the temple. We stood again in an ancient park, of magnificent old trees, with several shrines, and with lanterns or light-pillars innumerable, and before a gateway hung, like those at Isé, with white veils. Here, however, the veils were three in number, side by side, and were looped apart in the middle, to facilitate the viewing of the interior buildings. There were the pilgrims kneeling and sitting as at Isé, first washing the hands and throwing down their coins before uttering their brief prayers, and, let us hope, devising their prophecies of good. This temple of Atsuta is very ancient, having been founded, for the purpose of receiving the sacred sword, in the second century after Christ, by the sister of the heroic Yamato-Daké, after he had made a successful war against the eastern savages by aid of the sword.

The account of the sword given to me at the temple was, I must admit, a sufficiently clear one, being to the effect that the sacred weapon had originally belonged to the sun-goddess, Tensho-Dai-jin, from whom it was stolen by a serpent. The brother of Tensho, whose name was Susanoö-no-mikoto, recovered it from the serpent, and it was placed in a shrine on the sacred spot on which we stood, Tensho approving this as a very sacred place. At a much later period, viz. the beginning of the second century, Yamato-Daké, being commissioned by his father, the Mikado Keiko, to make war upon the savage inhabitants of the eastern part of the country, as previously stated, obtained permission to use the sacred sword, and after employing it with success deposited it in this shrine with increased claims to reverence, and ever since it has remained here, and has naturally enough been an object of veneration to millions who have come day and night to bow before it. It must be confessed, however, that this simple narrative begins to exhibit some legendary aspects when one remembers that the personage Tensho-Dai-jin is no other than the bright sun-goddess herself, that the serpent which carried off the sword had eight heads, and that Susanoö only got the sword back by intoxicating the monster, slaying him while in his cups, and extracting the sword from his tail. Even as regards Yamato-Daké, the story told to us (and told to the pilgrims and inhabitants of Miya likewise, in a printed paper) would have been more easily intelligible if one were not otherwise made aware that in the war against the savages the sword was used by him to stop a brushwood fire that was overwhelming his army, by cutting the grass in front of it, and that it likewise drove back the flames, to the overthrow and rout of the enemy that had kindled them. Hence the name " Grass-mower."

But it will be better to give the reader a somewhat fuller account of the matter which (since writing the last paragraph) I have found in the short paper on " The Sword of Japan," read at the Asiatic Society of Japan by Mr. T. H. R. McClatchie, one of the clever and accomplished staff of secretaries and interpreters by whom our minister, Sir H. Parkes, is surrounded in the British Embassy at Tokio. Mr. McClatchie says: " Saburodaiyu, in his preface to the 'Reference as to New Swords,' gives a short sketch of the

Japanese legends regarding the history of the weapon ; and though his allusions, in connection with his subject, to the mythology of his country may perhaps provoke a smile, still they are worthy of note as being the words of an author who is generally held to be a high authority on the matter of which he treats. The translation of this sketch reads as follows : 'If we search out in bygone days the origin of the sword, we find that our country excelled barbarian localities in regard to metal. In the olden times of the divine period, when Izanagi and Izanami-no-mikoto, standing upon the floating bridge of heaven, thrust down their glittering blade and probed the blue ocean, the drops from its point congealed and hardened and became an island, after which the deities created several other islands. These eventually became a large country composed of eight islands, and amongst the many names of this country they styled it too the 'Land of many blades.' In its early days there existed the divine swords To-nigiri and Ya-nigiri. Then, too, when Susanoö-no-mikoto smote the eight-clawed great dragon, and struck him on the tail, the sword of the deity became slightly nicked, and from the inside of the tail he drew out a single blade. 'This,' said he, 'is a marvellous sword,' and he caused it to be presented to Tensho-Dai-jin. This was styled the 'Sword of the Clustering Clouds of Heaven,' and also the 'Grass-mowing Sword.' Should not this be said to be the commencement of fixing the dates of swords ? That 'Sword of the Clustering Clouds' was made one of the 'Three divine precious things' (i.e. the seal, sword, and mirror held by the Mikados), it has had no equal in this country, and, being the gigantic weapon that watches over it, it is a thing of great dread even to speak of. Now, when our country had arrived at the heavenly rule of Sujin-Tenno, the tenth of the mortal emperors, he feared to dwell in the same palace with the 'Divine precious things,' and so he caused a person called Amakuni, a man of the department of Uda, in the province of Yamato, a far-removed descendant of Me-hitotsu-Gami, to forge an imitation of the sword ; and as for the 'Clustering Clouds,' that had descended from the divine age, he was pleased to offer it up to the shrine of Tensho-Dai-jin. Under the heavenly rule of Keiko-Tenno, Yamato-Daké-no-mikoto, at the time of his expedition against the east, went to pay reverence at the shrines of Isé. His aunt, Yamato Himé-no-mikoto, was the resident of the shrine at that period, and she besought that the divine sword of the 'Clustering Clouds' might be handed down to him from the shrine, and so gave it over to Yamato-Daké-no-mikoto, together with a tinder case attached. This is said to have been the origin of the custom of fastening a charm case to a sword as a guardian for children. Yamato-Daké-no-mikoto, having accomplished the subjugation of the east, offered up the sword at Atsuta, in the province of Owari. Up to the present day, the virtue of this sword, permanent and immutable even unto the end of myriads of ages, is the guardian of our country and our homes, and the protector of our own selves. In no way can it be fully described by the pen! The second 'precious sword' was buried in the western seas at the death of Antoku-Tenno (1185 A.D.)."

This may not be an unsuitable place to speak of the consideration which the sword has received in Japan. Being one of the three insignia of the divine authority of the Mikados, it became to the military class a symbol at once of their loyalty and their pride. "Cherished by the *samurai* as almost part of his own self, and considered by the common people as their protector against violence, what wonder," says Mr. McClatchie, "that we should find it spoken of in glowing terms by Japanese writers as 'the precious possession of lord and vassal from times older than the divine period,' or as 'the living soul of the *samurai*'?" The art of determining the maker and date of a sword-blade became one of more than ordinary interest, and many treatises have been written upon it. Those made before 1603 A.D. are called old swords; those made since new swords.

The old form of Japanese sword, or *ken*, was a long, straight, double-edged weapon, while the modern sword, *katana*, has a single edge, and is slightly curved, especially towards the point. A short sword or dirk, called the *wakizashi*, was until lately worn with the *katana*, as a sign of military or gentle birth. A short dirk without a guard, known as an *aikuchi*, was worn by doctors, artists, and persons of the fourth and fifth rank. Stilettos a foot long or less, known as *tanto* and *mamori katana*, were sometimes worn by nobles, officers, and gentlemen in place of the more cumbrous *wakizashi*. The *jintochi* was a large two-handed war-sword, usually borne by a sword-bearer when not in actual use. A sword of medium size, worn when hunting or rambling in the country, was called a *nodatchi*. Another kind, *tatchi*, of which there were several styles, was hung by two slings from the girdle.

The making of swords was considered an honourable profession, and men of good family were trained to it. It is mentioned of the emperor Gotaba (1184) that not only did he "give directions to the noted smiths of the various provinces and make them forge, but he also worked with his own hand"; later noted smiths, according to their evidence, received honorary rank from the court. The decoration and mounting of swords embraced a large and diversified field of art, which has been cultivated with distinction for centuries by some families. Upon the hilt are usually four highly ornamental metallic pieces—the ferrule on the head of the hilt, the ring next to the guard, and two pieces covering the rivet holes, which latter are partly covered by the silk binding of the hilt. The ferrule and ring are beautifully made, and ornamented with dragons or other figures handsomely wrought in relief, being often of solid gold, the other two pieces resembling these ornaments. The guard is often a "wonderful piece of workmanship in metal," usually handsomely and more or less quaintly ornamented, and often "worked up with gold, silver, etc., into a detailed picture" of battles, hunts, or natural scenery. Passing through the guard, and sheathing itself in the scabbard, is a narrow knife or stiletto about eight inches long, even the blade of which is often beautifully shaped and chased, while the exposed handle is richly ornamented with gold figures to match those of the hilt.*

The name of the maker of the sword with the date being engraved on one side of the hilt, upon the other side was sometimes inscribed a motto or a verse of poetry; such as

" There's nought 'twixt heaven and earth that man need fear who carries at his belt this single blade; "

or,

" One's fate is in the hands of heaven, but a skilful fighter does not meet with death; "

or,

" In one's last days one's sword becomes the wealth of one's posterity."

Swords often received specific names, and the swords of great men have been handed down as heirlooms. We saw, as elsewhere stated, the swords of Yoritomo in the temple of Hachiman at Kamakura. In an appendix to this volume I have added some notes on Celebrated Swords and their makers.

The angle at which the sword was carried in the belt was an indication of rank, and the etiquette of the sword was both complex and solemn. " To clash the sheath of one's sword against that belonging to another person was held to be a grave breach of etiquette; to turn the sheath in the belt, as though about to draw, was tantamount to a challenge; while to lay one's weapon on the floor of a room, and to kick the guard with the foot, in the direction of any one else, was a deadly insult, that generally resulted in a combat to the death. It was not even thought polite to draw a sword from its sheath without begging the permission of any other persons present." †

---

* " The small knife was used to throw at an enemy, the skewers to attach the heads of slain enemies to the girdle."—*Pfoundes.*

† See Mr. McClatchie's paper before quoted; also Mr. Pfoundes's

Notes. Mr. Pfoundes adds other particulars of sword etiquette: To enter a friend's house without leaving the sword outside, a breach of friendship. Those whose position justified the accompaniment of an attendant

From the Atsuta temple our *jinriki-shas* bore us—preceded by representatives of the civic authorities of Nagoya—to that celebrated city. Here we were taken to very comfortable quarters in an hotel (purely Japanese, of course), and after a short rest proceeded to fulfil an engagement to dine with the governing authorities of the Ken or county. The governor himself was absent, but his deputy acted as our host, and performed the office entirely to our satisfaction and pleasure. The place of the banquet was the exhibition building. A select display of the beautiful porcelain ware of Seto (Owari) had been brought together to interest us. There was much pleasing colouring in the articles displayed, with fine examples of modern " blue and white " in a great variety of forms, including temple-lanterns, street lamps, large decorative plaques, immense bowls and vases, and other very large examples, together with a choice series

---

invariably left the sword in his charge at the entrance, or, if alone, it was usually laid down at the entrance. If removed inside it was invariably done by the host's servants, and then not touched with the bare hand, but with a silk napkin kept for the purpose, and the sword was placed upon a sword-rack in the place of honour near the guest, and treated with all the politeness due to an honoured visitor who would resent a discourtesy. The long sword (if two were worn) was withdrawn, sheathed, from the girdle with the right hand, and placed on the right side—an indication of friendship, as it could not be drawn and used thus—never by the left hand, or placed on the left side, except when in immediate danger of attack. To exhibit a naked weapon was a gross insult, unless when a gentleman wished to show his friends his collection. To express a wish to see a sword was not usual, unless when a blade of great value was in question, when a request to be shown it would be a compliment the happy possessor appreciated. The sword would then be handed with the back towards the guest, the edge turned towards the owner and the hilt to the left, the guest wrapping the hilt either in the little silk napkin always carried by gentlemen in their pocket-books, or in a sheet of clean paper. The weapon was drawn from the scabbard and admired inch by inch, but not to the full length unless the owner pressed his guest to do so, when, with much apology, the sword was entirely drawn and held away from the other persons present. After being admired, it would, if apparently necessary, be carefully wiped with a special cloth, sheathed, and returned to the owner as before. The short sword was retained in the girdle, but at a prolonged visit both host and guest laid it aside. Women did not wear swords in their girdle by right or fashion, although when travelling alone it was often done. On the occasion of fires, the ladies of the palace sometimes placed side-arms in their girdles.

A DANCING GIRL.

To face page 213, Vol. II.

of articles of a smaller kind, and of purely Japanese design. The exhibition comprised some remarkable examples of modern porcelain, made in imitation of the old China ware which now is deemed of so much value; and also examples of vases with ornaments in relief, Dresden fashion, of great beauty and merit. Although these porcelain manufactures are mainly the productions of Seto, which is about ten miles from Nagoya, the artists employed upon them are chiefly resident in Nagoya itself; and the Owari district generally is famous for its porcelain productions. There was also exhibited a complete set of models, showing the appliances used in the manufacture from rice of the national wine or spirit, *saké*, the processes being explained to us by a manufacturer. At the banquet several of the officials and merchants of the city were present, and gave us a cordial welcome. In the course of the evening there was national music and dancing, and later on the vice-governor and some of the other officers and residents of the city were so kind as to make for me, offhand, at my request, some of those rough but very effective drawings and writings which, more than anything else, exhibit the national style both of drawing and of writing, and the close relationship of the one to the other. On leaving the entertainment at ten o'clock, we found many of the shops and stalls of the city still open, and flowing down on these, and us, and everything, the silent glory of the rising moon.

Next day—it being in contemplation to travel about forty-five miles along the Tokaido on the following day (the state of my muscular and nervous systems, which were far from satisfactory as yet, permitting)—we limited our enterprises to a visit to the famous castle, the finest of those now remaining in Japan, and to an inspection of the military establishments now existing there. The castle proved to be extremely interesting, as it contained, in a fair state of preservation, not only the largest tower or castle proper still remaining in Japan, but also a palace built and decorated for the accommodation, under the old system, of the Tycoon during his visits to Nagoya. In Tokio the largest tower of the Tycoon's castle has, with its other buildings, ceased to exist, and from Osaka Castle likewise the great tower has disappeared. In Nagoya Castle the towers exist and are in good condition, the great tower being a peculiarly fine and lofty edifice, surmounted with two large glittering fish, standing 8½ feet in height, and covered with plates of gold. In 1872 the last possessor of the castle presented these fish to the Mikado for preservation in his palace (the gold plates upon them having cost £6000), and one of them was afterwards sent to the Vienna Exhibition. On its passage back the vessel containing it was wrecked on the coast of Japan, but the treasure was afterwards recovered. The inhabitants of Nagoya not unnaturally desired to have these golden fish restored to their former position as ornaments of their tower and town, and his majesty having approved of the request, they now, to use a local phrase, "bathe the city in their brightness." It is related that on one occasion, many years ago, an attempt was made to obtain possession of the gold scales of these aerial creatures by a man who raised himself up to them for the purpose by means of an immense kite in a gale of wind at night; he was, however, detected, and boiled in oil for his pains. It is further said that the making of very large kites was afterwards prohibited throughout the district of Owari as a protection to these valuable objects.

This castle, according to the information given me on the spot, was built about two hundred and seventy years ago by the seventh son of the great Shogun Iyéyasu (first of the Tokugawas), more than twenty Daimios contributing towards its cost, as a compliment paid to the Shogun and his family.*

---

* The following account of the building of Nagoya Castle is given by Mr. W. T. Dixon, in a paper read before the Asiatic Society of Japan : "It was built in the year 1610 A.D., for Yoshinawo, the first prince of the Tokugawa house in Owari, and the seventh son of Iyéyasu For some two centuries before that date there had been a castle of Owari, situated at Kiyosu, a few miles west of Nagoya. This was founded by a Daimio named Shiba Takatsuné, a near relative of the Shogun Ashikaga, and remained in the possession of his descendants until the end of the sixteenth century, when it was seized by Ota Nobunaga, and made by that famous warrior the

The main tower was designed by the general Kato Kiyomasa, who, according to Mr. Griffis ('Mikado's Empire'), was a very ill-conditioned fellow indeed, who wore a helmet three feet high, quarrelled with his brother officers, inscribed prayers on his banners, became a member of the Nicheren sect, and "a bloody persecutor of the Christians in the sixteenth century." He appears, however, to have been a skilful architect of castles, if one may infer this from the style and construction of this great tower at Nagoya, and from the fact that he designed also the castle of Kumamoto, in Kiushiu, which I have seen described as another of the finest in Japan. He is now a deified personage. and some of my Japanese friends to whom I have spoken respecting him assure me that his colleague in the Korean expedition, with whom he refused to act cordially, was really a most objectionable individual; that the so-called Christians whom Kato Kiyomasa is said to have persecuted were of a bad sort; and that he is worthily worshipped as a great and good patriot, and now one of the gods of Japan, by a very large number of the Japanese people. It is not to be expected that I should decide between these opposite views of his character in a mere gossip about a tower of his design; so I will pass on to say that Nagoya Castle stands upon about four hundred acres of ground; that it is protected by two moats, with the power of inundating the country at the back of it, where its defence

---

centre from which to keep in check the neighbouring provinces. Some years afterwards, Tokugawa Iyéyasu, having survived all his rivals, recognised that his authority would be more secure if Owari, lying as it did at the junction of the two great highways between Kiyoto and Yedo, were defended by a strong castle. He would thus have more command over the western Daimios, some of whom had not yet acknowledged his sway. The castle at Kiyosu was found quite insufficient, on account both of its limited size and of the shallowness of its moats; so he resolved to build a new and more formidable one, and fixed upon the present site at Nagoya as the most advantageous for his purpose. Several Daimios, the principal of whom were Fukushima Masanori, prince of Aki, Kato Kiyomasa, prince of Higo, and Kuroda Nagamasa, prince of Chikuzen, were, after some threatening, prevailed upon to undertake the task. The materials of the old fortress of Kiyosu helped to compose the new stronghold, and it is said that 200,000 men were employed, who finished the work of erection in a few weeks."

is obviously weak; that it was until lately the castle of one
of three of the most powerful Daimios in Japan, who as
members of the Tycoon's family enjoyed many important and
exclusive privileges, and that although part of its inclosure
is now used for military purposes, another part is devoted to
the growth of vegetables, which is probably a better use, in
some respects, than was ever before made of it. We ascended
Kato's tower to the top floor, and obtained an extensive view
over the city and its suburbs, and for some miles of fruitful
ground around, but the atmosphere was not clear enough to
admit of a view of the mountains in either direction. It may
be interesting to mention that the plan adopted in the
designing of this tower was to make the area of the lowest
floor one thousand "mats," that of the next floor five
hundred, the others decreasing upwards by a hundred mats
per floor, the upper being of one hundred mats only. The
"mat" is a rectangle of about three feet by six feet, that
being the size given to the single piece of the matting in use
as the floor-covering throughout Japan. The sizes of rooms
are usually given in mats. A fine model of the great tower,
constructed before the tower itself was built, and therefore
nearly three hundred years old, was shown to us in the
Shogun's palace, and is in perfectly good condition. The
palace of the Tycoon, though intended for occasional occupation only, was of a far more costly character, both in its
construction and in its decorations, than that of the Mikado
at Kioto. The ceilings are panelled and decorated with some
of the most refined artists' work that I have seen in Japan,
while the carved work is lavish alike in its abundance and its
beauty. This palace seems to furnish an illustration of the
accuracy of those who tell us that under the system of
government which the Tycoons gradually brought about the
Mikado, the true emperor, was kept in a state of comparative
weakness, meanness, and privation, while the Tycoon revelled
in wealth, splendour, and power.

CHAPTER XII.

Our long land journey from the old capital (Kioto) to the
new (Tokio) was resumed on Thursday, March 13, at 7 A.M.
The later hours of the previous day had been devoted to
drenching rains outside and rest indoors, but the saving
of time was a matter of so much importance to me, and the
delays occasioned by my illness were tending to so much
congestion of duties, if I may so speak, in both Japan and
England, that we decided to start at an early hour next
morning, rain or sun, showers or torrents. Happily the
morning broke fine, with little or no sunshine, but with a
dry atmosphere, the rain wholly gone. Early as it was, the
vice-governor was kindly there to take leave of us, and, with
many little arrangements for enabling a rheumatic individual
of a certain age to make a journey of forty-five miles in a
hand-carriage without too much distress, off we went. All
the shops and places of business appeared to be open and in
operation as we rattled through Nagoya and Miya, although

the hour was so early. There were several very pretty
gateways in Miya which I should have been glad to have
sketched had time allowed, but a passing glance was all we
could devote to them. The shrines of Atsuta, with their
mystic sword, their towering trees, their crowded light-
pillars and simple ceremonies, were soon passed and left
behind, and behind us likewise loomed up the great Honganji temple, and beyond, the mountains—mountain-shrines,
shall we call them?—hung with curtain-screens like Atsuta,
but in this case the screens were blue, and wrought of
valley mist and morning light. Numerous temples, and
still more numerous shrines much simpler than temples,
were passed during the day, and at many of them, here as
elsewhere, the stone basins in front of them for the washing
of the hands received their water from spouting bronze
dragons of considerable size and much artistic merit.

Soon after leaving Miya we were again upon the great
Tokaido road, which throughout the day, as on some former
days, was a fine, smooth, well-kept road between the towns
and the villages, but was much neglected where it passed
through them—a point which would seem to require some
attention on the part of both the central and local governments.
The road traversed by bridges several large rivers, the beds of
which were raised above the neighbouring land-level by as
much as 10 feet. After a short halt at the town of Narumi,
where cotton-spinning is carried on, and transit through
another in which dyeing is successfully practised, we passed
through the famous battle-field in which the great Shogun of
three days, so to call him, Yoshimoto, engaged the redoubtable
Nobunaga in the sixteenth century, and was defeated by
him and killed.* A monument to his (Yoshimoto's) memory
was passed in a field on our right—a simple column of stone,
surrounded by a railing of wood. Luncheon was taken at
the town of Okazaki, the birthplace of Iyéyasu, at which are
the great granite quarries from which the capital, Tokio,
and many other places, are provided with that stone; the

---

* See vol. i. p. 185.

nearness of Okazaki to the bay of Owari and its branches greatly facilitating the supply of this stone to towns and cities near the coast. The remainder of the day's journey was completed at four o'clock in the apparently thriving town of Yoshida, which is situated on a branch of the great river Tenriu, which finds its way into the sea further eastward. This town does a considerable trade in timber, most of the roof-rafters for Tokio going hence. After the drive of forty-five miles a stroll in the town to the river bank and flower garden was a pleasant change. After dinner a gentleman, Mr. Watanabé Shoka, of great local fame as an artist, and considered by some of our party as one of the first now living in Japan, did us the honour of dropping in and helping to pass a wet evening pleasantly by knocking off a few large rough sketches of birds, each drawing being executed in times varying from five to ten minutes only. In this pleasing pastime he was joined by Mr. Hinoké, from Nagoya, who had accompanied us thus far, and who, like his friend just mentioned, possesses wonderful skill in producing fine effects with a few daubs and touches of the brush. I observed that in putting in trees and certain parts of birds Mr. Watanabé Shoka frequently employed two brushes simultaneously. I have seen a good deal of rapid sketching and drawing at different times, but with the exception of my friend Chevalier de Martino, the painter of great naval pictures, who is surprisingly skilled in the swift use of the ink-brush, I know no one who approaches Mr. Watanabé Shoka.

Early on Friday the 14th of March, after another night of rain, we pursued our journey eastward, in an atmosphere of delightful freshness, in a north-western breeze of considerable force, and in sunshine that made the morning perfect. We were soon skirting on our left ranges of wooded hills, rolling away to mountains in the distance. I was informed that on one of the finest and most sheer and lofty of these high wooded hills there was a temple. I had chosen a position in the procession of *jinriki-shas* well to the rear, so that I had before me the shifting picture of more than a dozen of these curious little carriages, with double that number of half-nude men trotting them along at a rate of six to seven miles an hour, their red and blue colours dancing with their movements, and little flags surmounted with bunches of bright heather, or something like it, waving at the side of each carriage. Among the villages passed through was one named Surazaga, concerning which we were told a little story to this effect. On a certain occasion the prince of Bizen, travelling on the Tokaido, stayed to sleep in this village. During his slumber a vision appeared to him—no other than that of the goddess Kwannon herself, in the guise of a priest, who woke him and told him to escape for his life, as the village would be flooded during the night. He accordingly arose and made his way in all haste to a neighbouring hill called Siomizaka (" the Height with a View of the Sea "), and sure enough the flood came, the village was inundated, and many of the inhabitants were drowned. This is the whole of the story as I heard it, but as it appeared to have been recounted to my informant by one of the *jinriki-sha* men it may have been but imperfectly told. Under other circumstances one might have been tempted to consider the prince of Bizen a very selfish sort of personage to leave the poor villagers to perish, he himself meanwhile escaping to a high hill; and having seen a short time afterwards how very high the hill is, one might further have inferred that Prince Bizen must have been very frightened indeed to have gone up so far. One might also have observed that the selfishness of the prince was matched by the negligence of the goddess, who appears to have cared only for the prince, and to have forgotten all about the people, who lost their lives for want of a warning similar to his. Further, how came the goddess to appear as a priest? If she wished to be taken for a priest, why was not her disguise effectual? If she intended to allow herself to be known, why did she assume the appearance of a priest? One might even ask whether, after all, it was not really a priest, and no goddess, who gave the warning, and whether the name of Kwannon was not taken in vain by the individual, whoever he was, who asserted that she had anything to do with the matter. But it is possible that all these seeming weaknesses are only in the story as it reached me, and that the priest was really the goddess, satisfactory evidence establishing the identification. The only difficulty remaining in that case would be the neglect of the poor inhabitants by the goddess, but that difficulty is as old as miraculous appearances themselves, the wonder always being in such cases that the gods and the goddesses and the virgins and the angels and the saints who from time to time come on earth to give private warnings to individuals should be so very, very callous as to those whom they do *not* warn, and who would be as grateful, if they could afford it, as the prince of Bizen himself. And grateful indeed he was, for when we came to Siomizaka, there, on the high cluster of granite rocks, several hundred feet above us, and on a summit to which it would be difficult to lift even a living and breathing life-size goddess, was a large bronze statue of Kwannon 13 feet high, gazing over land and over the sea, which we know by the name to be within her view, though we could not see it, and apparently not a little proud of her elevation—proud in the very presence of the sun-goddess herself, who, indeed, did not disdain to adorn her brazen brow with a touch of her own bright light.

Leaving the goddess to her lofty meditations, we rolled on through a fine country, very wild, and wooded and mountainous on our left, and very level, and cultivated and glistening with rice-swamps on our right. The road next led us up a succession of long hills, in ascending which I gladly availed myself of the opportunity thus afforded for a delightful morning walk. Presently we came out for a short time upon a comparatively open road, and a shrill voice exclaimed, "Fuji-yama!" and there indeed, somewhat away on our left (broad on our port bow, as a sailor would put it), was the superb mountain which we had not seen for five weeks, and which, as it now stood up, nearly ninety miles off, above the nearer and darker mountains—stood up, whiter with snow than if wrought of silver, purer than the very sky into which it towered, and more perfect in form than any mortal

hands could model—was a shrine of splendour worthy of the
true God, and a consecration to the land which is so fortunate
as to form its pedestal.   It was a native gentleman who saw
it first; not a poet, not an artist, not a seer of any sort; but
he was a man, and a Japanese, and he clapped his hands and
shouted with delight, and with the joy of seeing once again
the sacred mountain, and of turning the eyes of us strangers
towards it.

While we gazed with wonder and almost with worship upon
this "most awful Form," another voice shouted "The sea!" and
there on our right lay before us, and low beneath us, and rolling
far away over the horizon's arc, the living liquid splendour of
the sea indeed.   "Isn't it just like gauze!" shouted another
of the party from a distance; and, although one feels some
reluctance to associate with the ocean the name of so frail a
thing as gauze, yet there was so soft and semi-transparent
and delicate a look about the sea on this occasion, viewed
from our height, that one felt the verisimilitude of the
metaphor.   I never before saw the sea so utterly beautiful.
I have often hung above its splendour; often listened to its
alluring music on the shore, and its power of floating great
ships with truth and certainty has always had a certain
charm for me—a charm at which those may laugh who are
insensible to that viewless grace which lurks in all the
ways. and paths of science.   On the way out to Japan, on
the very part of the sea upon which we were now looking
down, we passed some hours in admiring the intense colour
of the sea-deeps and the pure whiteness of the surface as it
was torn into fragments by the gale; but on this sun-bright
morning, on which the breeze seemed saturate with sun, and
the sun blown through with breeze, both sun and breeze
seemed to mix with the sea, until the whole surface foamed
with light and life.

We now dipped down from the height, and after a short
run entered the village of Arai, which is—or rather was,
for the Tokaido has now taken another and newer route
near this place, and the gate is removed--one of the gates of
the Tokaido, giving upon an inlet of the sea over which

passengers have to be ferried. Our party at once embarked
in several boats which were waiting for us, and a strong
stern breeze drove us quickly over the two or three miles of
shallow water to the village of Mayezaka, in the province of
Totomi. Here we re-entered our *jinriki-shas* and started for
our luncheon-place, Hamamatsu. The road through Mayezaka, and for a few miles beyond—no longer a recognised
portion of the Tokaido—is a bad, sandy road, and we moved
over it, or rather through its sandy ruts, but slowly, thus
giving ourselves ample time to observe the large extent to
which the small fish that abound in the neighbouring sea
with its bays are caught and dried in the sun to serve as
manure. A large number of the inhabitants of Mayezaka and
the adjacent villages appear to be employed mainly in this
trade. As we passed under the hills we observed a number
of fishermen seated upon them, watching the sea for the fish-
shoals which they first descry from these heights, and then
descend and capture.

Before reaching Hamamatsu we pass the broad river of
Tenriu (Tenriugawa) by the longest bridge in Japan, nearly
four thousand feet in length. This river is navigable in its main
stream for one hundred and twenty miles from the sea, which
but few rivers of Japan are, owing to the narrowness of the
country, and the nearness of the mountains to the sea in very
many cases. Hamamatsu has some excellent native hotels, in
one of which, kept in admirable order, we took luncheon with
an avidity doubtless due in part to the sea-air, of which we had
breathed pretty freely in the course of the morning. The
breeze of the morning increased through the day, and we might
have sailed for the remainder of it in our *jinriki-shas*, had they
been supplied with masts and canvas. At length we entered
Kakegawa in a gale of wind, which found its way pretty freely
into our chambers, without the necessity of exercising much
ingenuity in getting there. The hotel, though the best in
the town—better having lately been destroyed by fire—is
an old one, and without the shelter of numerous screens and
rugs I feared my Yokkaichi pains and experiences might have
been renewed. Throughout the evening and night the house

shook with the wind almost incessantly, as if being nursed by an attentive earthquake.

The next day's journey lay chiefly over hills and river-beds, with occasional transits over lovely valleys. The strong north-westerly wind still swept down from the chill mountain heights, occasionally developing into brief gales of considerable force, threatening to sweep us from the hills. With more force still they swept the bridges over the torrent-beds of he Oigawa and the Abégawa, on the farther or left bank of which stands the city of Shidzuoka, which was to be our resting-place for the night. · In other respects the day was fine and bright. After driving a few miles, in our usual hand-carriages (or Pull-man cars, as they are jocosely called), we reached Missaka, where we alighted to cross the hills for four or five miles, either in *kagos* or on foot, the road, although practicable for *jinriki-shas*, being in large part so very steep and rough that no one would from choice be jolted up and down it. Those who cannot walk are taken in *kagos*, which are little carriages, either open or closed, carried upon the shoulders of men. There were several of them in readiness for our party, but none into which it appeared at all possible for me to squeeze or be squeezed; and I should have been among the most unreasonable and ungrateful of men, I thought, if I preferred such a mode of conveyance, being as far recovered as I was, to a fine mountain walk of a few miles.

And a fine walk indeed we had, through Swiss-like scenery, with occasional views over large extents of lowlands, now and then glimpses of the distant sea, and suddenly, after passing the first summit, such a full-fronted view of Fuji-yama as would have well repaid a far more laborious climb. Later on, after passing across a valley and ascending a second hill, we came upon another and still more beautiful view of the sacred mountain, the highest in Japan, which rises 13,000 feet clear away from the sea. We could not, however, see the base from our position, but we saw what was perhaps better as an object of beauty. Below its snow-covered summit and sides, the lower and darker part of the mountain appeared of the self-same blue as the sky above, so that the mountain of snow

seemed poised in heaven—perhaps suspended there after the
fashion in which one of our poets has imagined the world
to be—

"Hung by gold chains about the feet of God."

Below Fuji were lower ranges of mountains, darkly contrasting with it; then, nearer, came low wooded hills;
nearer still, the broad, rough, stony bed of the Oigawa, with
swift streams chasing down it, and sand-storms driving over
it; and nearer still a village, and tea-plantations, and the
Tokaido sweeping down with its wild borderings of old and
twisted trees. On all the sun shone brightly, and over all the
gale blew swiftly, so that we had before us such a scene as
artists well might paint and poets edit. Dipping down to
the village below, Kanaya, where other *jinriki-shas* awaited
us, we started in them for Fusieda. Our way lay first across
the Oigawa, and through the driving sand-storms which we
had enjoyed as part of a picture, but which were anything
but charming as atmospheres to be driven through We
were soon beyond them, however, and ere long comfortably
engaged in ascertaining the merits of a Fusieda luncheon in
a very good native inn or hotel. This matter sufficiently
determined to the satisfaction of all, we were speedily *en
route* again, and instead of skirting the hills to the southward, as I expected, turned towards the hills in front. After
passing through a village at their base, and racing down a
valley between them, we ascended a winding or alternating
roadway, which terminated at the entrance of a tunnel
through the mountain. This tunnel, much resembling that
of Pozzuoli, near Naples, and lighted, like it, with lamps at
intervals, was about a third of a mile in length. It terminated in a beautiful valley, down which the road plunged,
and up which—as up the steep roads of the morning, by-
the-bye—several *kagos* were being borne, the travellers
usually walking to spare the carrying *ninsokus*, as this class
of labourers and *jinriki-sha* men are called. After a few
miles of further travelling we saw before us the roofs of
a large town, and between them and us the bed of another

large river, which I rightly took to be the Abégawa, the
town or city beyond being the terminus of our day's run,
Shidzuoka.*

Here we were cordially received at an excellent native
hotel, by the governor of the large district or Ken which
takes its name from this place, and also by the vice-governor
or chief secretary, who indeed had already received us on our
entrance into the Ken earlier in the day, and had pushed on
before us to welcome us in the city. The kindness of these
gentlemen deserves more than a passing tribute here, for in
addition to their welcome to the place, they entertained us
at a private banquet in the evening, and made us valuable
presents of specimen productions of the district, including
lacquer work, inlaid work, articles of delicacy and beauty made
of the bamboo cane, teas as prepared for both the home and
the European markets, etc. They also had a large quantity
of the lacquer, inlaid, and bamboo work of the district placed
for our inspection in the hotel. While looking in an upper
room at some of these very pretty productions of Shidzuoka,
the selling prices of which I found on inquiry to be singularly,
quite wonderfully, low, a door was slid open, just after sunset, and disclosed a superb view of Fuji-yama, on which the
light lingered, and to which it clung, certainly with loveliness, apparently with love. I do not wonder that in
these parts of Japan this wondrous, this sublime, object is
impressed, more or less imperfectly, upon almost every
article to which the arts are applied—and in Japan what is
there to which art is not applied? After dinner we tried
the Shidzuoka tea as prepared for the European, or, more
correctly speaking, for the American, market, and found it
excellent. The European taste is somewhat different, as we
know, but this also is now being provided for. The export
of tea from Shidzuoka Ken amounts in value to £200,000,
and in one year, when tea was scarce, the export reached
two and a half times that amount. It is hoped by the
authorities that it will greatly increase, the cultivation of

---

* Formerly Fuchiu, and known also as Sumpu.

the tea-plant in this Ken being developed with great care and energy, as was apparent throughout the day's journey.

This town is the most notable of all in relation to the great Tokugawa family, which gave to Japan its Shoguns and Tycoons from the year 1603 down to 1868, when the system of government by a Shogun was brought to an end. The first of the Tokugawa Shoguns, Iyéyasu, finally took up his residence in Shidzuoka after his great victory over his rivals at Sekigahara, near Lake Biwa—a victory which determined, as we saw, the government and fate of Japan from the beginning of the seventeenth century onwards to our own day. Here at Shidzuoka, then known as Sumpu, Iyéyasu had long before built himself a great castle, and resided in it. He now returned to it, and left it again only for two short intervals, to suppress rebellious attempts. Here he devoted himself mainly to literature, collecting and preserving so many old manuscripts, and otherwise so exerting himself that it is said to be largely due to him that much of the ancient Japanese literature is now in existence.[*]

---

[*] " The Sumpki quoted by Hirata mentions a large number of works brought to Iyéyasu from various parts of the country, some from Kioto and others from Kamakura, and a few from the monastery of Minobu San, in Koshiu. Before his death he gave directions that the library of Japanese and Chinese books which he had formed at Sumpu should be divided between his eighth son, the prince of Owari, and his ninth son, the prince of Kiushiu. The former received the greater part of the Japanese books, the latter the Chinese books. Under the directions of the prince of Owari were composed the ' Jingihoten ' and ' Ruijiu Nihongi.' One of Iyéyasu's grandsons, the famous second prince of Mito (1622-1700), known variously as Mito no Komon Sama and Mito no Giko (Mitsukini was his *nanori*), also collected a vast library by purchasing old books from Shinto and Buddhist temples, and from the people. With the aid of a number of scholars, amongst whom tradition says were several learned Chinese who had fled to Japan to escape the tyranny of the Manchu conquerors, he composed the ' Daini-honshi,' or History of Great Japan, in two hundred and forty books. This book is the standard history of Japan to this day, and all subsequent writers on the subject have taken it as their guide. He also compiled a work on the ceremonials of the imperial court, consisting of more than five hundred volumes, which the Mikado condescended to give the title of Reigi riuten. To defray the cost of producing these two magnificent works, the prince of Mito set aside at least 30,000 *koku* of rice per annum (some accounts say 50,000, others 70,000)."—Ernest Satow, in ' Transactions ' of Asiatic Society of Japan.—The *koku* is a little less

As the first, so the last of the Tokugawa Tycoons has made
Shidzuoka his place of residence, for here now resides the dethroned Tycoon, who lives in great privacy and simplicity.
He sees but few people, frankly acknowledging that the
reassertion of the Mikado's authority is just, and not
desiring to give any countenance to a contrary feeling.   He
devotes himself mainly to field-sports, but as I saw in the
house of one of the ministers of state in Tokio a very pretty
drawing from his (the ex-Tycoon's) hand, I cannot doubt
that he indulges himself likewise in the exercise of the
artist's skill.   As some compensation for their loss of employment, the Mikado's government presented a large tract
of land in this district to the former personal attendants and
servants of the Tycoon, much of which is cultivated under a
system of partnership, the tea-plant for which the soil is
peculiarly favourable being the principal thing grown here.

The literary reminiscences suggested by a visit to Shidzuoka are not limited to the doings of the Tokugawas, and I
must mention the circumstance that it was to this city that
the learned Hirata Atsutané secretly retired in the year 1812
to compose his great work, the 'Koshi-seibun,' which has
previously been quoted.   After offering up a prayer to all
the gods for their aid, he is said to have set to work on the
fifth of the month, and to have completed it by the end of it.
"As a proof of his remarkable memory," says Mr. Satow,
"it is said that he composed the three volumes of the text
and several volumes of the prolegomena, entitled 'Koshi-cho,'
without making a single reference to the works from which
his materials were drawn.   The 'Koshi-seibun' was apparently intended to have been brought far down into what is
usually called the historical period, but the part which
relates to the divine age is all that has at present appeared."

On our way over the mountains to-day we picked up a few
matters of fact which are worth mention here.   By the side

---

than five imperial bushels, and ten
koku per acre is given as a good
average production from the rice-
lands.   The prince of Mito thus devoted the produce of at least 3000
acres of rice-land to these literary
enterprises.

of one of the tea-houses, near the summit of the hill rising
from Missaka, was a large rounded stone of remarkable form,
which is known as the "night-crying stone." The story
connected with it, as told to me here at Shidzuoka, is as
follows:—

More than two thousand years ago (in the time of the
emperor Kogen, who reigned from 214 to 158 B.C., and died
at the good old age of 116), a woman who was—well, who
was a thorough wife, and whose husband had been away
but a few months, went to seek him in the region of what
is now the modern capital of the country. There met her, or
overtook her, on the way, one of those two-sworded gentlemen the *samurai*, who with all their advantages were not
always as gentle or as virtuous as they might have been,
as we shall presently see. This one fell in love with his
fellow-traveller, and employed all his arts, both on the road
and at the inn at which he took care they both should stay,
to establish that which some in our own country are at
present sighing for—a condition of "reciprocity." Failing
in this object, he appears to have lost his temper, and with
it what he called his love, for he drew his sword and
actually slew the poor woman on the spot. A month later
and she would have been nursing an infant at home; but as
it was, to keep the child alive required the aid of superior
power. That, fortunately, was not wanting, and the goddess
Kwannon had everything done that was necessary, even to
the naming of the child, Otahachi, and to having it brought
up upon a sort of "toffee" made from rice. That the crime
might not be kept secret, the goddess also caused the stone
previously mentioned to cry out, and a pine-tree standing
near to cry out likewise. When young Otahachi grew up
he went to a sword-grinder's, a Mr. Gengero's, to learn his
art, and while there one day, who should go in to have
his sword sharpened but the wicked *samurai* who slew his
mother! Gengero, on looking at the sword, pronounced it,
although of excellent quality originally, so worn and with so
little steel left in it as to be nearly useless. This led to a
conversation which convinced Otahachi, who overheard it,

that the *samurai* was the very man on whom he desired to
revenge his mother's death, and the spirited young fellow
at once challenged him to mortal combat. Ashamed as a
samurai to refuse, though desiring to escape (these swash-
buckler gentry who cut and slash at the weak always do
desire to escape when a strongish young fellow tackles
them !), he accepted the challenge, fought and fell, and thus
was the poor mother avenged by Kwannon's well-nourished
protégé. And what is the moral? Well, the great moral,
which tells so much for virtue, is obvious; and another is
that the Japanese rice-toffee is remarkably good food for
children, and can be purchased even to this day at the tea-
house of the "night-crying stone," and also at many another
tea-house up and down this Missaka mountain, and I dare say
at a great many places besides. I tried a little of it myself,
but I was so sure that my illustrious physician, Sir Henry
Thompson, would not consider it good for me that I scarce
did more than taste it. For two thousand years and more,
however, it has helped to nourish Japanese babes, and
plumper children I never desire to see.

Another of these matter-of-fact stories carries us back
still earlier, even to the time of the emperor Koan, who
reigned from 392 to 291 B.C., and died at the very ripe age
of 137. It tells of a wondrous pheasant which had wings
and a tail formed of swords, and was therefore far more
terrible, let it be understood, than any porcupine with mere
spears, however large. Worse a great deal than the cruel
samurai of the last story, this ferocious bird used to descend
upon the neighbouring village of Koya-nakayama, carry off
people, slay and eat them. The villagers not unnaturally
got so worried by these cruel depredations that they petitioned
the Mikado Koan to have the sworded pheasant hunted and
killed, and his majesty sent down a certain Prince Yashimasa
to effect this. The bird was so difficult to find, however,
and so artful in its devices for evading Yashimasa, sometimes
appearing as a woman mixing up with the villagers, sometimes
taking the form of a tree, and sometimes disappearing altogether, that the prince was long detained in the house of Atago

Shoji, a local gentleman, whose guest he had become. So long was he detained that he fell in love with a young girl named Shiragika, who happened to be at the same time an emissary of the goddess Kwannon and a daughter of Atago Shoji, and who returned the love of Yashimasa with warmth and loyalty. At last Yashimasa found the nest of the pheasant on the top of a neighbouring hill, and took his precautions for bagging it by arranging a bamboo screen with a hole to see through, and sitting behind it armed with a bow and arrows till the pheasant came. When it came there was no mistaking it, with its gleaming steel wings and its eyes which sparkled like stars, and Yashimasa at once brought it to the ground with an arrow through its cruel heart. He now had to return to the Mikado to report his success, and perforce left Shiragika behind, she deeming herself as a village girl unfit to accompany a prince to court, and sure to discredit him if she did so. Unfortunately, however, there was one result of their mutual love which could not be concealed for long, and which she was ashamed to have known, and poor Shiragika therefore thought it better that she should perish. She accordingly loaded her dress with stones and dropped into a deep part of the river off the rocks between Kame and Sakura, which are called to this day (I do not see why) the Chrysanthemum and Cherry-blossom Rocks. When Yashimasa got old and feeble he left the court and went and spent his last days at the spot, and died in the adjacent village of Kikugawa.

A further story was connected with the above, inasmuch as it concerned a well which the ghost of the sword-pheasant troubled and caused to boil and foam. The well was on the top of Mount Mokanza, and the name of it was Awagadaky. Notwithstanding that it was a well on the top of a mountain, it had an underground connection with the sea, for the water in it rose and fell with the tide. By the foaming of the well a sort of crust was formed, which got converted into a bell—one of three very famous bells in Japan, those of Mii and Anoyé being the others. All these bells were considered gifts of the sea-god. This Awagadaky bell had a very peculiar property, for if you struck it you would obtain whatever you desired at the time; but the fulfilment of your wish was ultimately followed by a terrible penalty, for you were sent to the worst of all places, which shall be nameless here, though it is as easy to spell as "bell," and you there found part of the established tortures to be that of satisfying innumerable leeches, food and other things thrown into the well curiously enough turning into leeches. At the foot of the mountain, in the village of Amatzuba, lived a man, Narinobel by name, who appears to have camped out on the mountain near the well's mouth for some reason of his own, and while there a man intruded upon him and thus offended him. On being angrily questioned on the subject, the man informed Mr. Narinobel that he was son and heir-apparent of the county *samurai* house of Ozawahiogo, and therefore had the right to enter uninvited. He at once left, however, and cherished the desire to revenge himself on Narinobel for his insolence. He decided, against the will of his father, whom he consulted on the point, to strike the bell and thus obtain ample means for taking his revenge in his own way. To prevent this his father went up the mountain in the night and buried the bell out of the son's way, and buried it so effectually that it has never since been found. The son was extremely angry to find it gone, and searched a great deal for it, even going to the length of burning down a temple in the hope of finding it among the ashes. A ferocious wind thereupon sprang up, and in it came one of the Gongen gods (deified Japanese celebrities), and either wind or god, or both together, hurled the heir of Ozawahiogo down a precipice, and thus brought his brief career to an end. "Mark," says the native narrative, "the power of God," and the reverent reader will not fail to do so.

With these very ancient stories I may fitly conclude the record of an evening at Shidzuoka, where they were written down as my interpreters roughly translated them from papers picked up on our mountain-walk during the day.

CHAPTER XIII.

FUJI-YAMA AND THE HAKONÉ MOUNTAINS.

As we have now come in full view of the great sacred mountain, and shall have it almost continually before us for a day or two to come, this appears to be a proper time and place to say a little more about it. And I would first observe that I see no reason for suggesting any explanations derived from profound considerations either for its being treated as a sacred mountain, or for its predominance in the works of artists of all kinds. The great height, solitude, and solemn beauty of the mountain would have had these results in any country in the world in the early stages of its life, and all these qualities would be quite certain to make even a deeper impression upon the life and thought and sentiment of such a people as the Japanese than upon those of most nations.

It has been said that there are on the summit of Fuji eight peaks, which have been likened to the eight petals of the sacred lotus-flower, and that this may have had some influence in confirming the popular belief in the sacredness of the mountain; and this may be true, for people will be influenced by almost any kind of consideration in the way of confirming themselves in beliefs already formed. But the best evidence of the sacred character of Fuji is to be found, I think, in the fact that every person who speaks or writes about it seems naturally to rise more or less into a reverent state of feeling as he does so. It has a real, a strong, and a solemnising influence on all who behold it. Even when it is viewed from beyond other mountains, its sovereign character is very striking; and when it is seen springing with one tremendous and sublime flight from sea to sky, it is of more sovereign character still. I am sorry to have to admit that there are not many places on the Tokaido from which this single unbroken curve of Fuji can be seen. He has a hump—not a very large or ungraceful one fortunately—upon his south-eastern side, known as Hoyei-san, which was thrown up at his last eruption in the year 1707, after a terrible fashion. A tremendous earthquake shook even distant provinces, and from the side of Fuji, about three thousand feet from the top, there burst out such masses of ashes that portions of them were carried a hundred miles away. The noise of the eruption was heard in Yedo, more than seventy miles away.

Mr. Brunton, in his large map of Japan, which I have found so very useful,[*] gives the height of Fuji-yama as 13,000 feet, and describes it as an extinct volcano. Mr. D. H. Marshall, M.A., however, in his 'Notes on some of the Volcanic Mountains in Japan,' read at the Asiatic Society,[†] gives the height as 12,365 feet—from a very careful determination with an omnimeter by Mr. R. Stewart, of the Govern-

---

[*] I have a copy of this map, but as it is mounted on a roller I did not take it to Japan. Mr. McRitchie, the accomplished engineer of the imperial Japanese lighthouse department, was kind enough to lend me a folding copy, which was so very useful.

[†] In what follows I propose to make a free use of the information given in this interesting paper, which was read as recently as 1878.

ment Survey Department—and says that it is erroneous to speak of it as extinct. "It has been dormant for not more than one hundred and seventy years, but the world-known Vesuvius itself is known to have been dormant for periods comparable with this, *e.g.*, prior to 79 A.D., between 79 and 203, and between 203 and 472. Again, Scrope writes that during the quiescent interval between the eruptions of 1137 and 1306 the whole surface of Vesuvius was in cultivation, and pools of water and chestnut-groves occupied the sides and bottom of the crater, as is at present the case with so many of the extinct craters, of Etna, Auvergne, etc. Fuji is therefore better called a dormant volcano." Mr. J. Rymer Jones descended into the crater, and found it to be 500 feet deep. As to the origin of Fuji, some native chroniclers claim for it even a less age than the present reigning dynasty, for whereas they allege that Jimmu-Tenno, the founder of the present Mikado's family, began to reign 660 years before Christ, they state that Fuji-yama was only created 285-6 years before Christ, Fuji being elevated and the bed of Lake Biwa being sunk both in one night. We are not, however, bound in any way to believe this, and modern investigators do not accept it. It appears to have been a pretty active volcano from the eighth to the eleventh century (A.D.). In the *Nihonki* it is written that in 799 the summit of Fuji burnt and emitted showers of ashes with thundering noises; the waters of the rivers at its base became red, and at night brilliant flames were seen. Again, in the *San-sai-dzuyé* it is recorded that in 864 the flames rose from the summit of Fuji to a great height; there were frequent earthquakes, and the sea for a distance of more than seventy miles along the shore receded five miles, large quantities of fish perishing. Fuji is cultivated to a height of from one to two thousand feet; above this is a belt of what has been called "prairie ground," and above this again is "a vast belt of forest which encircles the mountain for half its height." In this forest there is a great variety of trees, "including coniferous trees of various kinds—crypto-merias, pines, firs, etc., chestnut, elm, *dzusa*, a tree from the leaves of which oil is extracted, maple, elder, willow, boxwood, etc." The only plant that is said to be found above the forest is a curious one called *nikuji*, which is supposed to cure diseases.* The ascent of this mountain is a sacred pilgrimage, and there are accordingly several roads to the summit, with nine huts or shelters on each. The sight of the pilgrims, dressed in white robes, and praying to the rising sun, is said to greatly interest foreigners. Mr. Marshall says he has known two or three hundred of these white-robed devotees turn out of the numerous sheds on the summit "and chant their prayers most melodiously to the rising ruler of the day." He adds: "From the summit of Fuji on a clear day the view is superb of mountains, lakes, rivers, valleys, plains, and seas. . . . Sometimes the higher mountains are hidden by stormy seas of snow-white cloud, but even then the mountaineer feels the splendour of the scene ample reward for his labour."

Leaving Shidzuoka early on the morning of the 16th of March, we pursued our course eastward, lunching at Kambara, and staying for the next night at Mishima. Our route lay for several hours with Fuji-yama on our left and the sea on our right, and as the day was one of rare fineness, and of very remarkable atmospheric clearness, we enjoyed scenery which is not to be surpassed in the world. For some hours the whole 13,000 feet of Fuji-yama was without the faintest phantom of a cloud—an almost unprecedented fact, according to the local statements made to us—and when clouds formed they merely constituted a sort of experimental display, as if the governor of the district had carried his courtesy to the length of showing us how prettily clouds can be produced up there out of nothing; how much softer than any silk, and how much more transparent than any gauze, they can be woven when sunbeams interlace with vapours of snow; how slowly they can sail past the steadfast

---

* In a discussion on Mr. Marshall's paper, Mr. Satow stated that in an ascent of Fuji-yama which he had made in 1877, he had found plants growing as far up as the seventh station, and had seen tufts of grass as far up even as the ninth.

mountain front, and quicken their speed as they pass around and beyond it; with what consummate art they can veil any blemish on the mountain's beauty; and how, by deepening their own shade and darkening their own shadows, they can intensify by contrast even the cold, white, solid-seeming splendour of the mountain itself. As for the sea, as it lay lake-like but vast in the beautiful Suruga Bay, sparkling in a setting of coloured mountains, its solicitations to the eye were urgent and perpetual. A morning or two before it seemed, as I have previously remarked, to fairly foam with brightness; but on this occasion its brightness was more definite and intense, more like one might expect it to appear if its whole surface were surging with liquid diamonds. I have no power to describe the combined beauty of the mountain on the one hand and the sea on the other, on this middle day of March; but to assist the reader in imagining it, I ought to repeat that for hours we had full before us the immense sweep of this huge tower of silver and blue, from the summit, high in heaven, clear down to the sparkling sea. O for the skill of some more than mortal artist with which to fix before the eye this glorious picture!—and indeed those many pictures of this hallowed mountain as it appeared from our ever-shifting points of view throughout the day.

Where a branch of Suruga Bay comes close up to the hills, the Tokaido passing along the strand between, stands the beautiful Buddhist (Zen-shu) temple of Seikenji ("Clear View Temple")—beautiful for its position, overlooking the bay and the mountains beyond; beautiful for its buildings, which are among the best that we have seen of the purely Japanese type; and beautiful for its garden at the back, formed from the mountain-side, with a small natural torrent pouring down it, and with trees of great variety scattered in a highly picturesque manner over its rocky amphitheatre. In front of this temple is a plum-tree, planted by the hand of the great Iyéyasu nearly three hundred years ago. The residential buildings of the temple were in part rebuilt eleven years ago, and have been occu-

pied for a short time by the now reigning Mikado, who
once stayed here on account of the salubrity of the place.
We halted and visited this temple, the chief priest kindly
showing us its treasures, among which were letters of
Iyéyasu and Hideyoshi. There were likewise three silver
cups given to the temple by the present Mikado in remembrance of his visit. *A propos* of these cups, I was informed
that persons now subscribing to the funds of public institutions in Japan receive from the Mikado a present of cups.
If the subscription is of ten thousand *yen* (dollars) or upwards, the cups are of gold; if it be less than ten thousand
but of or over one thousand *yen*, they are of silver; and if
for less, they are of some material of less value. The
venerable chief priest of this temple has held the office for
thirty years.

Most of the villages passed through on the day now under
notice were on or near to the shore of Suruga Bay, along
which the Tokaido sweeps, and the villagers were largely
occupied in drying fish for manure. There was also carried
on in favourable places, and on a large scale, the method of
obtaining salt from the sea, by throwing sea-water over
prepared beds of sand, and allowing the sun's heat to
evaporate the water and leave the salt. The largest river
crossed was Fuji-kawa, which runs down from the inland
mountains past the western side of Fuji-yama, entering the
sea close to the base of that mountain. Its main channel
is about seventy miles long. When we passed it was
flowing with swiftness through one main channel of suf-
ficent width to compel us to cross in ferry-boats in the
absence of a bridge, but the bed of the river, which must
be nearly two miles wide, was dry. Three times a year
the whole of the broad bed is covered with the torrent.
The Tokaido proper crosses this river by a bridge much
higher up; but we took a short cut, and with it a very bad,
sandy road, so that I doubt if we gained anything in time.
I for one, however, gained the exercise and pleasure of the
walk across the river bed, which was very enjoyable. At
one period of the day, as we approached Mishima, we lost for

a time the company of his excellency Admiral Kawamura, who went off to inspect a quantity of Tiaki timber cut for his department in the forests on Mount Amaki, not allowing me to accompany him or to know beforehand of his going, on account of the disturbed state of my health.

It was five o'clock before we arrived at Mishima, having visited some pleasant gardens at Hara, after lunching at Kambara. Immediately after alighting from our *jinriki-shas*, in which we had been with brief intervals for nearly ten hours, we proceeded to visit the great Shinto temple of Mishima Gengin, at the invitation of the chief priest, Mayada, a temple so ancient as regards its foundation that no one knows when it was founded, and a chief priest so pleasant that I do not wish to meet a pleasanter. This is the temple by which Japanese pledge themselves when they wish to make a very solemn and binding engagement. Two of the junior priests received us at the outer *torii*, and led us to the temple proper, where the chief priest awaited us with the temple band playing. Some of us went through the simple ceremony of washing the hands and putting a branch of the sacred tree into its place. We then examined the treasures of the temple, including a very ancient vase, said to belong to the period of the gods—dating, that is, from before the reign of Jimmu-Tenno, the first Mikado, which commenced, according to the histories, six hundred and sixty years before Christ; an imperial order or warrant to the temple from the empress Gensho, written nearly twelve hundred years ago; likewise numerous small articles which once belonged to Yoritomo and his mother (twelfth century), having been brought here from the palace of Kamakura; a very ancient flute, known as the flute of ivory; a sword which was used by the Daimio of Hizen in subduing the Christian Japanese; and collections of other swords and of robes of distinction which have from time to time, during many centuries, been presented to the temple, and many of which, as the reader will suppose, were viewed with interest. The chief priest presented us with some of the "god's-food" in the form of boxes of sweetmeats which had been offered to the

god at the altar, and had remained there the usual time;
and likewise with a written description of the temple, and
some of the simple temple remembrances such as pilgrims
take away with them. He was good enough afterwards to
bring me (to the excellent hotel at which we stayed in
Mishima) some photographs of the temple which he had
considerately had taken during the day for the purpose.
Our hotel at Mishima was that of Mr. Saiko, which was in
admirable condition, having been renovated for the reception
of the Mikado on his Tokaido journey.

The next day our route lay over the Hakoné mountains,
the pass of which, although broad and in the main of
moderate gradients, is in places so steep, and everywhere
paved with such large rough stones, as to be almost impracticable for *jinriki-shas;* and although, as we saw, these
little carriages were occasionally dragged over, they are
taken over empty, the passenger having to travel on foot
the greater part of the distance from Mishima to Hakoné.
The usual course is therefore to resort to the *kago,* or
light carriage, borne on the shoulders of men. But before
describing *our kagos,* let me mention another sort of *kago*
which we met in the street on our way out of Mishima,
and which was no less than the *kago* of the god. It appears
that just as the god had at Isé ponies to take him for a
ride on great occasions, so he has a *kago* to serve a similar
purpose on festival days; and this ornamental little carriage,
mounted partly above the bearing-poles, instead of being
slung below them, was the *kago* of Mishima's god. I am
told that here as elsewhere the god has at the great festivals,
known as " Matsurei," no less than forty bearers, all dressed
in white, who sway from side to side of the road, singing
sacred songs, and at intervals hoisting the *kago* as high
in the air as possible. All the shops are closed at such
festive times, and there is general rejoicing. And in what
form is the god? the reader will ask, at least I hope she *

---

* I agree with a writer who re-   reading—I forget where—that we
cently set forth in an article I was   are very much in want of a pronoun

SOLDIERS IN TIME OF PEACE.

From HOKUSAI. Reproduced for this Work by a Japanese Engraver.

will, because that question will enable me to point out the power of the Japanese imagination : for the god has no form at all, except that with which the imagination invests him ; he is simply represented, after a fashion, by *goheis*, which, as the reader knows, are neither more nor less in themselves than bits of paper cut in jagged strips and attached to sticks.

Our kagos are of two kinds, the one being closed like a dwarf sedan-chair, with the bottom serving as the seat, and sliding doors at the sides ; the other, known as *yama-kago*, or mountain-*kago*, being a mere suspended open framework of bamboo to rest on, with a light screen over it. In both cases they are suspended from a pole running lengthwise, and the bearers carry folded handkerchiefs as a shoulder-pad, and a bamboo stick to rest the pole on when they "change shoulders," which they do after very short intervals. The largest *kago* of each kind that could be obtained in Mishima was placed at my disposal, and I tried both before starting, and found, as I thought, that either would do ; but we all started from Mishima on foot, and when, after a long and tiring climb, I forced myself into them and attempted to travel in them, I found that neither was endurable for more than a few minutes, especially as the bearers changed shoulders frequently, and kept me so incessantly gyrating through large angles that they gave me a sort of longitudinal swimming in the head, to which a reasonable regard for the readers of this book would not allow me to submit myself for more than a very few hundred yards. I was obliged, therefore, to make my own way on foot to Hakoné, and a toilsome way I found it. At Hakoné, after luncheon, a much larger *yama-kago* was obtained, and adapted for four bearers, so that the remainder of the day's journey to Yumoto was relieved as much as I found necessary. Speaking generally, these *kagos* are a detestable means of conveyance to all but Japanese, owing to the cramped position which you are required to assume in them. They appear to be comfortable

---

to stand for either he or she in cases of this sort. In this instance I give the lady the preference, as is meet and right.

enough, indeed very comfortable, to the natives of the country, because they are habituated from infancy to sit upon their feet, or upon the floor with their feet turned under. But for those of us (Europeans, Americans, and others) who are accustomed all our days to sit on chairs, it is very difficult to assume at all the position necessary for *kago*-sitting or *kago*-lying, and almost impossible to preserve it long. "In these vehicles," says Mr. Griffis, "I always fall asleep at the wrong end; my head remaining wide awake, while my feet are incorrigibly somnolent. I lie in all shapes, from a coil of rope to a pair of inverted dividers, with head wrapped from the cold, and hardly enough face visible to make a monkey."

We had a very suitable day for crossing these Hakoné mountains, the atmosphere being clear and inclined to brightness, but with continuous screens of cloud to protect us from the fiercer heat and light of the sun's direct beams. We obtained as we ascended glorious views over the country we were leaving, from Fuji-yama westward over the fruitful Shidzuoka Ken, and southward over the fine bay of Suruga and the Idzu hills and vales. The road is pillared on either side throughout with ancient pine-trees, that make it like a vast continuous cathedral aisle, but one unlike all human architecture in its ascents and descents, in the twisted, contorted earth-grasping character of its column-pedestals, and in the shifting lights and shadows that stream through its rustling roof. Occasionally we heard the melodious notes of the *uguisu*, a wood-bird much celebrated in the poetry of the country. It has a note like one of the best "phrases" of the nightingale, if the musical world will allow the expression; but its range is limited. It is, however, a pretty though a brief bit of nightingale melody, and is sufficient of itself (although it is not by any means alone) to make answer to those who say that bird-song has been omitted altogether from the delights of Japan.* The *uguisu* is said by the

---

* Since writing the above I have been looking over the proof of a paper by my friend Capt. Hawes, of Tokio, descriptive of a tour made by him in

poets "to come warbling with the plum-blossom." And as one is here speaking of birds, it may not be amiss to add that throughout most of the country, and more still throughout the towns of Japan of which I have had experience, there has been a marked abundance of hawks and eagles on the wing—these being, in fact, with wild ducks and wild geese, the birds most usually seen here. We observed on this road the process of preparing the bark of the *koso* for paper manufacture. There were also—if I may be allowed to vary the subject of my remarks with something like the rapidity with which the objects of observation varied on the roadside—numerous small shrines at intervals, and occasionally a rough monumental tablet to the memory of some long-deceased person of eminence. It was touching to note that here, high up on this mountain road, the memory of persons who had been dead for centuries was kept green still by a living hand placing before the stone, in a bit of bamboo cane, a branch of fresh spring verdure.

Our hard walk over the mountain was relieved by frequent stoppages for rest and the slight but welcome refreshment of a cup of Japanese tea. There were numerous tea-houses by the way, and at any of them this could be got; but having the honour of travelling with a cabinet minister of the country, and one of the most thoughtful and kindly of hosts, our necessities had all been anticipated by his officers, or by those of the Ken or county. A long way up the mountain we halted at a spot whence the view westward was thought to be the finest on the pass, and where consequently a little view-house had been erected for his majesty the emperor on his journey previously mentioned. Our view of the great solitary king of mountains, Fuji, was already, by our change

---

the interior of Japan, in which I find a similar view stated. After describing the delicious perfume of the air as not unlike the fragrance of the meadow-sweet at home, he adds: "This, combined with the clear note of the cuckoo, which sounded pleasantly through the woods, the warble of the nightingale, and the harsher song of the jay, which were heard all around, does certainly rather upset the theory of some writers who assert that 'Japan is a country in which the birds do not sing and the flowers have no smell.'"

of position, getting seriously compromised by other mountains intervening, and he had donned a sort of helmet or crown of cloud; a little later on he became like our own King Arthur, on the night of his final leave-taking from the queen, for the rolling vapour

> " Enwound him fold by fold, and made him gray,
> And grayer, till himself became as mist,"

and he was seen again no more before the close of our journey to the capital.

Soon after the descent commenced we reached the dividing line between the Kens of Shidzuoka and Kanagawa, which was notified by notice-posts, and was further marked in the present instance by a change of police, it being an order of the emperor to the governing bodies of the Kens, since the murder of the late minister Okubo, that cabinet ministers travelling in the interior shall be attended by a small escort of police. Some people who observe this police escort jump to the conclusion that the ministers live in fear for their lives, and that it is by their own desire that the escort is provided; whereas I am able to state from personal knowledge and experience that the escort is felt by some of the ministers to be irksome rather than otherwise, and is submitted to in deference to the commands of his majesty. No such thing as a general fear for the lives of the ministers is probably felt either by themselves or by his majesty; but the country has undergone vast changes during the last few years, and vast changes of necessity beget dissatisfaction in many, and there is always a risk that among many dissatisfied there may be here and there a fanatic who would revenge himself in blood if he could, and this is no doubt the reason why the emperor desires that for the present his cabinet advisers should usually have the protection of either a military or civil guard to prevent at least anything like hasty or casual attempts against them. Another reason for the precaution is to be found in the fact that the ministers are considered by the people to be peculiarly responsible for the regulations which foreign powers impose upon the government of Japan, and which are known to give to foreigners many privileges at the expense of the native population. This is a perpetual source of danger to the government.

After changing guard and commencing the descent towards Hakoné, we came upon a fine view of the pretty little lake of that name, which has an area of 3½ square miles, and upon the bank of which stands the village.* Mr. Marshall, in the paper already quoted, tells us that Lake Hakoné, like Avernus, is supposed to be an ancient crater, and quotes what Kaempfer wrote in his description of his journey to the court of the Shogun in 1691, when he passed the lake about the middle of March, and therefore at the same period as that at which we passed it. He wrote : "This lake is everywhere surrounded with high mountains, which shut it up on both sides in such a manner that there is no room to apprehend its overflowing the adjacent country. Though the mountains that encompass it be of a very great height, yet the top of Fuji-yama rises still higher, being seen to the W.N.W. by the inhabitants of Togitsu (Hakoné). We were told that in former times this place sank in by a violent earthquake, and that in lieu of it sprang up this lake. In proof of this they advance the great quantity of *sugi* or cedar trunks of an uncommon size which lie at the bottom, and are fetched up from thence by divers, when the lord of the place commands it, or hath occasion for them. For the neighbourhood produces everywhere great plenty of this tree, and the tallest and finest cedars that are to be found anywhere in Japan. The lake of Hakoné being entirely surrounded with mountains hath no other outlet but through one of these mountains, being the same which is called Futago-yama, and which lets the waters come through three different openings, from whence they fall down the mountain-side in the nature of cataracts to a considerable height, and, soon receiving other rivulets from the neighbouring mountains, form them-

---

* This and the neighbouring villages as far on as Yumoto are noted for the excellence and cheapness of their ornamental articles in wood, and more especially of their inlaid work. Shops for the sale of them abound in all these villages.

selves into a river, which with a frightful horrid noise crosses
the valley, running down over stones and sometimes precipices
towards the sea." In this last sentence he refers, says Mr.
Marshall, to the river Haya, which flows through the Miyano-
shita, which is really the outlet of the lake; and he was led
by the people of Hakoné into the error regarding the connection between the Haya and the lake by the people telling him
of an artificial outlet which the farmers on the other side of
the mountains to the west of the lake made in order to secure
water for their fields in all seasons. This is a tunnel piercing
the mountains, and is an engineering work of great magnitude, requiring much skill for its execution. Mr. Marshall
makes no reference to the age of this great engineering work;
but Mr. Griffis states that it was performed centuries ago,
"and now through the rocky sluices flows a flood sufficient to
enrich the millions of acres of Suruga province."

In passing out of Hakoné we saw the site of the old
Tokaido gate, and the remains of the gate buildings. In the
days of the Tycoons this Tokaido high road was blocked by
three defensible gates, which people were allowed through
only with passports. These gates were known as *séki*, as
already intimated, and appear to have been kept with great
care down to the close of the Tycoon's government, as I have
heard from those who travelled over the Tokaido in comparatively recent times of the difficulties experienced in getting
quickly through the gates, and of the insistence of those in
charge upon all passengers, even the sick and weak, alighting
from their *kagos* to pass through. I have also heard, however,
that even the officers of the terrible Tycoon were not at
all times more absolutely incorruptible than other such
functionaries, and that the passage was facilitated by a due
regard to the financial convenience of the "obstructives."
The *sekis*, in the feudal days, which were days of feuds, were
important strategic points, and their sites were of course so
selected that they might be.

The road beyond the old Hakoné gate, going eastwards
(as we were), rises again occasionally, but to no very great
extent—if my observation from a *yama-kago*, in a nearly

horizontal position, may be trusted—but there were long descents, with many very steep and winding places, to be made before our destination, Yumoto, was reached. The scenery was fine, and for the greater part wooded, with a torrent tumbling down the valley, and the hedges enlivened by violets and by a variegated bamboo plant with green and yellow in each stem and leaf. It being a bad thing to go to sleep under such circumstances, although still ill, I did what I could to avoid it, but the easy, synchronous, sonorous movements of the *kago*, the lulling though half-sibilant voice of the torrent, the soothing beauty of the green aisle through which one was gliding, and, most of all, the fatigue of a long mountain walk succeeding a short night's sleep, were sometimes and short times overpowering, and I had to yield to them. Unlike Mr. Griffis, however, I went to sleep at the right end. I completed the last two miles of the journey on foot, tempted by the glimpses ahead of the bright and beautiful Sea of Sagami, out of which opens the bay on which stand both Yokohama and Tokio. The earth drinks up nearly all the light the sun sheds on it; but the water reflects a part of it, and so brightens the landscape with sheets of light. It is, no doubt, this reflection of the light—whether of the direct rays of the sun or of rays already reflected from sky or cloud—that gives to water part of the charm which one never fails to feel in the presence of river, lake, or sea.

Our day's work terminated in a new, and as yet unfinished, hotel, with a European-looking exterior and a purely Japanese interior. It contains a couple of baths of the hot-spring water of Yumoto, and is beautifully situated on the bank of the resounding river that leaps and scrambles down to the valley. The landlord, Mr. Saiko, does not like Europeans or Americans, I was told—at least he sets his face against having them as guests in his hotel, because while he takes a great pride in having it clean and bright, and in perfect Japanese order, they have not the good manners to take their boots off and behave as becomes the place. Therefore he objected very seriously to my son and myself going there as involving an infringement of a rule which he intended to be absolute and to maintain unbroken, and how his objection was got over I don't know. But it was got over, and we found ourselves in charming quarters, making due allowance (as you always must make in a house of Japanese style) for the absence of any warmth beyond what can be got out of small open charcoal fires in *hibachis*, and likewise for the presence of draughts all round you. The best was, however, done with screens, as usual in such cases, and the best was not bad in this case.

Too fatigued to sleep much, nevertheless, I was glad when six o'clock came, and with it the preparations for the last start of our Tokaido trip. Before leaving I looked carefully through Mr. Saiko's hotel, and found it very interesting. It was most excellently built as regards workmanship, and several beautiful woods were used in its construction, in all cases being left, as usual in Japan, untouched by paint or polish. Some of the ceilings were formed of planks cut from a tree dug from such a depth below the soil and in such a position as to prove that it was of great antiquity. Time and darkness and the grave had only veined and stained it with peculiar beauty, and, laid in strakes alternating with others of modern wood, it had a very bright and pleasing effect. Another ceiling was formed with plank of extreme breadth and clearness of texture, and was quite a curiosity of construction. The house had other constructive merits which I need not dwell on. I confess, however, that I was a little startled to find the old Japanese system of a common bath for men and women preserved in this beautiful modern establishment. There were but two baths to the house, one public, in which ladies, gentlemen, and young people of both sexes were supposed to refresh themselves, and the other a private bath, the privacy of which consisted solely, so far as I could see, in a partition separating part of it from the other, the bath itself being open in front. I presume Mr. Saiko's motto is "Honi soit qui mal y pense!"

Yomoti is fifteen *ris* six *chios* from Kanagawa. A *ri*

is thirty-six *chios*, and a *chio* is sixty fathoms and a little more. But as there are people alive who were educated before Mr. Forster introduced the School Boards, I had better put the case more simply, and say that the distance was 15⅙ *ris*, and that a *ri* is equal to nearly two and a half miles (more exactly 2·46); let us call it thirty-seven and a half miles. We left, by my watch (which was wrong, having Nagoya time, but that does not matter), at a quarter past seven; we arrived in Kanagawa at a quarter before two. We stopped three or four times; we spent one hour in lunching and resting at Fuji-sawa; and the road was to a considerable extent very hilly, and to a larger extent very bad, being a sand road with so many holes in it that a frequent slackening of pace was inevitable. Yet, deducting the luncheon hour, we travelled in the *jinriki-shas*, with two men to each (three to mine most of the way), the thirty-seven and a half miles in five and a half hours, which was an average of nearly seven miles an hour. From Fuji-sawa to Kanagawa the distance is over fifteen English miles: we travelled it in exactly two hours, or at the rate of over seven and a half miles an hour, although this part of the journey included the most and worst of the hills, and the worst part of the road. On a smooth good road, such as the Tokaido often is beyond the Hakoné mountains, and where there are but few towns upon it, the *jinriki-sha* men frequently ran us along at eight miles per hour. I believe the poor fellows who get their living in this way are very, very poorly paid indeed—as a general rule, I mean, of course— and many of them have wives and families. The stress of life must therefore bear heavily on them; still, more willing or more industrious fellows I have never seen, and I sincerely hope they are able to bear their hard lot without too much of that pain which we must all feel in thinking of it.

I have mentioned the bad state of the Tokaido between Odawara—that famous town of the siege of which I have elsewhere spoken—and Tokio. I may add that hearing, as I had often done, of the excellence of this great highway between what were formerly the capitals of the Mikado and the Tycoon, I was quite astonished at the state in which I saw it in most of the towns and villages through which it passed. One would have expected that the presence of a populous town, where labour must be cheap, while on the one hand increasing traffic and damaging the highway, would on the other be made available for more than compensating for the extra traffic, and for keeping the road in a thoroughly satisfactory state. But the contrary is the case, and the local traffic is allowed to destroy the highway with seeming impunity, and thus to entail upon long-journey travellers delays, fatigues, and even dangers which are wholly unnecessary. I am quite aware that owing to the abolition of the Daimio traffic, and the existence of steamship communication between the former and present capitals, the Tokaido has become a less frequented highway than it was aforetime; but on the other hand the maintenance and improvement of its internal means of communication are of such great importance to the country, and the western part of the Tokaido is so well kept between the towns and villages, that one could not but continually regret the absence of satisfactory means for compelling the local people to keep the main road good and efficient within their own limits.

But whether the Tokaido be good or bad, our journey upon it was now over. The interior of Japan had swept past us for many days, decorating the hall of memory with many a splendid picture, not to be forgotten until its walls turn again to dust. At the Kanagawa railway station we were met by many friends, upon several of whom the naval uniform glittered in the afternoon sun. A few minutes more and we were speeding back to the capital behind the horse of fire; and yet a few minutes more and we were once again under a roof where kindness blooms continually, and again the guests of a hostess whose gentle but hearty welcome suffered nothing from her want of English words.

APPENDIX.

TREATIES AND CONVENTIONS.

TREATY BETWEEN GREAT BRITAIN AND JAPAN,

Signed at Yedo August 26, 1858. Ratifications exchanged at Yedo July 11, 1859.

HER MAJESTY the Queen of the United Kingdom of Great Britain and Ireland, and His Majesty the Tycoon of Japan, being desirous to place the relations between the two countries on a permanent and friendly footing, and to facilitate commercial intercourse between their respective subjects, and having for that purpose resolved to enter into a Treaty of Peace, Amity, and Commerce, have named as their Plenipotentiaries, that is to say :—

Her Majesty the Queen of Great Britain and Ireland, The Right Honourable the Earl of Elgin and Kincardine, a Peer of the United Kingdom, and Knight of the Most Ancient and Most Noble Order of the Thistle :—

And His Majesty the Tycoon of Japan, Midzuno Chikugo no Kami ; Nagai Gemba no Kami ; Inouye Shinano no Kami ; Hori Oribe no Sho ; Iwase Higo no Kami ; and Tsuda Hanzaburo, who after having communicated to each other their respective full powers and found them to be in good and due form, have agreed upon and concluded the following Articles :—

I. There shall be perpetual peace and friendship between Her Majesty the Queen of the United Kingdom of Great Britain and Ireland, her heirs and successors, and His Majesty the Tycoon of Japan, and between their respective dominions and subjects.

II. Her Majesty the Queen of the United Kingdom of Great Britain and Ireland may appoint a Diplomatic Agent to reside at the city of Yedo, and Consuls or Consular Agents to reside at any or all the ports of Japan, which are opened for British commerce by this Treaty.

The Diplomatic Agent and Consul-General of Great Britain shall have the right to travel freely to any part of the Empire of Japan.

His Majesty the Tycoon of Japan may appoint a Diplomatic Agent to reside in London, and Consuls, or Consular Agents, at any or all the ports of Great Britain.

The Diplomatic Agent and Consul-General of Japan shall have the right to travel freely to any part of Great Britain.

III. The ports and towns of Hakodaté, Kanagawa, and Nagasaki shall be opened to British subjects on the first of July, one thousand eight hundred and fifty-nine. In addition to which, the following ports and towns shall be opened to them at the dates hereinafter specified :—

Nee-e-gata, or, if Nee-e-gata be found to be unsuitable as a harbour, another convenient port on the west coast of Nipon, on the first day of January, one thousand eight hundred and sixty.

Hiogo, on the first day of January, one thousand eight hundred and sixty-three.

In all the foregoing ports and towns, British subjects may permanently reside. They shall have the right to lease ground, and purchase the buildings thereon, and may erect dwellings and warehouses; but no fortification, or place of military strength, shall be erected under pretence of building dwellings or warehouses; and to see that this Article is observed, the Japanese authorities shall have the right to inspect, from time to time, any buildings which are being erected, altered, or repaired.

The place which British subjects shall occupy for their buildings, and the harbour regulations, shall be arranged by the British Consul and the Japanese authorities of each place, and if they cannot agree, the matter shall be referred to and settled by the British Diplomatic Agent and the Japanese Government. No wall, fence, or gate shall be erected by the Japanese around the place where British subjects reside, or anything done which may prevent a free egress or ingress to the same.

British subjects shall be free to go where they please, within the following limits, at the opened ports of Japan :—

At Kanagawa to the River Lokugo (which empties into the Bay of Yedo, between Kawasaki and Sinagawa), and ten *ri* in any other direction.

At Hakodaté ten *ri* in any direction.

At Hiogo ten *ri* in any direction, that of Kioto excepted, which city shall not be approached nearer than ten *ri*. The crews of vessels resorting to Hiogo shall not cross the River Enagawa, which empties into the bay between Hiogo and Osaca.

The distance shall be measured by land from the goyosho, or town hall of each of the foregoing ports, the *ri* being equal to four thousand two hundred and seventy-five yards English measure.

At Nagasaki, British subjects may go into any part of the Imperial domain in its vicinity.

The boundaries of Nee-e-gata, or the place that may be substituted for it, shall be settled by the British Diplomatic Agent and the Government of Japan.

From the first day of January, one thousand eight hundred and sixty-two, British subjects shall be allowed to reside in the city of Yedo, and from the first day of January, one thousand eight hundred and sixty-three, in the city of Osaca, for the purposes of trade only. In each of these two cities a suitable place, within which they may hire houses, and the distance they may go, shall be arranged by the British Diplomatic Agent and the Government of Japan.

IV. All questions in regard to rights, whether of property or person, arising between British subjects in the dominions of His Majesty the Tycoon of Japan, shall be subject to the jurisdiction of the British authorities.

V. Japanese subjects, who may be guilty of any criminal act towards British subjects, shall be arrested and punished by the Japanese authorities according to the laws of Japan.

British subjects who may commit any crime against Japanese subjects, or the subjects or citizens of any other country, shall be tried and punished by the Consul, or other public functionary, authorised thereto, according to the laws of Great Britain.

Justice shall be equitably and impartially administered on both sides.

VI. A British subject having reason to complain of a Japanese, must proceed to the Consulate and state his grievance.

The Consul will inquire into the merits of the case, and do his utmost to arrange it amicably. In like manner, if a Japanese have reason to complain of a British subject, the Consul shall no less listen to his complaint, and endeavour to settle it in a friendly manner. If disputes take place of such a nature that the Consul cannot arrange them amicably, then he shall request the assistance of the Japanese authorities, that they may together examine into the merits of the case and decide it equitably.

VII. Should any Japanese subject fail to discharge debts incurred to a British subject, or should he fraudulently abscond, the Japanese authorities will do their utmost to bring him to justice, and to enforce recovery of the debts; and should any British subject fraudulently abscond, or fail to discharge debts incurred by him to a Japanese subject, the British authorities will, in like manner, do their utmost to bring him to justice, and to enforce recovery of the debts.

Neither the British or Japanese Governments are to be held responsible for the payment of any debts contracted by British or Japanese subjects.

VIII. The Japanese Government will place no restrictions whatever upon the employment, by British subjects, of Japanese in any lawful capacity.

IX. British subjects in Japan shall be allowed the free exercise of their religion, and for this purpose shall have the right to erect suitable places of worship.

X. All foreign coin shall be current in Japan, and shall pass for its corresponding weight in Japanese coin of the same description.

British and Japanese subjects may freely use foreign or Japanese coin, in making payments to each other.

As some time will elapse before the Japanese will become acquainted with the value of foreign coin, the Japanese Government will, for the period of one year after the opening of each port, furnish British subjects with Japanese coin in exchange for theirs, equal weights being given, and no discount taken for recoinage.

Coins of all description (with the exception of Japanese copper coin), as well as foreign gold and silver uncoined, may be exported from Japan.

XI. Supplies for the use of the British navy may be landed at Kanagawa, Hakodaté, and Nagasaki, and stored in warehouses, in the custody of an officer of the British Government, without the payment of any duty; but if any such supplies are sold in Japan, the purchaser shall pay the proper duty to the Japanese authorities.

XII. If any British vessel be at any time wrecked or stranded on the coasts of Japan, or be compelled to take refuge in any port within the dominions of the Tycoon of Japan, the Japanese authorities, on being apprised of the fact, shall immediately render all the assistance in their power; the persons on board shall receive friendly treatment, and be furnished, if necessary, with the means of conveyance to the nearest Consular station.

XIII. Any British merchant vessel arriving off one of the open ports of Japan shall be at liberty to hire a pilot to take her into port. In like manner, after she has discharged all legal dues and duties and is ready to take her departure, she shall be allowed to hire a pilot to conduct her out of port.

XIV. At each of the ports open to trade, British subjects shall be at full liberty to import from their own or any other ports, and sell there, and purchase therein, and export to their own or any other ports, all manner of merchandise, not contraband, paying the duties thereon, as laid down in the Tariff annexed to the present Treaty, and no other charges whatsoever. With the exception of munitions of war, which shall only be sold to the Japanese Government and foreigners, they may freely buy from Japanese, and sell to them, any articles that either may have for sale, without the intervention of any Japanese officers in such purchase or sale, or in making or receiving payment for the same; and all classes of Japanese may purchase, sell, keep, or use any articles sold to them by British subjects.

XV. If the Japanese Custom-house officers are dissatisfied with the value placed on any goods by the owner, they may place a value thereon, and offer to take the goods at that valuation. If the owner refuses to accept the offer, he shall pay duty on such valuation. If the offer be accepted by the owner, the purchase money shall be paid to him without delay, and without any abatement or discount.

XVI. All goods imported into Japan by British subjects, and which have paid the duty fixed by this Treaty, may be transported by the Japanese into any part of the Empire without the payment of any tax, excise, or transit duty whatever.

XVII. British merchants who may have imported merchandise into any open port in Japan, and paid duty thereon, shall be entitled, on obtaining from the Japanese Custom-house authorities a certificate stating that such payment has been made, to re-export the same, and land it in any other of the open ports without the payment of any additional duty whatever.

XVIII. The Japanese authorities at each port will adopt the means that they may judge most proper for the prevention of fraud or smuggling.

XIX. All penalties enforced, or confiscations made under this Treaty, shall belong to, and be appropriated by, the Government of His Majesty the Tycoon of Japan.

XX. The Articles for the regulation of trade which are appended to this Treaty, shall be considered as forming a part of the same, and shall be equally binding on both the Contracting Parties to this Treaty, and on their subjects. The Diplomatic Agent of Great Britain in Japan, in conjunction with such person or persons as may be appointed for that purpose by the Japanese Government, shall have power to make such rules as may be required to carry into full and complete effect the provisions of this Treaty, and the provisions of the Articles regulating trade appended thereto.

XXI. This Treaty being written in the English, Japanese, and Dutch languages, and all the versions having the same meaning and intention, the Dutch version shall be considered the original; but it is understood that all official communications addressed by the Diplomatic and Consular Agents of Her Majesty the Queen of Great Britain to the Japanese authorities, shall henceforward be written in English. In order, however, to facilitate the transaction of business, they will, for a period of five years from the signature of this Treaty, be accompanied by a Dutch or Japanese version.

XXII. It is agreed that either of the High Contracting Parties to this Treaty, on giving one year's previous notice to the other, may demand a revision thereof, on or after the first of July, one thousand eight hundred and seventy-two, with a view to the insertion therein of such amendments as experience shall prove to be desirable.

XXIII. It is hereby expressly stipulated that the British Government and its subjects will be allowed free and equal participation in all privileges, immunities, and advantages that may have been, or may be hereafter, granted by His Majesty the Tycoon of Japan, to the Government or subjects of any other nation.

XXIV. The ratification of this Treaty, under the hand of Her Majesty the Queen of Great Britain and Ireland, and under the name and seal of His Majesty the Tycoon of Japan, respectively, shall be exchanged at Yedo, within a year from this day of signature. In token whereof, the respective Plenipotentiaries have signed and sealed this Treaty.

Done at Yedo, this twenty-sixth day of August, in the year of our Lord one thousand eight hundred and fifty-eight, corresponding to the Japanese date, the eighteenth day of the seventh month of the fifth year of Ansei, Tsuchinoye 'mma.

ELGIN AND KINCARDINE.
MIDZUNO CHIKUGO NO KAMI.
NAGAI GEMBA NO KAMI.
INOUYE SHINANO NO KAMI.
HORI ORIBEI NO SHO.
IWASE HIGO NO KAMI.
TSUDA HANZABURO.

REGULATIONS UNDER WHICH BRITISH TRADE IS TO BE CONDUCTED IN JAPAN.

I. WITHIN forty-eight hours (Sundays excepted) after the arrival of a British ship in a Japanese port, the captain or commander shall exhibit to the Japanese Custom-house authorities the receipt of the British Consuls, showing that he has deposited all the ship's papers, the ship's bills of lading, etc., at the British Consulate, and he shall then make an entry of his ship, by giving a written paper, stating the name of the ship, and the name of the port from which she comes, her tonnage, the name of her captain or commander, the names of her passengers (if any), and the number of her crew, which paper shall be certified by the captain or commander to be a true statement, and shall be signed by him; he shall, at the same time, deposit a written manifest of his cargo, setting forth the marks and numbers of the packages and their contents, as they are described in his bills of lading, with the names of the person or persons to whom they are consigned. A list of the stores of the ship shall be added to the manifest. The captain or commander shall certify the manifest to be a true account of all the cargo and stores on board the ship, and shall sign his name to the same.

If any error is discovered in the manifest, it may be corrected within twenty-four hours (Sundays excepted) without the payment of any fee, but for any alteration or post entry to the manifest made after that time, a fee of fifteen dollars shall be paid.

All goods not entered on the manifest shall pay double duties on being landed.

Any captain or commander that shall neglect to enter his vessel at the Japanese Custom-house within the time prescribed by this regulation, shall pay a penalty of sixty dollars for each day that he shall so neglect to enter his ship.

II. The Japanese Government shall have the right to place Custom-house officers on board of any ship in their ports (men-of-war excepted). All Custom-house officers shall be treated with civility, and such reasonable accommodation shall be allotted to them as the ship affords.

No goods shall be unladen from any ship between the hours of sunset and sunrise, except by special permission of the Custom-house authorities; and the hatches, and all other places of entrance into that part of the ship where the cargo is stowed, may be secured by Japanese officers between the hours of sunset and sunrise, by fixing seals, locks, or other fastenings; and if any person shall, without due permission, open any entrance that has been so secured, or shall break or remove any seal, lock, or other fastening that has been affixed by the Japanese Custom-house officers, every person so offending shall pay a fine of sixty dollars for each offence.

Any goods that shall be discharged, or attempted to be discharged, from any ship, without being duly entered at the Japanese Custom-house, as hereinafter provided, shall be liable to seizure and confiscation.

Packages of goods made up with an intent to defraud the revenue of Japan, by concealing therein articles of value which are not set forth in the invoice, shall be forfeited.

If any British ship shall smuggle, or attempt to smuggle, goods in any of the non-opened harbours of Japan, all such goods shall be forfeited to the Japanese Government, and the ship shall pay a fine of one thousand dollars for each offence.

Vessels needing repairs may land their cargo for that purpose, without the payment of duty. All goods so landed shall remain in charge of the Japanese authorities, and all just charges for storage, labour, and supervision shall be paid thereon. But if any portion of such cargo be sold, the regular duties shall be paid on the portion so disposed of.

Cargo may be transhipped to another vessel in the same harbour without payment of duty; but all transhipments shall be made under the supervision of Japanese officers, and after satisfactory proof has been given to the Custom-house authorities of the *bonâ fide* nature of the transaction, and also under a permit to be granted for that purpose by such authorities.

The importation of opium being prohibited, any British vessel coming to Japan for the purposes of trade, and having more than three catties' weight of opium on board, the surplus quantity may be seized and destroyed by the Japanese authorities; and any person or persons smuggling, or attempting to smuggle opium, shall be liable to pay a fine of fifteen dollars for each catty of opium so smuggled or attempted to be smuggled.

III. The owner, or consignee of any goods who desires to land them, shall make an entry of the same at the Japanese Custom-house. The entry shall be in writing, and shall set forth the name of the person making the entry, and the name of the ship in which the goods were imported, and the marks, numbers, packages, and the contents thereof, with the value of each package extended, separately in one amount, and at the bottom of the entry shall be placed the aggregate value of all the goods contained in the entry. On each entry, the owner or consignee shall certifiy in writing that the entry then presented exhibits the actual cost of the goods, and that nothing has been concealed whereby the Customs of Japan would be defrauded, and the owner or consignee shall sign his name to such certificate.

The original invoice or invoices of the goods so entered shall be presented to the Custom-house authorities, and shall remain in their possession until they have examined the goods contained in the entry.

The Japanese officers may examine any or all the packages so entered, and for this purpose may take them to the Custom-house; but such examination shall be without expense to the importer or injury to the goods, and, after examination, the Japanese shall restore the goods to their original condition in the packages (so far as may be practicable), and such examination shall be made without any unreasonable delay.

If any owner or importer discovers that his goods have been damaged on the voyage of importation before such goods have been delivered to him, he may notify the Custom-house authorities of such damage, and he may have the damaged goods appraised by two or more competent and disinterested persons, who, after due examination, shall make a certificate, setting forth the amount per cent. of damage on each separate package, describing it by its mark and number, which certificate shall be signed by the appraisers, in presence of the Custom-house authorities, and the importer may attach the certificate to his entry, and make a corresponding deduction from it.

But this shall not prevent the Custom-house authorities from appraising the goods in the manner provided in Article XV. of the Treaty to which these Regulations are appended.

After the duties have been paid, the owner shall receive a permit, authorising the delivery to him of the goods, whether the same are at the Custom-house or on shipboard.

All goods intended to be exported shall be entered at the Japanese custom-house before they are placed on shipboard.

The entry shall be in writing, and shall state the name of the ship by which the goods are to be exported, with the marks and numbers of the packages, and the quantity, description, and value of their contents.

The exporter shall certify, in writing, that the entry is a true account of all the goods contained therein, and shall sign his name thereto.

Any goods that are put on board of a ship for exportation before they have been entered at the Custom-house, and all packages which contain prohibited articles, shall be forfeited to the Japanese Government.

No entry at the Custom-house shall be required for supplies for the use of ships, their crews and passengers, nor for the clothing, etc., of passengers.

IV. Ships wishing to clear shall give twenty-four hours' notice at the Custom-house, and at the end of that time they shall be entitled to their clearance; but if it be refused, the Custom-house authorities shall immediately inform the captain or consignee of the ship of the reasons why the clearance is refused; and they shall also give the same notice to the British Consul.

British ships of war shall not be required to enter or clear at the Custom-house, nor shall they be visited by Japanese Custom-house or police officers.

Steamers carrying the mails of Great Britain may enter and clear on the same day, and they shall not be required to make a manifest, except for such passengers and goods as are to be landed in Japan. But such steamers shall, in all cases, enter and clear at the Custom-house.

Whale ships touching for supplies, or ships in distress, shall not be required to make a manifest of their cargo; but if they subsequently wish to trade, they shall then deposit a manifest, as required in Regulation I.

The word "ship," wherever it occurs in these Regulations, or in the Treaty to which they are attached, is to be held as meaning ship, barque, brig, schooner, sloop, or steamer.

V. Any person signing a false declaration or certificate, with the intent to defraud the revenue of Japan, shall pay a fine of one hundred and twenty-five dollars for each offence.

VI. No tonnage duties shall be levied on British ships in the ports of Japan, but the following fees shall be paid to the Japanese Custom-house authorities:—For the entry of a ship, fifteen dollars; for the clearance of a ship, seven dollars; for each permit, one dollar and a half; for each bill of health, one dollar and a half; for any other document, one dollar and a half.

VII. Duties shall be paid to the Japanese Government on all goods landed in the country, according to the following Tariff:—

CLASS I. All articles in this class shall be free of duty:—Gold and silver, coined or uncoined; wearing apparel in actual use; household furniture and printed books, not intended for sale, but the property of persons who come to reside in Japan.

CLASS II. A duty of five per cent. shall be paid on the following articles:—All articles used for the purpose of building, rigging, repairing, or fitting out of ships, whaling gear of all kinds, salted provisions of all kinds, bread and breadstuffs, living animals of all kinds, coals, timber for building houses, rice, paddy, steam-machinery, zinc, lead, tin, raw silk, cotton and woollen manufactured goods.

CLASS III. A duty of thirty-five per cent. shall be paid on all intoxicating liquors, whether prepared by distillation, fermentation, or in any other manner.

CLASS IV. All goods not included in any of the preceding classes shall pay a duty of twenty per cent.

All articles of Japanese production which are exported as cargo shall pay a duty of five per cent., with the exception of gold and silver coin, and copper in bars.

Rice and wheat, the produce of Japan, shall not be exported from Japan as cargo, but all British subjects resident in Japan, and British ships for their crews and passengers, shall be furnished with sufficient supplies of the same.

Foreign grain brought into any open port of Japan in a British ship, if no part thereof has been landed, may be re-exported without hindrance.

The Japanese Government will sell from time to time, at public auction, any surplus quantity of copper that may be produced.

Five years after the opening of Kanagawa, the import and export duties shall be subject to revision, if either the British or Japanese Government desires it.

> ELGIN AND KINCARDINE.
> MITZUNO CHIKUGO NO KAMI.
> NAGAI GEMBA NO KAMI.
> INOUYE SHINANO NO KAMI.
> HORI ORIBEI NO SHO.
> IWASE HIGO NO KAMI.
> TSUDA HANZABURO.

TARIFF CONVENTION,

Signed at Yedo, in the English, French, Dutch, and Japanese
Languages, on the 25th day of June 1866.

THE Representatives of Great Britain, France, of the United States of America, and Holland, having received from their respective Governments identical instructions for the modification of the Tariff of Import and Export Duties contained in the Trade Regulations annexed to the Treaties concluded by the aforesaid Powers with the Japanese Government in 1858, which modification is provided for by the VIIth of those Regulations;

And the Japanese Government having given the said Representatives, during their visit to Osaka, in November 1865, a written engagement to proceed immediately to the Revision of the Tariff in question, on the general basis of a duty of five per cent. on the value of all articles imported or exported;

And the Government of Japan being desirous of affording a fresh proof of their wish to promote trade, and to cement the friendly relations which exist between their country and foreign nations;

His Excellency MIDZUNO IDZUMI NO KAMI, a Member of the Gorojiu and a Minister of Foreign Affairs, has been furnished by the Government of Japan with the necessary powers to conclude with the representatives of the above-named four Powers, that is to say—

Of Great Britain, Sir HARRY S. PARKES, Knight Commander of the Most Honourable Order of the Bath, Her Britannic Majesty's Envoy Extraordinary and Minister Plenipotentiary in Japan; Of France, Monsieur LEON ROCHES, Commander of the Imperial Order of the Legion of Honour, Minister Plenipotentiary of His Majesty the Emperor of the French in Japan; Of the United States of America, A. L. C. PORTMAN, Esquire, Chargé d'Affaires ad interim; And of Holland, Monsieur DIRK DE GRAEFF VAN POLSBROEK, Knight of the Order of the Netherlands Lion, Political Agent and Consul General of His Majesty the King of the Netherlands—

The following Convention, comprising Twelve Articles.

I. The contracting Parties declare, in the names of their respective Governments, that they accept, and they hereby do formally accept as binding upon the subjects of their respective Sovereigns, and the citizens of their respective countries, the Tariff hereby established, and annexed to the present Convention.

This Tariff is substituted not only for the original Tariff attached to the Treaties concluded with the above-named four Powers, but also for the special Conventions and arrangements relative to the same Tariff, which had been entered into at different dates up to this time.

between the Governments of Great Britain, France, and the United States on one side, and the Japanese Government on the other.

The New Tariff shall come into effect in the port of Kanagawa (Yokohama) on the first day of July next, and in the ports of Nagasaki and Hakodaté on the first day of the following month.

II. The Tariff attached to this Convention being incorporated from the date of its signature in the Treaties concluded between Japan and the above-named four Powers, is subject to revision on the first day of July 1872.

Two years, however, after the signing of the present Convention, any of the contracting parties, on giving six months' notice to the others, may claim a readjustment of the duties on tea and silk, on the basis of five per cent. on the average value of these articles during the three years last preceding. On the demand also of any of the contracting parties, the duty on timber may be changed from an *ad valorem* to a specific rate six months after the signature of this Convention.

III. The permit fee hitherto levied under the VIth Regulation attached to the above-named Treaties is hereby abolished. Permits for the landing or shipment of cargo will be required as formerly, but will hereafter be issued free of charge.

IV. On and from the first day of July next, at the port of Kanagawa (Yokohama), and on and from the first day of October next at the ports of Nagasaki and Hakodaté, the Japanese Government will be prepared to warehouse imported goods on the application of the importer or owner without payment of duty. The Japanese Government will be responsible for the safe custody of the goods, so long as they remain in their charge, and will adopt all the precautions necessary to render them insurable against fire. When the importer or the owner wishes to remove the goods from the warehouse, he must pay the duties fixed by the Tariff; but if he should wish to re-export them, he may do so without payment of duty. Storage charges will in either case be paid on delivery of the goods. The amount of these charges, together with the regulations necessary for the management of the said warehouses, will be established by the common consent of the contracting parties.

V. All articles of Japanese production may be conveyed from any place in Japan to any of the ports open to foreign trade, free of any tax or transit duty other than the usual tolls levied equally on all traffic for the maintenance of roads or navigation.

VI. In conformity with those Articles of the Treaties concluded between Japan and Foreign Powers which stipulate for the circulation of foreign coin at its corresponding weight in native coin of the same description, dollars have hitherto been received at the Japanese Customhouse in payment of duties at their weight in Boos (commonly called

Ichiboos), that is to say, at a rate of Three Hundred and Eleven Boos per Hundred Dollars. The Japanese Government being, however, desirous to alter this practice, and to abstain from all interference in the exchange of native for foreign coin, and being also anxious to meet the wants both of native and foreign commerce by securing an adequate issue of native coin, have already determined to enlarge the Japanese Mint, so as to admit of the Japanese Government exchanging into native coin of the same intrinsic value, less only the cost of coinage, at the places named for this purpose, all foreign coin or bullion in gold or silver that may at any time be tendered to them by foreigners or Japanese. It being essential, however, to the execution of this measure, that the various Powers with whom Japan has concluded Treaties should first consent to modify the stipulations in those Treaties which relate to the currency, the Japanese Government will at once propose to those Powers the adoption of the necessary modification in the said stipulations, and on receiving their concurrence will be prepared, from the first of January 1868, to carry the above measure into effect.

The rates to be charged as the cost of coinage shall be determined hereafter by the common consent of the contracting parties.

VII. In order to put a stop to certain abuses and inconveniences complained of at the open ports, relative to the transaction of business at the Custom-house, the landing and shipping of cargoes, and the hiring of boats, coolies, servants, etc., the contracting parties have agreed that the Governor at each open port shall at once enter into negotiations with the foreign Consuls, with a view to the establishment, by mutual consent, of such regulations as shall effectually put an end to these abuses and inconveniences, and afford all possible facility and security, both to the operations of trade and to the transactions of individuals.

It is hereby stipulated that, in order to protect merchandise from exposure to weather, these regulations shall include the covering in at each port of one or more of the landing-places used by foreigners for landing or shipping cargo.

VIII. Any Japanese subject shall be free to purchase, either in the open ports of Japan or abroad, every description of sailing or steam vessel intended to carry either passengers or cargo; but ships of war may only be obtained under the authorisation of the Japanese Government.

All foreign vessels purchased by Japanese subjects shall be registered as Japanese vessels, on payment of a fixed duty of three boos per ton for steamers, and one boo per ton for sailing vessels. The tonnage of each vessel shall be proved by the foreign register of the ship, which shall be exhibited through the Consul of the party interested on the demand of the Japanese authorities, and shall be certified by the Consul as authentic.

IX. In conformity with the Treaties concluded between Japan and the aforesaid Powers, and with the special arrangements made by the Envoys of the Japanese Government in their note to the British Government of the sixth of June 1862, and in their note to the French Government of the sixth of October of the same year, all the restrictions on trade and intercourse between foreigners and Japanese alluded to in the said notes have been entirely removed, and proclamations to this effect have already been published by the Government of Japan.

The latter, however, do not hesitate to declare that Japanese merchants and traders of all classes are at liberty to trade directly, and without the interference of Government officers, with foreign merchants, not only at the open ports of Japan, but also in all foreign countries, on being authorised to leave their country in the manner provided for in Article X. of the present Convention, without being subject to higher taxation by the Japanese Government than levied on the native trading classes in Japan in their ordinary transactions with each other.

And they further declare that all daimios or persons in the employ of daimios are free to visit, on the same conditions, any foreign country, as well as all the open ports of Japan, and to trade there with foreigners as they please, without the interference of any Japanese officer, provided always they submit to the existing police regulations, and to the payment of the established duties.

X. All Japanese subjects may ship goods to or from any open port in Japan, or to and from the ports of any foreign Power, either in vessels owned by Japanese or in the vessels of any nation having a Treaty with Japan. Furthermore, on being provided with passports through the proper department of the Government, in the manner specified in the Proclamation of the Japanese Government, dated the twenty-third day of May 1866, all Japanese subjects may travel to any foreign country for purposes of study or trade. They may also accept employment in any capacity on board the vessels of any nation having a Treaty with Japan.

Japanese in the employ of foreigners may obtain Government passports to go abroad on application to the Governor of any open port.

XI. The Government of Japan will provide all the ports open to foreign trade with such lights, buoys, or beacons as may be necessary to render secure the navigation of the approaches to the said ports.

XII. The undersigned being of opinion that it is unnecessary that this Convention should be submitted to their respective Governments for ratification before it comes into operation, it will take effect on and from the first day of July, one thousand eight hundred and sixty-six.

Each of the Contracting Parties having obtained the approval of his Government to this Convention, shall make known the same to the others, and the communication in writing of this approval shall take the place of a formal exchange of ratifications.

IN WITNESS WHEREOF the above-named Plenipotentiaries have signed the present Convention, and have affixed thereto their seals.

Done at Yedo, in the English, French, Dutch, and Japanese languages, this twenty-fifth day of June, one thousand eight hundred sixty-six.

(L. S.)   HARRY S. PARKES,
*Her Britannic Majesty's Envoy Extraordinary
and Minister Plenipotentiary in Japan.*

(L. S.)   LEON ROCHES,
*Ministre Plénipotentiaire de S. M. l'Empereur
des Français au Japon.*

(L. S.)   A. L. C. PORTMAN,
*Chargé d'Affaires a. i. of the United States
in Japan.*

(L. S.)   D. DE GRAEFF VAN POLSBROEK,
*Politiek Agent en Consul Generaal der Neder-
landen in Japan.*

(L. S.)   MIDZUNO IDZUMI NO KAMI.

LIST OF EMPERORS.

Name.	Date, beginning with the Emperor Jimmu.	Date, beginning with Christian Era.	Name.	Date, beginning with the Emperor Jimmu.	Date, beginning with Christian Era.
Jimmu	1	B.C. 660	Sushun	1248	588
Suisei	79	581	Suiko (Empress)	1253	593
Annei	112	548	Jomei	1289	629
Itoku	150	510	Kokioku *}	1302	642
Koshio	185	475	(Empress)}		
Koan	268	392	Kotoku	1305	645
Korei	370	290	Saimei * (Empress)	1315	655
Kogen	446	214	Tenji	1328	668
Kaikua	503	157	Kobun	1332	672
Sujin	563	97	Temmu	1333	673
Suinin	629	31	Jito (Empress)	1350	690
Keiko	731	A D. 71	Mommu	1357	697
Seimu	791	131	Gemmei (Empress)	1368	708
Chuai	852	192	Gensho (Empress)	1375	715
Jingu (Empress)	861	201	Shomu	1384	724
Ojin	930	270	Koken † (Empress)	1409	749
Nintoku	973	313	Junjin	1419	759
Richiu	1060	400	Shotoku † }	1425	765
Hansho	1065	405	(Empress)}		
Inkiyo	1071	411	Konin	1430	770
Auko	1113	453	Kuwammu	1442	782
Yariaku	1116	456	Heizei	1466	806
Seinei	1140	480	Saga	1470	810
Kenso	1145	485	Junna	1484	824
Ninken	1148	488	Nimmio	1494	834
Buretsu	1159	499	Montoku	1511	851
Keitai	1167	507	Seiwa	1519	859
Ankan	1194	534	Yozei	1537	877
Senkuwa	1196	536	Koko	1545	885
Kimmei	1200	540	Uda	1553	893
Bitatsu	1232	572	Daigo	1558	898
Yomei	1246	586	Shujuku	1591	931

* The names thus marked belonged to the same empress, who reigned twice. See vol. i. p. 108.

† The names thus marked likewise belonged to the same empress. See vol. i. p. 110.

Name.	Date, beginning with the Emperor Jimmu.	Date, beginning with Christian Era.	Name.	Date, beginning with the Emperor Jimmu.	Date, beginning with Christian Era.
Murakami	1607	947	SOUTHERN DYNASTY.		
Reizei	1628	968	Go-Murakami	1999	1339
Engu	1630	970	Go-Kameyama	2028	1368
Kuwazan	1645	985			
Ichijo	1649	987	NORTHERN DYNASTY.		
Sanjo	1672	1012	Komio	1996	1336
Go-Ichijo *	1677	1017	Shuko	2009	1349
Go-Shujaku	1697	1037	Go-Kuwoogen	2012	1352
Go-Reizei	1706	1046	Go-Enyu	2032	1372
Go-Sanjo	1729	1069	Go-Komatsu	2053	1393
Shirakawa	1733	1073	Go-Komatsu	2053	1393
Horikawa	1747	1087	Shoko	2073	1413
Toba	1769	1108	Go-Hanazono	2089	1429
Shutoku	1784	1124	Go-Tsuchi-Mikado	2125	1465
Konoye	1802	1142	Go-Kashiwabara	2161	1501
Go-Shirakawa	1816	1156	Go-Nara	2187	1527
Nigo	1819	1159	Oki-Machi	2218	1558
Rokujio	1826	1166	Go-Yozei	2247	1587
Takakura	1829	1160	Go-Miwo	2272	1612
Antoku	1841	1181	Miosho (Empress)	2290	1630
Go-Toba	1846	1186	Go-Komio	2304	1644
Tsuchi-Mikado	1859	1199	Gozai-in	2315	1655
Juntoku	1871	1211	Reigen	2323	1663
Chukio	1881	1221	Higashiyama	2347	1687
Go-Horikawa	1881	1221	Naka-Mikado	2370	1710
Shijo	1891	1231	Sakura-Machi	2396	1736
Go-Saga	1904	1244	Momozono	2407	1747
Go-Fukakusa	1907	1247	Go - Sakura-Machi		
Kameyama	1926	1266	(Empress)	2423	1763
Go-Uda	1930	1270	Go-Momozono	2431	1771
Fushimi	1948	1288	Kokaku	2440	1780
Go-Fushimi	1959	1299	Niako	2477	1817
Go-Nijo	1961	1301	Komei	2507	1847
Hanazono	1968	1308	Mutsu - Hito (the		
Go-Daigo	1979	1319	present Emperor)	2527	1867

* Equivalent to "Ichijo the Second." See footnote, vol. i. p. 112.

LIST OF YEAR-PERIODS.

THE Japanese have two modes of reckoning time in years: one by means of 12 year cycles, named after the twelve signs of the Japanese Zodiac; the other by means of short periods of arbitrary length, varying from one to twenty years, or even more. Each of these latter periods is distinguished by a name given by the Mikado. The present one (*Meiji*) commenced Oct. 12, 1868.

Name.	Date, beginning with the Emperor Jimmu.	Date, beginning with Christian Era.	Name.	Date, beginning with the Emperor Jimmu.	Date, beginning with Christian Era.
Taikua	1305	645	Kuanpei	1549	889
Hakuchi	1310	650	Shiotai	1558	898
Sujaka	1332	672	Yengi	1561	901
Hakuho	1333	673	Yencho	1583	923
Shucho	1346	686	Shiohei	1591	931
Taikua	1355	695	Tengio	1598	938
Taicho	1357	697	Ten Riyaku	1607	947
Taiho	1361	701	Tentoku	1617	957
Kei-un	1362	704	Wowa	1621	961
Wado	1368	708	Koho	1624	964
Hoki	1375	715	Anwa	1628	968
Yozo	1377	717	Tenroku	1630	970
Jinki	1384	724	Tenyen	1633	973
Tenpio	1389	729	Jogen	1636	976
Tenpio Shoho	1409	749	Tengen	1638	978
Tenpio Hoji	1417	757	Yeikuan	1643	983
Tenpio Jingo	1425	765	Kuanwa	1645	985
Jingo Kei-un	1427	767	Yeiyen	1647	987
Hoki	1430	770	Yeiso	1649	989
Teno	1441	781	Shioriyaku	1650	990
Yenriyaku	1442	782	Chotoku	1655	995
Daido	1466	806	Choho	1659	999
Kuonin	1470	810	Kuanko	1664	1004
Teneho	1484	824	Chowa	1672	1012
Jowa	1494	834	Kuannin	1677	1017
Kasho	1508	818	Chian	1681	1021
Nin-ju	1511	851	Manju	1684	1024
Saiko	1514	854	Chogen	1688	1028
Tenan	1517	857	Choriyaku	1697	1037
Jokuan	1519	859	Chokiu	1700	1040
———	1537	877	Kuantoku	1701	1044
Ninna	1545	885	Yenjo	1706	1046

Name.	Date, beginning with the Emperor Jimmu.	Date, beginning with Christian Era.	Name.	Date, beginning with the Emperor Jimmu.	Date, beginning with Christian Era.
Tenki	1713	1053	Kenyei	1866	1206
Kohei	1718	1058	Shogen	1867	1207
Chiriyaku	1725	1065	Kenriyaku	1871	1211
Yenkiu	1729	1069	Kenpo	1873	1213
Joho	1734	1074	Jokiu	1879	1219
Joriyaku	1737	1077	Jowo	1882	1222
Yeiho	1741	1081	Gennin	1884	1224
Otoku	1744	1084	Karoku	1885	1225
Knanji	1747	1087	Antei	1887	1227
Kaho	1754	1094	Kuanki	1889	1229
Yeicho	1756	1096	Joyei	1892	1232
Shotoku	1757	1097	Tenpuku	1893	1233
Kowa	1759	1099	Bunriyaku	1894	1234
Choji	1764	1104	Katei	1895	1235
Kajo	1766	1106	Riyakunin	1898	1238
Tennin	1768	1108	Yenwo	1899	1239
Tenyei	1770	1110	Ninji	1900	1240
Yeikiu	1773	1113	Kuangen	1903	1243
Genyei	1778	1118	Hoji	1907	1247
Ho-an	1780	1120	Kencho	1909	1249
Tenji	1784	1124	Kogen	1916	1256
Daiji	1786	1126	Shoka	1917	1257
Tensho	1791	1131	Shogen	1919	1259
Chosho	1792	1132	Bunwo	1920	1260
Hoyen	1795	1135	Kocho	1921	1261
Yeiji	1801	1141	Bunyei	1924	1264
Koji	1802	1142	Kenji	1935	1275
Tenyo	1804	1144	Ko-an	1938	1278
Kiuan	1805	1145	Showo	1948	1288
Niupei	1811	1151	Yeinin	1953	1293
Kinju	1814	1154	Sho-an	1959	1299
Hogen	1816	1156	Kengen	1962	1302
Heiji	1819	1159	Kagen	1963	1303
Yeiriyaku	1820	1160	Tokuji	1966	1306
Oyei	1821	1161	Yenkei	1968	1308
Chokuan	1823	1163	Ocho	1971	1311
Yeiman	1825	1165	Showa	1972	1312
Ninan	1826	1166	Bunpo	1977	1317
Kawo	1829	1169	Genwo	1979	1319
Sho-an	1831	1171	Genko	1981	1321
Angen	1835	1175	Shochu	1984	1324
Jijo	1837	1177	Kareki	1986	1326
Yowa	1841	1181	Gentoku	1989	1329
Juyei	1842	1182	Genko	1991	1331
Monji	1845	1185	Kemmu	1994	1334
Kenkiu	1856	1190			
Shoji	1859	1199	SOUTHERN DYNASTY.*		
Kennin	1861	1201	Yengen	1996	1336
Genkin	1864	1204	Kokoku	2000	1340

* There were two dynasties during the time (1336–39 A.D.), and separate year-periods were used.

Name.	Date, beginning with the Emperor Jimmu.	Date, beginning with Christian Era.	Name.	Date, beginning with the Emperor Jimmu.	Date, beginning with Christian Era.
Shohei	2006	1346	Koji	2215	1555
Kentoku	2030	1370	Yeiroku	2218	1558
Bunchu	2032	1372	Genki	2230	1570
Tenju	2035	1375	Tensho	2233	1573
Kowa	2041	1381	Bunroku	2252	1592
Genchu	2044	1384	Keicho	2256	1596
			Genna	2275	1615
NORTHERN DYNASTY.			Kuanyei	2284	1624
Rekiwo	1998	1338	Shoho	2304	1644
Koyei	2002	1342	Kei-an	2308	1648
Teiwa	2005	1345	Showo	2312	1652
Kuanwo	2010	1350	Meireki	2315	1655
Yenbun	2016	1356	Manji	2318	1658
Owa	2021	1361	Kuanbun	2321	1661
Toji	2022	1362	Yenpo	2333	1673
O-an	2028	1368	Tenwa	2341	1681
Yeiwa	2035	1375	Jokio	2344	1684
Koreki	2039	1379	Tenroku	2348	1688
Yeitoku	2041	1381	Hoyei	2364	1704
Shitoku	2044	1384	Shotoku	2371	1711
Kakei	2047	1387	Hokio	2376	1716
Kowo	2049	1389	Genbun	2396	1736
Miotoku	2050	1390	Kuanpo	2401	1741
Oyen	2054	1394	Yenkio	2404	1744
Seicho	2088	1428	Kuanyen	2408	1748
Yeikiyo	2089	1429	Horeki	2411	1751
Kakitsu	2101	1441	Meiwa	2424	1764
Bunan	2104	1444	Anyei	2432	1772
Hotoku	2109	1449	Tenmei	2441	1781
Kiotoku	2112	1452	Kuansei	2449	1789
Kosho	2115	1455	Kiowa	2461	1801
Choroku	2117	1457	Bunkua	2464	1804
Kuansho	2120	1460	Bunsei	2478	1818
Bunsho	2126	1466	Tenpo	2490	1830
Onin	2127	1467	Koka	2504	1844
Bunmei	2129	1469	Kayei	2508	1848
Chokio	2147	1487	Ansei	2514	1854
Yentoku	2149	1489	Manyei	2520	1860
Miowo	2152	1492	Bunkiu	2521	1861
Bunki	2161	1501	Genji	2524	1864
Yeisei	2164	1504	Keiwo	2525	1865
Taiyei	2181	1521	Meiji	2528	1868
Kioroku	2188	1528	Meiji, ninth year	2536	1876
Tenbun	2192	1532			

COMPARATIVE TABLE OF WORDS IN JAPANESE, WEST AFRICAN, AND OTHER LANGUAGES.

Prepared for this Work by HYDE CLARKE, ESQ., *V.-Pres. Anthropological Institute, Corr. Mem. American Oriental Soc.*

ENGLISH.	JAPANESE.	AFRICAN.	INDIAN, ETC.
Child . . .	ko	nẽgo, Toma.	
		mo-koa, Balu.	
Boy	waratse . .	woronorun, Akurz-kura.	
Elder brother .	kei	koyo, Mandenga.	
		oke, Isoama.	
		yaka, Bornu.	
	aui	nuane, Ishiele.	
		nia, Abese.	
Younger brother	tsi	pantsi, Nyombe.	
		kadshi, Kupa.	
Servant . . .	sin	dshono, Mandenga, etc.	
		usamp, Pajade.	
		dshon, Soso.	
		ashunku, Banyun.	
		issung, Berber.	
King	kami . . .	komasa, Mandenga.	
		fankama, Pajade.	
		nkumu, Bumbete.	
		dukumu, Bumbete.	
		nkoma, Nyomban.	
		kamambuku, Undaza.	
God	shivo . . .	oshowo, Ekamtulufu	siva, Indian.
		oshowo, Udom . .	saba, Arabic.
		nsambi, Kasanj, etc.	
		njambi, Babuma.	*The following are American :—*
		ndzambi, Nyombe.	
		saba, Phrygian .	shiwa, Mexico.
		saba, Prisco-Hellenic	sibu, Bribri.
		saba, Lydian . .	sibu, Cabecar.
			zibo, Tiribi.
		seb, Egypt . . .	zuba, Terraba.
		assabi, Ethiopian .	sibo, Brunka.

Central America. (bracketing the Central American entries)

English.	Japanese.	African.	Indian, etc.
Sky	sora	sar, Jelana, etc. . dshensara, do. .	zeru, Basque. sorgi, Dhimal. sarang, Magar. sarangi, Sunwar. sarange, Rajmahali. sargam, Rutluk. sirma, Kol. sarg, Chentsu. sarag, Newar.
Foot	asi . . . . . achi. (shanna, Loo- cho)	sonkonyo, Toronka (sanna soso, *leg* ?).	shan, Annam. tachang, Naga. aji, Savara. hejje, Karnataka.
Mouth . . .	kuti . . . kuchi . . .	kedshi, Bornu . nashue, Mandenga	kuga, Garo. khouga, Bodo. kha, Takpa.
Shoulder . .	katta . . .	katta, Nyamban. kosoe, Ngola. kata, Matatan. katana, Mano.	
Hand . . .	ta . . . te . . .	ckei, Babuma . koe, Gio, etc. . . tagi, Tene . . .	tayuk, Gyarung. da, Brahui. tekka, Naga. kaKumi. tay, Annam. kha, Ahor., etc. ti, Kol, etc.
Belly . . .	fara . . .	pura, Mose. fure, Okuloma. tefunu, Ashantee. for, Jelana. furi, Soso. puri, Kisi.	
Blood . . .	tsi . . . chee . . .	aze, Oloma . . . atsi, Oloma . ozai, Ihewe . dsheyi, Mandenga edshi, Eshitako . ndze, Momenya .	azu, Naga. tashi, Gyarung. usu, Chourasya. chiwi, Bhramu. chi, Garo. chui, Deoria Chutia.
Skin . . .	kawa .	ngewe, Momenya . nekuwe, Matatan . koro, Kisi . koro, Toma . . . okuba, Orunga .	koppa, Serpa. tugap, Naga. kwakte, Chourasya. kombo, Lepcha. chupta, Uraon.
Breast . .	mone	mean, Kisi. nine, Toma.	
Bone . . .	hone .	akuau, Bayon . hoare, Soso.	wan, Naga.

ENGLISH.	JAPANESE.	AFRICAN.	INDIAN, ETC.
Neck . . .	kabi . . . kale (Loochoo)	kapuru, Toma. kompol, Mano. koerambi, Soso. kase, Soso. kano, Mandenga. kougo, Okuloma.	
Fire . . .	hi . . . . fi	fene, Okuloma. veia, Bongo. firi, Bonny. afu, Mandara. wia, Diwala. ive, Benin. veva, Baseke.	
Water . . .	mizzu . . .	mazea, Kabunga . maza, Mimboma. mazi, Meto, etc. mingi, Okuloma. mendan, Kosi.	atzu, Naga.
Day . . .	ka . . . . fi . . . . hi . . . . nitsi . . .	kan, Bornu . . afo, Sobo . . . furo, Toma . . notsu, Ngoala .	nhi, Newar. nyi, Chepang. anyi, Naga. nathi, Sunwar.
Night . . .	yo . . . . yoru . . .	yoro, Guresa . . nyoru, Gurma . . irahu, Egbira . naifore, Soso . ohuora, Orungu . eridai, Egbele .	yotin. jori, Manchu. dobori, Manchu. ya, Chepang. phiru, Lhopa. phar, Garo. ira, Tamil, etc.
Village . . .	mura . . .	maro, Barba . muri, Kiriwan. muri, Melon .	merong, Singpho. uri, Basque.
House .	iya . . . . taku .	uá, Boko. oyo, Abaja. hu, Timbuktu. kata, Nupe. daki, Houssa.	
Iron . .	tetsu . . .	sisu, Barba. . . asho, Juku. kitsulo, Marawi. su, Bornu. sisu, Barba., etc.	shi, Manyak.
Stone .	ishi . . .	adshie, Koro . . dudsi, Houssa.	kache, Naga.
Moon .	bsuki. otsoki (Loo- choo) . .	isogo, Yarriba. suru, Barba. iguki, Oloma. sung, Mandenga.	

ENGLISH.	JAPANESE.	AFRICAN.	INDIAN, ETC.
Sand . . .	sona . . . sinna (Loo-choo) . .	sonma, Bagba. nsagi, Muntun, etc. shionde, Kisi.	
Yam . . .	imo . . . tsu-kemono .	yomo, Baseke . . aso, Ngoala . . ekama, Filham. .	thoma, Thibet. homan, Shan. shi, Naga.
Door . . .	kado . . . to . . . . te	kogu, Koro . . ko, Mandenga. kitseko, Marawi. kendara, Kono. kodia, Soso. kondo, Kisi.	ka, Akkad.
Itch	kaya . . .	kuo, Musu. kato, Mandenga. gaye, Pulo. kasua, Houssa. kasgun, Bornu. kasi, Soso.	
Medicine . .	kusuri . . .	sera, Kisi. share, Soso. sali, sare, Abese. sorum, Karekare.	
Monkey . . .	saru . . .	sirowa, Bijogo . . on-shere, Egbira . sula, Mandenga.	sara, Kuri. sarrha, Kol. saheu, Lepcha.
Mouse . . .	no	ene, Boko.	
Rat		nino, Mandenga. no, Guresa.	
Elephant . .	zo	se, ese, Ngoala . . se, Toma.	tsu, Naga.
Bull	sai	so, Nhalemoe. osues, Alege. esua, Nki. sa, Kandin.	(So Tiribi, Central America, tapir.)
Buffalo . .	wo-osi . . . suigue . . . (wo-oshi, Loo-choo.)	wosanque, Baseke. okeshu, Ishiele. esuwe, Sobo.	
Cow . .	ushi . . . me-usi . . . (mi-oehi, Loo-choo) . . .	misi, Bambara. . esuwe, Sobo . .	masi, Naga. mosa, Chupang. musho, Bocle. chuma, Serpa. mosu, Deoria Chutia.
Cat	nekko . . .	nyago, Momenya . nyanguma, Bam-bawa . . . . unogbo, Sobo. nyayo, Kisi.	uyen, Thoungthu. ningyau, Singpho.

ENGLISH.	JAPANESE.	AFRICAN.	INDIAN, ETC.
Dog . . .	inu . . . moinu. (ing, Loochoo)	mengu, Ngoala.	
Bird	tori	tori, Pulo . . . nwori, Toma . . tore, Soso.	chori, Basque. chari, Darhi, etc.
Snake . . .	hebi . . . (= fish) febi .	kowo, Kisi. uwa, Guresa. ewa, Goali. ewu, Koro.	
Fish . . . . (= snake)	siwo . . . uwo . . .	siowo, Goali . . suwo, Kisi . . . yewo, Mandenga . soa, Barba. nsi, Wi Sagara. iwowo, Egbira.	sapa, Pakhya. sapa, Tharu. sapa, Chentsu.
To-day . . .	kon-nichi . .	nano, Oloma . . nume, Sobo. . . nyanse, Nyamban . ku, Bornu.	enengi, Manchu. innaki, Tamil.
Yesterday . .	saku-sichu .	suka, Goali. matsega, Babuma.	
To-morrow . .	myo-nichi .		nesu, Yerukala.
No . . .	nai	na, Mano . . .	nu, Georgian.
Not	na . . . . . suruna. . .	na, Abese . . . ne, Bornu . . . serunu, Kra . . yerunu, Krebo . .	na, Kuswar. nah, Kooch. nonga, Naga. nao, Kami.
Great . . .	oki . . . . ooi . . . . day	oku, Isoama. okokoi, Sobo. akolo, Kono.	
Small .	saino-dsi . . sai-hito . . tsiisa . . .	isone, Isuwu . . dshetito, Pangela . dshi-dsho, Kabenda asoso, Oloma . . ose, Sobo . . . oshobere, Kisi .	osokhou, Manchu. syouti, Gyami. sanu, Pakhya. sai, Naga. sanka, Uraon. sani, Kuri.
White . .	siro . . .	setire, Tene. fera, Timne. ma-zela, Kasanj, etc. pan-fera, Baga. fali, Houssa.	
Black . . .	kuroi . . . kuro . . .	kuru kuru, Oku- loma . . . . kereshe, Aloje .	kara, Turkish. kariya, Tharu. mokhara, Uraon.
Good . .	yo	eye, Ashantee . . e-nyu, Anfue.	yo, Magyar.

ENGLISH.	JAPANESE.	AFRICAN.	INDIAN, ETC.
Bad	waru . . .	waira, Pajade.	
		wori, Mampa.	
Greedy . . .	siva . . .	saweneh, Murundu.	
		tsawil, Bornu.	
		songoàu, Kisi.	
Hot	atsui . . .	ososo, Sobo . . .	tefsa, Naga.
	nuku . . .	dshou, Bornu . .	tetsok, Naga.
		odshu, Baghrmi.	
		esiese, Gio.	
		dukuna, Houssa.	
Cold . . .	samu . . .	esine, Isuwu . .	masunn, Yerukala.
	sabu . . .	samsu, Bornu . .	sim, Thaksya.
		sumane, Mandenga	semba, Limbu.
		adsoabet, Kanyop .	simba, Murmi.
Straight . .	masugu . .	masegi, Kambali .	saiko, Gondi.
		sung-amini, Mimboma	sukaga, Keikadi.
		dshok, Bornu . .	kasumi, Madi.
Crooked . .	magalie . .	gongoro, Timbuktu	vankara, Yerukala.
	magaro . .	okure, Kra . . .	kokurai, Deoria Chutia.
		kerigata, Bornu .	koikolo, Naga.
			makur, Basque.
Old	furu . . .	eru, Ngoala.	
	oyu . . .	wuara, Bornu.	
	oitaru . . .	kiari.	
		fori, Soso.	
New	arata . . .	yareade, Whydah.	
Young . . .			
Sleep . . .	neri . . .	sinoro, Mandenga .	nama, Semitic.
	nemu . . .	kenem, Bornu . .	nyan, Tibetan.
		danima. Pulo . .	nawa, Bhramu.
		tamese, Sobo.	
		nawunuro, Akumakura.	
Speak . .	ivi	owo, Mbamba . .	hawe, Khyeng.
		mve, Yasgua.	
		we, Mano.	
		hawe, Nhalomoe.	
Tell	mangatalo .	magana. Houssa.	
	nannaworusa .	neman, Bornu.	
		man, Bornu.	
Give .	yaru . . .	yaru, Bini.	
	ataye . . .	yeri, Murundo.	
	tamave . .	eyere, Aro.	
		dimamo, Ashantee.	
		dima, Mandenga.	
Drink . . .	nomi .	nyoma, Isuwu .	nomu, Amoy.
		numu, Momenya .	punamu, Khond.
		num, Ashantee.	

ENGLISH.	JAPANESE.	AFRICAN.	INDIAN, ETC.
Come . . .	kuru . . .	gire, Kra, etc. . saka, Houssa.	karo, Naga.
	tsuki . . .	iseski, Bornu.	
Go . . .	yuki . . iku. . . susumi. .	ko, Timne, etc. ko, Landoma . ko, Ashantee . shaimi, Ham .	kas, Naga. eka, Rajmahali. yenga, Bhramu.
Play . . .	asobi . .	sabaso, Kisi. sowero, Marawi. sewa, Orungu. gun-sbab, Balu.	
Sell . .	uri . . .	fereke, Mandenga. fere, Tene.	
Boil .	ni .	na, Ekamtulufu.	
Cook		nua, Ashantee. ny, Sobo. nyin, Soso.	
Sit .	swaru .	dshara, Lezba . . dshara, Kasm. dsbowo, Kiamba. susoan, Oloma.	eserri, Basque.
See .	mi . . miru .	mo, Whydah, etc. shimora, Pangela.	
Love .	so . suki	so. Houssa. se, Toma. soge, Mano. shotka, Bode.	
Strike .	tata	tudsa, Kanyop.	tatup, Gyarung.
Beat .	utsi	bute, Mandenga .	tat, Mon. teda, Savara. thattu, Malabar.
Understand .	wakaru kadensuru.	woeri, Gbe. dshoro, Orungu.	
Laugh . .	waravi . .	yuwuru, Bornu. unarawi, Yasgua. yurasan, Ekamtu- lufu.	
Kill .	korosú	kuri, Gurma. kur, Jelana . .	kolusu, Yerukala.
Cry	naku .	akua, Isoama .	negaregin, Basque. nagh, Brahui.
Weep . . .			
Run . .	fashiri . . kakoru . .	shiran, Oloma . berase, Toma . . kurde, Pajade.	korri, Basque. ghure, Dumi. garitan, Mon.

CELEBRATED SWORDS AND MAKERS.

THE following are the notes I promised, in Chapter XI., Vol. II., to give. They are taken from Mr. Pfoundes's ' Fu so Mimi Bukuro.'

Old weapons are frequently presented to Kami shrines, especially those dedicated to Hachiman and Dai-jin Gu.

The following are some of the numberless renowned blades and their forgers.

Ama-kuni of Yamato, who lived about 700 A.D., was a celebrated maker. One of his blades is said to have been carried off by a crow during the reign of Kanmu-Tenno, 782 A.D., and has since been known by the name of the *Kogarasu maru** (little crow). In 940 A.D. Taira Sadamori became the possessor of this sword, which was drawn by him in the wars with Masakado, who was until lately deified at Kanda, Yedo.

Shin-soku, who lived at Usa no Mia of Buzen, was ordered to forge a blade for the son of the emperor Heizei-Tenno in 806 A.D., and he cut his name on the blade, the first time this was done. There is a legend that Riu Jin† came to his assistance.

Of ninety-nine swords he is said to have made, only eight had his name on them, and the Hachiman shrines are named as being in possession of most of these blades, many of which are now little else than a mass of rust.‡

---

* Names were given to swords, as to vessels, horses, and other favourite possessions, the commonly used affix *maru* meaning " perfect " in this sense, and still used for ships. Formerly even the young sons of nobles were thus styled, as Take chi yo maru, a common title for the heir to the Tokugawa line ; as also to castles, such as Hon maru (true perfect) or Nishi maru (west perfect).

† Riu Jin is the same as the old man living at the bottom of the sea in Riugu (Dragon Shrine). The father of Toyotama himé Hiko quarrelled with his brother, and descending into the depths of the sea became enamoured of Toyo, and lived with her in coral caves until she was about to bring forth her child. Hiko then built her a hut on the sea-shore, roofing it with cormorants' wings. Here Fuki was born, and his mother Toyo then became a crocodile and returned to her home in the deep, Hiko having displeased her. She left her sister Tama-yori-himé behind, who married Fukiawasedzu, and Jimmu-Tenno was their fourth child.

‡ There are some of these old blades in the Exhibition at Tokio. One is marked as valued at 700 *yen.*

Ohara Taru daiyu Yasutsuna of Hoki, a contemporary of Shin-soku, forged a blade which in 947 was used by Raiko (Minamoto Yorimitzu) to kill Shi ten doji, a celebrated robber. He dreamed that this sword, then still at the Isé shrine, alone had power to break through the spell of invincibility that surrounded this celebrated robber, who is even now known to children as a ghoul. This sword was placed in the Isé Mai as an offering by Tamura Shogun. Another sword of the same make was likewise placed at Kehi-miojin in Echigo by the Shogun Toshihito.

Ohara Sane-mori, another maker of celebrated swords, lived at the same time. One of his blades was called *Nuke maru*, from its having flown out of its sheath and destroyed the *Ja* (enormous serpent) that came to swallow up Taira Tadamori, who had laid the weapon sheathed beside his pillow when lying down to rest. Another blade, called *Korgarashi maru*, also in the possession of the Heiki family, was reputed to cause trees to wither if it was laid down touching them.

985 A.D. Yukihira was another celebrated sword-maker. One of his swords was used by Watanabé, the follower of Yorimitzu (Raiko), to cut off the arm of the Onié* (ghoul) when sent by Raiko to exter-minate the wicked ghouls, dragons, *ja*, &c.

987 A.D. Mune chika, a sword-smith living in Sango Street, Kioto, in the province of Yamashiro, made a blade called *Cho maru*, possessed by Gonguro of Kamakura. *Cho maru* was so called from a *cho* (butter-fly) being worked into the *forte* of the blade. Another was placed in the temple of Fudo son at Echigo, and became the property of Wada Saburozaiemon, who repaired the temple at his own cost. The blade was thereafter called *Fudo maru*.

Another was called *Koyitsune maru* (little fox), from its having been forged by the assistance of Inari (Uga no mitama), when Ichi jo no In (887 A.D.) ordered one of the finest workmanship. The name of the maker, Mune chika, was cut on the obverse, and the name *Kokitsune* on the reverse side (*tska*).

Tomonari of Bizen was a noted sword-maker of the same period.

1004 A.D. there lived in Yamashiro Yoshi iye, to whom appeared Sumiyoshi Daimio Jin (of the temple at Osaka) and ordered the best blade that could be welded. When it was finished, the maker was on his way to the temple, as ordered, but while crossing the water he dropped the sword into its depths. A cormorant dived, and finding, flew away with it. Shortly afterwards a new sword was found at the Shrine of Sumi yoshi, which proved to be the lost blade, and it is now called *Wuno maru* (*wu*, a cormorant).

* *Vide* Stories (*Kodomo Banashi*).

1186 A.D. Gotoba no In was partial to sword-makers,* the most celebrated of whom were sent for by him in rotation, as follows :—

1st month,	Bizen no Norimune.
2nd ,,	Bitchiu no Sadatsugu.
3rd ,,	Bizen Nobufusa.
4th ,,	Awadaguchi no Kuniyasu.
5th ,,	Bitchiu no Tsunetsugu.
6th ,,	Awadaguchi no Kunitomo.
7th ,,	Bizen no Muneyoshi.
8th ,,	Bitchiu no Tsuguieye.
9th ,,	Bizen no Sukemune.
10th ,,	Bizen no Yukikuni.
11th ,,	Bizen no Sukenari.
12th ,,	Bizen no Sukenobu.

The blades made by Gotoba no In are marked with a chrysanthemum and a stroke beneath (*kiku ichi mon ji*).

1204 A.D. Yoshimitzu of Awadaguchi, in the province of Yamashiro, commonly known as Toshiro. His make of swords, having cut through a druggist's metal mortar (called *yagen*), are known as *Yagen Toshiro.*

Rai-taro Kuni-yuki is the name of a celebrated maker of this period. In 1248 Kuni-mitzu flourished; in 1250, Kuni-yoshi. In 1279 Nagamitzu made a sword, afterwards worn by Iyéyasu, called *Adzuki naga mitzu* from its cutting a bean (*adzuki*) thrown into the air.

Other celebrated makers are :—

A.D.	
1293.	{ Rai Kuni toshi. { Shin to go Kuni mitzu.
1303.	Yuki mitsu of Sagami.
1319.	Sadamune of Sagami.
1320.	Go no Yoshi hiro of Yetchiu.

The last is the most celebrated of these renowned makers. He proudly refused to cut his name on the blades, saying that their superiority would be recognised without this.

1322 A.D., Mura-masa of Senjiu mura, in Isé, commonly spoken of as Senjiu-in Mura-marsa. His swords would, it is said, cut a sheet of paper floating on the stream if the sword were only held in the water to meet the paper. Such was the reputed keenness of these weapons, and so great the desire to test it possessed the owners, that when a fitting opportunity occurred, the Tokugawa government forbade their being worn.†

* Many of the imperial family and Daimios imitated this Mikado, and patronised amateur and professional word-making.

† The compiler of these notes possesses one, and has experience of

In 1326 Masa-mune, the most celebrated of sword-makers, forged some of his best blades, now still in existence. The welding shows a peculiar golden tinge, like forked lightning through a dark cloud. He folded his metal from four sides, beat it out and refolded it in a peculiar manner.

In 1338 there lived in Mino, at the village of Seki, Shidzu saburo Kani-uji, a pupil of Masa mune.

In 1362, Okane-mitzu, a celebrated maker of sabres, having more sweep in them than the blades of other makers.

1370 A.D., Kane-sada was a reputed sword-smith of Seki.

All swords made since 1570 are called *Shinto* (new swords), and the old but inferior blades are included with these. The swords of previous make are called *Koto* (old swords).

Horikawa Kuni-hiro, 1600 A.D., was the best of the new (*Shinto*) makers.

In Setsu (Osaka) Tsuda Echizen no kami Suke-hiro was another maker of about the same period (1624).

Subsequent makers are numerous, but as there are no special legends connected with their blades or particular characteristics pertaining to them, the list of their names is omitted here.

The edge of the Japanese sword is tempered separately from the body, by being covered with clay when placed in the fire, and this process brings out the marking peculiar to these swords called *ya-ki ba* (burnt head).

These processes vary, and are called :—

Suguha, or straight edge : the style of Kuni mitzu.

Hoso suguha (fine thin), straight edge; the Yamashiro style.

Oömidare, large, irregular, wavy : the Sagami and Bizen style.

Komidare, small, irregular, wavy; same style.

Choji, like cloves laid side by side : Bizen style.

Jinku, overlaid petals, like flower petals : Bizen style.

Hitatsura, marked with cloudy spots : Soshiu style.

O Notare, large wavy line; common to all.

Ro Natare, a small wavy line ; common to all.

Saka ashi, serrated; principally Bizen.

Gunome or *gonome*, five curves and a straight line alternating : Mino and Seki style.

Sambonsugi, three serrated marks and a straight line alternating.

*Niye** are spots on the hard metal of the edge, peculiar to certain makes; and *Niyoie*, cloudings and markings in the welding. The

the fear and superstitious reverence evinced by natives of all classes for the swords of this maker.

* Swords are said to retain the stain of human blood if it is not ground out speedily after the death of the victim.

markings on the point, called *boshi*, are of several kinds, denoting the peculiar makes.

All these details must be thoroughly studied by every Japanese gentleman, and *Hon Nami* (experts) were pensioned by the Tokugawa government to teach the " true marks."

The shapes of blades were classed as following :—

Ken, two-edged falchions.

Tatchi, swords with a greater curve.

Katana, the common large sword.

Wakizashi, the ordinary medium blade.

Tanto, the short sword, of late most worn with the *Katana*.

Yoroidoshi, a short thick blade.

Yari, a lance.

Nagina'a, a large-headed lance.

Unokubi tskuri (cormorant's-head-shaped), a blade flattened out at the point.

Kamuri otoshi, a small pointed stiletto.

Shobutskuri, like a flag-leaf, flat-backed.

Hiratskuri, broad-shaped.

Iwomune, sloping-backed.

Hako mune, square-backed.

Ogisaki, round-pointed.

Kiromono are grooves or hollows in the blades filled with crimson lacquer or carvings of *Fudo*, *Marishiten* (dragons), and sometimes Bonji (Sanskrit) letters and Chinese characters, such as read *kimi ban zei* (" will cut for ten thousand years "); *ten ka tai hei* (" peace beneath heaven "); *sei shin ho koku* (" honest heart and patriotic"). Some swords have been engraved with poetry of thirty-one syllables.

The shapes of the haft (*komi*, or *nakago*) and the marks thereon are a serious study to all true swordsmen.

Yasuri me (file-marks), to keep the hilt from slipping.

Hirayasuri, Yokoyasuri taka no ha, Ya hadzu, are the various styles each having some peculiarity of the maker.

INDEX.

THE END.

LONDON: PRINTED BY WILLIAM CLOWES AND SONS, LIMITED, STAMFORD STREET
AND CHARING CROSS.

50, ALBEMARLE STREET,

October, 1880.

MR. MURRAY'S

LIST OF

FORTHCOMING WORKS.

ILIOS,

A COMPLETE HISTORY OF THE CITY AND COUNTRY OF THE TROJANS.

THE RESULT OF DISCOVERIES AND RESEARCHES
ON THE SITE OF TROY AND THROUGHOUT THE TROAD
IN 1871-3, 1878-9.

INCLUDING AN AUTOBIOGRAPHY OF THE AUTHOR.

By Dr. HENRY SCHLIEMANN, F.S.A., &c. &c.,
Author of "Troy and its Remains," and "Mycenæ and Tiryns."

With Preface, Appendices, and Notes by *Professors Virchow, Brugsch Bey, Sayce, Max Müller, Mahaffy, Ascherson, Mr. Calvert,* and *Mr. Duffield.*

With nearly 2,000 Illustrations.   Imperial 8vo.

UNBEATEN TRACKS IN JAPAN.

TRAVELS OF A LADY IN THE INTERIOR,

INCLUDING VISITS TO THE ABORIGINES OF YEZO AND TO THE SHRINES OF
NIKKO AND ISÉ.

By ISABELLA BIRD,
Author of "A Lady's Life in the Rocky Mountains," &c.

With Map and Illustrations.   2 vols.   Crown 8vo.   [*Ready.*

DUTY.

WITH ILLUSTRATIONS OF COURAGE, PATIENCE, AND ENDURANCE.

By SAMUEL SMILES, LL.D.

A Companion Volume to "*Self-Help,*" "*Character,*" "*Thrift.*"

Post 8vo.

MRS. GROTE: A SKETCH.
By LADY EASTLAKE.
Post 8vo.

PERSONAL LIFE of DAVID LIVINGSTONE, LL.D., D.C.L.
FROM HIS UNPUBLISHED JOURNALS AND CORRESPONDENCE.
(With the sanction of his Family.)
By WILLIAM GARDEN BLAIKIE, D.D., LL.D.
New College, Edinburgh.
Portrait and Map.   8vo.

LIFE AND LETTERS OF JOHN, LORD CAMPBELL,
LORD CHIEF JUSTICE, AND AFTERWARDS LORD CHANCELLOR OF ENGLAND,
BASED ON HIS AUTOBIOGRAPHY, JOURNALS, AND CORRESPONDENCE.
Edited by his Daughter the Hon. Mrs. HARDCASTLE.
Portrait.   2 Vols.   8vo.

JAPAN: ITS HISTORY, TRADITIONS, AND RELIGIONS.
WITH THE NARRATIVE OF A VISIT IN 1879.
By SIR EDWARD J. REED, K.C.B., F.R.S., M.P.
With Map and Illustrations.   2 vols.   8vo.

CHRISTIAN INSTITUTIONS:
ESSAYS ON ECCLESIASTICAL SUBJECTS.
By ARTHUR PENRHYN STANLEY, D.D.,
Dean of Westminster.

CONTENTS:

BAPTISM.	ABSOLUTION.
THE EUCHARIST.	ECCLESIASTICAL VESTMENTS.
THE EUCHARIST IN THE EARLY CHURCH.	BASILICAS.
THE EUCHARISTIC SACRIFICE.	THE POPE.
THE REAL PRESENCE.	THE LITANY.
THE BODY AND BLOOD OF CHRIST.	THE BELIEF OF THE EARLY CHRISTIANS.

8vo.

THE EASTERN QUESTION.

By the late **VISCOUNT STRATFORD DE REDCLIFFE, K.G., G.C.B.**

BEING A SELECTION FROM HIS WRITINGS DURING THE LAST
FIVE YEARS OF HIS LIFE.

With a Preface by DEAN STANLEY.

Post 8vo.

A PILGRIMAGE TO NEJD,

THE CRADLE OF THE ARAB RACE, AND A VISIT TO THE
COURT OF THE ARAB EMIR.

By LADY ANNE BLUNT.

Author of the " Bedouins of the Euphrates Valley."

With Illustrations from the Author's Drawings. 2 vols. Post 8vo.

We were passed on by the Bedouins from kinsman to kinsman, and were everywhere received as friends; nor is it too much to say that while in Arabia we enjoyed the singular advantage of being accepted as members of an Arabian family. This gave us an unique occasion of seeing and of understanding what we saw; and we have only ourselves to blame if we did not turn it to very important profit. . . . . We are, I believe, the only European travellers who have made the complete journey from Damascus to Häil, or from Häil to Bagdad, while only two Europeans besides ourselves have visited Jebel Shammar at all.—*From Editor's Preface.*

MEMOIR OF THE PUBLIC LIFE OF THE RIGHT HON. JOHN CHARLES HERRIES,

DURING THE REIGNS OF GEORGE III., GEORGE IV.,
WILLIAM IV., AND QUEEN VICTORIA.

FOUNDED ON HIS LETTERS AND OTHER UNPUBLISHED DOCUMENTS.

By his Son EDWARD HERRIES, C.B.

2 vols. 8vo.

INDIA IN 1880.

By Sir **RICHARD TEMPLE**, Bart., **G.C.S.I., C.I.E., D.C.L.**

Late Governor of Bombay, Lieut.-Governor of Bengal, and Finance Minister of India.

CONTENTS:

CLAIMS OF INDIA ON THE CONTINUOUS ATTENTION OF ENGLAND.	PRODUCTS, AGRICULTURAL AND INDUSTRIAL.
OBJECTS OF BEAUTY AND INTEREST.	COMMERCE, INTERNAL AND EXTERNAL.
MATERIAL PROGRESS OF THE NATIVES.	FAMINES.
MENTAL PROGRESS OF THE NATIVES.	PUBLIC HEALTH AND SANITATION.
NATIONAL EDUCATION.	PHYSICAL SCIENCE.
RELIGIOUS MISSIONS.	LEARNED RESEARCH.
NATIVE STATES AND CHIEFSHIPS.	WILD SPORTS.
OFFICIAL CLASSES, EUROPEAN AND NATIVE.	FOREIGN RELATIONS.
NON-OFFICIAL EUROPEANS.	ARMIES.
LAW AND LEGISLATION.	NAVY AND MARINE.
REVENUES.	FINANCES.
CANALS AND IRRIGATION.	STATISTICAL SUMMARY.
ROADS AND RAILWAYS.	EFFECTS AND PROSPECTS OF BRITISH RULE.

8vo.

LIFE OF SAMUEL WILBERFORCE, D.D.,

LATE BISHOP OF OXFORD, AND WINCHESTER,

WITH EXTRACTS FROM HIS DIARIES AND CORRESPONDENCE.

Edited by his Son, REGINALD WILBERFORCE,

ASSISTED BY SEVERAL CLERICAL AND LAY FRIENDS OF HIS FATHER.

With Portrait. VOL. II. 8vo.

A HISTORY OF GREEK SCULPTURE.

FROM THE EARLIEST TIMES DOWN TO THE AGE OF PHEIDIAS.

By A. S. MURRAY,

Of the Department of Antiquities, British Museum.

With 70 Illustrations. Royal 8vo.

MEMOIRS OF THE LIFE AND EVENTFUL CAREER OF F.M. THE DUKE DE SALDANHA,

SOLDIER AND STATESMAN.

WITH SELECTIONS FROM HIS CORRESPONDENCE.

By the CONDE DA CARNOTA.

With Portrait and Maps. 2 vols. 8vo.

CONTENTS :—Services in the Peninsula under the Duke of Wellington—Campaigns in the Brazils—Imprisonment at Lisbon and Exile—Prime Minister of Portugal—Commander-in-Chief in War of Succession in Portugal—Supports Donna Maria against Dom Miguel—Battles and Sieges—Successes as Commander of Queen's Forces—Places her on the Throne—Ambassador at Madrid, Vienna, London, Paris, and Rome—Special Missions to England—Civil War in Portugal—Defence of the Queen and her Throne—Secures Peace for his Country.

THE MANIFOLD WITNESS FOR CHRIST.

BEING AN ATTEMPT TO EXHIBIT THE COMBINED FORCE OF VARIOUS EVIDENCES OF CHRISTIANITY, DIRECT AND INDIRECT.

Part I.—CHRISTIANITY AND NATURAL THEOLOGY.
Part II.—THE POSITIVE EVIDENCE OF CHRISTIANITY.

THE BOYLE LECTURES FOR 1877-78.

By ALFRED BARRY, D.D., D.C.L.,

Principal of King's College, London; Canon of Worcester; and Honorary Chaplain to the Queen.

8vo.

THE POWER OF MOVEMENT IN PLANTS.

By CHAS. DARWIN, LL.D., F.R.S., assisted by FRANCIS DARWIN.

With Woodcuts. Crown 8vo.

MADAME DE STAEL:

A STUDY OF HER LIFE AND TIMES.

THE FIRST REVOLUTION AND THE FIRST EMPIRE.

By A. STEVENS, LL.D.

With Portraits. 2 Vols. Crown 8vo.

THE LIFE, LETTERS, AND JOURNALS OF FIELD-MARSHAL SIR WM. MAYNARD GOMM, G.C.B.

COMMANDER-IN-CHIEF IN INDIA, CONSTABLE OF THE TOWER, AND COLONEL OF THE COLDSTREAM GUARDS, 1784—1879.

Edited by FRANCIS CULLING CARR GOMM,

H.M. Madras Civil Service.

With Portrait. 8vo.

SPEECHES AND ADDRESSES,

POLITICAL AND LITERARY.

DELIVERED IN THE HOUSE OF LORDS, IN CANADA, AND ELSEWHERE.

By the Right Hon. The EARL OF DUFFERIN.

Late Governor-General of Canada. Ambassador at the Court of St. Petersburg.

8vo.

HISTORY OF EGYPT UNDER THE PHARAOHS.

DERIVED ENTIRELY FROM THE MONUMENTS.

WITH A MEMOIR ON THE EXODUS OF THE ISRAELITES AND THE EGYPTIAN MONUMENTS.

By Dr. HENRY BRUGSCH BEY.

Translated by PHILIP SMITH, B.A. and H. DANBY SEYMOUR.

Second Edition, revised, with a new Preface and original Notes by the Author.

With Maps. 2 vols. 8vo.

RAMBLES AMONG THE HILLS:

OR WALKS IN THE PEAK OF DERBYSHIRE.

INCLUDING VISITS TO CHATSWORTH, BOLSOVER, HARDWICKE, ASHOPTON, THE WOODLANDS, CASTLETON, THE KINDERSCOUT, AND SHERWOOD FOREST. Also

WALKS IN THE SOUTH DOWNS,

FROM PETERSFIELD TO BEECHY HEAD, WITH DESCRIPTIONS OF SOUTHDOWN VILLAGES AND MANORS, ASHBURNHAM, WISTON, &c. ; and

DESCRIPTIONS AND SKETCHES OF OLD HOUSES, CHURCHES, AND PEOPLE BY THE WAY.

By LOUIS J. JENNINGS,
Author of "Field Paths and Green Lanes in Surrey and Sussex."

With Illustrations. Post 8vo.

THE CAT.

AN INTRODUCTION TO THE STUDY OF BACK-BONED ANIMALS, ESPECIALLY MAMMALS.

By ST. GEORGE MIVART,
Author of "Lessons from Nature," &c., &c.

With numerous Illustrations. 8vo.

A POPULAR ACCOUNT OF THE INTRODUCTION OF PERUVIAN BARK

FROM SOUTH AMERICA INTO BRITISH INDIA AND CEYLON AND OF THE PROGRESS AND EXTENT OF ITS CULTIVATION.

By CLEMENTS R. MARKHAM, C.B., F.R.S.

With Maps and Woodcuts. Post 8vo.

ENGLISH STUDIES

OF THE LATE

REV. J. S. BREWER, M.A.,

OF THE RECORD OFFICE, AND PROFESSOR OF MODERN HISTORY, KING'S COLL., LONDON.

CONTENTS :

NEW SOURCES OF ENGLISH HISTORY.	HATFIELD HOUSE.
GREEN'S SHORT HISTORY OF THE ENGLISH PEOPLE.	THE STUARTS.
	SHAKSPEARE.
THE ROYAL SUPREMACY AND THE HISTORY OF ITS INTRODUCTION.	HOW TO STUDY ENGLISH HISTORY.
	ANCIENT LONDON.

8vo.

SIBERIA IN EUROPE.

A NATURALIST'S VISIT TO THE VALLEY OF THE PETCHORA IN NORTH-EAST RUSSIA,

WITH DESCRIPTIONS OF BIRDS AND THEIR MIGRATIONS.

By HENRY SEEBOHM, F.Z.S., F.L.S., F.R.G.S.

With Map and Illustrations.   Crown 8vo.

SKETCHES OF EMINENT STATESMEN AND WRITERS, WITH OTHER ESSAYS.

REPRINTED FROM THE "QUARTERLY REVIEW," WITH ADDITIONS AND CORRECTIONS.

By A. HAYWARD, Q.C.

CONTENTS:

THIERS.	MONTALEMBERT.	SEVIGNÉ.
BISMARCK.	WELLESLEY.	DU DEFFAND.
CAVOUR.	BYRON AND TENNYSON.	HOLLAND HOUSE.
METTERNICH.	VENICE.	STRAWBERRY HILL.
MELBOURNE.	ST. SIMON.	

2 Vols.   8vo.

THE GARDENS OF THE SUN.

A NATURALIST'S JOURNAL ON THE MOUNTAINS AND IN THE FORESTS AND SWAMPS OF BORNEO AND THE SOOLOO ARCHIPELAGO.

By F. W. BURBIDGE,
Trinity College Botanical Gardens, Dublin.

With Illustrations.   Crown 8vo.

A NEW LIFE OF ALBERT DURER,

AND A HISTORY OF HIS ART.

By MORITZ THAUSING,
Keeper of Archduke Albert's Art Collections at Vienna.

Portrait and Illustrations.   2 vols.   Medium 8vo.

LECTURES ON ARCHITECTURE,

DELIVERED BEFORE THE ROYAL ACADEMY.

By the late EDWARD BARRY, R.A.

8vo.

THE HUGUENOTS:

THEIR SETTLEMENTS, CHURCHES AND INDUSTRIES IN ENGLAND AND IRELAND.

By SAMUEL SMILES, LL.D.

New Edition.   With Frontispiece.   Crown 8vo.

THE PSALMS OF DAVID.

WITH NOTES EXPLANATORY AND CRITICAL,

By G. H. S. JOHNSON, Dean of Wells; C. J. ELLIOTT, Canon of Christ Church; and F. C. COOK, Canon of Exeter.

New and Revised Edition.   Medium 8vo.

(DETACHED FROM THE SPEAKER'S COMMENTARY.)

A DICTIONARY OF HYMNOLOGY.

INTENDED AS A COMPANION TO EXISTING HYMN BOOKS.

SETTING FORTH THE ORIGIN AND HISTORY OF THE HYMNS IN COMMON USE, A DESCRIPTION OF THE MOST POPULAR HYMNALS, AND BIOGRAPHICAL NOTICES OF THEIR AUTHORS AND TRANSLATORS.

By Rev. JOHN JULIAN, F.R.S.L.,
Vicar of Wincobank, Sheffield.

8vo.

N.B.—This Work is designed to embrace the following subjects :—

1. THE HISTORY OF EVERY HYMN IN GENERAL USE IN ENGLAND, IRELAND, AND SCOTLAND, EMBRACING ORIGINALS AND TRANSLATIONS.
2. BIOGRAPHICAL NOTICES OF AUTHORS, TRANSLATORS, AND COMPILERS OF HYMNS.
3. AN INVESTIGATION INTO ANONYMOUS AUTHORS OF HYMNS.
4. HISTORICAL ARTICLES ON GREEK, LATIN, AND GERMAN HYMNODY — ON SERVICE BOOKS, MISSALS, BREVIARIES, EARLY HYMN BOOKS, &c.; AND NOTES ON FRENCH, DANISH, AND OTHER HYMNS, FROM WHICH TRANSLATIONS HAVE BEEN MADE INTO ENGLISH.
5. DETAILS OF THE SOURCES OF ENGLISH HYMNOLOGICAL INFORMATION.

As the field of research is exceedingly wide, the assistance of eminent hymnologists has been secured to ensure the fullest and most accurate information possible.

CONTINUATION OF ELWIN'S EDITION.

THE WORKS OF ALEXANDER POPE;

POETRY, Vol. III.

CONTAINING THE SATIRES, THE MORAL ESSAYS, &c., WITH
INTRODUCTIONS AND NOTES.

By W. J. COURTHOPE, M.A.

8vo.

LIFE OF JONATHAN SWIFT.

By HENRY CRAIK, B.A.,
Late Scholar and Snell Exhibitioner, Baliol College, Oxford.

8vo.

THE LIFE AND WRITINGS OF ST. JOHN THE DIVINE.

By the LORD BISHOP OF DERRY AND RAPHOE.

2 vols. 8vo.

A HANDBOOK FOR TRAVELLERS IN BENGAL.

FROM CALCUTTA TO JAGHERNAULT ON THE WEST, ALLAHABAD
ON THE NORTH, AND RANGOON ON THE EAST.

By E. B. EASTWICK,
Author of "Handbook to Bombay" and the "Handbook to Madras."

With Maps and Plans. Post 8vo.

HANDBOOK FOR BOMBAY.

A New Edition, most carefully Revised on the spot, and for the most part rewritten.

By E. B. EASTWICK.

With Map. Post 8vo.

DUCANGE'S MEDIÆVAL LATIN-ENGLISH DICTIONARY.

Re-arranged and Edited in accordance with the Modern Science of Philology.

By E. A. DAYMAN, B.D.,
Prebendary of Sarum, formerly Fellow and Tutor of Exeter College, Oxford,

and J. H. HESSELS.

Small 4to.

A MANUAL OF NAVAL ARCHITECTURE.

By W. H. WHITE,
Assistant-Constructor, Royal Navy.

Second and revised Edition, with 130 Illustrations.   8vo.

The STUDENT'S MANUAL of the GEOGRAPHY of INDIA.

By GEORGE SMITH, LL.D.,
Author of the " Life of Dr. Wilson, Dr. Duff," &c.

Post 8vo.

A GLOSSARY OF PECULIAR ANGLO-INDIAN COLLOQUIAL WORDS AND PHRASES.

ETYMOLOGICAL, HISTORICAL, AND GEOGRAPHICAL.

By HENRY YULE, C.B., and ARTHUR BURNELL, Ph.D.

8vo.

NEW DICTIONARY OF THE ENGLISH LANGUAGE.

FOR PRACTICAL REFERENCE, METHODICALLY ARRANGED, AND BASED UPON THE BEST PHILOLOGICAL AUTHORITIES.

Medium 8vo.

THE STUDENT'S HISTORY OF MODERN EUROPE.

FROM THE END OF THE MIDDLE AGES TO THE TREATY OF BERLIN, 1878.

Post 8vo.

BEING A NEW VOLUME OF "MURRAY'S STUDENTS' MANUALS."

LONDON: PAST AND PRESENT.

By the late PETER CUNNINGHAM, F.S.A.
Revised and Edited by JAMES THORNE, F.S.A.,
Author of the " Handbook to the Environs of London."

In this work will be found much antiquarian, historical, and entertaining information, together with ample descriptions of all the streets and buildings of note now to be seen, as well as those no longer existing ; and every place endeared to Englishmen by *Interesting* and *Historical* associations.   *New Library Edition.*   3 Vols.   8vo.

THE
SPEAKER'S COMMENTARY on the NEW TESTAMENT.

Edited by F. C. COOK, M.A.,

Canon of Exeter, late Preacher at Lincoln's Inn, and Chaplain in Ordinary to the Queen.

To be completed in 4 Vols.   Medium 8vo.

Vol. III.

ROMANS	E. H. GIFFORD, D.D., Hon. Canon of Worcester, Rector of Much Hadham, and Examining Chaplain to the Bishop of London.
CORINTHIANS	T. S. EVANS, Canon of Durham, and Professor of Greek in Durham University. J. WAITE, M.A., Vicar of Norham, Northumberland.
GALATIANS	J. S. HOWSON, D.D., Dean of Chester.
PHILIPPIANS, EPHE-SIANS, COLOSSIANS, THESSALONIANS, and PHILEMON	J. A. JEREMIE, D.D., late Dean of Lincoln. Rev. Prebendary MEYRICK, and the DEAN OF RAPHOE. WM. ALEXANDER, D.D., Bishop of Derry and Raphoe.
PASTORAL EPISTLES .	JOHN JACKSON, D.D., Bishop of London.
HEBREWS	W. KAY, D.D.

Vol. IV.

EPISTLE of ST. JAMES	ROBERT SCOTT, D.D., Dean of Rochester.
EPISTLES of ST. JOHN	WM. ALEXANDER, D.D., Bishop of Derry and Raphoe.
ST. PETER & ST. JUDE	Canon COOK, and J. R. LUMBY, D.D., Norrisian Professor of Divinity at Cambridge.
REVELATION OF ST. JOHN	WM. LEE, D.D., Archdeacon of Dublin.

. VOLS. I. & II. *are now Published.*

THE APOCRYPHA,

WITH A COMMENTARY, EXPLANATORY & CRITICAL,

BY VARIOUS WRITERS.

Edited by Rev. HENRY WACE, M.A.,

Preacher of Lincoln's Inn, Professor of Ecclesiastical History, King's College, London.

2 Vols.   Medium 8vo.

(UNIFORM WITH THE SPEAKER'S COMMENTARY.)

THE
STUDENT'S COMMENTARY on the OLD TESTAMENT.

ABRIDGED FROM THE "SPEAKER'S COMMENTARY."

Edited by JOHN M. FULLER, M.A.,

Vicar of Bexley, and formerly Fellow of St. John's College, Cambridge.

Vol. IV.—ISAIAH TO MALACHI.   Crown 8vo.   7s. 6d.

50, ALBEMARLE STREET,
October, 1880.

MR. MURRAY'S

LIST OF

NEW & RECENT PUBLICATIONS.

Handbook to the Mediterranean.

FOR TRAVELLERS IN GENERAL, AND ESPECIALLY FOR YACHTSMEN.

DESCRIBING THE PRINCIPAL CITIES, SEAPORTS, HARBOURS, AND BORDER LANDS,

THE COASTS OF AFRICA, SPAIN, ITALY, DALMATIA, GREECE, ASIA MINOR.

FORMING A GUIDE TO

CORSICA, SARDINIA, SICILY, MALTA, THE BALEARIC ISLANDS, CRETE, RHODES, CYPRUS, &c.

By Colonel R. L. PLAYFAIR,

Author of "Travels in the Footsteps of Bruce," "Handbook to Algeria and Tunis."

With nearly 50 Maps, Plans, &c.   Post 8vo.

A Smaller Manual of Modern Geography.

FOR SCHOOLS AND YOUNG PERSONS.

By JOHN RICHARDSON, M.A.

Diocesan Inspector of Schools, and Author of "The School Manual of Modern Geography."

250 pp.   Post 8vo.   2s. 6d.

Old French Plate.

FURNISHING TABLES OF THE PARIS DATE-LETTERS AND FACSIMILES OF OTHER MARKS.

A HANDBOOK FOR THE COLLECTOR.

By WILFRID J. CRIPPS, M.A., F.S.A.,

Author of "Old English Plate."

With Illustrations.   8vo.   8s. 6d.

A Handbook to Political Questions of the Day.

WITH THE ARGUMENTS ON EITHER SIDE.

By SYDNEY C. BUXTON.

Second Edition. 8vo. 5s.

A History of Ancient Geography among the Greeks and Romans,

FROM THE EARLIEST AGES TILL THE FALL OF THE ROMAN EMPIRE.

By E. H. BUNBURY, F.R.G.S.

With 20 *Maps.* 2 *Vols.* 8vo. 42s.

The Student's Hume.

A HISTORY OF ENGLAND FROM THE EARLIEST TIMES TO THE TREATY OF BERLIN, 1878.

NEW EDITION, REVISED, CORRECTED, AND PARTLY RE-WRITTEN.

By J. S. BREWER, M.A.

Late of the Record Office, Professor of Modern History, King's College, London.

Maps and Woodcuts. (830 *pp.*) *Post* 8vo. 7s. 6d.

The Convocation Prayer Book;

BEING THE BOOK OF COMMON PRAYER, WITH ALTERED RUBRICS,

SHOWING WHAT WOULD BE THE CONDITION OF THE BOOK IF AMENDED IN CONFORMITY WITH THE RECOMMENDATIONS OF THE CONVOCATIONS OF CANTERBURY AND YORK IN 1879.

Post 8vo. 5s.

The Metallurgy of Silver and Gold.

PHYSICAL PROPERTIES AND CHEMISTRY OF SILVER, IN RELATION TO METALLURGY.

ALLOYS.

ORES.

ASSAYING.

PARTING OF SILVER AND GOLD.

SMELTING OF SILVER ORES.

AMALGAMATION OF SILVER ORES, IN PART, ENDING WITH THE CAZO PROCESS.

By JOHN PERCY, M.D., F.R.S.,

Lecturer on Metallurgy to the Advanced Class of Officers of the Royal Artillery, and Honorary Member of the Institution of Civil Engineers, of the Society of Engineers, and of the Iron and Steel Institute.

With numerous Illustrations. 8vo. 30s.

Life of Samuel Wilberforce,

LATE BISHOP OF OXFORD AND AFTERWARDS OF WINCHESTER.

WITH EXTRACTS FROM HIS DIARIES AND CORRESPONDENCE.

By A. R. ASHWELL, M.A., late Canon of Chichester.

FIFTH THOUSAND. VOL. I. *With Portrait.* 8vo. 15s.

History of British Commerce,

AND OF THE PROGRESS OF THE NATION, FROM 1763 TO 1878.

By LEONE LEVI, F.S.A.,

Barrister-at-Law, Professor of the Principles and Practice of Commerce and Commercial Law, King's College, London.

New, Revised, and Enlarged Edition. *With Diagrams.* 8vo. 18s.

St. Chrysostom: His Life and Times.

A SKETCH OF THE CHURCH AND THE EMPIRE IN THE IVTH CENTURY.

By W. R. W. STEPHENS, M.A.,

Prebendary of Chichester, and Author of the "Life of Dean Hook."

Second and revised Edition. *With Portrait.* 8vo. 12s.

Life of Dr. John Wilson (of Bombay):

FIFTY YEARS MISSIONARY, PHILANTHROPIST AND SCHOLAR.

By GEORGE SMITH, LL.D.

Popular Edition. With Portrait and Illustrations. Crown 8vo. 9s.

Nile Gleanings:

THE ETHNOLOGY, HISTORY, AND ART OF ANCIENT EGYPT, AS REVEALED BY THE PAINTINGS AND BAS-RELIEFS.

WITH DESCRIPTIONS OF NUBIA AND ITS GREAT ROCK TEMPLES TO THE SECOND CATARACT.

By VILLIERS STUART, of Dromana, M.P.

With 58 Coloured Lithographs and Plates from Impressions from the Monuments. Royal 8vo. 31s. 6d.

The Civil and Political Correspondence of the Duke of Wellington. Vol. VIII.

Edited by his SON.

CONTENTS:

REFORM BILLS OF 1831-32.—THE DUKE ON CORPORAL PUNISHMENT.—O'CONNELL. —SEPARATION OF HOLLAND FROM BELGIUM.—SIEGE OF ANTWERP.—BRITISH EXPEDITION IN AID OF DOM PEDRO OF PORTUGAL, &c., &c.

8vo. 20s.

The Greek Verb.

ITS STRUCTURE AND DEVELOPMENT.

From the German of Professor CURTIUS.

Translated by A. S. WILKINS, M.A., Prof. of Latin and Comp. Philology; and E. B. ENGLAND, M.A., Assistant Lecturer in Classics, Owens College, Manchester.

8vo. 18s.

Gleanings of Past Years, 1843–78.

By the Right Hon. W. E. GLADSTONE, M.P.

CONTENTS.

VOL. I.—THE THRONE AND THE PRINCE CONSORT, THE CABINET, AND CONSTITUTION.	VOL. III.—HISTORICAL & SPECULATIVE.
	VOL. IV.—FOREIGN.
	VOLS. V. & VI.—ECCLESIASTICAL.
VOL. II.—PERSONAL AND LITERARY.	VOL. VII.—MISCELLANEOUS.

Small 8vo. 2s. 6d. each.

A Lady's Life in the Rocky Mountains.

By ISABELLA BIRD,

Author of "A Residence in the Sandwich Islands," &c.

Third Edition. With Illustrations. Crown 8vo. 10s. 6d.

The Cities and Cemeteries of Etruria.

By GEORGE DENNIS.

A NEW EDITION. REVISED AND INCORPORATING ALL THE MOST RECENT DISCOVERIES.

With Maps and 200 Illustrations. 2 Vols. Medium 8vo. 42s.

Memoir of the late
Robert Milman, D.D., Bishop of Calcutta,

AND METROPOLITAN OF INDIA.

WITH A SELECTION FROM HIS CORRESPONDENCE AND JOURNALS.

By his Sister FRANCES MARIA MILMAN.

With Map. 8vo. 12s.

Memoirs of
Edward, Catherine, and Mary Stanley.

By the DEAN OF WESTMINSTER.

Third Edition. Crown 8vo. 9s.

The Synoptic Gospels,

THE DEATH OF CHRIST, THE WORTH OF LIFE, AND OTHER ESSAYS.

By WILLIAM THOMSON, D.D., Lord Archbishop of York.

Crown 8vo. 9s.

The Lex Salica;

THE TEN TEXTS WITH THE GLOSSES, AND THE LEX EMENDATA.

Edited Synoptically, by J. H. HESSELS.

WITH NOTES ON THE FRANKISH WORDS IN THE LEX SALICA.

By H. KERN,
Professor of Sanscrit, University of Leyden.

4to. 42s.

" In the Salic Laws and the Pandects of Justinian we may compare the first rudiments and the full maturity of Civil wisdom."—GIBBON.

The Moral Philosophy of Aristotle.

COMPRISING

A TRANSLATION OF THE NICOMACHEAN ETHICS, AND THE PARAPHRASE ATTRIBUTED TO ANDRONICUS.

WITH INTRODUCTORY ANALYSES.

ADAPTED FOR STUDENTS AT THE UNIVERSITIES, ETC.

By WALTER M. HATCH, M.A.,
Late Fellow of New College, Oxford.

8vo. 18s.

Illustrated Lectures on Gothic Architecture.

DELIVERED AT THE ROYAL ACADEMY

By the late Sir G. GILBERT SCOTT, R.A.

With 450 Illustrations. 2 Vols. Medium 8vo. 42s.

Twenty Years in the Wild West of Ireland;

OR, LIFE IN CONNAUGHT.

By Mrs. HOUSTOUN,
Author of " A Yacht Voyage to Texas."

Post 8vo. 9s.

Life of Dr. Erasmus Darwin.

WITH A STUDY OF HIS SCIENTIFIC WORKS.

By CHARLES DARWIN, F.R.S., and ERNEST KRAUSE.

Portrait and Woodcuts. 8vo. 7s. 6d.

The Ancient Egyptians.

By Sir J. GARDNER WILKINSON, F.R.S.

THEIR MANNERS, CUSTOMS, PRIVATE LIFE, GOVERNMENT, LAWS, ARTS, MANUFACTURES, RELIGION, AGRICULTURE, EARLY HISTORY, ETC.,

DERIVED FROM A COMPARISON OF THE PAINTINGS, SCULPTURES, AND MONU-MENTS STILL EXISTING, WITH THE ACCOUNTS OF ANCIENT AUTHORS.

A New Edition Revised by SAMUEL BIRCH, LL.D.

With 500 Illustrations, Coloured Plates, &c. 3 Vols. Medium 8vo. 84s.

The River of Golden Sand.

NARRATIVE OF A JOURNEY THROUGH CHINA TO BURMAH.

By Capt. WILLIAM GILL, R.E.

WITH AN INTRODUCTORY PREFACE

By Col. HENRY YULE, C.B.

With 10 *Maps and various Illustrations.* 2 *Vols.* 8*vo.* 30*s.*

Rheinsberg:

MEMORIALS OF THE EARLY DAYS OF FREDERICK THE GREAT AND PRINCE HENRY OF PRUSSIA.

By ANDREW HAMILTON.

2 *vols.* *Crown* 8*vo.* 21*s.*

The Ascent of the Matterhorn.

By EDWARD WHYMPER.

Third Thousand. *With Maps and* 100 *Illustrations.* *Medium* 8*vo.* 10*s.* 6*d.*

The Wild Sports and Natural History of the Highlands of Scotland.

By CHARLES ST. JOHN.

New Edition, with 70 *Illustrations by* WHYMPER, CORBOULD, COLLINS, ELWES, *and* HARRISON WEIR. *Crown* 8*vo.* 15*s.*

Mycenæ and Tiryns.

A NARRATIVE OF RESEARCHES AND DISCOVERIES.

By Dr. HENRY SCHLIEMANN.

With 500 *Illustrations.* *Medium* 8*vo.* 50*s.*

British Burma and its People;

SKETCHES OF THE NATIVES, THEIR MANNERS, CUSTOMS, AND RELIGION.

By Capt. C. J. F. S. FORBES, F.R.G.S., M.R.A.S., &c.,
Late Officiating Deputy-Commissioner, British Burma.

Crown 8vo.   10s. 6d.

An Atlas of Ancient Geography.

BIBLICAL AND CLASSICAL.

INTENDED TO ILLUSTRATE SMITH'S CLASSICAL AND BIBLICAL DICTIONARIES, AND THE "SPEAKER'S COMMENTARY ON THE BIBLE."

Compiled under the Superintendence of WM. SMITH, D.C.L., and GEORGE GROVE, F.R.G.S.

WITH DESCRIPTIVE TEXT, GIVING THE SOURCES AND AUTHORITIES, INDICES, &c.

Forty-three Maps and Plans.   Folio, half-bound.   £6 6s.

DR. WM. SMITH'S NEW DICTIONARIES.

A Dictionary of Christian Antiquities.	A Dictionary of Christian Biography.
The History and Institutions of the Christian Church, from the Time of the Apostles to the Age of Charlemagne.	Literature, Sects, and Doctrines. From the Time of the Apostles to the Age of Charlemagne.
By VARIOUS WRITERS. Edited by WM. SMITH, D.C.L., and ARCHDEACON CHEETHAM, D.D. With Illustrations. **2 Vols.** Medium 8vo. £3 13s. 6d.	By VARIOUS WRITERS. Edited by WM. SMITH, D.C.L., and HENRY WACE, M.A. [*To be completed in 4 vols.*] Vols. I. and II. Medium 8vo. 31s. 6d. each.
** This work can be had in 14 monthly parts, 5s. each.	** This work will be issued in monthly parts, 5s. each.

NEW BOOKS OF DR. WM. SMITH'S EDUCATIONAL SERIES.

English Composition.

With copious Illustrations and Practical Exercises.

By THEOPHILUS D. HALL, M.A., Fellow of University College, London. 12mo. 3*s*. 6*d*.

Italian Principia.

A Grammar, Delectus, Exercise Book, with Vocabularies.

By SIGNOR RICCI, Professor of Italian at the City of London College. 12mo. 3*s*. 6*d*.

The Bedouins of the Euphrates Valley.

By Lady ANNE BLUNT. With some Account of the Arabs and their Horses. With Map and Illustrations. 2 vols. Crown 8vo. 24*s*.

Cyprus; its History, Art, and Antiquities.

By LOUIS DI CESNOLA. 400 Illustrations. Medium 8vo. 50*s*.

BIOGRAPHIES BY SAMUEL SMILES.

Life of Thomas Edward, Shoemaker of Banff, Scotch Naturalist.

15*th Thousand*. With Portrait and 30 Illustrations. Crown 8vo. 10*s*. 6*d*.

Life of Robert Dick, Baker of Thurso, Geologist and Botanist.

10*th Thousand*. With Portrait and 50 Illustrations. Crown 8vo. 12*s*.

The Cathedral : its Place in the Life and Work of the Church.

By the BISHOP OF TRURO. *Second Edition*. Crown 8vo. 6*s*.

The Witness of the Psalms to Christ and Christianity.

By the BISHOP OF DERRY. *Second Edition*. 8vo. 14*s*.

The Temples of the Jews at Jerusalem.

By JAMES FERGUSSON, F.R.S. Plates and Woodcuts. 4to. 42*s*.

Memoir of Caroline Herschel.

By Mrs. JOHN HERSCHEL. *New Edition*. Portraits. Crown 8vo. 7*s*.6*d*.

Travels and Researches Among the Lakes and Mountains of Eastern and Central Africa.

By Capt. J. FREDERICK ELTON, and H. B. COTTERILL. With Maps and Illustrations. 8vo. 21s.

The Talmud.

Selected Extracts illustrating the Teaching of the Bible.

By Dr. BARCLAY, BISHOP OF JERUSALEM. 8vo. 14s.

Nyassa.

The Missionary Settlement of "Livingstonia."

By E. D. YOUNG. Second Edition. With Maps. Post 8vo. 7s. 6d.

Life of St. Hugh of Avalon, Bishop of Lincoln.

And some Account of his Predecessors in the See of Lincoln.

By GEO. G. PERRY, Canon of Lincoln, Author of "The Student's Manual of the History of the English Church." Crown 8vo. 10s. 6d.

A Little Light on Cretan Insurrection.

By A. F. YULE. Post 8vo, 2s. 6d.

The Satsuma Rebellion.

An Episode of Modern Japanese History.

By AUGUSTUS H. MOUNSEY, F.R.G.S., H.B.M. Secretary of Legation at Athens; recently H.B.M. Secretary of Legation in Japan. Maps. Crown 8vo. 10s. 6d.

Life of the Right Hon. William Pitt.

By Earl STANHOPE. New Edition. Portraits. 3 vols. 8vo. 36s.

Lives of the Early Flemish Painters; and their Works.

By CROWE and CAVALCASELLE. Third Edition. Woodcuts. Post 8vo. 7s. 6d.

Burckhardt's Cicerone, or Art Guide to Picture Galleries in Italy.

Translated from the German. New Edition Revised by J. A. CROWE. Post 8vo. 6s.

Handbook to St. Paul's Cathedral.

Condensed from the Larger Work.

By DEAN MILMAN, D.D. With 20 Illustrations. Crown 8vo. 10s. 6d. (Forming a Volume of "Murray's English Cathedrals.")

The Agamemnon of Æschylus.

Translated by the EARL OF CARNARVON. Small 8vo. 6s.

Scepticism in Geology, and the Reasons for it.

An Assemblage of Facts from Nature refuting the Theory of "Causes now in Action."

By VERIFIER. *Second Edition, Revised*. Woodcuts. Post 8vo. 6s.

My Boyhood.

A True Story of Country Life and Adventures for the Old and Young.

By H. C. BARKLEY. With Illustrations by CORBOULD. Post 8vo. 6s.

Leaves from my Sketch Book.

Paris — Arles—Monaco — Nuremburg —Switzerland — Rome—Egypt — Venice — Naples — Pompeii — Pæstum—The Nile, &c.

By E. W. COOKE, R.A. 50 Plates. 2 vols. Small folio. 31s. 6d. each.

Aristotle.

By GEORGE GROTE, F.R.S. With Additional Essays. 8vo. 18s.

The Odyssey of Homer. Books I.—XII.

Rendered into English blank verse by GENL. SCHOMBERG. 8vo. 12s.

Six Months in Ascension.

An Unscientific Account of a Scientific Expedition.

By Mrs. GILL. Prefaced by a Brief and Popular History of the Methods employed to Discover the Sun's Distance from the Earth by DAVID GILL, Astronomer Royal, Cape of Good Hope. *Second Edition*. With Map. Crown 8vo. 9s.

Field Paths and Green Lanes.

An Account of Rambles chiefly in Surrey and Sussex.

By LOUIS J. JENNINGS. Illustrations. Post 8vo. 10s. 6d.

The Etched Work of Rembrandt Van Rhyn.

A Descriptive Catalogue, preceded by a Life and Genealogy.

By CHARLES H. MIDDLETON, B.A. With Plates. Medium 8vo. 31s. 6d.

Hortensius.

By WILLIAM FORSYTH, Q.C. With Illustrations. 8vo. 7s. 6d.

The Speaker's Commentary on the Old Testament:

EXPLANATORY AND CRITICAL, WITH A REVISION OF THE TRANSLATION.

Edited by F. C. COOK, M.A., Canon of Exeter.

Now Ready, complete in 6 Vols.   Medium 8vo.   £6 15s.

VOL. I.—PENTATEUCH. 30s.

Genesis	EDWARD HAROLD BROWNE, D.D., Lord Bishop of Winchester.
Exodus	The EDITOR, and SAMUEL CLARK, M.A., late Rector of Eaton Bishop.
Leviticus	SAMUEL CLARK, M.A.
Numbers	T. E. ESPIN, B.D., Chancellor and Canon of Chester. J. F. THRUPP, M.A., late Vicar of Barrington.
Deuteronomy	Canon ESPIN, B.D.

VOLS. II. & III.—HISTORICAL BOOKS. 36s.

Joshua	Canon ESPIN, B.D.
Judges, Ruth, Samuel	Lord ARTHUR HERVEY, D.D., Lord Bishop of Bath and Wells.
Kings, Chronicles, Ezra, Nehemiah, Esther	GEORGE RAWLINSON, M.A., Canon of Canterbury, and Camden Professor of Ancient History at Oxford.

VOL. IV.—POETICAL BOOKS. 24s.

Job	The EDITOR.
Psalms	G. H. S. JOHNSON, M.A., Dean of Wells. The EDITOR. C. J. ELLIOTT, M.A., Hon. Canon of Christ Church, and Vicar of Winkfield.
Proverbs	E. H. PLUMPTRE, M.A., Prebendary of St. Paul's, Vicar of Bickley, and Professor of Pastoral Theology, King's College, London.
Ecclesiastes	W. T. BULLOCK, M.A., Prebendary of St. Paul's, and Chaplain at Kensington Palace.
Song of Solomon	T. KINGSBURY, M.A., Prebendary of Salisbury, and Vicar of Burbage.

VOL. V.—ISAIAH AND JEREMIAH. 20s.

Isaiah	W. KAY, D.D., Hon. Canon of St. Albans, and Rector of Great Leighs.
Jeremiah, Lamentations	R. PAYNE SMITH, D.D., Dean of Canterbury.

VOL. VI.—EZEKIEL, DANIEL, AND THE MINOR PROPHETS. 25s.

Ezekiel	G. CURREY, D.D., Prebendary of St. Paul's, and Master of the Charter House.
Daniel	H. J. ROSE, B.D., late Archdeacon of Bedford. J. M. FULLER, M.A., Vicar of Bexley.
Hosea, Jonah	E. HUXTABLE, M.A., Prebendary of Wells.
Amos, Nahum, Zephaniah	R. GANDELL, M.A., Prebendary of Wells, and Professor of Arabic, Oxford.
Joel, Obadiah	F. MEYRICK, M.A., Rector of Blickling with Erpingham.
Micah, Habakkuk	SAM. CLARK, M.A., and the EDITOR.
Haggai, Zechariah, Malachi	W. DRAKE, M.A., Hon. Canon of Worcester, and Rector of Sedgebrook.

BRADBURY, AGNEW, & CO., PRINTERS, WHITEFRIARS.

www.ingramcontent.com/pod-product-compliance
Lightning Source LLC
Chambersburg PA
CBHW032339280326
41935CB00008B/380